The History Of Christianity In India: From The Commencement Of The Christian Era : Second Portion: Comprising The History Of Protestant Missions, 1706-1816 / By James Hough, Volume 1

James Hough

THE HISTORY

OF

CHRISTIANITY IN INDIA

FROM THE COMMENCEMENT OF THE CHRISTIAN ERA.

BY THE

REV. JAMES HOUGH, M.A., F.C.P.S.

PERPETUAL CURATE OF HAM:

LATE CHAPLAIN TO THE HONOURABLE EAST-INDIA COMPANY AT MADRAS.

VOL. I.

PUBLISHED BY R. B. SEELEY AND W. BURNSIDE:
AND SOLD BY L. AND G. SEELEY,
FLEET STREET, LONDON.
MDCCCXXXIX.

1639

PRINTED BY L. AND G. SEELEY, THAMES DITTON, SURREY.

TO

THE RIGHT REVEREND

CHARLES RICHARD,

LORD BISHOP OF WINCHESTER,

PRELATE OF THE MOST NOBLE ORDER OF THE GARTER,

ETC. ETC. ETC.

THE LIBERAL PATRON

OF

CHRISTIAN MISSIONS

TO THE

HEATHEN WORLD.

THIS ATTEMPT TO RECORD THE RISE AND PROGRESS

OF

CHRISTIANITY IN INDIA

IS,

WITH HIS LORDSHIP'S PERMISSION,

GRATEFULLY INSCRIBED

BY HIS OBEDIENT SERVANT

THE AUTHOR.

PREFACE.

A HISTORY of Christianity in India has long been desired by persons interested in the progress of the Gospel in the East. The only general work of the kind, is the *Histoire du Christianisme des Indes*, by La Croze: a work little known in England, and, though of great value, yet not full enough for a mere translation of it to supply the desideratum. For the earlier annals of the Indian Church, the materials are very scanty; and they are mixed up with much that tends to obscure, rather than elucidate, the few fragments of history that are unquestionably authentic. But there is no lack of information on the subject during the last three centuries, for readers who have leisure to explore its ample resources; which, however, is by no means the case with all who are interested in their contents. So numerous are the volumes, consisting chiefly of portions of history and missionary correspondence, that have been published; they are written in such a variety of languages; and some of the most important of them are become so scarce; that they are inaccessible to the generality of readers: and even of the persons who are competent and have opportunity to examine this variety of records, only a small proportion have time for the task. There can be no question, therefore, as to the importance of a work of moderate size that shall combine the information scattered over so wide a surface.

In publishing the present History, I do not pretend to have supplied the desideratum; for a much more extensive work would be desirable, had I leisure for the performance, and the means of incurring the responsibility of its publication. Neither am I entitled to, the credit of entering upon the present limited undertaking merely for the purpose of meeting the general wish for such a work. The duties and responsibilities of my situation are too great for me to have thought of engaging in so laborious a task, had I not been constrained by a conviction of duty to the Church of Christ. No other motive could have induced me to sit down to write history, or to persevere in it when begun; for it is not without much inconvenience and many scruples that I have devoted to these volumes the time that they have required.

If asked, what constituted this constraint, I answer, —The pertinacity of the romanists in continuing to misrepresent the state of their own and the protestants' foreign missions. Like M. P. Norbert, a Romish missionary in India, who tells us that he was compelled by the Jesuits' libels to publish many things in justification of himself and his brethren;* so have I

* Memoires Historiques, &c. tom. III. p. 423, &c. *Les Apologistes de la Société par leurs Libelles ont constraint le P. Norbert à se justifier par des Pieces qu'il auroit tenu cachées.*

been urged, on former occasions as well as the present, from a similar cause, to expose the fallacy of their statements. In 1824 I was called upon to answer the Abbé Dubois's *Letters on the State of Christianity in India;* and evidence was given in my Reply to reverse the picture he had drawn, that, I have reason to know, proved satisfactory to readers of candour, and disabused the minds of several persons who had been misled by the opposite statements. The only attempt I heard of to answer my work, was an angry letter by a Bishop at Pondicherry, published in the Madras papers, to which I replied on the spot: and as nothing more appeared for some time on the subject, I ventured to hope that no similar attempt would be made to mislead the public mind. In this expectation, however, I have been disappointed. About six years ago writers of the Romish Church resumed the charge, repeating the calumnies of former authors, especially the misrepresentations of the Abbé Dubois, whom they quoted as an unquestionable authority, without noticing the confutation of his assertions. This disingenuous conduct came to my notice in November, 1833, and I met it immediately with a letter to the *Editor of the Record*, repeating the substance of my Reply. But this produced little effect upon the opposite party, whose confidence was then gathering strength to publish whatever they chose: and their subsequent proceedings soon convinced me, that to maintain a controversy with men so utterly regardless of their opponents' answers, was a hopeless contention. They write chiefly for their own people, very few of whom venture to read what is written on the protestant view of the subject; and thus the repetition of falsehood confirms them in the belief of its truth. The success of these statements even upon protestants is much more extensive than may be suspected. For some persons, not sufficiently informed on the matter, are carried away by the confidence with which these writers put forth their assertions; and though they may read a pamphlet on the other side of the question, yet it soon shares the fate of most pamphlets, which are frequently put out of sight, and dismissed from the mind. Accordingly, when they hear the calumnies that it answered repeated, they have forgotten the arguments and facts that at one time, perhaps, seemed to them satisfactory, and they begin to feel inclined to think that there must be some truth in that which had appeared to be false. It is by no means uncommon to find persons of intelligence on other subjects so ill-informed upon this, as to credit the statements of these authors for no other reason but because positively made. When remonstrated with upon the impropriety of allowing themselves to be carried away by falsehoods so easy of detection, you shall often hear them reply—Such confident assertions can hardly be without some foundation:—and herein is proved the sagacity of Voltaire, as well as his want of probity, in the advice that he is said to have given to a controversialist to go on repeating his falsehood, without noticing its confutation, assuring him that at last it would be believed.

Such were the circumstances that convinced me that no satisfactory result was to be looked for from a mere controversy with these antagonists, however conducted, or to whatever length protracted. A History of Christianity in India seemed to present the only hope of fortifying the public mind against their assaults; and this thought first suggested the undertaking to my mind.

Of the manner in which the task is executed, the public will judge : but, while very far from indifferent what judgment may be pronounced upon it, I will confess that my chief solicitude has been <u>about facts</u>. This was demanded, as well for the integrity of the history, as for the sake of the parties chiefly implicated in the transactions here recorded. Exposing as they do the infamous conduct of Romish Missionaries, it was specially necessary to ascertain the truth of every statement, and for this reason I have omitted some of doubtful authority. I am not aware of having stated one fact that did not appear to me unquestionable ; and *I pledge myself to withdraw every thing that can be* PROVED *contrary to the truth.* But I do not promise to take notice of any assertions that have already been confuted. My sole object has been to put the public in possession of a History that shall enable them to understand the merits of the question raised by the romanists to the prejudice of the protestant cause : and the end I desire to promote is, the glory of the Lord—an end not to be accomplished without the most scrupulous adherence to truth. Under this conviction, I shall deem nothing that may seem to affect the *integrity* of the work too unimportant to claim the best attention I can command.

During the past six years the confidence of romanists in England has increased more than, perhaps, at any former period since the Reformation. Their chapels and seminaries have been multiplied, but it does not follow that their converts have kept pace with them ; for it is their well-known policy first to provide the building, and then to exert themselves to fill it. While, therefore, there is enough in their activity to keep protestants on the watch against their encroachments, we should take care not to allow ourselves to be deluded by these appearances into the belief, that their progress is equal to their pretensions. Glad would they be to make such an impression on the public mind ; for it would tend to paralyse the timid, and to confirm the lukewarm in their indifference. They are now preparing extensive means of aggression, and threatening great things : but, in reliance upon the God of truth, we tell them, " Let not him that girdeth on his harness boast himself as he that putteth it off." (1 Kings xx. 11.)

Besides these exertions, we are informed, by the Hon. & Rev. George Spencer, that he has proposed to the Romish Clergy abroad to unite in prayer for the conversion of England to the Roman Church, and that they, especially the Archbishop and Clergy of Paris, have entered with zeal into his proposal. Of this there could be nothing to complain, if they would confine themselves to prayer for the Divine blessing on their instructions. No doubt nothing more is to be apprehended from the reverend gentleman with whom the proposal originated : but he does not yet know his newly adopted fraternity, if he imagines that they will be guided by his pacific suggestions, as soon as they shall have attained power to use means more in accordance with the history, the character, and the pretensions of their Church. The record of their proceedings in India here presented to the public, may teach him, and England, what we have to expect, should they ever obtain the object of their prayers.

But is this probable ? What prayers are the Romish priests using for the purpose ? The reverend gentleman informs us, that he was greatly encouraged in his proceedings for England's conversion, on being assured, by some French priests, that they had made a beginning *by offering mass* on the first Thursday that occurred after his proposal. Surely he must have forgotten, or never could have rightly understood, the Creed and Liturgy of the Church he has forsaken, if he expects such prayers to obtain the answer desired. When we consider the character of this Mass—its adoration of a consecrated wafer; its invocation of the Virgin and other Saints; we feel that we have nothing to fear from it for the Protestant institutions of our country. Though the whole body of the Romish clergy should unite in this service, we believe that such prayers can injure none but those who offer them. Should the Lord be pleased again to bring Great Britain under the yoke of Rome, it will be, not in answer to these prayers, but in punishment for her own sins.

In the letter of a Romish Bishop in India alluded to above, one principal cause of the writer's displeasure was, my use of the term *Papist,* instead of *Catholic,* in the Reply to the Abbé Dubois. Nothing was more foreign from my intention than to give offence by using an obnoxious term, and therefore, in the present History I have adopted the word romanist. The term papist occurs indeed, but it will be found generally, if not exclusively, in quotations from other authors. If asked, why I have not called them *Catholics,* since it is the name which they prefer, I answer—Because of the advantage that they disingenuously take of our use of the term. The Church of England retains the word *Catholic* in her Liturgy, and the romanists know that we do not use it in their exclusive sense, but apply it universally to all that have been baptized in the name of the Trinity, hold the true faith in Jesus Christ, have " the pure word of God preached " to them, and the Sacraments " duly administered according to Christ's ordinance in all those things that of necessity are requisite to the same." (Article xix.) The Church of England regards all other churches who answer to this character as united with her to Jesus, their common Head, by communion of the same Spirit. Though varying in outward circumstances, and in matters not essential to salvation, they form various branches of the Catholic, or Universal Church. Yet romanists well know, that many members of both our Church and theirs do not make this distinction, but apply the term exclusively to that of Rome: and, taking advantage of this ignorance in some, and negligence in others, they charge us with inconsistency in using the term, while we protest against their Church. Whereas, they know that protestants use it in its legitimate sense; and the inconsistency is theirs, in applying it only to their own communion.

Are we then to be charged with illiberality for refusing to concede to them this name, while they persist in making so unfair a use of the concession? This is not a mere logomachy. Truly has it been said— "Names are things." For protestants to call romanists *Catholics*, is to put a weapon in their hands which they neglect no opportunity to wield against us. While in courtesy yielding the name, they pretend that we concede the principle it implies; and hereby we expose our brethren, who do not take trouble, or have not ability to discriminate, to the designs of these enemies to the truth and freedom of the Gospel. The single point they keep in view is, that theirs is the only Catholic Church; that all Christians out of her pale, by whomsoever baptized, owe allegiance to the Pope; and that every term is to be repudiated that implies the existence of any Church independent of Rome. *Catholic* is the name that bests accords with these arrogant pretensions; no wonder, therefore, that they so strenuously contend for it: but for the same reason should protestants resist their exclusive appropriation of it to their own communion. *Papist* is, undoubtedly, their most appropriate designation, for it implies an acknowledgment of the Papal supremacy and infallibility, which they alone believe; and the learned Bossuet, and others of their best writers were not ashamed to use it. In the days of those authors, indeed, it was not in such bad odour as it is at present, and this is the real cause of the modern romanists anxiety to get rid of it: but unless their character is altered, they will gain nothing by changing their name. There are countries where even the word *Catholic* is as odious* as the term *Papist* ever was in Europe: and wherever the light and liberty. of the Gospel shall predominate, no mere appellation will shield the darkness and tyranny of Rome from general abhorrence. Should the account of the Roman Church in India given in the following pages, tend to awaken the public mind to the danger of her present encroachments, I shall be grateful to God for the result, and deem myself amply recompensed for all my pains.

The Synod of Diamper is the leading event of the Romish Missions in Malabar, and it developes the character of their entire history. There could be no ques-

---

* See Smith and Dwight's Missionary Researches in Armenia. p. 392, &c.

tion, therefore, as to the necessity of giving in detail the account of its proceedings, together with the circumstances that preceded and followed it. At the same time, the length of its Decrees created some difficulty. As they contain the only authentic account extant of the doctrines and practice of the Syrian Church in Malabar, previous to this atrocious Synod, I could not consent to curtail them. Yet, if given in the body of the work, they would nearly have filled a volume of the ordinary size; and an analysis of them is, no doubt, sufficient for the general reader of history. Such an analysis is given by La Croze, for which he has incurred the censure of some Romish writers. It seemed, therefore, essential to the character of the work, as well as due to myself, to publish them entire; and while consulting the reader's convenience by giving a brief abstract of them in the text, the whole are printed in smaller type in the Appendix. Persons who have neither leisure nor curiosity to consult such records, may deem this unnecessary; but I shall be disappointed if the student of ecclesiastical history does not consider them a valuable appendage to the work.

During the progress of these volumes, a paragraph appeared in the public papers, stating that the Bishop of Calcutta was composing a similar history, for which he was said to have collected some valuable materials during his recent visit to the Syrian Church in Malabar. I applied immediately to the Bishop's son, the Vicar of Islington, to ascertain the fact, and was assured by that gentleman that he believed the report to be without foundation. I then wrote to the Bishop himself, and as his Lordship's answer, while it confirms his son's opinion, also shows the importance that he attaches to such a work, I venture to transcribe that part of it which relates to the subject.

"I wish I were writing, my dear friend, THE HISTORY OF CHRISTIANITY IN INDIA. It is a glorious theme to those who have health, materials, leisure— of none of which three have I the least portion. How the report got into the papers, I cannot for a moment conjecture, unless it were, that, upon hearing of my 20,000 miles of travel, some one had confounded the opportunity, with the health, materials, and leisure of such an undertaking. It never entered my thoughts." Then, in answer to my request for such information as he might have to communicate, his Lordship states, that he has not collected any; assures me, that "the rumoured collections of the Syrian Churches are all a dream;" and refers me to several sources of information from which I had previously drawn. In conclusion, he earnestly persuades me to "to pursue the work with vigour," and encourages me to persevere: and I cannot refrain from acknowledging thus publicly the kindness of his proposal carefully to revise a few sheets of the work, though it is too late to avail myself of the advantage it would have derived from such a revision. Considering his Lordship's incessant avocations, this was a favour I did not venture to ask; but I should certainly have been induced to wait for it, had I contemplated the probability of his finding time to give any attention to the manuscript.

In the prosecution of the undertaking, I have spared no pains to obtain access to all the authentic documents extant; and as their titles, together with, in some cases, a description of their authors and their contents, are given when first quoted, it is unnecessary to enu-

merate them here. I am not aware of having made
use of one work of doubtful authority; and the facts
that were likely to be questioned by romanists if not
well authenticated, I have been specially careful to
establish by reference to authors of their own communion. It has been a weary task to wade through
such a mass of legendary tales, and to find so little of
the light of truth to relieve the toil of the investigation.
Volume after volume of ecclesiastical matter have I
read, jaded and disappointed to discover nothing like
Christianity to extract; and more than once I have
doubted whether it were right to retain the present
title of the work, so little does it answer to the general character of the Syrian Church and the Romish
Missions in India. With this feeling I quite respond
to the sentiment of a friend who has taken the trouble
to read the entire manuscript. In returning the papers,
he writes—" They are painfully interesting — but can
you get no scrap of history that discovers divine faith
or Christian graces in the poor Syrian Churches?
They had the Scriptures among them, and surely they
were not like dead corpses all through their history.
Does Fabricius give nothing in his *Lux Evangelii?* It is
greatly to be regretted that the interior and spiritual
history is absent and lost. Where is the faith, hope
and love of the Gospel? Where is the *Blessed with all
spiritual blessings in heavenly things in Christ?* You cannot *make* what the remnants of history do not give you;
but no doubt there could not have been such a conflict
with Rome, and such a victory, without some internal
principles of real and evangelical truth at the bottom.
The great spiritual lessons of the history are left in
obscurity for want of insight into their actual spiritual

state, and this will only fully be given hereafter in the day of the Lord."

Though not in my power to supply the great deficiency here so affectingly deplored, yet I have occasionally given expression to the feelings that afforded relief to my own mind, and have now only to desire that they may produce a similar effect upon that of the reader. If they do not show all that I desire to exhibit of the true Spirit of Christ and His people, together with their heavenly life, yet the contrast it is attempted to present may enable readers, in some measure, to see the partial character of the History in its present development, and induce them to wait with patient devotion, a future discovery of its meaning and intent. In God's own time and way, He will bring hidden things to light; and, therefore, will we always patiently abide His pleasure, and praise Him more and more.

The two volumes now published will be found to include the History of the Syrian Church and the Romish Missions to the commencement of the present century. The remaining two volumes will give the history of the Protestant Missions. Some progress is made in them, but it was deemed advisable, in the mean time, to give this first Section to the public: and while I regret that it contains so little to satisfy the mind that is chiefly interested in the progress of Divine Truth, I can venture to promise that the latter Section will correspond better to the title of the work.

CONTENTS OF VOL. I.

BOOK FIRST.

CHAPTER I.

A BRIEF DISSERTATION ON THE OPENING OF THE INTERCOURSE BETWEEN THE WESTERN NATIONS AND THE EAST-INDIES.

CHAPTER II.

INTRODUCTION OF CHRISTIANITY INTO INDIA.

CHAPTER III.

RISE AND PROGRESS OF NESTORIANISM.

CHAPTER IV.

RISE AND PROGRESS OF MAHOMEDANISM, AND ITS EFFECT ON THE INDIAN CHURCH.

BOOK SECOND.

CHAPTER I.

CONTINUATION OF THE REVIEW OF THE COMMERCIAL INTERCOURSE WITH INDIA UNTIL THE DISCOVERY OF THE PASSAGE BY WAY OF THE CAPE OF GOOD HOPE.

CHAPTER II.

RISE AND PROGRESS OF THE SECULAR AND ECCLESIASTICAL POWER IN THE CHURCH OF ROME.

CHAPTER III.

MISSION OF FRANCIS XAVIER.

CHAPTER IV.

INQUISITION AT GOA 212

CHAPTER V.

FIRST ATTEMPT TO BRING THE SYRIAN CHURCH OF MALABAR UNDER SUBJECTION TO ROME.

CHAPTER VI.

THE NATIVE POWERS RESIST THE ENCROACHMENTS AND INTOLERANCE OF THE PORTUGUESE.

CHAPTER VII.

CONTINUATION OF THE ROMANISTS' ATTEMPTS AGAINST THE LIBERTY OF THE SYRIAN CHURCH.

CHAPTER VIII.

ARRIVAL OF DON ALEXIO DE MENEZES IN INDIA : HIS PRELIMINARY MEASURES AGAINST THE SYRIAN CHURCH.

BOOK THIRD.

CHAPTER I.

CHAPTER II.

CHAPTER III.

CHAPTER IV.

PROGRESS OF THE ARCHBISHOP'S ENCROACHMENTS.

CHAPTER V.

MENEZES' CONTINUED PROGRESS : OVERCOMES THE ARCHDEACON.

CHAPTER VI.

A HISTORY

OF

CHRISTIANITY IN INDIA.

BOOK I.

CHAPTER I.

A BRIEF DISSERTATION ON THE OPENING OF THE INTERCOURSE BETWEEN THE WESTERN NATIONS AND THE EAST INDIES.

Of all histories, the history of the kingdom of God in the world is the most important. Christianity is the commencement of that kingdom in its spiritual character, and the account of its progress will interest the mind according to our estimate of its worth. If we regard the achievements of men as of superior moment to the conquests of truth, we shall feel more concern in the rise and fall of temporal dominions, than in the advancement of Christ's religion upon earth: but, if duly penetrated with the consequences of the fall, and with gratitude to God for the means which He has provided to remedy those

Preliminary remarks.

B

evils, no record of human conquests, whatever civil benefits they may secure, will be read with half the interest we shall take in the progress of a religion that brings " Glory to God in the highest, and on earth peace, good will toward men.[1]

This feeling will gather strength, as we turn our thoughts from the universal church, to any section of it in which we are more immediately concerned. The interest felt in the general diffusion of the Gospel cannot fail to be increased when our attention is directed to its successes in our own country : and since Eastern India now forms so considerable a portion of the British empire, the history of Christianity in that extensive region, ought to be read with somewhat of the augmented interest that we take in the evangelizing of the land that gave us birth.

To further the cause of Christianity is a sacred duty incumbent upon all who have avouched Jesus Christ to be their Lord ; for His last command to His disciples, to go " into all the world, and preach the gospel to every creature," claims their attention in all ages and in every land, to the extent of their capabilities. How vast then the responsibility of Great Britain, to whom the Almighty has intrusted the empire of India ! But we are too much accustomed to lose sight of our individual duty in the general obligation of the state. Every Christian is responsible to God for whatever means and opportunity he may possess, to make known the tidings of salvation among men : and while a nation, in its collective character, can suffer only in the present world for the neglect of its responsibilities, each

---

[1] Luke ii. 14.

individual will be judged in the next. Instead then of overlooking our own obligations, in the contemplation of those that belong to our country, they ought rather to be kept the more vividly in view. Sitting down to the present history with the mind thus disposed for instruction, we may, with the Divine blessing, derive improvement from what we read, and be stimulated thereby to enter upon the work to which it will invite us with an energy commensurate to its importance.

1. The Saviour's command first claims our attention. "Jesus came and spake unto the disciples, saying, All power is given unto me in heaven and in earth. Go ye therefore, and teach all nations, baptizing them in the name of the Father, and of the Son, and of the Holy Ghost: tea ning them to observe all things whatsoever I have commanded you : and, lo, I am with you alway, even unto the end of the world."[1] These were His last words to those whom He had chosen to lay the foundation of His kingdom in the world. They did not enter immediately upon their commission, but, in obedience to their Lord's directions, awaited the descent of the Holy Ghost, which He had led them to expect, saying, " Behold, I send the promise of my Father upon you : but tarry ye in the city of Jerusalem, until ye be endued with power from on high."[2] Accordingly, when " He was parted from them, and carried up into heaven," " they worshipped Him, and returned to Jerusalem with great joy : and were continually in the temple, praising and blessing God."

The Saviour's command to His apostles.

[1] Matt. xxviii. 18—20.   [2] Luke xxiv. 49, 51—53.

CHAP.
I.

Holy Ghost
descends
upon them.

2. " And when the day of Pentecost was fully come, they were all with one accord in one place. And suddenly there came a sound from heaven as of a rushing mighty wind, and it filled all the house where they were sitting. And there appeared unto them cloven tongues like as of fire, and it sat upon each of them. And they were all filled with the Holy Ghost, and began to speak with other tongues, as the Spirit gave them utterance."[1] Endued thus miraculously with grace and ability for the work, " they went forth, and preached every where, the Lord working with them, and confirming the word with signs following."[2] With such diligence did the first preachers of Christianity attend to their Lord's instructions, that within thirty years from the descent of the Holy Ghost upon them, St Paul applied to their unparalleled exertions to instruct mankind in the Gospel, the very terms in which David described the revolution of the heavenly bodies.— " Their sound went into all the earth, and their words unto the ends of the world."[3] It is not probable that the apostle meant these expressions to be understood literally of all the countries then known to the civilized world. They are to be taken metaphorically, as descriptive of the vast extent to which the glad tidings of salvation had already been conveyed.

Uncertain
whether In-
dia was vis-
ited by an
apostle.

3. Whether India was honoured with the presence of an inspired apostle, is a question involved in great uncertainty. Of its probability, or otherwise, we may perhaps be able to judge, from a brief review of the events which led to the opening of that continent to the natives of the West. Geography is truly said

---

[1] Acts ii. 1—4.   [2] Mark xvi. 20.   [3] Rom. x. 18.

to have been chiefly indebted for its improvement to the wars and commerce of nations ; and the all-wise Ruler of the world has made the same means subsidiary to the diffusion of Divine truth.　Mankind, intent on the objects of their ambition, are as unconscious as the winds that blow, of the subserviency of their exertions to the Almighty's designs.　Even the hearts of kings are in His rule and governance, and He disposes and turns them as it seemeth best to His godly wisdom.[1]　And as of monarchs, so of their subjects, all their projects and exertions are under the absolute control of the King of Kings.　When He causes them to prosper in the world, they have their reward ; but it is earthly, and fadeth away suddenly like the grass.　The permanent fruit of their endeavours is reaped by the church of God, and the glory that may result from them must ultimately return to Him.

4. With this recognition of a wise and gracious Providence guiding all human affairs to accomplish His own designs, we regard Alexander the Great, King of Macedon, as an important agent raised up by the Almighty, to prepare a way for the Gospel in the East. For that ambitious prince first opened India to the people of the West, and the opening that he effected was never again entirely closed.　The country, indeed, had long been partially known to the natives of Egypt and Syria, by means of the commerce carried on between those countries. The most ancient navigators of whom we read, are the Egyptians and Phenicians, whose first voyages were made in the Mediterranean, called in sacred writ, the Great Sea, and the Sea of

India first known to the Egyptians and Phenicians.

---

[1] Prov. xxi. 1.　Eng. Liturgy. Com. Service.

Tarshish. Their trade, however, was not long confined to the countries bordering on its shores. Acquiring early possession of some ports on the Arabian Gulf, they extended the sphere of their commerce, and are represented as the first people of the West who opened a communication with India by sea.[1]

Egyptians relinquish maritime pursuits.

5. The Indian trade was soon engrossed by the Phenicians, who for many ages continued in undisturbed possession of the monopoly, the Egyptians becoming indifferent about the commerce, while they could obtain the commodities of the East without personal risk or trouble. The fertile soil and temperate climate of Egypt producing the necessaries and comforts of life in rich profusion, rendered the inhabitants almost independent of other countries; and they laid aside their maritime pursuits for so long a season, that they began at last to think themselves the greatest nation in the world ; and it became an established maxim of their policy, to renounce all intercourse with foreigners. In consequence of this, they held other people, as well as the Hebrews,[2] in abomination ; and they especially regarded all sea-faring persons as impious and profane. In the end they carried this prejudice so far, that they actually fortified their harbours, and refused admission to strangers.

B. C. 1491.

Sesostris revives them. He marches across India.

6. The enterprising ambition of Sesostris, king of Egypt, disdaining the restraints imposed upon it by these contracted ideas of his subjects, prompted him to render the Egyptians a commercial people ; and in the course of his reign he so completely accomplished this, that, if we

[1] Robertson's Historical Disquisition concerning antient India, p. 5.

[2] Gen. xliii. 32 ; xlvi. 34.

may give credit to some historians, he was able to fit out a fleet of four hundred ships in the Arabian Gulf, which conquered all the countries stretching along the Egyptian sea to India. At the same time, his army, led by himself, marched through Asia, and subjected to his dominion every part of it, as far as the banks of the Ganges: whence, crossing that river, he advanced to the Eastern Ocean. Some are of opinion that these efforts produced no permanent effect:[1] but others have very reasonably conjectured, that they wrought a considerable change in the manners of the inhabitants, and that several laws and customs now prevailing in India, which resemble those of ancient Egypt, were introduced by Sesostris at the time of his invasion.[2] His subjects, however, were too proud, or too indolent, to derive any immediate benefit from his exertions. They appear to have been so contrary to the genius and habits of the Egyptians, that, on the death of Sesostris, they resumed their ancient maxims, and many ages elapsed before the commercial connexion of Egypt with India came to be of much importance.[3]

7. The Egyptians willingly abandoned the toils and the gains of commerce generally, as well as those of India, to the more enterprising inhabitants of Phenicia, the situation of whose country was favourable to the commercial spirit. The territory which they possessed was neither large nor fertile. It was from trading with

Phenicians permitted to hold the monopoly of the Indian trade;—theirs the earliest route of communication with India.

---

[1] Robertson's India.

[2] La Croze. Histoire du Christianisme des Indes, p. 434. This subject will be noticed more particularly in the account to be given of the Mythology and Customs of India.

[3] Herodotus, Diodorus Siculus. See Rollin, vol. i. pp. 78—83.

other countries only that they could derive either opulence or power. Accordingly, the traffic carried on by the Phenicians of Sidon and Tyre, was extensive and adventurous; and, both in manners and policy, they resembled the great commercial states of modern times, more than any people in the ancient world. Among the various branches of their commerce, that with India may be regarded as one of the most considerable and lucrative. As by their situation on the Mediterranean, and the imperfect state of navigation, they could not attempt to open a direct communication with India by sea; the adventurous spirit of ambition prompted them to wrest from the Idumeans some commodious harbours towards the bottom of the Arabian Gulf. From these they had a regular intercourse with India on the one hand, and with the eastern and southern coasts of Africa on the other. The distance, however, from the Arabian Gulf to Tyre, was considerable, and rendered the conveyance of goods thither by land carriage so tedious and expensive, that it became necessary for them to take possession of Rhinocolura, the nearest port in the Mediterranean to the Arabian Gulf. Thither all the commodities brought from India were conveyed over land by a route much shorter, and more practicable, than that by which the productions of the East were, at a subsequent period, carried from the opposite shore of the Arabian Gulf to the Nile. At Rhinocolura they were shipped again, to be transported by an easy navigation to Tyre, and thence distributed through the world. This is the earliest route of communication with India of which we have any authentic description; and it had so many advantages over any other ever known before the

modern discovery of a new course of navigation
to the East, that the Phenicians could supply
other nations with the productions of India in
greater abundance, and at a cheaper rate, than
any people of antiquity. This circumstance,
for a considerable time, secured to them a
monopoly of that trade; and so extraordinary
was the wealth of individuals, that it rendered
the " merchants of Tyre, princes, and her
traffickers the honourable of the earth:"[1] while
the power of the state itself became so extensive, that it first taught mankind to conceive
what vast resources a commercial people possess, and what great exertions they are capable
of making.[2]

8. The Jews, by their vicinity to Tyre, had
a favourable opportunity to observe the wealth
which flowed into that city, from the lucrative
commerce carried on by the Phenicians, and
they were induced to aim at obtaining a share
of it. This they effected under the prosperous
reigns of David and Solomon, partly by the
conquests which they made of a small district
in the land of Edom, whereby they obtained
possession of the harbours of Elath and Esion-
geber on the Red Sea. They were assisted
also by the friendship of Hiram, king of Tyre,
who enabled Solomon to fit out fleets, which,
under the direction of Phenician pilots, sailed
to Tarshish and Ophir.[3] In what region of the
earth we should search for these famous ports,
which furnished the navy of Solomon with the
various commodities enumerated by the sacred
historians, is an inquiry that has long exercised
the industry of learned men. Ophir was early

B. C.
992

B. C.
992
The Jews'
attention
drawn to
this com-
merce.

---

[1] Isaiah xxiii. 8.   [2] Robertson.
[3] 1 Kings ix. 26; x. 22.

supposed to be situated in some part of India, and the Jews were thought to be one of the nations which traded with that country. But the opinion now more generally adopted is, that Solomon's fleets, after passing the straits of Babelmandel, held their course along the south-west coast of Africa, as far as the kingdom of Sofala, a country so celebrated for its rich mines of gold and silver, that it has been deno-minated by Oriental writers—the Golden Sofala. It abounded also in all the other articles which composed the cargoes of Solomon's ships.[1] The Jews, then, we may conclude, have no title to be reckoned among the nations which carried on intercourse with India by sea.

B. C.
510.
Persians ob-
tain the first
foreign esta-
blishment in
India.

9. The first establishment of any foreign power in India, which can be ascertained by evidence meriting any degree of credit, is that of the Persians ; and even of this we have only a very general and dubious account. Darius, the son of Hystaspes, king of Persia, possessed an active and enterprising spirit. Having sub-jected to his dominion many of the countries which stretched south-east from the Caspian Sea towards the river Oxus, his curiosity was excited to acquire a more extensive and ac-curate knowledge of India, on which they bordered. But his conquests do not seem to have extended beyond the district watered by the Indus, nor was any general knowledge of India diffused at that time in consequence of his expedition.

B. C.
326.
Alexander
the Great
covets the
Indian com-

10. About one hundred and sixty years after the reign of Darius Hystaspes, Alexander the Great undertook his celebrated expedition into India. Soon after his first successes in Asia, he

[1] Calmet's Dictionary on Tarshish and Ophir.

seems to have formed the idea of establishing a universal monarchy, and to have aspired to the dominion of the sea as well as of the land. From the wonderful efforts of the Tyrians in their own defence, when left without any ally or protector, he conceived a high opinion of the resources of maritime power, and of the wealth to be derived from commerce, especially that with India, which he found engrossed by the citizens of Tyre. With a view to secure this commerce, and to establish a station for it that should be preferable in many respects to that of Tyre, as soon as he had completed the conquest of Egypt, he founded a city near one of the mouths of the Nile, which he honoured with his own name. With such admirable discernment was the situation chosen, that ALEX-ANDRIA soon became the greatest trading city in the ancient world ; and, notwithstanding many successive revolutions in empire, it continued during eighteen centuries to be the chief seat of commerce with India. Amidst the military operations to which Alexander was soon obliged to turn his attention, the desire of acquiring the lucrative trade which the Tyrians had carried on with the East, was never relinquished. Events soon occurred, that not only confirmed and added strength to this desire, but also opened to him a prospect of obtaining the sovereignty of those regions which supplied the rest of mankind with so many precious commodities.

11. After his final victory over the Persians, in his pursuit of the last Darius, and of Bessus, the murderer of that unfortunate monarch, he was led to traverse that part of Asia which stretches from the Caspian Sea beyond the river Oxus. He advanced towards the East as

B. C. 326.

merce—he founds Alexandria to facilitate the communication.

Commences his first expedition to India.

CHAP.
1.

far as Maracanda, then a city of some import-ance, and destined in a future period, under the modern name of Samarcand, to be the capital of an empire not inferior to his own either in extent or power. In a progress of several months, through provinces hitherto un-known to the Greeks; in a line of march often approaching near to India, and among people accustomed to much intercourse with its in-habitants; he learned many things concerning the state of a country that had been long the object of his thoughts and ambition, which in-creased his determination to invade it. Decisive in all his resolutions, and prompt in their execu-tion, he soon set out from Bactria, and crossed that ridge of mountains which, under various denominations, forms what oriental geographers have called the Stony Girdle. This range of gigantic hills environs Asia, and constitutes the northern barrier of India.

Is compelled to return.

12. After passing the Indus, Alexander marched forward in the road that leads directly to the Ganges and the opulent provinces to the south-east, now comprehended under the general name of Hindoostan. But on the banks of the Hydaspes, known in modern times by the name of the Jhylum, he was opposed by Porus, a powerful monarch of the country, at the head of a numerous army, whom he overcame, and received the submission of Porus himself and his allies. This and other interruptions that he met with, induced him to alter his route. Stimulated by the descriptions he had received of the Ganges, he continued to press onward towards that mighty river and the regions through which it flows : but on reaching the banks of the Hyphasis, the modern Beyah, in the Punjab of Lahore, his army with one voice refused to

advance further. They had already done so much, and suffered so severely, chiefly from excessive rains and extensive inundations, that their patience and strength were exhausted: and they persisted with such sullen obstinacy in their determination to return, that even Alexander, though possessed in the highest degree of every quality that gains ascendency over the minds of military men, was obliged to yield, and to issue orders for marching back to Persia.

B.C. 326.

13. Before setting out from the Hydaspes for the East, Alexander left some officers behind, with orders to build and collect as many vessels as possible during his absence: and on his return to that river, he found that they had executed his instructions with so much diligence, that a numerous fleet was waiting his arrival. Amidst the hurry of war and the rage of conquest, he never lost sight of his pacific and commercial schemes. The destination of his fleet was to sail down the Indus to the Ocean, then to proceed from the mouth of that river to the Persian Gulf, that a communication by sea might thus be opened with India and the centre of his dominions. The distance between the ocean and the place on the Hydaspes where this fleet was fitted out, cannot be less than one thousand British miles. Soon after they reached the mouth of the Indus, Alexander, satisfied with having accomplished this arduous undertaking, led his army by land back to Persia. The command of the fleet, with a considerable body of troops on board, he left to Nearchus, who, after a coasting voyage of seven months, conducted it safely up the Persian Gulf into the Euphrates.

Opens a communication by sea with India and his dominions.

14. In this manner did Alexander first open the knowledge of India to the people of Europe,

Customs and manners of India at that

period con-
tinue unal-
tered.

and an extensive district of that vast country was surveyed with greater accuracy than could have been expected from the short time that he remained there. From the accounts of the campaign written by three of his principal officers[1] we learn, that at that early period India was divided into regular monarchies of considerable extent. They describe with accuracy the climate, soil, and productions of the country. Their descriptions of the inhabitants, with their manners, customs, and even dress, correspond minutely with what we now observe, though at the distance of more than two thousand years.

Extent of
Alexander's
projects.

15. When Alexander invaded India, he had something more in view than a transient campaign. It was his object to annex that extensive and opulent region to his empire; and though the refractory spirit of his army compelled him, at that time, to suspend the prosecution of his design, he was far from relinquishing it. Having established a medium of communication with the interior of Hindoostan, he proposed to convey the valuable commodities of that country down the Indus, then to transmit them from the Persian Gulf into the interior parts of his Asiatic dominions; while by the Arabian Gulf they were to be carried to Alexandria, and thence distributed to the rest of the world.

His death.

16. Grand and extensive as these schemes were, the precautions taken against disappointment, and the arrangements made for carrying them into effect, were so various, and so judicious, that Alexander had reason to entertain sanguine hopes of their proving successful. But his race was run. A premature death put

[1] Ptolemy, the son of Lagus, Aristobulus, and Nearchus.

an end to all his ambitious calculations. He had fulfilled the purpose for which Divine Providence had raised him up; [1] and in little more than a year after his expedition to India, this mighty conqueror was carried off in a fit of intemperance. How humiliating a spectacle of human greatness destroyed by human weakness! No hand can lay a mortal so prostrate as his own. He for whose ambition the world was too small, could not conquer his vicious propensities, and they mastered him at the zenith of his glory. "Lord, what is man?" A compound of inconsistencies. The good in him that mercy has permitted to survive the fall, cannot preserve him from the evil that he inherits; and, but for Divine grace preventing, his passions will predominate over the best feelings of his heart, and lay his honour in the dust.

B. C. 326.

17. Not long after Alexander's death, his vast empire was divided between his four principal officers, but not without many severe contests in the partition. Macedon and Greece were given to Cassander: Thrace, with several provinces of lower Asia, fell to the share of Lysimachus: Egypt was the portion of Ptolemy, afterwards surnamed Soter: and upper Asia became the dominion of Seleucus. Accordingly it devolved on the latter two, Ptolemy and Seleucus, to carry into effect Alexander's intention regarding the commerce with India; and they both showed themselves willing and com-

B. C. 323. Division of his empire between four of his officers.

[1] The devout reader of the Bible, and the attentive observer of the ways of God with men, will not hesitate to subscribe to this sentiment. The removal of Alexander, and the immediate division of his empire, were in exact accordance with the prophecies of these events delivered more than two hundred years before they occurred. (Dan. vii. 6; viii. 8.)

Seleucus,
king of Sy-
ria, pursues
Alexander's
scheme of
conquest in
India, which
is ultimately
abandoned
by his suc-
cessors.

petent to prosecute the undertaking which he had so ably planned and commenced.

18. Seleucus, king of Syria, possessed much of the ambitious spirit of his master, as well as the eastern division of his conquests. He, like all the officers formed under Alexander, entertained such high notions of the advantages to be derived from a commercial intercourse with India, as induced him to march into that country to secure them. We have no particular account of his expedition. All we know is, that his pretext for undertaking it was some hostile demonstrations, real or imagined, on the part of Sandracottus, king of the Prasii;[1] against whom he carried on a successful war, advancing considerably beyond the utmost boundary of Alexander's progress eastward. Compelled to return for the defence of his dominions against Antigonus, he concluded a treaty of peace with Sandracottus, and sent a confidential officer, Megasthenes, to cultivate a friendly intercourse with that prince. The Prasii over whom he reigned were a powerful nation on the banks of the Ganges. Megasthenes executed his commission with fidelity, resided in the capital of the Prasii many years, and was probably the first European who beheld the river Ganges. The position of Palibothra is, with great probability, supposed to be the same with that of the modern city of Allahabad, at the confluence of the two great rivers, Jumna and Ganges. Alexander did not advance further than the spot where the modern city of Lahore is situated.

---

[1] 'The Prasii were the descendants of Pooru of Poorag, visited by Megasthenes, ambassador of Seleucus, and the principal city of the Yadus, ere it sent forth the four branches from Satwati.'—Annals and Antiquities of Rajast'han, by Lt. Col. JAMES TOD, Vol. I., p. 39.

Megasthenes, who was an officer in his army, became thoroughly acquainted with all that was hitherto known of India : he was, therefore, well qualified to describe, for the information of his countrymen, the nature and importance of the regions he had traversed. Though he was too fond of the marvellous, yet his accounts are considered, on the whole, worthy of credit. From his writings the ancients seem to have derived almost all their knowledge of the interior of India ; and from comparing the three most ample accounts of those regions extant, by Diodorus Siculus, Strabo, and Arrian, they appear manifestly, from their near resemblance, to be a transcript of the words of Megasthenes.

His embassy to Sandracottus, and another of Daimachus to his son and successor, Allitrochidas, are the last transactions of the Syrian monarchs with India of which we have any account. Nor can we either fix with accuracy the time, or describe the manner, in which their possessions in India were wrested from them. It is probable that they were obliged to abandon that country soon after the death of Seleucus, which happened forty-two years after the decease of Alexander. The petty kings of Bactria continued to carry on military operations in India with considerable success. Their country was separated from India by the mountainous range whence both the Indus and the Oxus flow : and recovering possession of the district near the mouth of the Indus which Alexander had subdued, they penetrated far into the interior of the country. They held peaceable possession of their conquest, until, about one hundred and twenty-six years before the Christian era, a powerful horde of Tartars wrested it from them. Driven by necessity

B. C
323.

B. C.
126.

c

from their native seat on the confines of China, and obliged to move towards the West by the pressure of a more numerous body that rolled on behind them, they passed the Jaxartes, and pouring in upon Bactria, like an irresistible torrent, overwhelmed that kingdom, and put an end to the dominion of the Greeks there, after it had been established near one hundred and thirty years.

19. Our attention is next turned to Ptolemy Soter, king of Egypt, whose exertions to carry into effect Alexander's commercial schemes, proved more successful than those of his cotemporary, Seleucus, in prosecuting their master's designs of conquest in the East. Under Ptolemy's auspices and vigilance, Egypt soon became the seat of an intercourse with India that promised to be successful and permanent; and it is not without admiration that we observe how soon and how regularly the commerce with the East came to be carried on by that very channel, in which the sagacity of Alexander destined it to flow. Ptolemy, when established in the empire of Egypt, fixed the seat of his government in Alexandria; and the celebrity of its mart, and the immunities which the king granted to traders of all nations, soon attracted vast numbers of foreigners, and induced them to take up their abode in that capital. Ptolemy was one of Alexander's most confidential officers, and he knew that his masters' chief object in founding Alexandria was to secure the advantages arising from the commerce with India. The king of Egypt showed that he was able to appreciate this design, and knew how to render the advantages of his situation available for its accomplishment. Alexandria, commanding the commerce with

the East and the West, soon became the emporium of the world. The Egyptians might now be
called a maritime nation, and there was better
prospect of their continuing to pay attention to
nautical pursuits than under the reign of Sesostris. For the protection of their shipping,
Ptolemy built a magnificent light-house on the
Island of Pharos, at the mouth of the harbour
of Alexandria, which was esteemed one of the
seven wonders of the world. A long and prosperous reign enabled him to bring his design
to some degree of maturity ; and in the year
before Christ 284, he was succeeded by a son,
Ptolemy Philadelphus, who entered with no
less ardour into all his father's commercial
arrangements.

20. In this reign the trade with India began
to revive at Tyre, its ancient mart. But the
King of Egypt, in order to retain this lucrative
monopoly, projected, and indeed commenced,
the formation of a spacious canal between the
Red Sea and the eastern branch of the Nile, by
means of which, had it been completed, the
productions of India might have been conveyed
to Alexandria wholly by water. When, from
some cause which cannot now be ascertained,
this project failed, Ptolemy Philadelphus built
a city on the western coast of the Red Sea, to
which he gave the name of Berenice. The site
of this city was well chosen ; the goods from
India were transported from Berenice to Coptos
by land, about two hundred and fifty-eight Roman miles, through the desert of Thebais. From
Coptos they were conveyed to the Nile, about
three miles distant, by means of a navigable
canal, and thence carried down the stream to
Alexandria. In this channel the intercourse
between the East and West continued to be

Margin notes:

B. C.
126.

Ptolemy
Philadel-
phus ; his
judicious
measures to
secure the
Indian
trade.

carrieᴜ on during two hundred and fifty years that is to say, as long as Egypt remained an in dependent kingdom.

21. It is not known how far the Egyptiaɪ voyagers proceeded along the coast of India but they appear for a considerable time to havɪ limited their commerce to that part of the coun· try which Alexander had visited and subdued As their vessels were small, they sailed near thɪ shore; so that their voyages must have been cir· cumscribed within comparatively narrow limits. and under the Ptolemies no considerable pro· gress was made in the discovery of India. Somɪ writers maintain that they stretched as far aː the northern part of the Malabar coast; yet thiɪ they allow to have been the extent of their pro· gress. It seems very doubtful, however, whe· ther they proceeded so far, or even advanced beyond the mouth of the Indus.

22. During this period, the Persians were nc less desirous than the people around them tc possess the valuable productions and rich manu- factures of India. Averse to navigation, they left to the Egyptians the undisputed monopoly of the commerce by sea; while they trans- ported the commodities of India on camels from the banks of the Indus to those of the Oxus and the Caspian Sea: and thence, by means of na- vigable rivers and canals, or by land-carriage, they conveyed them to all parts of the Persian dominions.

23. Such were the channels of intercourse with India by sea and land, while the em- pires of Egypt and Persia continued to be go- verned by their own sovereigns: but all this power and these resources, together with the other known parts of the world, were soon to be concentrated in one government. The time

drew near for the advent of Him, whose appearance was to bring glad tidings of great joy to all people. As the consummation of His reign on earth is to be universal peace; so all nations were at peace at the time of His appearing. The arms of Rome, after many severe contests and frequent alternations of victory and defeat, at last triumphed successively over Sicily and Carthage, Greece and Syria; and finally, Alexandria was taken by Octavius thirty years before the birth of Jesus Christ, and Egypt reduced into the form of a Roman province. Three years after, by a decree of the Roman senate, Octavius obtained the proud title of Augustus Cæsar, and an absolute exemption from the laws; an elevation which none before had legally occupied, so that he was properly the first Roman emperor. Left without a rival in the world, he shut the temple of Janus, in token of universal peace.

24. In that year Christ was born. It had been revealed seven hundred years before, that He should make His first appearance in Bethlehem:[1] and the Providence of God so overruled the proceedings of the Roman emperor, that his attention to the internal arrangement of his vast dominions, compelled the mother of the Messiah to journey from Nazareth, where she dwelt, to Bethlehem, previous to the birth of her miraculous child. The event is thus recorded in Holy Writ.—" And it came to pass in those days, that there went out a decree from Cæsar Augustus, that all the world should be taxed. And all went to be taxed, every one to his own city. And Joseph also went up from Galilee, out of the city of Nazareth, into Judæa, unto the city of David, which is called Beth-

B. C. 27.

B. C. 4.

These events lead to the birth of Jesus Christ at Bethlehem.

[1] Micah v. 2.

lehem, (because he was of the house and lineage .of David) to be taxed with Mary his espoused wife, being great with child. And so it was, that, while they were there, the days were accomplished that she should be delivered. And she brought forth her first-born son, and wrapped him in swaddling clothes, and laid him in a manger ; because there was no room for them in the inn."[1]

A manifest
arrange-
ment of
Divine Pro-
vidence
worthy of
our grateful
adoration.

25. Who can bring his mind to doubt whether all this was the arrangement of a wise and almighty Being? Who can believe that these events concurred accidentally to bring to pass a prediction so ancient and so circumstantially given? Who can think that there is nothing worthy of special remark in the circumstances attending the Redeemer's birth? Surely the same God, whose infinite wisdom ordained and foretold the wondrous event, brought it to pass by His all-pervading power. It is written, " Known unto God are all his works from the beginning of the world ;"[2] and the devout Christian verily believes, that he remembers " the former things of old ;" " declaring the end from the beginning, and from ancient times the things that are not yet done, saying, My counsel shall stand, and I will do all my pleasure." For He is " God, and there is none else ;" He is " God, and there is none like" Him.[3]

Such was the position of the world when the Sun of Righteousness arose upon it with healing in His wings.[4] " He came a light to lighten the Gentiles, and the glory of His people Israel."[5] If ' an undevout astronomer is mad ;' what shall be said of an undevout historian ? If *he* is

---

[1] Luke ii. 1—7.   [2] Acts xv. 18.   [3] Isa. xlvi. 9, 10.
[4] Malachi iv. 2.   [5] Luke ii. 31, 32,

denied the title of a rational being, who can contemplate without devotion the harmony of the celestial spheres; what right can that man have to the name, who can regard without piety and gratitude a succession of circumstances so much more within our range of observation, and bringing about a result so interesting to the human race? To elevate a mind like this, and teach it to contemplate the sublimities of religion, demands supernatural power and instruction. In such a case, the Redeemer's own question is quite in point.—" If I have told you earthly things, and ye believe not, how shall ye believe, if I tell you of heavenly things?"[1]

26. Thus far we have seen how Divine Providence had progressively opened the way, and prepared facilities, for the universal diffusion of that light with which the Redeemer was to illumine the world. The active pursuits of commerce were rapidly bringing the eastern and western worlds into closer union with each other. The Romans were no less desirous to obtain the productions of India than the nations they had subdued, and their thirst for those luxuries increased with their power to command them. For many ages they continued to flow through the two channels projected by Alexander, and opened by his successors: but as these modes of conveyance did not adequately supply the growing demands of Rome for the commodities of the East, a third medium of communication was opened between Mesopotamia and other provinces on the banks of the Euphrates, and those parts of Syria and Palestine which lay near the Mediterranean. By this route Abraham, upwards of 2000 years before, journeyed from " Ur of the Chaldees, to

Romans prosecute the Indian trade with activity. They open a third channel of communication through Mesopotamia; Solomon traded with the East by the same route.

_____
[1] John iii. 12.

go, at the command of God into the land of Canaan."[1] Solomon, when he turned his attention to commerce, considered this station of so much importance, that he built a city in the desert of Syria, towards the Euphrates, to facilitate his intercourse with the East. To this city he gave the Syriac name of Tadmor,[2] which subsequently received the Greek name of Palmyra, both appellations referring to the beauty and abundance of the palm tree which grew there. Under the Romans, the city of Palmyra became a place of great importance; and considering the natural disadvantages of its situation, its opulence can be attributed only to the vast extent of its commerce.

A. D.
50.
Hippalus
opens a di-
rect com-
munication
with India
across the
Arabian sea.

27. These modes of intercourse with India continued with little variation, until about the fiftieth year of the Christian era, at which time a discovery was made that materially shortened the voyage from Egypt, and rapidly led to a more extensive knowledge of the continent and islands of the East. Hitherto, as already described, their small coasting vessels had crept along the northern shore of the Arabian Sea. In the course of their voyages, the Greek and Egyptian pilots could not fail to observe the regular shifting of the periodical winds, now called Monsoons, which blow with little variation from the north-east and south-west at different seasons of the year. Encouraged by attending to this circumstance, Hippalus, the commander of an Egyptian vessel engaged in the Indian trade, ventured, about this time, to relinquish the slow and circuitous course hitherto taken; and boldly stretching from the mouth of the Arabian Gulf across the ocean, he was

---

[1] Gen. xi. 31.　　　　[2] 1 Kings ix. 18.

carried by the south-west monsoon to Musiris,
a harbour on the western coast of India. This
was the greatest adventure of navigation that
had hitherto been made by the Egyptian traders,
and the passage thus opened continued to be
the best communication by sea between the
eastern and western nations, during the next
fourteen centuries. The voyage from the mouth
of the Arabian Gulf to Musiris was performed
in forty days.

28. It is uncertain at what part of the Malabar coast this first emporium of India was
situated; but the opinion now generally adopted
is, that it was somewhere between Goa and
Tellicherry. The elder Pliny describes this
harbour, and that of Barace, which was not far
distant from it, as very incommodious for trade,
in consequence of the shallowness of the water.
This inconvenience would induce the merchants
to look out for a more convenient port, and they
soon found one on the same coast. Its name
was Barygaza, and Strabo's description of its
approach and situation corresponds with that of
Baroach, on the great river Nerbudda, a few
miles north of Surat. This soon became a mart
of far more consideration than Musiris, carrying
on an extensive commerce with the vessels of
Egypt, and bartering the productions of the
East for the manufactures of the West. A
thirst for gain, excited by the increasing facilities
for its acquisition; and the spirit of research,
awakened by the accounts of those distant
regions brought home by different voyagers, led
the active and enterprising Romans to extend
their survey of the Indian coasts. The elder
Pliny, who lived about fifty years after Strabo,
added to the geographical information already
possessed, an account of the Island of Ceylon,

which he calls Taprobane.[1] But it is to Ptolemy we are chiefly indebted for an account of the knowledge that was soon afterwards acquired of the countries still further to the eastward.

Ptolemy's Geography of India.

29. Ptolemy wrote about eighty years after the elder Pliny. Though he never visited the East, yet, residing in Alexandria at a period when the trade with India was carried on there with great activity, he was favourably situated for obtaining information from persons who had visited that country, and was indefatigable in collecting materials for his geography. Considering the infancy of the science, we cannot be surprised to find his geographical delineations of the places he described very erroneous. Nevertheless, they are sufficiently accurate to convey an idea to what extent those regions were known at that early period. His description of the eastern coast of the Indian continent, as far as the river Ganges, is more correct than might have been expected; and it favours the inference we have drawn, that he received his accounts of it from voyagers who had themselves surveyed those parts. But his delineations of the regions beyond are too imperfect to warrant such a conclusion, and lead to the conjecture, that the persons from whom he collected his information, received it themselves from the native traders who brought the commodities of those distant countries to the marts of India. This observation applies to his Golden Chersonesus, supposed to be the peninsula of Malacca, the eastern boundary of the bay of Bengal. In that case, the great bay which he describes to the eastward, would be the Gulf of Siam. He speaks of Catigara as the utmost limit of navi-

[1] For a more particular account of this island, see Chap. III. of the present Book.

gation in those times, though he mentions a place beyond, which he calls Thinæ, or Sinæ Metropolis. This is the most remote spot named in his geography, and it has been conjectured, from the similarity in the name, to be some port in China. M. D'Anville concludes, and his conclusion seems to be more probable, that the situation of Sin-hoa, in the western part of Cochin China, corresponds with Ptolemy's description of the site of Sinæ Metropolis. This point must be left for those interested in the inquiry to determine. It is enough for the purpose of this history to have noticed the probable boundary of the navigation eastward at that early period.

Besides this vast extent of coast, Ptolemy has described the island of Ceylon, or Taprobane, on the western, and the Andaman and Nicobar islands on the eastern side of the bay of Bengal.

30. While the Romans were thus extending their researches in this direction by sea, they were no less active in pursuit of the same object by land. The trade carried on with India through the provinces North of Syria, as already described, was continued with great activity, and in the course of a few years it extended to the borders of China. The Romans then endeavoured to render their intercourse with the country more secure by entering into a negotiation with one of the monarchs of that great empire. It is worthy of remark, that this information is derived, not from Greek or Roman, but from Chinese historians, who record [1] "that Antoun (the Emperor Marcus Antoninus) the king of the people of the Western Ocean, sent

[1] Memoire sur les Liaisons et le Commerce des Romains, avec les Tartares et les Chinois, par M. de Guignes. Mem. de Literat. xxxii. 355 &c. Robertson's Disquisition, p. 78.

The extent
of the know-
ledge of the
East in the
second cen-
tury.

an embassy with this view to Oun-ti, who reigned over China in the hundred and sixty-sixth year of the Christian æra."

31. The farthest point East in this direction to which their knowledge extended, was a town which Ptolemy calls Sera Metropolis, which appears, from various circumstances, to have been in the same situation with Kant-cheou, a city of some note in Chen-si, the most westerly province of the Chinese empire. This industrious and intelligent geographer collected some general information concerning various nations towards the North, which, according to the position he gives them, occupied parts of the great plain of Tartary, extending considerably beyond Lassa, the capital of Tibet.

Such were the limits of the eastern countries known to the Romans in the second century of the Christian æra. They, and the powers who successively followed them in the sovereignty of the western world, were for many ages content with the commercial advantages resulting from the connexion with India, all thoughts of conquest being relinquished until the fifteenth century, and the nations of Europe aiming at nothing more, than to secure an intercourse of trade with that opulent country.

This rapid sketch of the history of events that led to the opening of India to the nations of the West, may serve to dispel the mystery which, to some persons, seems to hang over the earlier records of European intercourse with the East. It may also, in some measure, enable the reader to judge of the probability of the account next to be given of the introduction of Christianity into those distant regions. [1]

[1] The reader, who may wish to fill up the outline described

in the text, will find ample materials for the purpose in the following works;

Strabo's Geography; Arrian's History of the Indies; Pliny's Natural History; Ptolemy's Geography.

The accounts of these writers are involved in much obscurity, which M. D'Anville has endeavoured to remove. In the execution of his task, he has shown considerable diligence and ability, and many of his conclusions are now generally adopted.

His principal works are, Limites du Monde connues Anciens au-dela du Gange. Mem. de Literat. Ant. de l'Inde.

This chapter is drawn up chiefly from Robertson's Historical Disquisition, concerning the knowledge which the ancients had of India, in which work may be found a very useful digest of the above-mentioned authors. Rollin's Ancient History will furnish a still more circumstantial account of the principal events here related.

CHAPTER II.

INTRODUCTION OF CHRISTIANITY INTO INDIA.

Improbability of any Apostles having preached in India.

1. WHILE mankind were establishing the commercial intercourse between Europe and Asia, described in the preceding chapter, the providence of God was preparing the way for the propagation of the Gospel in the East. At what precise period it was introduced into India, is uncertain. Tradition dates it as early as the apostolic age, and ascribes it to the preaching of Apostles; this, however, is very doubtful, as will presently be shown. There is satisfactory evidence indeed that it was carried to India at a very early period; but, considering the tedious mode of communication with that country, and the ancients' limited knowledge of its inhabitants until towards the close of the first century, it is not probable that any of the Apostles of our Lord embarked on such a voyage. Instead, however, of prejudging this interesting question, let us see what the earliest historians of the Church have written upon the subject.

The account of St. Bartholomew's preaching there incredible.

2. Eusebius, the father of Ecclesiastical history, relates, that St. Bartholomew preached the Gospel in India.[1] This assertion is repeated

[1] Eccl. Hist. lib. v. c. 10. Eusebius lived in the fourth century. He was consecrated Bishop of Cæsarea, in Palestine, A. D. 313, and died A. D. 338. His history of the Church of Christ is carried on from the commencement to the year 309.

by Socrates,[1] who, referring to the division of the gentile world among the Apostles which Eusebius had related,[2] says, that India was assigned to St. Bartholomew.[3] He describes this country as situated upon the confines of Ethiopia, calls it the innermost India, and relates that it was inhabited by several barbarous nations, who spake numerous languages. From this description it is uncertain what precise country he meant; but "no doubt," says Cave," it was the Asian Œthiopia:"[4] that is, the country beyond Ethiopia, with which the merchants of Alexandria carried on the extensive commerce which has been described in the former chapter.

That St. Bartholomew was ever in India is very problematical indeed. Eusebius does not name that Apostle in his account of the division of the heathen nations to which Socrates refers; and it is only incidentally that he alludes, in a subsequent part of his history, to the journey in question.[5] Socrates also mentions it without reference to any authority for his assertion, and asserts, at the same time, that India was not enlightened with the doctrines of Christianity before the reign of Constantine the Great.[6]

[1] Socrates followed in the fifth century, taking up the history where Eusebius left off, and continuing it to the year 440.

[2] Ecc. Hist. lib. iii. c. 1.

[3] Socrates Scholasticus. Ecc. Hist. lib. i. c. 19. Rufinus, Tillemont, Baronius, and others after them, have followed in the wake of this assertion, without appearing to have investigated its probability. Fabricius. Lux Evangelii, c. 36, p. 626.

[4] Cave's Apostles and Fathers. St. Bartholomew, fol. edit. A. D. 1677.

[5] Euseb. Eccles. Hist. lib. v. c. 10. Vide the Note of Valesius in loco.

[6] Socrates. Ecc. Hist. lib. i. c. 19.

After an attentive investigation of the subject, I do not hesitate to affirm, that the whole story is built upon a foundation too slender to sustain it. It appears to have originated in a vague rumour, that the Gospel of St. Matthew was found in India about the beginning of the third century. Eusebius mentions this as a report, without attempting to corroborate it. Du Pin [1] and others speak of it in similar terms: and Milner, though he deemed it worth mentioning as a current tradition, yet much doubted its truth. [2] Such a report, however, would be received without much hesitation in a credulous age; and those who believed it would find little difficulty in imagining, or crediting, the story of St. Bartholomew's visit to India, in order to account for the alleged discovery of the Gospel in those parts.

The story of St. Thomas also unworthy of credit.

3. The tradition which attributes to the Apostle Thomas the introduction of Christianity into India, is of very early date: but, though now more generally credited than that which ascribes it to St. Bartholomew, it derives less support from authentic history. Eusebius does not even mention it. That historian says, that tradition assigns to St. Thomas the region of Parthia; [3] but he does not appear anywhere to allude to this Apostle's travels and preaching in India. Socrates also is silent on the subject, and the same may be said of all the earlier historians of the church. Cave takes his account of St. Thomas' journeys in the East from Nicephorus, a Greek historian of the fourteenth century; and also from the Portuguese, "in want,"

---

[1] Du Pin's Eccl. Hist. fol. edit. 1693, p. 62.
[2] Milner's Church Hist. cent. 3. c. 3.
[3] Eccl. Hist. lib. iii. c. 1.

he admits, " of better evidence from antiquity." [1]

La Croze has drawn up the following account of this tradition from all the authorities he could collect, but declares, at the same time, that it does not appear to be entitled to credit. [2]

[1] Cave's Apostles and Fathers, pp. 186, 187. The Abbé Fleury pronounces Metophrastus, *Nicephorus*, and other writers of about the same day, as of little authority in questions of such antiquity. Eccles. Hist. Dissertation 1st.

[2] The following note, taken from Turner's History of the Anglo-Saxons, vol. ii. p. 147, will convey some idea of the puerile character of this tradition. " In the Saxon life of " St. Thomas, in MS. Calig. A. 14., which is ascribed to Elfric " in Jul. E. 7., the legendary account there is, ' The Saviour " himself came to him from heaven, and said to him,' ' A king " of the Indians, who is called Gundoforus, will send his " gerefa to Syria's land to seek some labourer who is skilful in " arts. I will soon send thee forth with him.' Thomas " answered, ' Send me whither thou wilt, except to the In-" dians.' But, on the command to go being repeated, he " assented; and, when the regal officer came, they went toge-" ther to the ship, and reared their sail and proceeded with " the wind; and they sailed forth then seven nights before " they reached a shore, but it would be long to tell all the " wonders that he did there. They came next to the king in " India, and Abbanes boldly brought Thomas to the speech of " the king, who said to him, ' Canst thou build me a kingly " mansion in the Roman manner?' Thomas tried and suc-" ceeded, and had then liberty to preach, and baptized, and " constructed a church, and Migdonia, the king's wife's sister, " believed what he taught."—Cott. MSS. Calig. A. 14. pp. 112—118.

The native Christians of the Roman Church relate a miraculous story of St. Thomas which, probably, refers to this building. " The sea having cast up a tree of a vast bulk, the " king, who was desirous to use it in the building of a house, " had employed a great number of men and elephants to bring " it from thence, but in vain, the wood being not to be moved " from the place. St. Thomas standing by, told the king, " that if he would present him with the piece of wood, he " would carry it alone to the city, then ten leagues from the " shore. The king looking upon him as a mad man, told him, " He should do with it what he pleased. Whereupon St.

D

" " In the division of all the parts of the world
" which was made among the holy Apostles,
" India fell to the lot of St. Thomas, who, after
" having established Christianity in Arabia Felix
" and in the Island of Dioscoride, now called
" Socotora, arrived at Cranganore, where the
" principal king of the coast of Malabar then
" resided. It was there that the fabulous ad-
" ventures happened, of which we read in this
" Apostle's life, written by the pretended Ab-
" dias of Babylon. The holy Apostle having
" established many churches at Cranganore,
" passed to Coulan,[1] a celebrated town of the
" same coast, where he converted many persons
" to Christianity. Having departed to the other
" coast, now known by the name of Coroman-
" del, he stopped at Meliapore, a town which
" the Europeans call St. Thomé, where he is
" said to have converted the king and all the
" people. He went from thence to China, and
" remained in a town called Camballé, where he
" made numerous conversions, and built many
" churches.

" St. Thomas returned from China to Melia-
" pore, where the great success that attended

" Thomas, tying his girdle to one of the branches, and
" making the sign of the cross, drew the whole tree after him
" with a great deal of ease, followed by a vast number of peo-
" ple: and coming to the city, erected a stone cross there,
" telling the spectators, That whenever the sea should rise up
" to that place, God would send certain strangers from far
" distant places to settle the Christian religion here. This the
" Portuguese would have to be verified by their coming there;"
and there is reason to suspect that they are the inventors of
the story. Baldæus' Description of Malabar and Coromandel.
c. 20. Churchill's Voyages, &c. vol. iii. p. 575. Baldæus
refers to Lucena, Osorius, and Baronius, (tom. i.) for an account of a cross made by this Apostle's blood, " and a vast
number of miracles wrought by it."

[1] Quilon.

"his labours among the heathen excited against
"him the hatred and envy of two Brahmins,
"who are the priests of the idolatrous super-
"stition of India. These two men stirred up
"the people, who combined to stone the holy
"apostle. After his execution, one of the
"Brahmins, observing that he still breathed,
"pierced him with a lance, which put an end
"to his life."

"I shall not lose time," says the historian,
"in refuting this narration of the death of the
"holy apostle, which is not apparently less
"fabulous than the coming of St. Thomas into
"India."[1]

I should follow the example of this author,
and immediately pass on to more authentic records, were it not that several writers and tra-

[1] La Croze, pp. 39, 40. This author refers to the Portuguese historian, A. Gouvea, an authority implicitly followed
by Asseman and other Romish writers who have repeated this
legend. Asseman refers indeed to other authorities of greater
antiquity, as the following note will show: but it will be seen
how little they support the particular tradition which they are
adduced to sustain.

"Thomas, cui Judæ nomen fuisse, ex Ephræmo Syro et
Tabulariis Edessenis constat, non Syrorum modo et Chaldæ-
orum, sed Parthorum etiam, Persarum, Medorum Indorumque
Orientalium Apostolus fuit. Origines, (Lib. iii. in Genes.)
Euseb. (Lib. iii. Histor. Eccl. cap. 1.) Rufinus, (Lib. i.
cap. 9), Auctor libri Recognitionem, (Lib. ix. cap. 29),
Socrates, (Lib. i. cap. 15.) aliique, Parthiam Thomæ obtigisse
scribunt. Persidem Fortunatus Parthiæ substituit. (Lib. i.
Carm. 1.) Parthiam, Persidem, et Indiam Thomæ assignat
Hippolytus. (In Synopsi), Nazianzenus, (Orat. 21), et mar-
tyrologi omnes, (Baron. in not. ad Martyrolog. Roman.
21 Decemb.) Loca prædicationis Sophronius apud Hierony-
mum sic recenset. *Thomas Apostolus, quemadmodum tra-
ditum est nobis, Parthis, et Medis, et Persis, et Carminis, et
Hyrcanis, et Bactris, et Margis, prædicarit Evangelium
Domini, (Sophronius,* cap. 8). Asseman, Bib. Orient. Tom.
iii. pars. 2. p. 25.

vellers of the last and present century, have given more credit to this tradition than it appears to deserve.[1] A very short acquaintance with the Greek and Latin authors who have preserved and amplified it, will be quite enough to satisfy most readers of their extreme credulity, whatever credit may be thought due to this particular tradition. Many of them seem to have treasured up, as a sacred relique, every report that floated in the atmosphere of ignorance and superstition.

Some persons have thought it quite as probable that St. Thomas should visit the eastern, as that St. Paul should travel to the western extremity of the regions then known. But this opinion must surely have been formed without reference to the comparative state of the two hemispheres, during the first century of the Christian era. The Roman arms had penetrated even as far as Britain, and every part of the continent of Europe was accessible to an ordinary traveller. Not so the continent of India. It has been shown above, that until about the middle of the first century, the voyage to India was long and tedious; and considering the infancy of the commerce with that country, it is not probable that any but traders would venture so far eastward before the second century. The extension of the story to China greatly diminishes its credibility, as it is very doubtful indeed whether any Egyptian or Roman

[1] " Bishop Heber, (Journal, Vol. ii. p. 278), and Archdeacon Robinson, (Last Days of Bishop Heber, p. 317), incline to favour the claim of the Syro-Malabaric Church to this apostolic origin." Dean Pearson's Life of Swartz, Vol. i. p. 4. The author followed by these and other writers inclined to adopt this opinion, is Paulinus, author of " Orientalis Christiana," see pp. 127—145.

navigator penetrated beyond the river Ganges for several ages after the discovery of India.

This legend is not universally received by Romish writers: The learned Tillemont, in his ecclesiastical history of the first six ages,[1] treats the whole story as worthy of little or no credit. Eusebius Renaudot, in his translation of the travels of two Mahomedans into India and China in the ninth century, says,[2] " Notwithstanding all that has been written by the Portuguese, and others, about St. Thomas preaching in China, it can never stand upon the feeble support of far-fetched conjecture, and bare probability." Then, a few pages further, he accounts with great candour for the origin of the story.[3] " Two or three authors, who but copy from each other, suffice to give birth to a notion which spreads unexamined by those who follow them: this throws a mist over history, and gives an opportunity to confound truth with falsehood, and what is certain with what is mere conjecture. For example, Father Trigaut, misunderstanding some passages of Syriac,[4] declares it very probable that St. Thomas preached in China. A few years afterwards they find the Chinese and Syriac inscription, which talks of a mission from Judæa or Syria ; whereupon it was by some asserted, that the persons, thereinmentioned, must have been St. Thomas ; and

---

[1] Tom. i. pp. 284—290. Fol. ed.
[2] Preface, p. xxviii.   [3] Id. p. xxxv.
[4] In the *Beit Gaza*, or *Breviary* of the Syrian Church, where these words occur. *By* St. Thomas *the error of Idolatry has been confounded in the Indies. By* St. Thomas *the Chinese and Ethiopians have been converted to the knowledge of the truth. By* St. Thomas *the kingdom of Heaven hath taken its flight, and ascended quite up to China.* Vide Memoirs of Matthew Ricci, one of the first missionaries to China. E. Renaudot's Inquiry into the origin of the Christian Religion in China, p. 77. London ed. 1733.

at once they prick you down the track he must have followed, and give you a map to convince you it was so. " But these systems," he asserts, " are confessedly an absurdity : yet most who have touched on this matter in our times, do, upon no other testimony than Trigaut has offered, lay it down as an indubitable truth, that St. Thomas himself preached in China ; it is not doubted, says one of the last of them, but St. Thomas preached the faith in the Indies." Then, after quoting what this author[1] asserts respecting the introduction of Christianity into China, he thus remarks upon the legend in reference to India.[2] " It is true indeed, the common tradition of the Malabar Churches has it, that St. Thomas preached in the Indies, and the same has been admitted into the Roman Martyrology, where it is said he suffered martyrdom at Calamina : but there is no memorial left of any city so called in those parts, and the conjectures which some of the learned have advanced, concerning this name, are quite intolerable. Father Kircher pretends we must read Calurmina, instead of Calamina, and that the word signifies *upon a stone;* because in that country they still show a stone figured with some crosses, and other ensigns of Christianity, and upon this stone the Malabars tell you, he was pierced by a brahmin."

The Abbe Fleury, another candid historian of the Roman Church, has spoken of the ac-

<hr>

[1] Mem. de la Chin. tom. ii. p. 195.

[2] Renaudot's Inquiry, &c., pp. 79, 80. It would answer little purpose to enter here upon the discussion that has been raised about the name of a place mentioned by the two Mahomedan travellers as well known on the shores of India. It is called *Betuma,* which has been interpreted, the house, or church of St. Thomas.

tions of both St. Bartholomew and St. Thomas as involved in great uncertainty:[1] and the more carefully the two questions are consulted, the better will the intelligent reader be satisfied, that neither of them rests on a valid foundation. Protestant historians have taken a similar view of them. We have seen that no one credits the story about St. Bartholomew; and little more can be said for the legend of St. Thomas. The learned Fabricius, quoting the earliest authorities that at all bear upon it, classes it with other *questionable* traditions.[2] After citing the passage from Sophronius, which speaks of that apostle's falling at Calamina, he expresses himself as dubiously about this place as did Renaudot.[3] The two chief protestant historians of the Church, Mosheim and Milner, take no notice of the subject: and since the latter has

[1] Fleury's Discourse on Ecclesiastical History, p. 42. London edit. 1721. See also his Ecclesiastical History on the same subject.

[2] Traditiones minus certæ. Lux Evangelii. 4to edit. 1731. pp. 108—110.

[3] *Calaminam* existere tantum in Utopia et cerebro male feriato, scribit Steph. le Moyne notis ad varia sacra, p. 1060, qui suspicatur καλιρόην sive Edessam subillo nomine latitare, ubi S. Thomæ ostentatæ fuere reliquiæ. Kircherus vero Chinæ illustratæ c. 79. Calaminam interpretatur, *Maliapuram* S. Thomæ civitatem dictam a Lusitanis, Narsingæ ultra Indum fluvium metropolin, cum veteres ad citeriorem modo Indiam Thomam penetrasse testentur, unde illi sententiæ fidem detrahit præter laudatum Lemonium Samuel Basnage ad A. C. 46. n. 32. seq.

Baldæus agrees with Father Kircher in his interpretation of *Calurmina*, that it is not the name of a place, but merely descriptive of the spot where the apostle is said to have been martyred, *upon a rock*, or stone. In the Tamul language, which is spoken on the Coromandel coast, *callu* or *calur* is a stone, and *mel*, *mina*, or *midu*, upon. Baldæus' Description, &c., ch. xx. Churchill's Voyages, &c., Vol. iii. p. 575.

referred to the story of St. Bartholomew, it may be concluded that he deemed the legend of St. Thomas even less credible. La Croze rejects it, and at the same time accounts for its origin in a satisfactory manner, as will soon appear: and he has been followed in his conclusion by an intelligent writer in the Asiatic Researches,[1] who declares, that " this story is supported by no historical proof whatever." Baldæus credits the tradition indeed, being, as he expresses it, " the most secure way, because," as he thinks, " founded upon no small probabilities :" but he does not give the grounds of these " probabilities," to enable his readers to judge of them ; and all the authorities which he has quoted he agrees to set aside as " uncertain relations." However desirous we may be to establish so interesting a fact as the visit of St. Thomas to India, yet historic truth is too important to admit an assumption, unsupported as this is by the faintest vestige of authentic history; and in itself, I must continue to think it most improbable.

Probable origin of the tradition about him.

4. While, however, we reject this account as applied to the South of India, we admit that there would be much less improbability in the tradition if supposed to refer to the northern provinces bordering on the banks of the Indus. There is no question that the several ancient writers referred to by Asseman, Fabricius, and others, speak of St. Thomas' travels in a way that proves, at least, the antiquity of the tradition that he visited India : and this may be easily accounted for. Assuming the truth of Eusebius' account of the division of the Gentile

[1] F. Wrede, esq., Account of St. Thomé Christians on the coast of Malabar. Asiatic Researches, Vol. vii. p. 364.

world among the Apostles, Parthia was assigned to St. Thomas, and he might, without much difficulty, have visited some of the upper provinces of Hindoostan. For Parthia was bounded on the East by the river Indus; and it has been shown, in the former chapter, that since the days of Alexander the Great, a constant communication had been maintained with India in this direction, and that the Romans, in the first century of the Christian era, carried on a brisk trade through the same channel. It is easy, therefore, to imagine, that the Apostles' holy zeal for the glory of his Lord and for the salvation of the heathen, would move him to endeavour to evangelize the regions bordering upon his province. Origen, who lived in the third century, says expressly, that this Apostle preached in Parthia, Media, Caramania, and Bactriana. Though he does not mention India, yet the last-named kingdom was bounded on the East by Indo-Scythia and the country of the Massagetæ, through which the Indus flowed: and whether the apostle himself crossed that river, or sent others to preach there, the proximity of his province may be thought sufficient to account for his receiving the appellation of *The Apostle of India.* This is the utmost that can be conjectured on the subject; for, after all, it is mere conjecture : but it has some show of probability, which cannot be said for the extraordinary tales of St. Thomas' voyages and travels in the South and East of India and China.[1]

---

[1] Some have carried the story so far, as to make this Apostle pass over, some way or other, even to the Brazils. Vide Historica Ecclesia, &c. See Asiatic Researches, Vol. vii. p. 364, &c.

The mass of legendary matter which has been mixed up with this story is wholly unworthy of credit. Whatever foundation there may have been for the tradition as preserved by the earlier Christians in India, yet, as exaggerated and dressed up by more modern writers, it is fabulous in the extreme. That it is not wholly without foundation in the annals of the church in the East, is readily conceded; as no less than three persons bearing the name of Thomas occur in the early history of the Indian Christians, to whom the different parts of the tradition may be applied. It would be premature here further to anticipate our narrative; but it is important that the reader should bear this fact in mind, that he may be on his guard against the conjectures and the marvellous legends with which the history of Christianity in India has been clouded and encumbered.

Tradition of the Eunuch of Ethiopia preaching at Ceylon.

5. Sophronius,[1] bishop of Jerusalem, a Greek writer of the seventh century, mentions, that the Ethiopian eunuch whose conversion by Philip is recorded in the Acts of the Apostles, sailed to the island of Taprobane [2] (Ceylon) where he preached the Gospel: that he is reported to have suffered martyrdom there, and to have received an honourable burial. This also the learned Fabricius [3] has classed with his questionable traditions, though it is perhaps as worthy of credit as that relating to St. Thomas. Cave likewise confirms this account, which he gathered from Dorotheus, and the current traditions of the country.[4]

---

[1] This writer has just been quoted from Asseman and Fabricius.　Vide Du Pin, Vol. vi. p. 17.
[2] Acts viii. 26—29.　　[3] Lux Evangelii, p. 115.
[4] Life of Philip the Deacon.

6. Though we cannot attribute to the church of Christ in India an apostolic origin, yet there are reasonable grounds for assigning to it a date very little posterior to the apostolic age. It is generally believed that St. Mark the evangelist founded the church at Alexandria. Writers are divided in opinion as to the time when he went into Egypt, some affirming that it was in the second, others, in the ninth year of Claudius, and others, in the third of Caligula. This point it is now as difficult as unimportant to determine. In this, however, all are agreed, that he passed the latter years of his life in that country, where he introduced the Gospel, and lived to see the church flourish under his superintendence.[1] It will be remembered, that at this period Alexandria was the emporium of the world. By means of its extensive commerce it had now acquired an importance second only to Rome herself. Like other mercantile towns, its population was composed of the inhabitants of all the nations with which they carried on trade. Of these the Jews formed no inconsiderable portion. There were also vast numbers of strangers, not only from Syria, Lybia, Cilicia, Ethiopia, and Arabia, but also from Bactria, Scythia, Persia, and *India*, who were drawn thither by the attractions of its mart.[2] Here the Evangelist Mark assembled a numerous church, which, like the first fruits of the Gospel at Jerusalem, would be composed of converts from all the nations which Divine Providence had thus brought together, that they might hear the glad tidings of salvation. They came for the sake of this world's traffic indeed; but they found, in the knowledge of

Probable account of the early origin of the Indian Church through Mark the Evangelist, and founder of the Church of Alexandria.

[1] Eusebius. Ecc. Hist. Lib. ii. ch. 16.
[2] Fleury. Ecc. Hist. Lib. ii. sect. 5.

the Gospel, infinitely more than they sought, and returned home freighted with the merchandize of heaven.

It is not likely that Mark, who had travelled so much with Paul and Barnabas, in their journeys to spread abroad the kingdom of Christ in the world, should neglect the facilities that his situation afforded him, to send the Gospel to all countries to which he could gain access, either by means of native traders or the members of his own church. It has been seen that the Indian trade was in his time the chief object of attraction at Alexandria; and the progress of Christianity to India at that early period may be traced with some probability.

The populous island of Socotora,[1] in the Arabian Sea, lay about midway between the two countries, and was of considerable importance to the merchants of Alexandria. Alexander the Great, knowing the importance of this station to the furtherance of his commercial designs, removed the native inhabitants, and established there a colony of Greeks, issuing special orders to the neighbouring powers that this colony should be carefully preserved. We are informed that they remained in custody of ' the island until God sent Jesus Christ into the world; when the Greeks of this same isle, being informed concerning his Advent, embraced the Christian faith, as the other Greeks had done before them; and in the profession of this faith they have persevered to this day, as well as all the inhabitants of the other isles.'[2]   By

[1] Called the Isle of Aloes, from the vast quantity and excellent quality of that useful drug which grew upon it. The discovery of this island is considered one of the most important incidents in Alexander's progress.— E. Renaudot.

[2] This was written in the ninth century by the Mahomedan

whom Christianity was introduced there is uncertain.　It has been attributed to St. Thomas,[1]
but without any authority being cited in support of the assumption.　It is more probable
that some Christians of the primitive church
of Alexandria, accompanying the Egyptian
voyagers sailing to the East, stopped at this
island, and preached to its inhabitants the Gospel of Christ: and as this was in the direct
course to India, nothing can be more reasonable than to conclude, that while some remained
behind at Socotora, others pursued the voyage
to the place of the vessel's destination.　While
the merchants of Alexandria coveted the treasure, and the voluptuous craved the luxuries of
the East; devout Christians, indifferent to both,
would seek to make the Indians a more ample
return for their merchandize than the marts of
Egypt could yield.　Obtaining information of
their country from those Indians who visited
Alexandria, they would desire to send them
home freighted with a richer treasure than they
brought, even the Gospel of salvation.　Nor is
it likely that they would be content merely to

travellers, whose account of India and China has been already
noticed, pp. 91, 92.　Marco Paolo relates of this island, that
its inhabitants were Christians, and that they had an Archbishop under a Zatolic, who resided at Bagdad; that is, a
Catholico, or Patriarch of the *Nestorians*.　The Portuguese
writers, on the contrary, maintain that they are Jacobites, or
subject to the Patriarchs of Antioch or Alexandria.　When
the Portuguese first came to this island, the inhabitants
appeared before them with crosses in their hands, to show
that they were Christians. (Barros, Dec. 2; lib. 1. c. 3.
Purch. p. 778).　But Odoardo Barbosa says (p. 292), that,
in his time, they had hardly any notion of baptism, and that
they had nothing left to distinguish them as Christians but
the bare name.—E. Renaudot.　Note GG on the two Mahomedan's Travels quoted in the text.

[1] Maffeii.　Historia Indica, Lib. ii. p. 82.

instruct these strangers, and leave it to them to teach their countrymen on their return. Such a method of propagating the religion which they loved, must have appeared too precarious to satisfy the holy zeal of primitive Christians. Some, inspired by the Spirit that has always animated the faithful missionary's bosom, would cheerfully leave their home, with all its endearments, and go forth to preach among those Gentiles " the unsearchable riches of Christ." " For there were many evangelical preachers " of the word even at that time, who, inflamed " with a divine zeal, in imitation of the Apos- " tles, contributed their assistance to the en- " largement of the Divine Word, and the build- " ing up men in the faith." [1] Who those heralds of mercy were, or to what extent the great Head of the Church vouchsafed to prosper their endeavours, the pen of history has not recorded. But this is of little moment. It is enough to know that their names are written in heaven ; [2] and that having diligently sowed the seed of immortal life, they will participate in the joy of those who have already reaped, or shall hereafter reap, its imperishable fruits. [3]

In this manner then we may account for the introduction of Christianity into India. As nothing is distinctly recorded of the period when it was introduced, or of the circumstances that led to it, there can be no sufficient data for a positive conclusion : and in balancing the probabilities that arise out of the general allusions found in the early annals of the church, he is on the safest side who keeps the most clear of the marvellous.

7. We know that the first Christian mission-

[1] Eusebius, Lib. v. ch. 10.   [2] Luke x. 20.
[3] John iv. 36.

aries to India, whoever they were, did not labour in vain, though there appears to be no authentic record of the church they established there before the second century. About that period, Demetrius, bishop of Alexandria, received a message from some natives of that country, earnestly requesting him to send a teacher to instruct them in the faith and doctrines of Christ.[1] It is probable that these Indians were converts, or children of former converts to Christianity, and that they sent their message to Demetrius by some of the vessels that were constantly visiting their shores from Egypt. At that time one Pantænus, a Stoic philosopher who had embraced the Christian religion, presided over the celebrated school at Alexandria. Hearing of the Indians' request, this scholar freely offered himself to the work. Renouncing for a season the honours and emoluments of his situation, regardless of the dangers and difficulties of the voyage, he went forth with a willing mind, to spread abroad the light of life among those who were sitting in the twilight of truth, or in the darkness and shadow of death. This is the teacher who is said to have found in India the Gospel of St. Matthew in Hebrew, which St. Bartholomew was supposed to have carried thither. But, for reasons just stated, this tale appears to have no foundation in fact.

It is not known how long Pantænus was absent, but after his return home, he resumed his public duties as a teacher, and continued to preside over the school at Alexandria. As an expounder of the sacred scriptures, he met with great acceptance ; but whether his preach-

Pantænus of
Alexandria
the first missionary to
India in the
2nd century.

[1] Eusebius, Lib. v. ch. 10. Milner's Ch. Hist. Cent. 3, ch. 3.

ing was as profitable as acceptable, may well be questioned. He published some commentaries on the Bible, which are lost; so that the only means of forming an opinion of his method of explaining its contents, are contained in the writings of Clemens Alexandrinus, his disciple; and also in the works of Origen and others who were brought up in the same school, and may be supposed to have inculcated the doctrines of their master. From these it appears, that in that age, and in the church to which they belonged, there was a sad declension from the simplicity of scriptural truth. Pantænus himself was more celebrated for his philosophy than his divinity; and some of his most distinguished pupils erred grievously from the faith. Nevertheless, there seems to be sufficient ground for the following favourable opinion that has been formed of his integrity.—" Candour requires us to look on him as a sincere Christian, whose fruitfulness was yet much checked by that very philosophy for which Eusebius so highly commends him. A blasting wind it surely was : but it did not entirely destroy Christian vegetation in all whom it infected.' [1]

Who is not glad to believe thus much of the first Indian missionary on record? Of his exertions and successes in that country we have no account; but we are willing to hope, notwithstanding the disadvantages of his station and habits, and the imperfection of his own creed, that he shone as a light in a dark place, among the idolaters of the East, and was made, through the inspiration of the Holy Spirit, the honoured instrument of guiding many into the way of

[1] Milner, Cent. 3, ch. 3.

salvation. If we cannot attribute to him the enlightened zeal of a missionary of brighter days, we may at least give him credit for motives equally unquestionable. Integrity of purpose in promoting the cause of divine truth, is by no means incompatible with a limited knowledge of its value. That man, indeed, who knows the most of his Redeemer, will love Him the best; and his love will constrain him, in exact proportion to its purity and strength, to follow the Lord Jesus' injunctions.[1] This obedience he will render at every call of Christian duty, but especially will he obey the command to make known the way of God upon earth, His saving health among all nations.[2] The same principle, however, may actuate a Christian of weaker faith and less enlightened understanding, diligently to employ his single talent in the service of his Lord. Such, we may venture to hope, was the motive of Pantænus, in offering himself to the arduous enterprise of carrying the Gospel to India.

But a question has of late been raised about the country which was the scene of this missionary's labours. It is said, "The doubt respecting the country called India, to which he is stated to have been sent, is most probably to be solved by our concluding that he went to Arabia, and not to that country in the east of Asia which is properly known by the name of India."[3] This remark[4] must not be passed with-

<hr>

[1] John xiv. 15, 23. [2] Psalm lxvii. 2; Mark xvi. 15.

[3] History of the Christian Church, by Dr. Edward Burton, late Regius Professor of Divinity in the University of Oxford, p. 252.

[4] Not indeed that the difficulty was raised by this author. (See Bishop Middleton's Address, &c. Report of the Christian Knowledge Society for 1813, p. 62. Mosheim, Vol. i. p. 149.) But the doubt seems principally to have been as to the *part of India* from which the ambassadors came.—Milner's Church Hist. Vol. i. p. 288.

out some notice in this place: for it is calculated to depreciate a fact of some consequence in the early history of the Indian church; and the name and station of its author may cause greater importance to be attached to it than he, probably, intended.

The doubt that long hung over the country called India will come more appropriately under discussion at the close of this chapter, when giving an account of another mission. At present we need only remark, that it does not appear that any ancient author felt any such difficulty in the case of Pantænus, and the country he visited: and there is strong collateral evidence in the writings of his favourite pupil and successor, Clemens Alexandrinus, that he went to India proper. This author, alluding to the inhabitants and customs of that region, describes particularly the jogees and brahmins, and speaks of the god Boodhu.

" [1] There are two descriptions of Indian Gym-
" nosophists, or barbarous philosophers: the
" one called *Sarmanes*, the other, *Brahmins.*
" The Sarmanes are also called recluses; [2] they
" do not live in towns, and have no houses;
" they cover their bodies with the bark of trees,
" and live on fruits. Their only beverage is
" water, which they drink out of the hollow of
" their hands. They do not marry, and live
" after the manner of the Encratites.[3] The
" brahmins are those Indians who obey the

---

[1] Stromat, L. i. p. 529, edit. Potteri. La Croze, Histoire du Christianisme des Indes, Liv. vi. p. 492, 493.

[2] ἀλλόβιοι, Solitaires.

[3] i. e. Temperate. These recluses were followers of the heretic Tatian, an unworthy disciple of Justin Martyr. This sect arose towards the end of the second century. They were also called *Continentes*, because they abstained from marriage, the use of wine, and animal food. Other names of the like signification were given to them. Mosheim, cent. 2, part 2, sect. ix.

" commandments of *Boutta*, whom they honour
" as a god, because of the holiness of his life."
Can it be doubted that these sarmanes and
brahmins were the Indian recluses and priests
of his day? And when we compare them with
the modern jogees and brahmins of Hindoostan,
is it not more than probable that he is describing the inhabitants of the same country? Then,
the god *Boutta* that he mentions, was, no
doubt, the same idol that Jerom[1] and other
early writers call *Boudda*, the ninth incarnation
of the Hindoo god Vishnoo, formerly an object of
general adoration in India, but now worshipped
chiefly in Ceylon. Assuming then that Clemens
is speaking of the inhabitants and idolatries of
India, from what source is he so likely to have
derived his information about that country as
from his master Pantænus, after his return?
If this does not amount to positive evidence of
this missionary's having been there, it is at
least a strong collateral proof of it. To say
that Rufinus, Jerom, Nicephorus, and other
early writers, spoke of it as a fact which no one
at that time thought of doubting, were, perhaps,
to beg the question; for it would still remain
to be proved what country they meant by
India.[2] But this cannot be objected to the
opinion of Fabricius, who quotes all the ancient
authorities on the subject, and styles him the
Apostle of India:[3] nor to that of Niecamp, who
expressly says, that Pantænus and other per-

[1] Hieronym. Lib. i. adversus Jovinianum, Tom. IV. p. 186,
col. 2. Apud *Gymnosophistes Indiæ* quasi per manus hujus
opinionis auctoritas traditur, quod *Buddam* principem dog-
matis eorum e latere suo virgo generavit. La Croze, pp. 492,
493, also 512, 513.

[2] See the Note of Valesius upon Eusebius, Lib. v. ch. 10.

[3] PANTÆNUS, INDIÆ APOSTOLUS. Lux Evangelii, cap. 36,
p. 627.

CHAP.
II.

sons were called from Alexandria to India.[1] For in the time of both these writers, and that of others yet more modern, the name *India* was well understood to mean the country at present so denominated.

With such testimony in support of the fact, we cannot assent to the assertion, that "There is no reason to suppose that Pantænus travelled in the direction of India;" nor to the conjecture, that the southern part of Arabia, which is washed by the waters of the Persian Gulf, was the scene of his labours, and that "the conversion of the inhabitants may have been principally caused by him."[2] This, if admitted, would reduce it to a question of probability; and there are strong grounds for the opposite opinion, whereas none are produced for that here cited. It has been shown above, that the intercourse between Alexandria and India was open and frequent almost from the commencement of the Christian era, and that there are satisfactory reasons to conclude that Christianity was introduced into that country from Alexandria before the time of Pantænus. In the absence then of all proof that Arabia was the scene of his mission, or of any testimony, or even circumstance, except, perhaps, the mere locality, to favour that notion; we must continue to maintain, that there *is* good reason to conclude that he went to the country now known by the name of *India*.

A. D.
306.

8. The beginning of the fourth century was a new epoch in the History of Christianity; for

[1] Id tamen certum est, jam anno post Christum natum CLXXXVIIII, *Pantænum*, nomine missionarii, æque ac postea metropolitas quosdam ex *Alexandria* in *Indiam* vocatos esse. Historia Missionis, P. i. c. 5, p. 30.

[2] Burton's History of the Christian Church. p. 252.

the Church then emerged from the state of depression into which she had sunk under the severity of the Dioclesian persecution. Constantius Chlorus, who was joint emperor of Rome, at that time commanded the Roman army in Britain, and had his head quarters at York, where he died in the year 306. Before his death, he nominated his son Constantine, afterwards called the Great, as his successor to the imperial throne, and caused the Roman army at York, and even the English there, to proclaim him emperor. But, notwithstanding this precaution, Constantine had to maintain his right with the joint-emperor, Galerius Maximinus, by force of arms. After defeating Galerius in several battles, in the year 308 he forced from him the recognition of his claim. But this did not prevent the two succeeding emperors also, Maxentius and Licinius, from disputing his right. He was equally successful, however, in maintaining it against them both: and after his final triumph over the latter, in the year 323, he became sole emperor of Rome, uniting both the eastern and western empires under his own government. He had hitherto shown a decided predilection for the Gospel of Christ, favouring and protecting the Christians, as their circumstances required, to the extent of his power. But now that he was sole master of his actions, he took the decided step of establishing Christianity as the religion of the state. There is too much reason to believe that his own faith and practice were very defective; but it is not difficult to account for the course he took in favour of a creed which he himself, as it appears, so partially understood. His father, Constantius,[1] had set him

A. D. 306.

Constantine the Great establishes Christianity as the religion of the state.

A. D. 323.

---

[1] Eusebius' Life of Constantine. Lib. i. ch. 13, 16, and 17.

the example, and, no doubt, inculcated upon him the duty, of countenancing the Christians. His mother, Helena, is said to have been a Christian,[1] and to have instructed him in the principles of the Gospel from his earliest years. This, however, is uncertain; but there can be little doubt that England was the country of his birth.[2] The Church of England had long existed under her own hierarchy, independent of the Gallic or Roman, or any other foreign church; and it had flourished for some time under the protection of Constantius.[3] It is, therefore, most probable, that Constantine had grown up under the tuition of the British ecclesiastics about his father's court. At the period of his final triumph over Licinius, his mother, Helena, though declining in years, was actuated by no ordinary zeal for the cause of Christ; and as her son paid her the highest respect, and entered with ardour into her suggestions in other matters relating to the church, he was, no doubt, influenced by her counsels to establish Christianity as the religion of the state.[4] The extraordinary vision also that he had seen in the air some years before, when marching against Maxentius, would combine with the example of

[1] The country and parentage of Helena are involved in uncertainty. It has been affirmed that she was a British princess: but the general opinion is, that she was of low parentage, and a native of Drepane, a city of Bithynia; and that she was one of Constantius' concubines, not receiving the title of Empress until conferred upon her by her son. Eusebius, Jerom, Cassiodorus, and Orosius: all referred to in Du Pin. Fourth century. Constantine, p. 11, note in the margin.

[2] Stillingfleet. Origines Britannicæ. Ch. iii. p. 90.

[3] The origin of the British Church will be explained in the sequel.

[4] Eusebius' Life of Constantine, Lib. iii. ch. 42 to 47. See also the notes of Valesius in the margin.

his father, the lessons of his Christian preceptors, and the advice of his mother, to induce him to act in a manner so becoming a Christian sovereign. He is related to have seen on the occasion referred to, a cross in the air, with this remarkable inscription, *In this conquer.* This occurred at noon-day, and the vision is said to have been represented to him again at night in a dream.[1] Assuming the truth of this relation, that circumstance would naturally induce him to patronise the religion of the cross, and to attribute to its Divine Author all his subsequent triumphs.

Thus Constantine and his mother, whom he had honoured with the title of *Augusta,* and elevated to the imperial dignity, are to be regarded as the first sovereigns in whom, under the Gospel dispensation, was fulfilled the promise to the church of the protection of earthly potentates: " Kings shall be thy nursing fathers, and their queens thy nursing mothers."[2] It is written in the word of God, " By me Kings reign:"[3] and He in justice requires that they reign for Him, as well as by Him. Hitherto Christianity had met with only partial suc-

[1] Eusebius' Life of Constantine, Lib. i. ch. 28—30. Notwithstanding the attempts to throw discredit on this story, (see Maclaine's Mosheim. Cent. 4. p 1. ch. 1. sec. 9. note), I cannot see why it should be deemed incredible. A similar vision appeared to Alexander the Great, when marching with hostile intentions towards Jerusalem, and for a similar purpose—the protection of the Church of God. While we believe that the hearts of kings are in the Almighty's rule and governance, and that He disposes and turns them as seemeth best to His godly wisdom, why is it to be thought undeserving of credit that He should use extraordinary means to control the hearts of these two sovereigns ? Josephus' Antiquities, Book ii. ch. 8. sec. 3—5. Rollin also gives the account of Alexander's vision. Ancient History, Vol. v. sec. 7. p. 106, &c.

[2] Isa. xlix. 23.   [3] Prov. viii. 15. Rom. xiii. 1.

cess in the world, being chiefly confined to towns, whose congregations may be supposed to have been numerous and wealthy enough to maintain their ministers. But there were not sufficient means for the Gospel's pervading the rural districts, where the population was more scattered, and the inhabitants devoid of the advantages essential to the support of its teachers. Accordingly, the villages had almost every where continued to worship the heathen gods, long after the cities had for the most part become Christian. This contrast was so general about that time, that villager and heathen had become synonimous terms, the word *pagan*[1] being applied indifferently to both. But when Constantine established Christianity as the religion of the state, preachers were enabled to go forth into all parts of the Roman empire, to introduce the Gospel where it had not been received, and to minister gratuitously to multitudes who had embraced it, but were unable, through the paucity of their numbers in any one place, to support them in their work.

While, however, under the emperor's auspices, the boundaries of the Church were extended in all directions, it is very doubtful whether the interests of the Christian religion, in its purity and integrity, were promoted in an equal degree. With regard to the church herself, in the ignorance of the Gospel which had long prevailed, and the consequent degeneracy of the Christian character, we cannot be surprised that the godliness which had weathered the storms of persecution, began to decay in the calm of imperial favour.

Mankind cannot bear so sudden a transition

---

[1] From *pagus*, a village, *paganus*, a villager.

A. D.
323.

from adversity to prosperity, without the coun-
teracting influence of a much fuller measure of
Divine grace than the Christians of that age
seem to have possessed. And as to the heathen,
the expectation of the emperor's favour proved
irresistible, multitudes flocking to the baptismal
font, where they were received with little regard
to their character, or to their knowledge of
the truth.   By these means the " cords " of the
Christian tabernacle were lengthened, indeed,
but " her stakes " not being equally " strengthened "[1] at the same time, she was rendered less
able to resist the heresies that soon, as a tem-
pest, burst upon her, and for a long season
swept away almost every vestige of truth.   In
many countries the profession of Christianity
was so disguised by superstition and encumbered with secularity, that little more was to be
seen of religion than the name.

But all this was accidental, and is to be attributed to the errors of the times, which had
been accumulating from the very age of the
Apostles.   It does not at all affect the abstract
question of the emperor's duty to establish
Christianity as the religion of his empire, however it may moderate the satisfaction that we
cannot but feel on reading of its general acknowledgment and support.   Constantine himself understood but little of the religion he professed, having adopted the prevailing heresy of
Arius. He remained also in the state of a
catechumen all his days, refusing to be baptized
till on his death bed, in order that, according
to the notions of baptism which then prevailed,
his sins might all be washed away when he
should have lost the power of contracting fur-

[1] Isa. liv. 2.

ther guilt.　He knew as little also of the duty he owed to those professing a purer faith than his own.　Instigated by Eusebius, an Arian Bishop of Nicomedia, towards the close of his reign he persecuted the orthodox, and went so far as to banish several prelates of great eminence.　Such intolerance would obscure the setting of even a brighter sun than that of Constantine.

A. D.
325.
Johannes,
Bishop of
Persia and
India, at
the council
of Nice,
A. D. 325.

9. Notwithstanding the assertion of Suidas,[1] that the interior Indians, as well as the Iberians and Armenians, were baptized in the reign of this emperor, it does not appear that the efforts made under his auspices to propagate the Christian religion, produced any immediate effect in India.　But two years after the establishment of Christianity as the religion of the empire, we find the next intimation of the existence of that remote Church.　At the celebrated Council of Nice, the first Œcumenical Council, which was convened by the emperor's order in the year 325,[2] one of the prelates assembled, named Johannes, subscribed as Metropolitan of Persia, *and of the Great India.*[3]　Hence it has been concluded, that the Indian church was at this time in a flourishing condition, and governed by her own prelates.　That Bishops did preside over that see is most probable, as, from the age of the Apostles to the present period, and for about twelve hundred years after, no instance occurs of a church established in any part of the world without being governed by its own prelates, as a distinct and superior order to the clergy engaged in the subordinate duties of the mini-

---

[1] Suidas, in voce Ἀρμένιοι.

[2] Eusebius, Life of Constantine, Lib. iii. c. 6, 7, &c.

[3] Act. Synod. Nicæn.　Pars Secunda, c. 28.　La Croze, p. 44, Ἰωάννης Πέρσης, τῆς ἐν Περσίᾳ πάσῃ, καὶ τῇ μεγάλῃ Ἰνδίᾳ.

sterial office. It can hardly be thought, however, that Johannes was the *resident* Bishop of India. All that may be inferred from his signature is, that his jurisdiction, as Metropolitan of Persia, extended to that vast continent, [1] where the Christians were, probably, at that time, as we know they were subsequently, supplied with Persian ecclesiastics.

10. The political circumstances of Persia at the time when the council of Nice was held, were favourable to this assumption of ecclesiastical authority by the metropolitan of that empire. About a century before, in the reign of Alexander Severus, emperor of Rome, the Persians, at the instigation and under the command of Artaxerxes, revolted against the Parthians, whom they overcame in a hard-fought battle, destroying the greater part of their army, and, after the action, putting their king, Artabanus, to death. The Parthians were now totally subdued, and became in their turn vassals to the Persians, whom they had held in subjection 475 years.

Artaxerxes, or Artaxares, [2] was a Persian of low origin, and of spurious birth, but possessed of consummate abilities, and stimulated by a restless ambition. After his conquest of the Parthians, he mounted the throne of Persia, assumed the pompous title of king of kings, and formed a design of restoring the empire to its ancient glory. Indignant at the thought of any part of the Persian dominions being regarded as a Roman province, he gave notice to the Roman governors of the provinces border-

Persia recovers her political independence about this period under Artaxerxes.

---

[1] This may have been similar to the jurisdiction of the Bishop of London in all the colonies of Great Britain, where there are no local E. ps.

[2] Ardisheer Babigan. Malcom's History of Persia, c. 6.

ing on his dominions, that he had a just right, as the successor of Cyrus, to all the lesser Asia; which he, therefore, commanded them immediately to evacuate, as well as the provinces on the frontiers of the ancient Parthian kingdom, which he had already reduced to his subjection. The consequence of this haughty message was a war with the emperor of Rome. The opposite parties in this contest each claimed the advantage: and the Roman emperor, Alexander Severus, went so far as to assume the titles of *Parthicus* and *Persicus*. They seem however to have been but empty names, as he does not appear from this period to have held much, if any, dominion in either country: while the Persian king retained full possession of his territories, which, after his decease, were ably defended by his successors against all the endeavours of the Romans to recover them.

Persians enter with activity into the Indian trade, both by sea and land.

11. These events opened to the Persians the direct intercourse with North India by land, and they soon became formidable rivals to the Romans in the commerce with that country by sea. They appear entirely to have surmounted the aversion of their ancestors to maritime pursuits, and to have made early and vigorous efforts in order to acquire a share in the lucrative commerce with India. All its ports of any consideration were frequented by traders from Persia, who bartered some productions of their own country that were in request among the natives of India, for the precious commodities of the East. These they conveyed up the Persian Gulf; and by means of the great rivers, Euphrates and Tigris, they were able to distribute them through every province of the empire. As the voyage from Persia to India was much

shorter than that from Egypt, and attended with less expense and danger, the intercourse between the two countries rapidly increased.[1]

A.D.
325.

12. This brief reference to the history of those times will serve to explain the signature of Johannes at the council of Nice. It will be seen in the sequel, when we shall speak of the first authentic record extant of Christianity in India, that in most of the cities of any note upon the coast of that country,[2] Christian churches were found at the beginning of the 6th century in a flourishing condition, and that the functions of religion were performed by priests ordained by the Archbishop of Seleucia, the capital of the Persian empire, to whose jurisdiction they continued to be subject. This is in agreement with the popular belief of the present race of Syrian Christians in Travancore. They affirm that the Syriac version of the Scriptures was brought to India before the council of Nice, which was held A. D. 325, and some of their present copies are acknowledged to be of a very ancient date.[3]

Signature of Johannes at the council of Nice accounted for.

---

[1] Cosmas Indic. Topogr. Christ. Lib. iii. pp. 178, 179. Robertson's India, p. 94.   [2] Id.

[3] Buchanan's Christian Researches, p. 139. The following statement, written in 1814, shows that there is some ground of probability for this belief. "Though written on a strong thick "paper, like that of some MSS. in the British Museum, com- "monly called Eastern paper, the ink has, in several places, "eat through the material in the exact form of the letter. In "other copies, where the ink had less of a corroding quality, "it has fallen off, and left a dark vestige of the letter; faint "indeed, but not in general illegible.

"There is a volume, which was deposited in one of the "remote churches, near the mountains, which merits a parti- "cular description. It contains the Old and New Testaments, "engrossed on strong vellum, in large folio, having three "columns in a page; and is written with beautiful accuracy.

On the whole then, this may be considered satisfactory evidence of the existence of this ancient episcopal church at that early period: and here again we cannot but recognise the power and wisdom of the Almighty, in so controlling the violence and ambition of earthly potentates, and the schemes of avaricious and adventurous men, as thereby to subserve His purposes of mercy for the world.[1]

Story of
Frumentius
and Œdesius.

13. An ancient author, cited by Suidas, says that the inhabitants of the interior of India were brought over to Christianity during the reign of Constantine the Great; and a story is related by Rufinus,[2] and repeated by Socrates,[3] Sozomen,[4] Theodoret and others,[5] which explains the cause of their conversion. A Christian and philosopher, named Meropius, a native of Tyre, reading the account which Metrodorus, another philosopher, had given of his travels in India, felt his curiosity raised to visit that distant region. Accordingly, he sailed to India, in company with two youths who were related to him. The name of the elder was Frumentius, and that of the younger, Œdesius. Having satisfied his curiosity as far as he could, and taken in provisions and water for the voyage home, Meropius prepared to return. The na-

" The character is Estrangelo Syriac, and the words of every " book are *numbered*. But the volume has suffered injury " from time or neglect. In certain places the ink has been " totally obliterated from the page, and left the parchment in " its state of natural whiteness: but the letters can in general " be distinctly traced from the impress of the pen, or from the " partial corrosion of the ink."

[1] La Croze, p. 44.   [2] Ruf. i. c. 9.
[3] Socrates, Lib. i. c. 19—Jortin's Remarks, Vol. iii. p. 126.
[4] Sozomen, ii. 24.
[5] Theodoret i. 23—Asseman. Bib. Orient. Tom. i. p. 359. Note 2.

tives, however, for what cause is unknown, put him to death, with all on board his vessel, except his two young kinsmen. These, probably out of compassion for their tender age, they spared, and presented them to their king, who was so much pleased with them that he made the elder, Frumentius, his secretary, and the younger, his cup-bearer. They continued to enjoy the king's confidence and favour until his death, when he bequeathed to them their liberty. The queen, being left in charge of the kingdom during the minority of her son, entreated these strangers to undertake the government of the nation until the prince should come of age. In compliance with her request, they undertook the management of affairs, Frumentius, as before, holding the most responsible office in the state. But, in the constant and arduous occupation of government, he did not forget his obligations, as a Christian ruler, to his God and Saviour. Deeming it a paramount duty to employ the influence of his station for the honour of the Redeemer, and for the encouragement and protection of his fellow-christians, he diligently inquired of the merchants who traded with that country, whether any Christians resided there. Being answered in the affirmative, he sent for them, made known to them his own creed, and exhorted them to assemble together in separate places of worship, for prayer and mutual edification; reminding them, at the same time, that such was the general practice of the followers of Jesus. He then erected a small temple, in which they met together for those purposes. Induced by his Christian instructions and example, and, probably, by the countenance he showed them, several of the natives became converts to the Christian profession, and joined in the public service of the church. Thus encouraged, their number continued to increase as long as Frumentius remained at the head of affairs : but as soon as the king came of age, he resigned to him the reins of government, and asked permission to return to his native land. He had administered the affairs of the kingdom so much to the satisfaction of the queen and her son, that they were most reluctant to part with him, and earnestly entreated him to remain, but without effect. He quitted India, in company with his brother Œdesius, who hastened to Tyre to visit his parents and kindred : but Frumentius was too intent on succouring the disciples he had left behind, to allow his private affections to interfere with what he regarded as a public duty to the church of Christ.

Arriving at Alexandria, he related the whole story to the Bishop, Athanasius, who had recently been elevated to that see. To this prelate he mentioned the circumstances of his voyage, and explained the grounds of his hope that the Indians generally, under suitable instructions, would embrace the Christian religion. He then urged Athanasius to send a Bishop and a clergyman thither, exhorting him not to neglect those distant sheep who already needed attendance, or others who were yet to be gathered into the fold. The prelate, taking into consideration how this end might best be accomplished, entreated Frumentius to take upon himself the bishopric, declaring that he thought there was no man better qualified than he for the important enterprise. To this proposal Frumentius acceded, and returned to India in the year 356, as Bishop of that country, where he became a zealous and successful preacher of the Gospel, and built many churches

A. D.
356.

for the converts made by means of his exertions. Socrates adds, that through Divine grace, he wrought many miracles and cured many men's bodies, together with their souls. That, however, was an age of ignorance and superstition, and therefore one of extreme credulity. Socrates was evidently too fond of the marvellous; and very few, if any, of his relations of this description are worthy of credit.

Rufinus,[1] who gives this interesting narrative, says that he received it from the mouth of Œdesius, the brother of Frumentius. But here also, as in the case of Pantænus, a question has been raised about the country to which Socrates refers, when speaking of the innermost, or most distant India, where the see of this good Bishop was situated. Athanasius, in his Apology to the Emperor Constantine, mentions one Frumentius, Bishop of Auxumis,[2] which was the capital of Ethiopia: and from this circumstance, Valesius, in his comment upon the History of Socrates,[3] has expressed an opinion that Frumentius was Bishop of the country now called Ethiopia, and not of India proper. This interpretation has been followed by Fleury,[4] Geddes[5] and other modern writers; but they do not appear to have investigated the grounds of the opinion they adopted.[6] Baronius, the martyrologist,[7] concluded that there were two Bishops named Frumentius, one presiding over the

---

[1] Hist. Eccles. Lib. i. c. 9.
[2] Socrates Scholasticus. Lib. i. c. 19. note (e.)
[3] Idem. note (d.) [4] Eccl. Hist. Lib. ii. sec. 38.
[5] History of the Church of Ethiopia, pp. 9, 10.
[6] The authorities for this conclusion are collected by Fabricius, Lux Evangelii. cap. xxxvi. S. FRUMENTIUS, ET ALII CHRISTIANI IN INDIA, pp. 627, 628. Some of the principal are referred to in the next note.
[7] Annotations on the Roman Martyrology.

F

church of Ethiopia, and the other over that of India proper; the reader will judge whether this is a more reasonable way of solving the difficulty, than by drawing a summary conclusion which would deprive the History of the Indian Church of this interesting narrative. Besides, Bishop Middleton, of Calcutta, spake of Frumentius as " the Apostle of Abyssinia," and said, that " no doubt is entertained, that he became an Indian Bishop." There can be no question that this learned prelate alluded to India proper; for he was addressing a missionary destined for that country,[1] and speaking of it as " certain that the peninsula possessed a knowledge of Christ early in the fourth century"— that is, by means of Frumentius.

It has already been stated, that the innermost India, called also Asian Ethiopia, is described by Socrates as the scene of St. Bartholomew's labours: and although, as we have seen, there is good reason to doubt whether that Apostle ever visited India, yet thus much at least may be gathered from the narrative, that the historian intended particularly to distinguish the two countries from each other; for he speaks of St. Matthew as the Apostle of Ethiopia, properly so called, in immediate connexion with his notice of St. Bartholomew's labours in India.[2] This at least

[1] The Rev. C. A. Jacobi. Report of the Christian Knowledge Society, 1813, p. 62.
[2] Lib. i. ch. 19, see sec. 2 of this chapter. Tillemont has truly said, that the name, India, is of a very undetermined signification among the ancients; and he is of opinion, that they applied it to all the countries southward and eastward with which they were unacquainted, and which lay out of the two empires of the Parthians and the Romans. Ecclesiastical Memoirs, tom. i. Sts. Thomas and Bartholomew. In the age of Homer, India was known by the name of Eastern Ethiopia. Part of Africa was called India by the Greeks (Theophylact,

favours the opinion, that Socrates meant to describe this region as the see of Frumentius, rather than Ethiopia. Cosmas also, a writer of the 6th century, who himself visited India, applied to the coast of Malabar the very name here supposed to be mistaken for Ethiopia.¹ Upon the whole then, the probabilities are, to say the least, quite as much in favour of the text of Socrates, as of the comment of Valesius.

It is needless, however, to pursue the inquiry further. But it will not be thought irrelevant thus far, if we consider the important lesson to be learned from the example it brings before us, combined with the probability that it forms a part of the History of Christianity in India. The moral of the story invests it with an interest and importance which otherwise it might hardly, perhaps, be thought to possess. The mere question about its geography is of little moment, compared with the instruction which the narrative conveys. Whatever the country that formed the bishopric of this devoted prelate, his example is worthy of all imitation; and it reminds us of the self-denial of Moses, in the cause of God and his brethren, who, " when he was come to years, refused to be called the son of Pharaoh's daughter; choosing rather to suffer affliction with the people of God, than to enjoy the pleasures of sin for a season, esteeming the

b. iii. c. 9. b. vii. c. 17.) Strabo calls the people of Mauritania, Indians or Hindoos (b. xvii. p. 828) ; and they are supposed to have been a colony of Indians (Herodotus). In the time of Marco Paolo, Abyssinia was called Middle India. (Asseman, Bib. Orient. tom. i. p. 359, note 1. Asiatic Researches, Vol. iii. pp. 367, 368). And we have just seen (sec. 7 of the present ch.), that the late Dr. Burton supposed that Arabia was called India, in the account of Pantænus.
¹ La Croze. p. 44. &c.

reproach of Christ greater riches than the treasures of Egypt: for he had respect unto the recompense of reward."[1] In like manner did this Christian statesman renounce all the power and emoluments of the highest station in the kingdom, and all the honours and pleasures of the court, for the arduous, the humble, the gratuitous work of a missionary to his poor brethren in Christ. In an age of so much ignorance and corruption, when the heresy of Arius was growing rank in the plenitude of imperial favour, and rapidly diffusing its baneful leaven through the church, our spirits find relief in the contemplation of such a picture of Christian fidelity, and we delight to imagine the happiest results from his disinterested exertions. In this application of it, the story appears as a light shining in a dark place; and it proves that the church was not even then wholly forsaken of her Lord. To those Christians who are reluctant to make any such sacrifices in the Redeemer's cause, this example speaks in terms of deep reproach: but it addresses the language of encouragement to that disciple who has indeed taken up the cross, and is ready to go forth to proclaim the word of life, wherever duty to his Lord, and the necessities of his fellow-creatures, demand this " labour of love."

[1] Heb. xi. 24—26.

CHAPTER III.

RISE AND PROGRESS OF NESTORIANISM.

1. REFERENCE has already been made to the writer, to whom we are indebted for the earliest authentic record of the state of Christianity in India. This was Cosmas, a merchant of Alexandria, surnamed, Indopleustes, or Indicopleustes,[1] that is the Indian voyager. In his time the commerce with India and the western world continued to be carried on in its former channel, and both Rome, the ancient capital of the empire, and Constantinople, the new seat of government, were still supplied with the precious commodities of the East by the merchants of Alexandria. But until the reign of Justinian, who ascended the throne, A. D. 527, we have no account of further information being gathered relating either to the internal state of India, or to the progress of geographical discovery in those distant regions. Though by this time the Persians had become formidable rivals to the Romans in this lucrative commerce, yet their merchants were not accustomed to visit the regions eastward of the Indian continent, being

A. D. 527. Cosmas Indicopleustes. His notions of astronomy and geography correspond with those of the Hindoos.

[1] Ἰνδικοπλεύστης. Asseman, Tom. xiii. part 2. p. 405. Cave's Historia Literaria, An. 576, p. 348.

generally satisfied with receiving their silk, spices, and other valuable productions, as they were imported by the native traders into Ceylon, and conveyed thence to the various marts of Hindoostan. [1]

During these two centuries, history is silent also respecting the state of the Indian churches, until Cosmas published the information which he collected in his travels. Wearied, probably, with the dangers and fatigues of mercantile adventures, he exchanged them for the tranquillity of the cloister, and in his retirement devoted himself to literary pursuits. There he wrote several works, the principal of which he named Christian Topography, or, the opinion of Christians concerning the world. This work is in twelve books, in which the author betrays extreme ignorance respecting the figure and surface of the earth. Disputing with the philosophers, who maintained that the earth was spherical, Cosmas labours to prove it an oblong plane, twelve thousand miles in length from East to West, and six thousand miles in breadth from North to South. He asserts also that it is surrounded by high walls, and that the firmament of heaven is spread over it as a spacious canopy. He accounts for the vicissitudes of day and night, by supposing the sun to revolve round a vast mountain at the extremity of the North, whose shadow involved in darkness those parts of the earth over which it was thrown. Hence night and day would alternate according to the position of the sun on either side of this huge mountain.[2] These absurd notions he un-

---

[1] Cosmas' Indic. Topogr. Christ. Lib. xi. 337. Robertson's India, p. 95.

[2] Lardner's Gospel History, Vol. xi. pp. 262, 263. Robertson's India, pp. 92, 93. Cosmas is said to have published

dertakes to prove from reason, Scripture, and Christian writers, who lived before him.[1] It is probable, however, that he gathered them from the inhabitants of India, into whose customs and opinions he had evidently inquired with great diligence. To this day the Hindoos entertain ideas of the earth very similar to those of Cosmas,[2] except where the light of European science has dissipated the darkness of their understandings. This is not surprising when we consider their limited knowledge of the earth, and that their conclusions are drawn from the appearances and revolutions within their own contracted range of observation. But it is unaccountable how a man like Cosmas, who had seen so much more of the world, should allow himself to regard the rude notions of an uneducated people as tending to confirm the truth, rather than the fallacy, of such vague ideas as had prevailed, in the days of ignorance, in other quarters of the globe.

2. But whatever were the origin of these reveries in the mind of this Egyptian voyager; and though we cannot but regret that a writer of so much intelligence on other subjects, should have committed himself in this manner on the

His account of the Christian Church in India in the sixth century.

his book at Alexandria, A. D. 547. But Asseman dates it A. D. 535, Tom. iii. pt. 2, p. 602. Diss. de Syris Nestorianis. This work was published in Greek by Melchisedec Thevenot, Relations Curieuse, part 1. Translated into French by Don Burnard de Montfaucon, and given in his Nova Collectio Patrum, Vol. II. pp. 113—346, which was published 1707. Asseman. Bibliotheca Orientalis, Tom. iii. pt. 2, pp. 601, 606. Gibbon's Decline and Fall, 4to. edit. Vol. iv. pp. 79, 596. Universal History, fol. 1750. Vol. viii. pp. 213, 214.

[1] Ap. B. Montfaucon, Nov. Collection, P.P. Tom. ii. 113, &c. 138. Lardner's Gospel History, Vol. xi. c. 148. p. 262.

[2] A more particular explanation of these will be found in a subsequent Book of this History.

sciences of astronomy and geography, which were at that time sufficiently advanced to have informed him better; yet it is acknowledged, that he seems to relate what he himself had observed in his travels, or what he had learned from others, with great simplicity and regard for truth.[1] The accuracy of his geographical description of the Malabar coast, and of the commerce with India, both by the Red Sea and the Persian Gulf, is unquestionable. His testimony also to the canon of sacred Scripture, as now received, is justly esteemed of great value:[2] and his account of the Christian Church in India is quoted, both by Protestant and Romish writers, as authentic history. It is thus given by La Croze,[3] who introduces it with the declaration, that he undertakes to write from good authorities the history of these Indian Christians, and that he cannot begin better than with the testimony of Cosmas, who was an eye witness to part of what he relates.

"There is," says he, "in the island of Ta-
"probane[4] (Ceylon), in the farthermost India,
"in the Indian sea, a Christian Church, with
"clergymen and believers. I know not whe-
"ther there are any Christians beyond this
"island. In the Malabar country also, where
"pepper grows, there are Christians, and in
"Calliana, as they call it, there is a Bishop,
"who comes from Persia, where he was con-
"secrated."[5] In this extract, as La Croze justly

---

[1] Robertson's India, p. 93.　　[2] Lardner, Vol. xi. c. 148.
[3] Histoire, pp. 37, 38.

[4] Σιελενδίβα, Cosmas. He calls the Christians there *Persians*, and says that they had priest and deacon, and all the Church Liturgy. Mahommedan Traveller's Account, &c. E. Renaudot, Note D.

[5] In quoting the original of this passage from Cosmas,

remarks, we have an undoubted testimony that Christianity was established in India in the sixth century. The present race of Christians in Malabar claim an antiquity much more remote indeed, and with justice, as already shown: but this is the most ancient authentic record of their existence, as a united and well ordered church, and also of the dependence of their Bishops and clergy upon the primate of Persia. All this may be fairly taken as presumptive evidence in favour of the conclusion drawn in the last chapter, that *India proper* was the country visited by Pantænus and others.

Thus is given in few words an account of one of the most ancient churches in the world. At the time of Cosmas' visit, they are said to have been Nestorians; and although they do not now hold the opinions of that sect, and it is no

Mr. Le Bas has added the following Note. " The names MAAE and KAAAIANA, fix the locality beyond all reasonable doubt. Μαλέ or Male, in the Malabar language, signifies *pepper*, from which product this region notoriously has its appellation. With regard to Καλλιάνα, it has been conjectured that it is identical either with Calicut, or Quilon, spelt also sometimes Coilan, (Coulan)." But it is more probable that the Calliana of Cosmas is the ancient city of Calianapore, of which some ruins are said to be still in existence near the sea-coast, two days' journey to the north of Mangalore.—See Paulinus, India Orientalis Christiana, p. 14. Romæ, 1794.

" It is, however, by no means impossible that Christianity may then have extended still farther north, to the district known at this day by the name of Calliance, or Calyani, ' a strong hilly country, extending along the sea-coast of the Aurungabad province, opposite to the island of Bombay, bounded on the east by the Western Ghauts, and situated between the 18th and 20th degrees of north latitude.' " Hamilton's Description of Hindoostan, vol. ii. p. 150). Life of Bp. Middleton, vol. i. c. 9. pp. 265, 266.

¹ It will be shown in the sequel what grounds there are for this conjecture.

where explained when and by whom their creed was altered; it may nevertheless be concluded that they were Nestorians at some former period, from the circumstance of their dependence upon the primate of Persia, who unquestionably held the Nestorian creed. This sect owed its origin to a Bishop of Constantinople, who lived about a century before the period when Cosmas visited the Indian churches: and it may tend to elucidate this part of our History, briefly to narrate the circumstances that gave rise to it, and to state its peculiar tenets.

Advancement of Nestorius to the see of Constantinople.

3. Nestorius, the prelate in question, was a native of Germanicia, a city of Syria, but he was brought up and educated at Antioch, where he was baptized. He lived in retirement in a monastery at Funeste, in the vicinity of Antioch, and there prepared for the sacred office of the ministry. After his admission to the order of priesthood, he became indefatigable in preaching the word of God, and soon acquired such reputation for eloquence in the pulpit, for piety and regularity of conduct, that the emperor, Theodosius II., promoted him to the bishopric of Constantinople, to which he was consecrated in the year 429. But it was his misfortune to be elevated to this arduous station, before his judgment and piety were sufficiently matured to qualify him for its important functions. It soon appeared that, however pure his motives, or irreproachable his character, he had not sufficient experience and discretion to fill so responsible a post. Constantinople being then the seat of government, its see ranked above the bishopric of Rome, and was considered second only to that of Alexandria. At that time numerous sects infested the church, Arians,

Novatians, Quartadecimans, Pelagians, Macedonians, &c. The situation of Nestorius placed
at his command a favourable opportunity to
counteract the influence of these heresies, and
to check their growth. But he wanted wisdom
to devise the needful plans, simple dependence
upon God to prosper his endeavours, patience
to await the developement of events, and judgment to improve any circumstances that might
arise to favour his good design. Instead of
acting the holy and judicious part becoming a
Christian Bishop, he proceeded in his work like
an infatuated zealot. In his first sermon after
his consecration, when preaching before Theodosius, he declared his determination to wage
war with all heretics, and called upon the
emperor to join him in this crusade. "Give
"me," said he, "O Emperor! the earth cleared
"from hereticks, and in recompense thereof,
"I will give you heaven. Assist me in des-
"troying hereticks, and I will assist you in
"vanquishing the Persians." This self-confi-
dence soon brought upon him a severe chastisement.

4. In those days, every Bishop, especially
when raised to a see of importance, was expected, in his first sermon, to give a full exposi-
tion of his doctrines, and to make a declaration
of the manner in which he intended to exercise
his jurisdiction. Accordingly Nestorius was
listened to on that occasion with more than
usual interest. His candour, therefore, in thus
meeting the expectations of his audience, may
be thought in some measure to extenuate his
indiscretion: but it cannot excuse his arrogance.
The wiser and better part of the auditors were
scandalized at his presumption. Had the act
itself been unexceptionable, yet they justly

His violent proceedings to extirpate heresy.

considered him premature in avowing, at so
early a stage of his episcopate, his intention to
persecute all that were not of his own sentiments. Too often, however, the pious and
discreet form the minority of even a Christian
assembly : while the multitude, more easily
wrought upon by the vehemence of an orator's
declamation than by the solidity of his argument, are carried away, under the impetus thus
produced, to the commission of the wildest
extravagancies. Such was the result on the
present occasion. The majority of the congregation approved of what they had heard from
their new Bishop, and encouraged him to proceed forthwith to the execution of his threats.
The Arians were the first objects of attack.
On the fifth day after his consecration, " Before," to use, as Socrates says, an ancient proverb, " he had tasted the water of the city," he
acted against them with unrelenting fury, and
attempted to demolish the church in which
they had hitherto secretly held their assemblies.
In this, however, they anticipated him. Driven
to desperation, and abandoning all hope of
saving the edifice, they burnt it to the ground,
together with several other buildings in its
neighbourhood. The fire excited great commotion in the city ; and being justly attributed
to the violent conduct of Nestorius, his enemies
ever after called him an incendiary.[1]

Emboldened by this success, he next directed
his persecution against the Novatians ; but the
emperor was now induced to interpose and stop
him in his rash career. Unable, therefore, to
proceed further in the city, he let loose his fury
against the Quartadecimans in Asia, Lydia and

---

[1] Πυρκαϊάν, Socrates. Lib. vii. ch. 29.

Caria. The only offence of this people was, that they thought proper to celebrate Easter on the 14th day of the moon (hence they received their designation), and for this deviation from the general practice of the church, many of them were put to death by the agents of Nestorius, both at Miletum and Sardis. With equal cruelty did he proceed against the Macedonians and Pelagians, sparing neither their persons nor their churches, wherever he could effect their destruction.

5. Such, however, were not the weapons with which Jesus Christ armed His disciples. He expressly declared, " All they that take the sword shall perish with the sword: "[1] and Nestorius soon felt the weight of this denunciation. His next act was one which stirred up against him the hostility of all parties: and he that had made such haste to banish others, was in his turn driven from his own church not long after his elevation.

The worship of the Virgin Mary " began to creep in among some superstitious people," about the middle of the fourth century, and for some time was regarded as the *Heresy of the Women*:[2] yet the other sex not long afterwards followed their example. These sectarians were called Collyridians,[3] who paid divine honours to the Virgin, and styled her *Theotocos*,[4] Mother of God. Although this name originated with

The cruelty
and injustice
of his ene-
mies.

---

[1] Matt. xxvi. 52.

[2] Epiphanus. Hæres. 78, 79. This father lived about that time. See also Archbishop Tillotson, on 1 Cor. iii. 15; Vol. iii. p. 98, fol. ed.

[3] From *collyridæ*, oblations of cakes, by which, with libations, sacrifices, and the like services, they judged it necessary to appease the Virgin's anger, and seek her favour and protection —Mosheim, cent. 4, p. ii. cap. 5. sect. 25. Binghams' Antiquities, &c. B. ii. ch. 22. s. 7.   [4] Θεοτόκος

the heterodox, and was undoubtedly very exceptionable : for Mary was the mother of Jesus' humanity indeed ; but it was blasphemy to call her the mother of the Divine Person that assumed humanity : yet afterwards, this title received the sanction of Basil, and many other fathers of a more orthodox faith, until it had grown into general use. Even Gregory Nazianzen, an illustrious ornament of the Greek church in the fourth century, and one of the most devout of Nestorius' predecessors in the see of Constantinople, had made use of the term, in his first epistle to Cledonius. It is true, the best of the prelates and fathers of those times had very indistinct views of divine truth ; and their general adoption of this erroneous appellation is one of the many proofs of the fact which might be adduced. While, therefore, Nestorius was right in protesting against it, for no human authority should be allowed to sanction error ; yet the age, the character, and the station of several who had adopted it, were entitled to some consideration, and ought to have induced Nestorius to be more temperate in his resistance. The courtesy which was due to his seniors would have been quite compatible with the most inflexible adherence to truth.

It ought, however, to be remarked, in extenuation of his violence, that it was chiefly the gross abuse of the obnoxious term, by the disciples of Apollinarius, which roused his zeal against it. For those heretics had taken occasion from it to confound the divine and human natures of Christ ; Nestorius, therefore, deemed it dangerous any longer to use it, and applied himself with energy to assert the distinction between our Lord's divinity and humanity, and to enforce its acknowledgment in the church. It does not appear that he wished to depart from the doctrines defined at the council of Nice, and since maintained by all orthodox writers. Indeed, when speaking of the two natures of Jesus Christ, he gives this unequivocal explanation of his sentiments. " I distinguish the natures, but I unite my adoration." These expressions, to which might be added others of like import, sufficiently prove that he admitted the two natures of Jesus Christ, inseparably united in one person. This explanation, however, did not satisfy the church. He was accused of reviving the errors of Paulus Samosetenus and Photinus, who taught that Jesus Christ was a mere man. Nothing could be more unjust than such an allegation. Nestorius, notwithstanding his intemperate zeal, was an advocate for the truth, and, no doubt, with proper management, might have been induced calmly to discuss the question at issue. But the minds of men were too much excited candidly to consider his apology. The monks, and even the orthodox prelates, combined against him. Several Bishops, more moderate, made an effort to stem the torrent. But the persons who undertook to restore peace to the church, seeing no impropriety in the expression, *Theotocos*, or, perhaps, not aware of its abuse, wrote to Nestorius, earnestly endeavouring to persuade him to acknowledge that Mary was the Mother of God. With their entreaties he refused to comply, lest he should appear to sanction the heresy founded upon the name. In such controversies names are tenets ; and so he regarded the title in dispute, maintaining that God could not be born, and that, therefore, the Virgin ought only to be called, the *Mother of Christ*. The Bishops, not satisfied with this, now joined his enemies against him. The council of Ephesus was convened for the purpose of trying him, and he was denounced as a heretic, in a summary and disgraceful manner. Without giving him the opportunity of explaining, defending, or retracting his sentiments, they deprived him at once of his see, and banished him from the city. He retired to his monastery, near Antioch, but his enemies would not allow him long to repose in its solitude. After four years he was removed to Tarsus, and then driven thence from place to place, until, worn out with grief and fatigue, he died of a broken heart.

We cannot take even this cursory view of these painful events, without deploring the intolerance and bigotry which both parties displayed. If, on the one hand, the sole object of Nestorius had been to protest against the Apollinarians' abuse of the term, *Mother of God*, and in his zeal to correct it, had proceeded with the discretion becoming a Christian prelate, he would have commanded the admiration of all devout and orthodox Christians, and the Lord would, doubtless, have prospered his work. Or if, on the other hand, in refusing to the Virgin Mary this title, he had really meant to deny the divinity of Jesus Christ, there would have been no injustice in his excommunication. For to hold such a heresy, is to subvert the fundamental doctrine of Jesus' atonement, and therefore to cease to be a Christian, in the proper sense of the term. It would then have been a manifest neglect of duty on the part of the other prelates to have allowed him to remain in communion with the orthodox: and, on his own part, he would have been practising gross hypocrisy by continuing in the church, and palpable dishonesty by retaining his preferment and emoluments. But it no where appears that he had the remotest intention so to dishonour the Lord: and had both parties mutually explained their views in a dispassionate manner, there can be little doubt that they would have come to a right understanding upon the disputed question. There seems, however, to have been too much of human passion in the contest to admit of an amicable adjustment. While Nestorius, like the furious Jehu, fancied that he was showing his " zeal for the Lord,"[1] it is to be feared that he was gratifying his own pride, or impetuosity of temper. And on the other hand, it cannot be denied that Cyril, in his treatment of Nestorius, was actuated by a spirit most unbecoming his character and station. For he presided at the council of Ephesus, which condemned him unheard, and is accused of bribing many to join him in proceeding against that unhappy prelate. His passion carried him so far, that, without waiting the arrival of the chief members of the council, and even of the Bishop of Antioch, he judged and condemned Nestorius at the first sitting, and had the cruelty to announce to him his condemnation in these terms. " To Nesto-" rius, a new Judas. Be it known to thee, that " thou art deposed, and stripped of all ecclesi-" astical rank," &c.

Conduct so opposed to the spirit of the Gospel, nothing can warrant; yet it is not difficult to account for it. Soon after Constantinople had become the seat of government, the Bishops of Alexandria, Antioch and Rome, began to observe with a jealous eye the growing influence of the prelate of that city: and there is too

---

[1] 2 Kings x. 16.

G

much reason to suspect that Cyril, who was Bishop of Alexandria, and chief actor in this disgraceful tragedy, was not sorry to have so plausible a pretext for humbling that rival prelate in the eyes of the universal church. How implacable is jealousy! It will pay no regard to the feelings of humanity, to the decision of justice, or to the voice of truth. May the Lord henceforth keep the unity of His Church from being disturbed by its baneful influence!

The progress of his sect and degeneracy of his tenets.

6. But while condemning the injustice of Cyril and his party, we must not fail again to notice the retributive justice of God, in giving up Nestorius to be chastened by such weapons as he had himself so unsparingly used. In this instance, however, as in most others, persecution had the contrary effect to that which was intended. The sentiment so violently opposed soon spread far and wide, like the waters of a river impeded in their course.[1] The churches of Syria, Egypt, Persia, and, according to Cosmas, that of India, embraced the obnoxious tenet of Nestorius: nor did they long confine themselves to his simple refusal to concede to the Virgin Mary the title in dispute.

It would answer little purpose here to discuss all the notions imputed to the unhappy founder of this sect. Suffice it to say, that the allegations which represent him as erring essentially from the orthodox faith, might all be shown to have as little foundation in truth as that just

---

[1] This observation applies also to the vehemence of Nestorius, his proceedings causing the very superstition he desired to correct to be the more tenaciously maintained: and the image of the Virgin Mary, holding the child Jesus in her arms, obtained the principal place among the idols in the churches, *in consequence of the Nestorian controversy.*— Mosheim, Cent. 5. pt. 2. c. 4. s. 2.

disproved. The historian, La Croze, has examined the question with his usual candour and
diligence; and he does not hesitate to affirm,
that the whole controversy was a mere logomachy. But this apology cannot be offered for
his followers, many of whom appear to have
enrolled themselves as disciples of his school
without comprehending his tenets. The duality
of *natures* for which he contended, soon degenerated into a duality of *persons*, which he
expressly denied. The difference between the
divine and human natures of Jesus, which they
attempt to define, is as unprofitable as unintelligible. It will be enough for our present purpose
to state the two distinguishing tenets of the
Nestorian heresy, as generally understood.
First, That in Christ there were not only two
natures, but two persons: of which, one was
divine, even the eternal Word; the other human,
even the man Jesus. Second, That Mary was
to be called the Mother of Christ,[1] and not the
mother of God.

7. This discussion,[2] brief as it is, might be
deemed too great a digression from our subject,

Importance
of this dis-
cussion in
reference to
the history
of Chris-
tianity in
India.

[1] Χριστοτόκος. Besides these leading tenets, they maintained
that the two persons of Jesus had only one aspect.—That the
union between the Son of God and the Son of Man was formed
at the moment of the Virgin's conception, and was never to be
dissolved. That it was not, however, a union of nature or of
person, but only of will and affection. That Christ was therefore to be carefully distinguished from God, who dwelt in Him
as in His temple.

[2] The following are the principal authorities for the account
here given of Nestorius, and of the heresy bearing his name.
Socrates Scholasticus, Lib. vii. c. 29—34. La Croze, Hist.
Lib. i. pp. 8—20. Fleury, Ecc. Hist. Lib. xxiv. s. 55. Du
Pin. Ecc. Hist. Tom. iv. pp. 40—43, 191, &c. Asseman,
Bib. Orient. Tom. iii. pp. 88, 388, 435, 448, 515, 516, 589,
606, &c. Also Tom. iii. pt. 2. Dissertatio de Syris Nesto-
rianis, pp. 605, 606.

were it not for the exaggerated and confused notions which Marius Mercator and other Latin authors impute to Nestorius, making him responsible for all the errors of his followers. [1] It were easy to account for these misrepresentations, were this the place for such a discus-

[1] Father Le Quien was too candid to join the turbulent outcry raised against this unhappy prelate. In his remarks upon the book of heresies composed by John Damascene, he has declared that Nestorius himself carefully avoided the assertion attributed to him, that there were two sons in the Lord Jesus Christ. Le Quien, though fond of scholastic subtilties, had yet too sound an understanding to be imposed upon by the unfounded assertions of prejudiced men, and too generous a spirit to impute to Nestorius a notion that he had disclaimed. Had all Romish writers treated his memory with equal justice, it would not have been loaded with half the opprobrium that is heaped upon it. But this was, perhaps, too much to be expected from the members of a church that has for centuries adopted the heresy against which he inveighed, and worshipped the Virgin Mary as the chief intercessor in heaven. It is presumed that no Romanist will contradict this assertion; but the two following specimens are given for the satisfaction of persons who may be reluctant to believe, that Christians of the present enlightened age can persist in such idolatry. They might be multiplied from the Roman Ritual, &c. to any extent required; but these, we presume, will suffice at present.

The first is taken from a Catechism, composed and published by order of the Pope in the year 1829.

Q. "Say now the Ave Maria. Hail Mary.

A. " God preserve thee Mary full of grace. The Lord is with thee, blessed art thou among women, and blessed is the fruit of thy womb, Jesus. Holy Mary, *Mother of God*, pray for us sinners now, and in the hour of our death. Amen."

Q. " Whose are these words?"

A. " Part are the words of the Archangel Gabriel, part of Saint Elizabeth, and part of the Church."

Q. " To what purpose do you say the Hail Mary after the Lord's prayer?"

A. " In order that by the intercession of the most blessed Virgin, I may more easily obtain that which I ask of God; because she is the advocate of sinners, and full of mercy, and at the same time is in heaven, above all the choirs of angels, and is most acceptable to God."

sion. As, however, our present object has been merely to give some account of the origin and character of the tenets attributed to the Indian Church at this period of her history, we shall proceed without further interruption.

The other specimen is a prayer taken from the Latin office of the Virgin.

" Oratio ad Reginam Omnium Creatorum."

" Serenissima Imperatrix," &c.

" A PRAYER TO THE QUEEN OF ALL CREATURES.

" 'Most serene Empress of heaven, Mother of the only-begotten Son of the Eternal Father, the Temple of the Holy Ghost, Mary purest virgin, full of grace and blessed above all women, I humbly adore thy bowels which did bear the fruit of life, through whom came salvation, and blessing to the whole world: to thee sinners have recourse as unto a mediatrix.—Sinners seek thee as the Mother of mercy. O most blessed mother, exalted above all the saints and above all the companies of angels, who next to thy most beloved Son, our Lord, possessest the highest throne of the heavenly court! O most refulgent Moon, who illuminatest the darkness of our gloomy night! O pious Mother, our benefactress, who ever called upon thee and experienced a denial! who ever hoped in thee and was confounded! Turn unto us those pitiful eyes of thine like the pools of Heshbon; for as in them there never wanted water, so in thy most kind eyes there never is wanting pity and compassion for our miseries. Incline, O most benignant Mother, the ears of thy kindness to our fervent prayers. Remember, O glorious Mother of God, the glorious things which are spoken of thee and have been done by thee. Thou art that fair and pious Virgin prefigured by Rebecca, who gave water not only to the servant of Abraham, who asked it of her, but also to his camels. Do thou, blessed Virgin, favour not only the righteous who are those that live according to reason, but favour the camels also, that is, sinners who, being crooked like camels, suffer themselves to be overcome of their lusts—to whom through thy mediation let the water of grace be communicated. Thou art that beloved Queen figured forth by the beautiful Esther, through whose intercession the great King Ahasuerus granted life to those whom he had condemned

CHAP.
III.

Nestorian-
ism of the
Indian
Church in
the sixth
century.

8. There is no reason to question the truth of the account given by Cosmas Indicopleustes, that the Christians of India in the sixth century were Nestorians, though he has not explained to what extent they embraced the dogmas of that sect. That he was himself a Nestorian, is satisfactorily proved from his writings; for he almost invariably adopts the Nestorian interpretations of sacred scripture, and makes use of their peculiar phraseology.[1] He was likewise the intimate friend of Thomas Edessenus, Archbishop of Persia, who was a leading prelate of that sect,[2] and is supposed to have been induced by Cosmas to send a Bishop, priests and deacons to Calliana.[3] It is, therefore, not improbable that Cosmas wrote under the influence of his own predilections when describing the creed of the Malabar Christians. Without,

to death: for thou, in like manner, beautiful and fair in the eyes of God the most High King, obtainest life eternal for many, who, by their sins, deserved damnation. Thou art that prudent Abigail who hinderedst the vengeance which David threatened against her unkind husband Nabal. Thou, like Judith, art the glory of Jerusalem, the joy of Israel, and the honour of the whole Christian people. Thou most excellent Lady—thou holy, thou glorious (Virgin).—Thou (who art) the joy of angels, strengthen by thy glorious countenance, and quicken our minds, that we may be able devoutly with the whole heart to contemplate the fifteen most profound mysteries of thy most sacred Rosary, to the eternal praise of thy only-begotten Son and thy glory, O most blessed Virgin.' "

The reader who has not access to the Romish ritual may see the original Latin in Mr. Cuninghame's work on the Apostasy of Rome, (pp. 12—14). The only remark necessary here to be made on the subject is, that we ought to receive with caution the invectives of a party so interested in depreciating the man that opposed this practice.

[1] La Croze, pp. 28—31. Lardner's Gospel Hist. Vol. xi. b. i. c. 148.

[2] J. S. Asseman, Bib. Orient. Tom. iii. pt. 2, pp. 405, 406.

[3] Calicut.

however, questioning their Nestorianism in his time, it is now well known, that their creed has for many ages past been more in accordance with that of the Jacobites; and there can be little doubt that it was changed at the time when their patriarch, at Seleucia, adopted the Jacobite tenets. In the second and third centuries of Mahomedanism, that is, the ninth and tenth of the Christian era, the Melchites and Jacobites obtained great privileges of the kalifs and sultans: in consequence of which they soon became the dominant sects in the eastern churches; and in many cities where the Nestorians had formerly been the only Christians, they were no longer in sufficient number to constitute a metropolitan church. Consequently, in some places they united with their neighbours; and in others they were totally extinct. The patriarch of Antioch adopted the Jacobite creed about the same period: and it is said, in the *Notitia* of *Nilus Doxapatrius*, "that his authority extended over all Asia, the East, and the Indies, whither he sent a Catholic bearing the title of Romogyris." "This title may have been kept up together with some others assumed by the *Greek* Patriarch of Antioch."[1] To what extent the churches of India conformed to the dogmas of the Nestorians or Jacobites at that early period, it is now impossible to ascertain: but it will be seen, that many ages after, they

[1] Κατεῖχεν ἅπασαν τὴν Ἀσίαν καὶ ἀνατολὴν αὐτήν τε τὴν Ἰνδίαν, &c. Origin of the Christian Religion in China. Eus. Renaudot, pp. 114—119. But this author asserts, that there is not the least vestige in history, since the seventh century at least, of Catholics, or Metropolitans sent to the Indies, either by the Orthodox or Jacobite Patriarchs of Antioch. The subsequent pages of this history will show how far he was mistaken in this assertion.

diverged into the opposite extreme of Nestori-
.anism, when compelled by the Jesuits to follow
the example of Rome, and pay divine honours
to the virgin Mary, as *Mother of God.*[1]

[1] The tenets held by the present race of Christians in
Malabar, will come more appropriately under discussion when
recording their emancipation from the arrogance and superstitions of the Roman Church.

N.B.—While this sheet is going through the press (September, 1838) the following notice has been published:—

‘The Archbishop of Paris has made a splendid offering to
the church of Notre Dame de Deliverance, in Normandy, in
fulfilment of a vow he had made conditionally on the conversion of Talleyrand. The offering, which is an image, has
inscribed on its pedestal, words to this effect:—“Offered to
the Holy Virgin, the mother of God, in grateful commemora-
tion of her Divine grace in bringing back a *stray lamb!* to
the fold of God's Church.”’

Will it be said after this, that the Romanists of the nineteenth century are too enlightened to sanction and perpetuate
such superstitions? or, that they are confined to the illiterate?
Is it not in perfect keeping with the darkness of the middle
ages? and does it not warrant the suspicion with which we
receive their denunciations against Nestorius?

CHAPTER IV.

RISE AND PROGRESS OF MAHOMEDANISM, AND ITS EFFECTS UPON THE INDIAN CHURCH.

1. ABOUT a century after the voyage of Cosmas, India was closed against the Greeks and Romans, in consequence of the extensive dominion which the Mahomedans then acquired in the East. In the year 608, Mahomet, the Arabian impostor, began to put forth his pretensions as, The Prophet of God. He recommended himself and his cause to the wild marauders of Arabia, by the prospect of plunder in this world, and of sensual indulgence in the next. Such promises easily induced those barbarians to leave their secluded haunts and barren desert, and to sally forth under their martial prophet to the work of desolation. They rushed on in one tide of prosperity, as resistless as impetuous, until the Mahomedan creed and dominion were extended from the Atlantic to the very confines of China. Egypt was one of their earliest conquests, and they soon learned to appreciate the advantages of the commerce which had been so long carried on between that country and India. From this period the traders of Greece and other countries could in no way obtain the productions of India, except through the Arab merchants of Alexandria. The Mahomedans

A. D. 606. Rise and progress of the Mahomedans, who monopolize and extend the Indian trade.

A. D. 640.

were equally successful in Persia, where also the warlike Arab was soon transmuted into an enterprising merchant. Thus possessing the two great marts for Indian commodities, they were able to monopolize the trade; and they continued for many ages to carry it on with an energy not inferior to that which they had displayed in the march of conquest and devastation. The progress of their voyagers towards the East soon extended far beyond the Gulf of Siam, hitherto the boundary of European navigation. They became acquainted with Sumatra, and the other islands of the great Indian Archipelago, and advanced as far as the city of Canton in China. Nor are these discoveries to be considered as the effect of the enterprising curiosity of individuals; they were owing to a regular commerce carried on between the Persian Gulf and China, and all the intermediate countries. Many Mahomedans, imitating the example of the Persians described by Cosmas Indicopleustes, settled in India and the countries beyond. They were so numerous in the city of Canton, that the emperor (as the two Arabian authors quoted above relate) permitted them to have a cadi, or judge, of their own sect, who decided controversies among his countrymen according to their own laws, and presided in all the functions of religion. In other places proselytes were gained to the Mahomedan faith, and the Arabian language was understood and spoken in almost every sea-port of any consequence. Ships from China and different places of India traded in the Persian Gulf, and by the frequency of mutual intercourse, all the nations of the East became better acquainted with each other.[1]

[1] "Ancient Accounts of India," &c. pp. 6, 7. E. Renau-

2. The review thus briefly taken of the rise and progress of that power which in after ages ruled over a vast proportion of the continent of Asia, should serve to keep the mind awake to the Divine Providence which never ceases to watch over the affairs of men, and to control their designs for the furtherance of His own purposes in the world.[1] "For," He hath declared, "as the rain cometh down, and the snow from heaven, and returneth not thither, but watereth the earth, and maketh it bring forth and bud, that it may give seed to the sower, and bread to the eater: so shall my word be that goeth forth out of my mouth; it shall not return unto me void, but it shall accomplish that which I please, and it shall prosper in the thing whereto I sent it." And wherever His wisdom has ordained that His word shall visit a people, either to bless those who receive it, or to bear witness against those who reject it, His providence usually directs the sword of the warrior or the sail of the merchant to open a way for its passage and reception.

3. Mahomet found among the Arabs great numbers who, having embraced the Christian profession under the leaders of different sects, had taken refuge within the borders of Arabia from

Marginal notes: A. D. 640. Manifestations of Divine Providence.

Marginal notes: Asiatic Christians tolerated by Mahomedan government. Persian Christians cherish the Indian Church.

dot's Note Q. See also Robertson's India, pp. 98—103, with his Notes in the Appendix, 37, 38.

During the middle ages, when Christendom was sunk in ignorance, literature was preserved from extinction, and even revived from the decline which had seized it, by the exertions of Mahomet's followers. The tenth century, which has been denominated the leaden age of Europe, was the golden age of Asia. (M'Crie's History of the Reformation in Spain, ch. ii). In confirmation of this remark we may refer to the fact, that history is indebted chiefly to the Arabian travellers whose writings we have referred to above, for all that is known of India about that period.

[1] Isaiah lv. 10, 11.

the proscriptions of the imperial edicts. He was too consummate a politician not to discover and improve the opportunity thus afforded him of strengthening his cause. For this purpose he incorporated their several notions with his religion, and granted a free toleration to those Christians, "and especially the Nestorians," within his dominions who did not embrace his faith.[1] For several ages this policy was pursued by the Mahomedan rulers in Asia; and while their merchants were busily engaged in commercial pursuits, their Christian subjects in Persia were no less active in cherishing the churches already planted in India, and in extending the knowledge of Christianity as far as they could reach. Their missionaries very soon followed the track of the enterprising trader, and their endeavours were crowned, both in India and China, with considerable success.

A. D.
660.

Letter of
Jesuyab, on
the decline
of the Indian
and Persian
Churches in
the seventh
century.

4. A letter is preserved by Asseman,[2] written by Jesuyab, metropolitan of Mosul, who died in the year of our Lord 660, from which it appears, that at that time the churches of India and Persia were in a declining state. This declension is attributed to the neglect of the patriarch of Persia, and is thus described. "In your region, since you have refused to observe the canons of the church, the succession of the priesthood has been cut off from the people of India, &c." "It appears that the patriarch of Persia had refused to acknowledge the authority of that of Seleucia, asserting that the Christians of Persia and India were Christians of St. Thomas, and were therefore not at all subject to

[1] Sale's Koran, Pre. Dis. sec. 2nd. Asseman, Bib. Orien. Tom. iii. pt. ii. p. 94. Eus. Renaudot, Origin of Christianity in China, p. 111, &c.
[2] Ib. Tom. iii. pt. ii. p. 438.

the followers of Mar[1] Moris, who is said to have propagated Christianity in Mesopotamia."[2]

5. The allusion here made to St. Thomas suggests a recurrence to the subject, especially as this seems to be the most suitable place to introduce the characters who are thought to have given rise to the tradition of that Apostle's having preached in India. The whole story is supposed to be a fable invented by the Manichees, a heresy that owed its origin to Manes, who lived towards the close of the third century.[3] His principal tenet was, the admission of two first causes independent of each other, whereby he endeavoured to account for the origin of evil. He is said to have sent one of his disciples, named Thomas, into India, to propagate his heresy. Jacobus Tollius suspected that this man was mistaken for the Apostle of that name. His suspicion is founded on the testimony of Theodoret, who relates the circumstance; and Tollius farther mentions an ancient tradition of the Malabar Christians, which makes mention of a certain magi[4] who visited them from Persia, and to whom they gave the name Mannacavasser, This name, as is very reasonably conjectured,

(margin) Thomas, a Manichee, visits India, another heresiarch of the same name, visits China; these supposed to have occasioned the legend about the Apostle Thomas.

[1] Mar is a title still given to the Syrian Bishops, and is nearly equivalent to our word—Lord.

[2] See "A brief History of the Syrian Churches in the South of India," drawn up by Professor Lee, for the Church Missionary Society, and published with their Seventeenth Report, Appendix IV.

[3] Eusebius, Lib. vii. c. 31. Beausobre's Hist. of Manichees.

[4] It is worthy of remark, that the religion of the Magi had recently been revived in Persia. The heresies of Manes and Mazdak had occasioned such violent dissensions throughout the empire as to threaten it with destruction. To save his country, the emperor Anushirwan, on the death of his father, Khosrú Kobád, " put Mazdak to death, with all his followers, and the Manichees also, restoring the ancient Magian religion." (Sale's Koran, Pre. Dis. sect 2, p. 48.)

signifies, a Manichee. According to the tradition, this man arrived in India before the churches of Malabar became subject to the patriarch of Persia; and he is said to have wrought miracles, and preached with so much success, that he drew vast multitudes after him. This narrative may serve to account for the story about St. Thomas, which in those dark and credulous ages would find too easy a reception.

The tradition, that Christianity was introduced into China by this Apostle, is equally unworthy of credit; but it may be traced to a similar origin. Magalhanes and other Jesuits assert it with their usual confidence: but M. Maigrot, Bishop of Conon and vicar apostolic in that kingdom, had too much candour to lend the credit of his name in support of so unfounded a tale. He was well acquainted with the history of China, and showed that the missionaries who gave currency to this tradition, mistook for the Apostle Thomas, "One Tamo, as notorious a rogue as ever visited China, who became a chief of one of the subdivisions of the sect of Foé, which they call the sect of contemplatives." The Bishop adds, that this man did not enter China till after the year 582.[1]

6. About the year 780, the church in India was again under the authority of the patriarch of Seleucia, to whom its Bishops were subject, and consequently they were Nestorians.[2] Not many years after, an Armenian merchant took up his abode in Malabar, who is said to have been the first to obtain for the Christians in

A. D.
780.
Probably
confirmed
by the settlement of
Mar Thomas, a rich
merchant of
Malabar.

[1] La Croze, pp. 41—43. Account of Syrian Christians. Asia. Res. vol. 7.

[2] See the last chapter, sec. 8. Also Professor Lee's Brief History.

those parts immunities of considerable importance.[1]   His name was Thomas Cana, or, as he
is usually called, Mar Thomas.   It appears
that his commercial pursuits first led him to
India.   The histories of the country describe
his dignity and affluence in magnificent terms,
and mention that he carried on trade to a great
extent.   He kept also two houses, one in the
South, in the kingdom of Cranganore, and the
other towards the North, whose situation is not
named, but it is thought to have been either at
Angamale or in its environs.   He is said to have
had two wives, the first, who is called his lawful wife, resided in the South; the residence of
the second was in the North.   She was a native
of the country, of the Naire, or military caste,
and is described as a slave,[2] who had been converted to the Christian faith.   It is thought
more probable that Mar Thomas espoused her
after the death of his first wife, than that he
followed the heathen practice of polygamy.   He
had a numerous family by each of these women,
among whom at his death he divided his immense wealth.   To the children of the former
he left his possessions in the South; and those
of the latter inherited his property in the North.
Both families continued rapidly to increase,
until, by intermarriages, they became so incorporated with the other Christians of the country, that in process of time the whole regarded
Mar Thomas as their common ancestor.   The
two lines of his posterity remained distinct, the
former being considered the more respectable;

[1] Gouvea, Histoire Orientale, tournée en François, par F.
Jean Baptiste de Glen.   En Anvers, l'an 1609, chap. 2.

[2] This is inconsistent with the present grades of society in
Malabar, the Naires being the nobility, and the slaves, the
lowest caste; indeed, these are literally outcasts.

and for many ages they were so proud of their priority, that they refused to contract marriages, or even to hold any intercourse with their northern brethren. So far did they carry this feeling, that they would not allow them even to enter their churches.

There is great difficulty in pronouncing upon these and similar transactions recorded in the early history of this church. Asseman has laboured hard to throw discredit upon the story of this Armenian merchant; for it presents too strong a confirmation of the independence of the Indian Church, at that remote period, to be admitted as authentic history by one, whose great object was to maintain the pretensions of Rome to the supremacy of the universal church, from the first ages of Christianity.[1] It is true, we cannot give much credit to certain stories related of the ancient

[1] This laborious compiler is to be followed with great caution, whenever he has a Romish tradition or pretension to maintain, or a protestant innovation to depreciate. In proof of the little reliance to be placed on his impartiality, we may quote the following note from Le Bas' Life of Bishop Middleton, Vol. i. c. 9. pp. 267, 268. " It is contended by Assemann, that this Thomas Cana was not an Armenian merchant, but a Nestorian bishop, who was dispatched to India, not in the sixth century, but about the year 800, by Timotheus the Nestorian patriarch. The worthy Maronite, indeed, seems to be sadly puzzled with the odd story of Thomas and his two wives, the one at Cranganore, the other at Angamala,—the one the parent of the nobility of the land, the other of the commonalty. It was an unheard of thing, he says, that even a Nestorian bishop should have two wives, together or successively: and (not knowing what else to make of this awkward and unseemly tradition), he concludes that it could be nothing more than a sort of allegory, signifying merely that Thomas had two churches to administer, namely, that of Cranganore, and that of Angamala; and that the Christians of each diocese may be traced to him, not as their carnal, but their spiritual progenitor." Assem. Biblioth. Orient., tom. iii. pars 2, p. 442.

Malabar Christians, for which there is no other authority than that of the Portuguese, a nation, as La Croze justly remarks, themselves but little enlightened, and determined enemies to these people. Nevertheless, the narrative just given derives confirmation from a tradition of the kind still preserved by the Syrian Christians in Travancore, and also from some customs that seem to prevail in consequence of these events. The most striking peculiarity that may be mentioned, as having the appearance of being derived from this origin, is, the two divisions, or castes, which they still preserve, the one in the South claiming superiority over the other in the North. And, assuming the truth of the whole account, which there is no just reason to question, we cannot but admit the probability of the historian's conjecture, that the name of this Armenian merchant, and all the circumstances relating to himself and his numerous posterity, have caused him to be confounded with the Apostle Thomas.[1]

7. Though it is uncertain at what time this Mar Thomas settled in India, yet there is no reason to doubt the assertion of Gouvea, who dates it in the ninth century, in the reign of Ceram Peroumal, Rajah of Malabar. As this is the first mention of a native sovereign of any consequence in the country, we shall here give some account of the origin of his power.

[2]The early history of Malabar is involved in obscurity, which, like that of India generally, is increased by the fabulous tales connected with it. This entire coast is believed, by the heathen, to have emerged from the sea; and

---

[1] La Croze, pp. 46, 47.

[2] Asiatic Researches, vol. v. Article 1. Historical Remarks on the Coast of Malabar.

its first appearance they ascribe to the piety or penitence of their god *Parasram*,[1] who, stung with remorse for the blood he had so profusely shed in overcoming the rajahs of the *Khetry* tribe, applied to Varoona, the god of the Ocean, to supply him with a tract of ground to bestow on the Brahmins; and Varoona having, in consequence of this petition, withdrawn his waters from the *Gowkern*, a hill in the vicinity of Mangalore, to Cape Comorin, this strip of territory, now called Malabar,[2] *Parasram* is believed, by its pagan inhabitants, to have parcelled out among different tribes of brahmins, and to have directed that the entire produce of the soil should be appropriated, first, to their maintenance, and, secondly, towards the erection of temples, and for the support of divine worship. From this fabulous tale, the country thus obtained still continues to be distinguished in their writings by the term of *Kermbhoomy*, or, The Land of Good Works for the Expiation of Sin.

Though none but a Hindoo can be expected to believe this account of the origin of this country; yet, from the nature of the soil, and the quantity of sand, oyster-shells, and other fragments of marine substances, met with in making deep excavations, in all parts of the country, it is extremely probable that the sea once came up to the foot of the Ghauts. The natives have a tradition, that it was recovered from the ocean about 2300 years ago; that it

---

[1] Or *Parasoo-Rama*, one of the incarnations of Vishnoo.

[2] Its original name, *Mulyalum*, was acquired from its situation, meaning, *Skirting at the bottom of the hills.* These hills are the range of mountains called, by the natives, *Sukhien;* by the Europeans, *the Ghauts.* Their proper name is *Sukhien Purbut,* or hills of *Sukhien,* pronounced with the guttural *kh.*

remained long in a marshy state, and was scarcely habitable ; insomuch, that the first occupants, whom *Parasram* is said to have brought into it from the eastern, and even the northern, part of India, again abandoned it, being more especially scared by the multitude of serpents with which its marshy soil abounded ; until they were taught by *Parasram* to propitiate those reptiles, by introducing the worship of them and their images, which are said to have become from that period objects of adoration.

When, by these and other means, the country was rendered habitable, the brahmins divided it into three equal proportions ; one of which was consecrated to supply the expense attending religious worship, another for the support of government, and the third for their own maintenance.[1]

The brahmins appear to have first set up, and for some time maintained, a sort of republic, or aristocratical government, under two or three principal chiefs, elected to administer the affairs of state. The business of the country was thus carried on, attended, however, with several intermediate modifications, 'till, upon jealousies arising among themselves, the great body of the brahmin landholders had recourse to foreign assistance : and this terminated, either by conquest or convention, in their receiving to rule over them a *Permal*, or chief governor, from the king of the neighbouring country of *Chaldesh*, a part of the southern Carnatic. This succession of governors, or viceroys, was regularly changed at the end of every twelve years : 'till at length one of those officers, the

[1] Other divisions and subdivisions are mentioned in the *Kerul Oodputtee*, or, *The emerging of the Country of Kerul.* Soc Asiat. Res. vol. v. pp. 2, 3.

renowned *Ceram Peroumal,*[1] appears to have rendered himself so popular during his government, that, at the expiration of its term, he was enabled, by the encouragement of those over whom his delegated sway had extended, to confirm his own authority, and to set at defiance that of his late sovereign, the king of Chaldesh. That prince, known in the native history by the name Rajah *Kishen Rao*, sent an army into Malabar, with a view to reduce this rebellious viceroy, and to recover his authority : but *Ceram Peroumal* defeated his army, and soon succeeded in establishing himself as sovereign of Malabar.

This event is supposed to have happened in the ninth century ; which is rendered probable, both by the date given as that of the building of Calicut, which is said to have been founded by this prince in the year 825 ;[2] and also by the coincidence of its being the epoch from which all the Rajahs and chief Naires, and the other titled and principal lords and landholders of Malabar, date their ancestors' acquisition of sovereignty and rule in that country. The greater part of their present representatives uniformly assert, that their possessions and prerogatives were derived from the grants made to their ancestors by *Ceram Peroumal*, some of whom being his relations, he thus enriched : and others, not related to him, he rewarded for their services in assisting to establish him on the throne. This distribution of the country, however, does not appear to have been made

---

[1] Named also in the native history, *Sheo Ram*, or, *Shermanoo Permaloo.*

[2] According to Scaliger, (Book v. de Emend. Temporum) in the year of our Lord 907, i. e. in 984 of the æra of India ; or, according to M. Vischer, A.D. 825.

by him until his death; and in this way do the natives account for the numerous petty rajahs that once filled the country.

During the reign of this prince, the division of the inhabitants of Malabar into castes which continues to the present day, is said to have been made; and it is attributed to one of their divinities, *Shunker*, a supposed son of *Mahadeo*, the principal of the Hindoo gods. The several castes, with their distinctions, are thus described. —1. The *Namboory Brahmins.*—2. *Naires*, who are the military tribe; but for some time past many of them have followed more menial professions.—3. *Teers*, who are cultivators of the soil, carpenters, smiths, goldsmiths, fishermen, &c.; but these are all freemen.—4. *Maleres*, who are musicians and conjurers, and also free. —5. *Poleres*, or *Poliars*,[1] who are bondmen, attached to the soil in the lower part of Malabar. These castes were restricted to their particular duties, and the inferior were forbidden to touch the superior, or even to approach them within certain prescribed limits. The bare meeting of any of the lowest caste on the road entailed pollution, for which the party of the superior caste was required to cleanse himself by ablution.

Whatever were the origin of these distinctions, they are believed to have been made soon after the defeat of *Kishen Rao's* army by *Ceram Peroumal*. This prince is described as having governed his kingdom with great magnificence and prosperity. The Mahomedans claim him as a convert, and affirm, that being desirous of dying at Mecca, he divided his dominions between his children and kinsmen, and then

---

[1] Called *Dêrs*, in Hindoostan. The caste above the Ghauts called Puniers, are likewise attached to the soil.

retired to the vicinity of their prophet's cave. One of his nephews he made his heir, with the title of Zamorin, or emperor, and assigned him the valuable territory of Calicut.[1] Whatever ground there may be for this alleged predilection of Ceram Peroumal for the Mahomedan creed, he was devoid of their bigotry, affording equal toleration to all classes of his subjects. So high and universal was the respect in which they held him, that after his decease, his heathen subjects numbered him among their gods; and it is said that their example was followed by those on the opposite coast. To his Christian subjects he granted many important privileges. Before his reign the Christians of the Coromandel coast underwent severe persecutions from the reigning sovereigns, and were compelled to flee for safety to the mountainous parts of the country. Encouraged by the paternal government of *Ceram Peroumal,* they left the hills, and finally settled in the interior of Cochin, Cranganore, and Travancore, where they still reside.

Under the reign of this prince, the Christians attained to some consequence. The opulence and extensive mercantile pursuits of the Armenian, Mar Thomas, would, doubtless, cause his family to be respected; and the rest of the Christians, who seem to have been so soon identified with them, would naturally participate in their immunities. They are said to have enjoyed the same rank as the Naires, who are the nobility of the country, and in every respect to have been placed in a state of equality with that caste. They were even made in great measure independent of the heathen authorities, being

[1] Barros, Decad 1, lib. ix. c. 5.　E. Renaudot's "Inquiry into the time when the Mahomedans entered China," p. 165.

left to the government of their own Bishops in civil, as well as ecclesiastical affairs.

8. The charters of their privileges were engraved on copper plates, in Malayalim, Canarese, Bisnagar and Tamul, which languages, are spoken in different parts of the western coast. They preserved them with great care until the sixteenth century, when they were lost; [1] and for many years the Christians had

[1] The following account has been given of the manner in which they were lost. Not long after the Portuguese arrived in India, the Christians of Malabar, observing their power, and induced by their profession of the same religion to confide in their expressions of regard, resolved, for greater security, to entrust these charters to their care. They were delivered by Mar Jacob, a Syriac Bishop of Angamale, to the custody of the Portuguese commissary at Cochin, by whom they were never returned. It is alleged, that he left them littering about in the magazine, and that they disappeared, no one knew how. Whether they were lost through carelessness or design, it is impossible to say, but the commissary might be unconscious of their value. However that may be, " Adrian Moens, a governor of Cochin in 1770, who published some account of the Jews of Malabar, informs us, that he used every means in his power, for many years, to obtain a sight of the famed Christian plates; and was at length satisfied that they were irrecoverably lost, or rather, he adds, that *they never existed.* The learned in general, and the antiquarian in particular, will be glad to hear that these ancient tablets have been recovered within this last month by the exertions of Colonel Macauley, the British resident in Travancore, and are now officially deposited with that officer."

"The Christian tablets are six in number. They are composed of a mixed metal. The engraving on the largest plate is thirteen inches long, by about four broad. They are closely written, four of them on both sides of the plate, making in all eleven pages. On the plate reputed to be the oldest, there is writing perspicuously engraved in *nail-headed* or triangular-headed letters, resembling the *Persepolitan* or Babylonish. On the same plate there is writing in another character, which is supposed to have no affinity with any existing character in Hindoostan. The grant on this plate appears to be witnessed by four Jews of rank, whose names are distinctly engraved in an old Hebrew character, resem-

nothing to show for their rights and immunities but prescription, and a reference to the names of the princes by whom they had from time to time been granted.

A. D.
883.
Alfred the
Great's am-
bassage to
the East:
his commer-
cial designs.

9. A fact is recorded in the early annals of England, which, taken in connection with this history, cannot fail to interest the English reader. Towards the close of the ninth century, Alfred the Great, a monarch in whose memory his country has such reason to exult, is said to have sent ambassadors to visit the shrine of St. Thomas in the East, which is supposed to be that which the Romanists now show at St. Thomé, in the vicinity of Madras. The principal ambassador was Sighelm; or, as some chroniclers call him, Suithelm, the Bishop of Shireburn. Having finished their devotions, which were the avowed object of their mission, Sighelm and his companions returned, bringing home a cargo of pearls and spices, which were

bling the alphabet called the *Palmyrene:* and to each name is affixed the title of ' *Magen,*' or chief, as the Jews translated it. It may be doubted, whether there exists in the world any documents of so great length, which are of equal antiquity, and in such faultless preservation as the Christian tablets of Malabar. The Jews of Cochin indeed contest the palm of antiquity: for they also produce two tablets, containing privileges granted at a remote period; of which they presented to me a Hebrew translation. As no person can be found in this country who is able to translate the Christian tablets, I have directed an engraver at Cochin to execute, on copper plates, a *fac simile* of the whole, for the purpose of transmitting copies to the learned societies in Asia and Europe. The Christian and Jewish plates together make fourteen pages."

Note.—" Most of the manuscripts which I collected among the Syrian Christians, I have presented to the University of Cambridge: and they are now deposited in the public library of that University, together with the copper plate fac similes of the Christian and Jewish Tablets."—Buchanan's Christian Researches, pp. 142, 143.

thought richly to repay their royal master's zeal. William of Malmsbury declares, that some of these gems were to be seen in his days, in the monuments of the church.

That the journey here alluded to was undertaken, there can be little question. " Neither the author of the Saxon Chronicle, in the year 883,[1] nor William of Malmsbury,[2] were capable in the twelfth century of inventing this extraordinary fact. They were incapable of explaining the motives and measures of Alfred ; and their hasty notice serves only to provoke our curiosity. William of Malmsbury feels the difficulty of the enterprise,"[3] which in that age is not to be wondered at : but others do not hesitate to say, " that the embassy was sent in discharge of a vow which the king had made."[4]

The fact then that such an ambassage was sent by Alfred may be received as unquestionable. Not so the assumption that the ambassadors accomplished all the object of their mission : for there is reason to doubt whether they reached India ; and it is strongly suspected that they collected both their cargo and legend in Egypt.[5] The situation of Egypt at that time tends to confirm this suspicion. We have

---

[1] Sax. Chron. p. 86.

[2] De Gestis Regum Angliæ, lib. ii. c. 4, p. 44. The mission and its safe return are mentioned also by Florence of Worcester, Radulph, Bromton, and other chroniclers, which are quoted in Turner's History of the Anglo-Saxons, vol. ii. b. v. ch. vi. pp. 145, &c. But the Saxon Chronicle and William of Malmsbury are the principal authorities.

[3] Quod quivis in hoc sæculo miretur.—Gibbon's Decline and Fall, ch. xlvii.

[4] Huntingdon, and Alured of Beverley. See Turner's Anglo-Saxons, vol. ii. p. 146. A fuller discussion of the question will be found in the Appendix to b. v. ch. vi of the same History.

[5] Gibbon's Decline and Fall, ch. xlvii.

already seen that the Arabian merchants were then in possession of that country, and that they monopolized the market of Alexandria, allowing no other traders to pass that way from the West to the East, though they freely supplied all who came to their mart with the commodities of India. They were not likely to be more indulgent to Christian strangers from England, than to those from Greece or Rome: and every account we have of journeys then performed in countries over which the Mahomedans exercised authority, shows what difficulty Christian travellers had to make their way even to the interior of Egypt and to Palestine;[1] and any attempt to penetrate to India would have had to encounter impediments, increasing at every stage, that must soon have been found insurmountable. It is thought probable that the Nestorians in the confidence of the Saracen caliphs, would exert their influence to facilitate the progress of the ambassage; but this is very doubtful. Considering the hostile feeling that subsisted between the Nestorians and the western churches, they would be more likely to impede than promote the advance of the English Bishop and his company.[2] On the whole then, there appears to be stronger grounds for the suspicion that they did not proceed beyond Alexandria, than for the assumption that they went as far as the eastern coast of India.

Alfred's real object in sending this ambassage to the East, may, perhaps, be gathered from

---

[1] Turner's Anglo-Saxons, vol. ii. pp. 162, &c.

[2] It has been shown in the former chapter, sect. 8, that the Nestorian influence in Persia was superseded about this time by the Jacobites: but the remarks in the text will apply to either of these sects.

what is said of his subsequent designs. His
original intention was, doubtless, more worthy
of his character and intelligence, than to send
his servants so far on a pilgrimage to the pretended tomb of a saint. It is more probable
that he had the interests of commerce in view;
for after their return, he is said to have entertained the largest projects of trade and discovery. The heart of Alfred, however, great
and patriotic as it was, could not have conceived
the vast dominion and prosperity which his
country was destined in future ages to attain in
the eastern world. The fact of this ambassage
in now comparatively unimportant, whatever
were its immediate object or place of destination. Yet, looking at the mighty empire and
extensive wealth since acquired by England in
the East Indies; and, above all, at the progress
of Christianity there during the nineteenth
century, and the wider prospects still opening
to the faith and benevolence of British Christians; it is indeed interesting to look back,
through a long vista of generations and events,
to the first opening of the eastern continent to
the enterprise of the British isles. May the
God of infinite mercy so prosper the union of
these distant regions, as to lead to the dawning
of eternal day upon millions yet unborn !

10. Some time after the foundation of Quilon,[1]
in the beginning of the tenth century, there is
an account of two Syrian ecclesiastics arriving
there from Babylon. Their names were, Mar
Sapores and Mar Pheroz. It is no where ex-

*A. D.
883.*

*A. D.
920.*
*Visit of Mar
Sapores and
Mar Pheroz,
Persian ec-
clesiastics,
to Malabar.*

[1] It is difficult accurately to determine these dates. According to the Portuguese historian, Gouvea, (fol. iv. col. 4,)
this period answered to the year 680 from the founding of
Coulan (Quilon). This epoch differs from that of Calicut.—
La Croze, p. 47.

CHAP.
IV.

plained for what purpose they came to India ; but it is probable that they were charged with some particular ecclesiastical commission from the Metropolitan of Persia, or that they came from him merely with the general intention of strengthening their Eastern brethren in the faith, and keeping up the communion already subsisting between them and their patriarch. But, whatever their object, they conducted themselves in a manner so becoming Christian missionaries, that they met with a fraternal reception from the Christians of the country, and were very successful in their endeavours to convert the heathen. The rajah of Travancore, seeing the respect that was paid to them by his Christian subjects, conferred upon them many favours. Among other privileges, he granted them free permission to preach throughout his dominions; left all his subjects who heard them at liberty, if they chose, to embrace their doctrines ; and allowed them to erect churches wherever they desired. In such estimation were these strangers held, that they were canonized after their decease, and the Christians added them to the catalogue of the saints, whose names they are to this day accustomed to call over at the time of public prayers. Several churches were also erected to their memory.[1]

---

[1] Some years after, when Menezes, a Romish Archbishop of Goa, visited the country, claiming jurisdiction over the Syrian Church, he erased the names of Sapores and Pheroz from the catalogue of their worthies, for no other reason, but because they were not found in his own Roman martyrology. He altered, likewise, the titles of the churches which had been consecrated in their names. If these were his only offences, they would have been comparatively unimportant : but it will soon appear that he inflicted a wound on this ancient church that she has not yet recovered.

11. The immunities conferred on the Indian Christians by Ceram Peroumal, insured for them the enjoyment of a long and uninterrupted course of prosperity; during which they became sufficiently powerful to assert their independence of their heathen rulers, whose yoke they at length shook off, and succeeded in raising a member of their own body to the throne. Their first Christian king was Baliartes, who assumed the title of Rajah of the Christians of St. Thomas. For some time they maintained their independence under their own kings, until one of them, having no children, adopted the Rajah of Diamper for his heir. This man was a heathen, and he succeeded to all the regal power over the Christians of India. By similar adoptions, a practice of frequent occurrence in that country, they became in the course of time subject to the heathen Rajah of Cochin, and other petty sovereigns of the country.[1]

A. D. 920.

Baliartes, the first Christian king in Malabar. They fall again under heathen sovereigns.

12. As chronological accuracy is essential to the right understanding of history, and greatly augments its interest, it is to be regretted that we cannot always depend upon the dates assigned for the events just narrated. An historian will omit no opportunity to connect the annals of a church or nation with each particular circumstance that he records. It must be remembered, however, that this is not the leading design of history; its primary object being to distinguish between *facts*, and those legendary tales with which the weakness of the credulous, the imagination of the extravagant, or the craft of the fraudulent, have too often imposed upon mankind. And thus much, we may hope, is here accomplished, notwithstanding the un-

The primary objects of civil and ecclesiastical history here attained.

[1] La Croze, pp. 47—49.

certainty of the periods at which several of the incidents just narrated occurred.

The history also of any particular church ought to consist of its polity, its doctrines, and its character. These constitute the chief subjects of interest in all ecclesiastical records. The Bible is the only authority to which Christians should refer in every matter relating to faith and godliness; and in the description of any local church, we are principally concerned to know how far it conformed to that infallible standard. If its annals be sufficiently authenticated, and its constitution and character are found to be in agreement with Holy Writ, the general object of history is attained, though the dates of particular events may be inaccurate or forgotten. Tried by this test, the impartial reader will be satisfied that the Syrian Church in India was a daughter of the primitive church of Christ. It partook, indeed, of that alloy which too soon corrupted the profession of Christianity in all parts of the world; yet we need not hesitate to affirm, that it would not suffer by comparison with any church in Christendom down to the period of its history at which we have now arrived.

Church of India episcopal: Dissertation on Episcopacy.

13. Its polity was that of the primitive church, being governed by Bishops, and served by the subordinate orders of priests and deacons. Without entering here into the discussion, raised at the Reformation,[1] as to the peculiar mode of

---

[1] The leading Reformers admitted, that Episcopacy was the primitive mode of church government. Calvin, especially, has shown, that this was universally the polity of the church from the times of the Apostles to his own, though it existed in a much more simple form, and was more efficient, until corrupted by the Roman Church. No episcopalian could deplore

ecclesiastical government established by the Apostles, which, it must be acknowledged, it is difficult to explain from the sacred text; we shall view it as an historical, rather than a scholastic question; and, by the concurrent testimony of all ages, beginning with that immediately succeeding the apostolic times, we find no church, whether orthodox or heterodox, that has existed under any other form of government.

The first church established out of Jerusalem was that of Antioch, where the disciples of Jesus Christ were first called Christians. The first Bishop[1] of Antioch, after the apostle Peter, was Euodius,[2] who continued chief pastor of that church twenty-three years, and died about the year of our Lord seventy. He was succeeded by Ignatius, who lived to preside over that church forty years. Ignatius is described as a devout and venerable man, and is said to have been the disciple and familiar friend of the Apostles.[3] In a church, then, established by the immediate disciples of our Lord, and flourishing

more than he did the utter subversion of *primitive* episcopacy, by the tyranny of the pope and hierarchy of Rome.—Institutiones Christianæ Religionis, Lib. iv. cap. 1, 4, 5.

[1] The name is sufficiently descriptive of the office. Saxon bishop. Gr. 'Επίσκοπος, an overseer, an inspector. When the disciples of the Lord were called Christians, (Acts xi. 26) Χριστιανοι, it is probable that the appellation was given in reproach, or contempt, as were Ναζαρηνοι and Γαλιλαιοι. Parkhurst, Greek Lex.

[2] Eusebius, Eccles. Hist. Lib. iii. c. 22.

[3] Ibid. c. 36. Apostolic Constitutions, Lib. vii. c. 47, p. 451. Mosheim, Cent. 1, pt. 2, c. 2, s. 20. See also the Acts of Ignatius, a piece of martyrology first published in 1647 by Archbishop Usher, "from two old manuscripts, which have stronger marks of credibility than is usual in such compositions."—Wake's Epistles. Milner's Church Hist. Vol. i. cent. 2. c. 1. p. 152.

for some years under their personal supervision, we may expect to find that form of government established which they, to say the least, approved.

That form is particularly described by Ignatius himself. In a letter which he addressed to the Magnesians, in favour of Damas,[1] their Bishop, who, like Timothy and Titus, was young for so responsible an office, he describes him as—" worthy of God," and goes on to remark, that " eminent grace in persons of tender years was sometimes in the primitive church distinguished by their advancement to the episcopacy." He thought it needful, however, after the example of St. Paul, to warn the Magnesians not to despise the youth of Damas, " but to imitate the holy presbyters, who gave place to him, but not to him so properly, as to the Father of Jesus Christ. Some persons, indeed," he adds, " call a man a Bishop, but do every thing independently of him. Such seem to me to have lost a good conscience, because their assemblies are not regulated with stedfastness and Christian order." He also makes honourable mention of Bassus and Apollonius, as *presbyters*, and of Sotio the *deacon*, " whose happiness," he adds, " may I partake of! because he is subject to the Bishop, as to the grace of God, and to the presbytery, as to the law of Jesus Christ."

" Here, as elsewhere, he evidently points out three distinct ranks in the primitive church,—the Bishop, the presbyters, and the deacons ;" and there is no reason to doubt, but every presumption in favour of the opinion, that the office, to which St. Paul appointed Timothy,[2] is that Bishop of

[1] Milner. Ch. His. Vol. i. p. 160, &c.
[2] 1 Tim. i. 3, 8.　2 Tim. ii. 2.

Ephesus, and Titus,[1] Bishop of Crete, was similar to that which Euodius and Ignatius held at Antioch. The same constitution was adopted by every other primitive church whose authentic annals have come down to us; and during the first three centuries, we have catalogues of the Bishops in regular succession, who presided over the patriarchal churches of Antioch, Rome, Jerusalem, Byzantium, and Alexandria.[2] In most other churches the succession of their Bishops has continued without intermission since their first foundation. We have the succession of the Bishops of every see in the collections entitled, *Christian Gaul, Sacred Italy*, and others of the same kind. Several churches have their particular histories; as to others, we from time to time meet with the names of the Bishops, in councils, and general histories, or other authentic acts.[3]

All these documents prove that episcopacy was the primitive constitution of the church of Christ; and, moreover, a fact already noticed tends to the same conclusion, that no church, whether orthodox or heterodox, is to be found in the annals of Christianity under any other form of government, prior to the 16th century.[4]

[1] Tit. i. 5, and iii, 10.

[2] Eusebius. Ecc. Hist. Cave's *Dyptica Apostolica.*

[3] Fleury's Ecc. His. Discourse 3rd. This able and candid historian says of several Gallic churches. " We can tell who have been the bishops of Lyons, from Potinus and Irenæus : of Tholouse, from Saturnine; of Tours, from Gratian; of Paris, from St. Denis. The churches likewise, whose origin is somewhat more obscure, have a known succession for about one thousand years." Discourse i.

[4] A thousand five hundred years and upward, the church of Christ hath now continued under the sacred regiment of Bishops. Neither for so long hath Christianity been ever planted in any kingdom throughout the world but with this kind of government alone ; which to have been ordained of

I

CHAP.
IV.

Through all the vicissitudes of doctrine and practice which took place in different parts of Christendom, the "sacred regiment of Bishops" was universally preserved. That the Nestorians continued it, has already appeared: and even the Novatians, and all other heretics, still retained their Bishops.[1]

Such has been the polity of the church of India from the earliest period to which her history can be traced; and we think this brief reference to the history of other churches from the commencement of Christianity, warrants the inference, that the episcopal constitution received the sanction of Apostles. The fact also of its existence from the beginning in a church so remote as that of Malabar, which, moreover, was for many centuries unknown to the western world, furnishes an additional argument for the origin assigned to the episcopal mode of government.[2]

Doctrines of the earlier Indian Church uncertain.

14. It is difficult to ascertain what precise tenets were held by the Indian Church at this early period of her history; but there can be

God, I am for mine own part as resolutely persuaded, as that any other kind of government in the world whatsoever is of God. In this realm of England, before Normans, yea before Saxons, there being Christians, the chief pastors of their souls were Bishops."—Hooker's Eccles. Polity, b. vii. s. i. pp. 85, 86.

[1] The Abbe Fleury has justly remarked, that this could not happen by chance; and that the grandeur and solidity of an edifice is the best proof of the wisdom of the architect and of the workman's labour. Ibid.

[2] But, however satisfactory the arguments of any church to prove her claim to the apostolical succession of her prelates, her character must be degenerated indeed, if she attaches more importance to this question, than to the proofs of her inheriting the Apostles' wisdom and holiness, diligence and love. While the episcopacy of these heretical churches tends to confirm the argument for the antiquity of that mode of government, it does not prove them to have been sections of the true

little doubt that they conformed generally to the doctrines, first of the Nestorian, and afterwards of the Jacobite Church in Syria, with which they were connected. Though we have no reason to conclude that they adopted all the errors of either of these sects, yet it is too probable, that with them also, as with other Nestorians and Jacobites, " the simplicity of the Gospel was fashioned and painted with the colours of the Syriac theology."[1]

They are said also to have held Eutychian, or Monophysite notions.[2] As this was the creed of the Church of Egypt, and the Indian Christians had from the first constant communication with that country, it is not improbable that their doctrines might be tinctured with the leaven of Eutychus. The opinion, however, of Renaudotius, that this sect was introduced into India as early as the year 696, has been satisfactorily confuted. Asseman dates its introduction in the year 1663;[3] it would, therefore, be premature in this place to enter further upon the question. At the present period of our history there are not sufficient data to warrant more than the general conclusion that has been drawn, that the doctrines of the Indian Church were in accordance with those of Nestorius, until they

church of Christ. Many of them were too manifestly of the synagogue of Satan. (Rev. ii. 9. iii. 9.) The orthodox creed and holy character of a church are the best evidence of her legitimacy; and these are now unquestionably possessed by churches that circumstances have led to adopt a different polity. —See Articles of the Church of England, Art. XIX.

[1] Gibbon, Decline and Fall, ch. xlvii.

[2] They are likewise called Monothelites, as well as Monophysites. There is often, however, much confusion in history with these names. The Monothelites sprang out of the Eutychians; while the Monophysites of the East are generally called Jacobites.

[3] Asseman, Tom. xiii. pars ii. p. 463.

received from Persia the Jacobite tenets. All historians are agreed, that during the seventh century these sects were propagated throughout the eastern world. Under the reign of the caliphs, first the Nestorian, and afterwards the Jacobite Church, was diffused from China as far as Jerusalem and Cyprus;[1] and their numbers together were computed to surpass those of the Greek and Latin communions. Twenty-five Metropolitans, or Archbishops, composed, at one time, the Nestorian hierarchy. The number of 300,000 is allowed for the whole body of that sect: the amount of Jacobites is not distinctly known. It is most probable that the majority, if not the whole, of the Indian Christians are included in this computation.

The Christians' good character inferred from the peace and prosperity they were permitted by their pagan rulers to enjoy.

15. Their moral and religious character also,[2] like that of their creed, is rather to be inferred from circumstances, than described. Hitherto we have had but little opportunity to observe how far the spirit of Christianity prevailed amongst them. Neither, on the other hand, do we meet with any thing prejudicial to their character: and we are, perhaps, justified in drawing a favourable conclusion from the fact of their growing prosperity, and from their freedom from molestation, during so long a course of years. It is very unlikely that their heathen rulers would have tolerated, much less encouraged them, had they been a vicious or disaffected people. Not, indeed, that devoted piety and an inoffensive deportment have always been security against the most cruel persecu-

[1] Gibbon, Decline and Fall, ch. xlvii. Jortin's Remarks, Vol. iv. 419, 440. Mosheim, cent. 6. c. 5. cent. 7. c. 1. cent. 16. c. 2. s. xi.

[2] We have no account of their Liturgy at this early period; it would therefore be premature here to enter upon it.

tion. On the contrary, too often, instead of commanding admiration, they have called forth the bitterest invectives and most barbarous treatment from the enemies of religion. When, however, a Christian community remains stedfast in the profession and practice of their religion amidst reigning idolatry, and their pagan governors continue to afford them protection, we are furnished with no dubious testimony in favour of their character. Few persons in authority, when uninfluenced by any particular motive, will attempt to bend the minds of others to their own opinions; and almost all rulers know how to appreciate the good conduct of men, whatever their creed. In the absence, therefore, of positive evidence to the contrary, we may fairly attribute the peace which these Christians were so long permitted to enjoy, to the accordance of their character with their profession: and on this assumption it is satisfactory to believe, that they shone as lights amid the darkness that surrounded them, and were thereby living witnesses for God to the multitudes who owned not His name.

BOOK II.

CHAPTER I.

CONTINUATION OF THE REVIEW OF THE COMMERCIAL INTERCOURSE WITH INDIA UNTIL THE DISCOVERY OF THE PASSAGE BY WAY OF THE CAPE OF GOOD HOPE.

1. BEFORE proceeding with the immediate subject of this history, it will prepare us for the contemplation of events about to be related, to resume the brief review already taken of the progress of the commercial intercourse between Europe and India. During the middle ages, that intercourse was too indirect to bring much accession to the knowledge of these regions already possessed by the inhabitants of the West. The avidity of the European nations for the productions of Asia now increased with the difficulty of obtaining them: and the powerful competition excited between several Italian states to secure a monopoly in the market, caused the trade to be carried on with an activity and an enterprise, which ultimately led to the opening of India to the western world, and to the supplanting of the Mahomedans by the Christian powers that embarked in the commerce of that country.

Increasing anxiety in Europe for the productions of India.

CHAP.
L.
Crusaders
recover the
Holy Land
from the
Mahome-
dans.

2. For many years after the conquest of Alexandria by the Mahomedans, the inhabitants of Europe were dependent upon the Arab merchants for the productions of India; but their intercourse with them was very precarious; indeed, it soon became extremely hazardous, in consequence of the animosity that existed between the Christians and the believers in Mahomet. When the crescent was planted in Palestine, all Christendom was animated with zeal to recover "the holy land" from the disciples of the Arabian impostor. In this cause, numerous hosts of crusaders were called forth from all parts of Europe, until, after much delay, and a profuse expenditure of lives and treasures, they finally succeeded in expelling the infidels, and in once more raising the standard of the cross on the battlements of Jerusalem.

A. D.
1204.
This event
opened the
Indian trade
to the Vene-
tians in the
thirteenth
century.

3. In the progress of the Christian arms, the interests of the Indian trade were not forgotten. The fourth crusade was undertaken about the beginning of the thirteenth century, at which time the republic of Venice had risen into importance by means of commerce. Many Venetian merchants accompanied the army of crusaders, to whom they rendered essential aid; and for this service, on the capture of Constantinople, they were rewarded with an extensive portion of the Imperial dominions in the East. Here they settled and carried on a lucrative trade, especially in silk and other productions of India, which had so long enriched that capital of the Greek empire.[1]

They are
supplanted
in the East
by the
Genoese.

4. But the Venetians did not long enjoy their prosperity, being dislodged from their possessions by the republic of Genoa, within sixty

[1] Hallam's Middle ages.—Robertson's Disquisition.

years after their settlement at Constantinople. The Genoese were envious of their rivals' growing power and wealth, and circumstances soon favoured their design to supplant them. Seeing the Greeks of the country impatient under a foreign yoke, they combined with them to overturn the throne of the Latin Emperor ; and, upon the success of this enterprise, they wrested from the Venetians all their commercial advantages. The Greek Emperor munificently recompensed the Genoese for these important services, and they improved their opportunities with so much industry and zeal, that Genoa soon became the chief commercial power in Europe.

5. In the meantime, the Venetians, driven from Constantinople and the Black Sea, did not sit down in despair, but endeavoured to repair their loss by resorting to the ancient mart of Alexandria for the commodities of the East. Here their exertions were soon rewarded beyond expectation. The prejudices and antipathies that had long subsisted between Christians and Mahomedans gradually subsided. The merchants of both religions, having one common object in view, the pursuit of commerce, suspended their religious animosities ; and their mutual interests induced them now to establish, for the first time, a fair and open trade between them.[1]

Venetians pursue the trade at Alexandria in conjunction with the Mahomedans.

6. While the affairs of commerce were thus advancing, under the Venetians and Genoese, a third power entered the field, the state of Florence. For some time the Florentines confined their attention to their domestic manufactures, and to pecuniary transactions with the other European states. At length, however,

In the fifteenth century the Florentines are admitted to a share of the commerce of Alexandria.

[1] Robertson. Dis. 121—125.

they began to covet a share of the Indian trade,
and in the beginning of the fifteenth century
they applied to the Soldan of Egypt, to admit
them to all the commercial immunities which
the Venetians enjoyed at Alexandria, and other
parts of his dominions.　Their application was
partially successful, as they were admitted to
the market of Indian productions: and soon
after this period we find spices enumerated
among the goods which the Florentines imported into England.[1]

Marco Pao-
lo's travels
in India and
China
awaken the
curiosity &
ambition of
Europe.

7. Of these three rival powers, the Venetians
appear to have been the most enterprising.　It
is foreign from the object of this history to
follow them in their active pursuit of new
channels for acquiring and circulating their
commodities: but it is quite within our province to notice the improved knowledge of
India for which the inhabitants of Europe were
at this time indebted to a citizen of Venice.　It
has been seen how effectually the Mahomedans
excluded the Christians of Europe from the East,
ever since they became masters of Egypt.
From that time to the period at which we have
now arrived, very little information had been
added to the account of India published in the
sixth century by Cosmas Indicopleustes.　But
in the thirteenth century, Marco Paolo, a Venetian of a noble family, brought great accessions
to the information already possessed.　He was
engaged in pursuits of commerce, and, after
trading for some time in Lesser Asia, was induced to penetrate further to the East, even to
the court of the Great Khan, on the frontier of
China.　During the course of twenty years,
employed partly in mercantile transactions, and

[1] Robertson. Dis. 125—127.

partly in conducting negociations with which the Great Khan intrusted him, he explored many regions of the East, through which no european had ever yet travelled. He proceeded through China [1] as far as Pekin; visited different parts of Hindoostan; and was the first who described Bengal and Guzzerat by their present names, as great and opulent kingdoms. He also made several voyages in the Indian Ocean, during which he visited Java, Sumatra, and Ceylon, with several other islands of minor importance, and sailed round the peninsula of India, as far as the Gulf of Cambay. Most of the places that he visited he called by the names which they at present bear. There are some inaccuracies in his topographical descriptions, which, considering the great disadvantages under which he travelled, may be easily accounted for; but they are sufficiently correct to identify them with the places to which they are applied. This was the most extensive survey of the East hitherto made, and the most complete description of it that had ever been given by any European : and in an age which had hardly any knowledge of those regions except what was derived from the geography of Ptolemy, not only the Venetians, but all the people of Europe, were very naturally astonished at the discovery of immense countries open to their view, beyond what had hitherto been reputed the utmost boundary of the earth in that quarter.

8. In the midst of the conjectures of the philosopher and the speculations of the merchant, to which these discoveries gave birth, an

---

[1] Marco Paolo calls it "the great kingdom of Cathay, the name by which China is still known in many parts of the East."—Robertson. 132, 133.

event occurred which soon drew a veil over the prospect opening to the imagination of the one, and to the cupidity of the other. They were tantalized respectively with a description of regions that promised a vast increase of knowledge and wealth, without the possibility of gratifying their curiosity and ambition. The event that occasioned this disappointment was, the closing of the mart of Constantinople against the people of Europe. In the year 1453, Mahomet II. finally conquered the Greek empire, and established the seat of government at that capital. The Genoese were obliged immediately to abandon their establishments in the neighbourhood, and were finally expelled from the Crimea in the year 1474. From that period the merchants of Europe carried on their Indian trade with the different parts of Syria, under all the restrictions that had long been imposed upon them by the Soldans of Egypt. The Genoese failed in every attempt to obtain a share in this trade; and during the remainder of the fifteenth century, the Venetians were almost the only people of Europe who were permitted to engage in that lucrative commerce.

9. Whatever regret the nations of Europe might then feel on finding themselves excluded from these markets, the Christian now perceives in that circumstance, another important link in the chain of events, with which Divine Providence was gradually drawing the people of the East and West together. The spirit of commerce was now becoming generally diffused among the inhabitants of Europe; and finding that the Mahomedans had raised insuperable barriers against them, they were induced to look abroad for other avenues to the object of their ambition. Necessity has ever been a

Portuguese, under Vasco de Gama, discover the passage to India by way of the Cape of Good Hope. They are soon obliged to return, but subsequently establish themselves in India.

strong incentive to adventure, as well as the mother of invention; and towards the close of the fifteenth century, it led to a discovery which at once defied all the Mahomedans' attempts to exclude other powers from India, and destroyed the Venetians' monopoly.

Under the auspices of the King of Spain, Columbus had undertaken to discover a western passage to India, but he was diverted from that remoter object by the discovery of America. The King of Portugal, however, stimulated by this voyager's account of that continent, was induced to seek a similar territory in the East. After several unsuccessful attempts, a squadron, consisting of three small armed vessels and one store ship, sailed from the Tagus, under the command of Vasco de Gama, who succeeded in reaching his place of destination. He was four months in making his passage to the Cape of Good Hope; and having with much difficulty sailed round that promontory, he bent his course along the south-east coast of Africa, as far as Melinda, where he obtained a Mahomedan pilot, who conducted him safely across the Indian Ocean. Reaching Calicut, on the Malabar coast, he landed there on the 22d May, 1498, just ten months and two days from the time of his departure from the port of Lisbon.

Not long after their arrival, a serious affray took place between the natives and the Portuguese, in which de Gama's confessor, Peter de Couillan,[1] was slain. The cause of this dispute is uncertain : but it is affirmed, that de Gama discovered a plot of the Mahomedan merchants for his destruction, upon which he effected his escape with all possible speed, and returned

---

[1] Life of Francis Xavier, Dryden's translation, p. 88.

home. He arrived at Lisbon in September, 1449, having lost the greater part of his crews through disease and excessive fatigue. But the trouble, expense, and sacrifices of the voyage were not lost : the Portuguese followed up the discovery they had made with such ability and perseverance, that in about twenty-four years they had acquired possession of several ports in India, where they began to exercise great influence over the natives, and for a long time carried on a thriving trade without rival or control.[1]

[1] Robertson's Dissertation, p. 134—150.

CHAPTER II.

RISE AND PROGRESS OF THE SECULAR AND
ECCLESIASTICAL POWER IN THE CHURCH OF
ROME.

1. BEFORE we proceed to detail the effect produced by the arrival of the Portuguese in India
upon the Christian Church established there, it
will prepare us for the subject briefly to review
the events that led to that assumption of power,
which at this period the Bishops of Rome exercised. The Abbé Fleury has the candour to
acknowledge, that the popes of the first five or
six centuries, usurped no such secular authority
as they afterwards claimed, and that they were
chiefly intent on promoting the spiritual interests of the Church.[1] This testimony is in
accordance with all the histories of that early
period.

The pope's limited jurisdiction prior to the sixth century.

2. In the fourth century the universal church
was divided into eleven patriarchates, whose
chief prelates, called Archbishops, or patriarchs,
were possessed of equal and independent authority within their respective provinces.[2] The

CENT. IV.

Universal church divided into independent patriar-chates.

[1] Ecc. History, Lib. 22. n. 45. lib. 30. n. 31. Discourses
on Ecc. His. Dis. 3rd. s. 9—25.

[2] Dissertations on the Papal Supremacy, Geddes. Bingham's Antiquities, B. ii. c. 16, 17. Palmer's English Ritual,
Vol. i. pp. 6, 7. Note.

Bishops of Rome, indeed, were for a long time less distinguished than the prelates who presided over the Churches of Alexandria and Constantinople: and the title of *Pope,* to which they have since laid exclusive claim, was then common to all Bishops.[1]

Independence of other national churches; that of Britain proved.

3. After the erection of patriarchal power, the metropolitans of several national churches retained their independence of each other; as those of Cyprus, Iberia, Armenia, and, it cannot but gratify the Englishman to be assured, the Church of Britain.[2]

Considering the attempts that are so incessantly made to prove the original dependence of the British Church upon the Bishop of Rome, it is satisfactory to know, that for the first six centuries she had not the slightest connexion with that prelate. It has already been shown, that the Church of England existed in a flourishing condition before the time of Constantine the Great, under her own hierarchy, and that she was at that time entirely independent of the Gallic, or Roman, or any other foreign Church.[3] There is reason to believe that Christianity was brought into this country in the Apostolic age, but by whom is not certain. Gildas fixes on the time that intervened between the triumph of Claudius for his victory, and the defeat of Boadicea by Suetonius Paulinus, in the first year of Nero, as the period for the introduction of Christianity into England.[4] And there is much greater

---

[1] παπα, Palmer's English Ritual, Vol. i. p. 86.

[2] Stillingfleet. Origines Britannicæ, Ch. iii. p. 108, &c. Bingham, B. ii. c. 18. s. 1.

[3] Book i. ch. ii, sec. 8,

[4] Warner's Ecclesiastical History of England, Vol. 1. b. 1. Also Bishop Lloyd's (of St. Asaph) ' Historical Account of church-government in Britain and Ireland, when they first received the Christian religion.'

probability that St. Paul preached here than St. Peter,[1] as Romish writers and preachers have endeavoured to prove. Like all other Apostolic churches, its polity was episcopal, and several of its Bishops were present at councils held in the 4th century. At the council of Arles, A. D. 314, there were three,[2] at the councils of Sardica, A. D. 347, and of Ariminum in 359, there were several prelates from this country, who represented their own church without any mandate from Rome, or other foreign Bishop.[3]

4. The British Churches continued to enjoy their ancient liberty until the arrival of Augustine and, with him, forty monks from Rome, in the 6th century. His object was to bring this country under subjection to the Roman Church; but feeling at a loss how to manage the British Bishops, he wrote to Gregory I., for instructions. That pope gave him the fullest commission he could desire, subjecting all the Anglican Bishops to his authority, directing him by his word, to teach the unlearned and strengthen the weak; and by his power, to correct the disobedient. Thus instructed, he requested, and, through the influence of Ethel-

Mission of Augustine the monk to Britain.

[1] Stillingfleet, Origines Britannicæ, Ch. i. pp. 35—48. Bingham's Christian Antiquities, B. ix. ch. i. sec. 12.

[2] Their names were, Eborius, Bishop of York; Restitutus, Bishop of London; and Adelsius, (de civitate colonia Londinensium), of Caer-Leon, upon Uske. There were also present, from the same province, a presbyter and a deacon. Stillingfleet, Ch. ii. pp. 75, &c. Bingham, B. ix. c. vi. s. 20. Sirmond, Concil. Gallic. tom. i. p. 9. Socrates, Schol. Lib. 5. c. 8. Note (*f*)

[3] Socrates. Ibid. Stillingfleet, ch. iii. p. 135. Also, " It seems probable that there were English bishops at the council of Nice in Bithynia, but the subscriptions preserved are so imperfect, that no names of British bishops can be distinguished." Dr. Short's History of the Church of England. Vol. i. p. 7.

K

bert, King of Kent, obtained, an interview with the Bishops in those parts. They met near Worcester; but Augustine found the Bishops too intractable for his purpose, and the assembly broke up without making the smallest concession to his demands. They gave him, however, a second meeting, which was attended by seven Bishops, and several ecclesiastics from the celebrated monastery at Bangor, with their learned Abbot, Dinothus, at their head. At this conference Augustine complained, that they did many things contrary to the Roman Church; but seeing how tenacious they were of their own usages, and desirous, above all things, of establishing the pope's supremancy in England, he offered to tolerate all their ' other customs, though contrary to their own,' provided they would conform to the Church of Rome in only three particulars,—the time of celebrating Easter, the mode of administering baptism, and the preaching of the word of God to the Saxons of the English nation who were not yet converted.[1] Augustine little thought what an important fact he was, by this proposal, establishing, in proof of the British Churches' independence of Rome before his arrival. But his concessions were now as unavailing as his entreaties had been at the former conference. Dinothus told him plainly, in the name of the Bishops present, and of all the Britannic Churches, that they owed the subjection of brotherly kindness and charity to the Church of God, and to the pope of Rome, and to all Christians, to love every one in his degree in perfect charity; but other obedience than that, they did not know to be due to him whom he called pope; and, for their parts, they were under the jurisdiction of the Bishop of Caer-

---

[1] Stillingfleet, Ch. iv. p. 216 &c. Bede, Hist. Ecc. Lib. ii. c. 2.

Leon upon Uske, who was, under God, their spiritual overseer and director. He also defended, ' with great learning and gravity,' the power of their own Metropolitan, and maintained that it was not for the British interest to own either the Roman pride or the Saxon tyranny.[1]

Upon this bold assertion of their freedom, Augustine lost all patience. Seeing how fruitless his endeavours to conciliate these fearless men were likely to prove, he resolved to make use of a very different expedient to bring them to subjection. He threatened them with war, which, at his instigation, " Ethelfridus, king of the Northumbrians, waged against them; wherein no less than twelve hundred British ecclesiastics were slain at one time." Even Bede relates, that they were put to death while engaged in prayer for the success of their countrymen,[2] when fighting in defence of their religion against the tyrannical assumptions of Rome.

The Church of England was as little indebted to Rome for her ritual, as for her orders. The offices she now uses were possessed by the pri-

---

[1] Stillingfleet, Ch. v, p. 356, &c. Bingham, B. ii. c. 18. s. 2. and B. ix c. 1, s. 11. The two principal authorities used by Stillingfleet and Bingham, as well as by more recent writers on this question, are, Gildas, a British Christian of the sixth century, just referred to; and Bede, an Anglo-Saxon of the seventh century. As the latter joined the Roman Church, his testimony in favour of the original independence of the British Church is very important. Eusebius, Theodoret, Epiphanius, Baronius, Leland, Usher, Alford, and other unquestionable authorities, are also quoted.

[2] Bede, Hist. Eccl. Gentis Anglorum, lib. i. c. 27; lib. ii. c. 2. See Mr. Wheelock's notes on the latter chapter. Also the notes of Valesius on Lib. v. c. 8, of Socrates Scholasticus Ecc. Hist. The whole of the Note (*f.*) on this chapter of Socrates, English translation, 1680, enters fully into the argument, and proves that the British Church was entirely independent of Rome, prior to the arrival of Augustine.

mitive church of Britain before her junction with Rome, when Augustine declared, as we have just seen, that they differed in many important respects, if not altogether, from the ritual of his own church. [1]

It is uncertain whence she obtained her forms of service; but from their close resemblance to the ancient offices of the Gallican church, they are with great probability supposed to have been derived from that source; [2] and it is well known that the original church of Gaul was independent of Rome, and that she maintained her independence long after the British church was compelled by force of arms to submit. [3]

[1] In reference to the question with which the members of the Church of England are sometimes taunted by Romish priests,—*Where was your Church before the Reformation begun by* Luther? Bishop Reynolds remarks,—" That reformation did not new make the Church, but purge it. And that it stood in need of purging, the papists themselves were fain to confess, and declare to the world in their Council of Trent. Only herein is the difference; the Council pretended a reformation in points of discipline and manners, and we made a reformation in points of doctrine too."—" We are not another Church newly started up, but the same which before from the Apostles' times held the common and necessary grounds of Faith and Salvation, which grounds being in latter ages perverted and overturned by Antichristianism, have been by valiant champions for the faith of Christ therefrom vindicated, who have only pruned the Lord's vine, and picked out the stones, and driven out the boars out of his vineyard, but have not made either one or the other new."—Bishop Reynolds on Psalm cx. v. 2. Fol. edit. p. 434.

[2] Stillingfleet. Orig. Brit. c. 4. pp. 216—237. It is worthy of remark, that during the existence of the Druids, the deities of Gaul and Britain were the same, and the Druids in both countries had the direction of all religious matters. This may be thought to strengthen the probability that the ritual of the primitive Christian church in Britain was derived from Gaul.—Warner's Ecclesiastical History of England, Vol. i. book i.

[3] Stillingfleet. Ibid. The tracts of the late Bishop Burgess, of Salisbury, *On the Origin and Independence of the Ancient*

The primitive church of Spain also is supposed to have furnished much that was contained in the offices of the British church: but
the fact is, that Spain herself had her liturgy
from Gaul, and it is most probable that England
received it from her. Indeed, the two churches
of Spain and England were "plainly of the
same mind, as to the royal and papal supremacy; and seem to have been unanimous in all
the other substantials of faith and worship."
It is proved, that before the eighth century,
"the Bishop of Rome had no jurisdiction or
authority in the Spanish church: and that
when, in the beginning of that period, he
first attempted to "introduce his supremacy
into Spain, that assumption was rejected and
condemned by the Spanish church, in a council
of all her Bishops." The ancient liturgy also
of this church, which was the Gothic, differs so
much from that of Rome, as to furnish "a strong
evidence of that church's having never been
subject to Rome."[1]

5. The church of Spain maintained her independence of Rome, and continued for a long time

Justinian
acknow-
ledges the
pope's su-
premacy in
533.

British Church, give an interesting and satisfactory view of
the whole question. The brief account here drawn up will, it
is presumed, be deemed sufficient for the purpose of this history.

[1] Geddes' Dissertation on the Papal Supremacy, Tracts,
Vol. ii. Palmer's English Ritual, Vol. i. sect. ix. x, xi,
pp. 143—176. Also the Antiquities of the English Ritual,
in which may be seen a collection of valuable matter on the
subject. It will suffice here to state, that the Ritual of Gaul,
which is traced through the Spanish church to Britain, was
itself that of Ephesus, and was brought from thence by Potinus and Irenæus, the first two Bishops of the church of
Lyons.

Several other writers declare that the Spanish church stood
her ground until the 8th century. M'Crie's History of the
Reformation in Spain, c. 1.. s. 3.

to resist all the pope's attempts to bring her under his subjection. At length, however, she was compelled to yield to the growing power of that haughty ecclesiastic. Some time prior to the mission of Augustine, in the year of our

Lord 533, the Emperor Justinian declared him to be THE HEAD OF ALL THE CHURCHES OF CHRISTENDOM, and placed under the jurisdiction of his HOLINESS, all the churches and priests of the eastern division of his empire. While Justinian lived, he maintained the Bishop of Rome in this extensive dominion: but after his decease, the Bishop of Constantinople, who had submitted with great reluctance to the Emperor's edict, refused to acknowledge the papal supremacy, and asserted his own independence. Indeed, his successor John, towards the close of the sixth century, himself assumed the title of UNIVERSAL BISHOP, and continued to retain it, in defiance of the invectives of Gregory, Bishop of Rome, who, singular to relate, now thought proper to denounce his competitor for this dignity,or any one else who should presume to usurp ecclesiastical supremacy, as *Antichrist*. And yet, while thundering his anathemas against this formidable rival in the East, he was labouring hard, as we have seen, to establish his own supremacy in the West. So little do ambitious men deem it needful to preserve consistency in their measures.

A. D.
606.
Ultimately
established
under Pho-
cas in 606;
its assump-
tion favour-
ed by cir-
cumstances.

6. A very few years after Gregory's protest against the Bishop of Constantinople, a Bishop of Rome, Boniface, resumed the title which he had pretended to disclaim. This was in the year of our Lord 606, when he engaged Phocas, the murderer of the Emperor Mauritius and the usurper of his throne, to deprive the Bishop of Constantinople of the title, and

to confer it upon himself. This wicked tyrant had sagacity enough to see the advantage that would accrue to him from the countenance of a prelate of so much influence as the Roman Bishop; and to this policy that ecclesiastic was indebted for the usurper's recognition of his pretensions, which he did not scruple to purchase of such a man on such terms. [1]

Not that the simple edict of Phocas settled the dispute between the rival primates of the East and the West. In a few years, however, circumstances transpired which left the Latin prelate in undisputed possession of the supremacy. About the commencement of this century arose, as we have seen, the Mahomedan power, after whose extensive conquests in Asia and Egypt, the Christians of those regions, though tolerated, ceased to be patronised by their rulers. Consequently, their primates soon declined into a state of comparative insignificance; and from that time the pope of Rome exercised more freely the authority conferred on him by Justinian and Phocas, and began also to assume a power to command in the affairs of nations, as extensive as that which he exercised in the church. Thus, in the beginning of the seventh century,[2] arose simultaneously the apostasy of

[1] In writing to the Emperor Mauritius, Gregory, Bishop of Rome, addressed him as his Lord, and acknowledged that it was incumbent on him to yield obedience to his commands, though in a matter that he disapproved. The obsequious and affectionate terms of his letters, in his prayers for the long life of the Emperor and his sons, were soon forgotten, when the murderer Phocas possessed the imperial dignity; for Gregory immediately addressed that usurper in terms equally flattering. The original letters may be seen in Geddes' *Appendix* to his Dissertation on the Papal Supremacy.

[2] Bishop Newton, Mr. Faber, and the most approved interpreters of prophecy, date the rise of the Eastern and Western apostasies in the year of our Lord, 606. The Mahomedan

Rome in the West, and the imposture of the false prophet in the East, according to the express revelation of the Spirit of prophecy many ages before those moral and intellectual blights appeared, to darken the world, and afflict the church of Christ.[1]

Former
Bishops of
Rome confined their
attention to
ecclesiastical affairs.

7. During the first ages of Christianity, the Bishops of Rome, as we have just shown from the Abbé Fleury, confined their attention, like most other prelates, to ecclesiastical affairs. The right of exercising authority in civil matters is expressly disclaimed by Gregory the Third, and several of the most distinguished Roman prelates. Even so late as the ninth century, Nicholas the First wrote to the Emperor of Constantinople in the following terms :—

" Before Jesus Christ there were kings who were also priests, as Melchisedek. The devil imitated this in the heathen emperors, who were high priests. But when He came, who is truly King and Priest, no longer did the emperor assume to himself the rights of the priest, nor the priest, the rights of the emperor. Jesus Christ divided the two powers : so that the Christian emperor stood in need of the priests,

---

æra, called the Hegira, or flight, commences, according to some writers, with the year of our Lord, 622 ; others date it from 630 and 633, when Mahomet fled, or rather, was expelled, from Mecca.

[1] As the interpretation of prophecy is not the object of these pages, the reader, who may desire to examine this question, is referred to Daniel vii. 8 — 27 ; viii. 9 — 14 ; xi. 34 — 45 ; xii. 7, 11, 12 ; 2 Thess. ii. 3—12 ; Rev. xi. 2, 3 ; xii. 14 ; 13, 14, and 17th chapters. These prophecies are interpreted by Bishop Newton, on the Prophecies, Diss. 17 and 22, and Analysis of Revelation, Part i. c. 11 ; Part ii. c. 12 and 13. Also by Mr. Faber, in his Dissertation, &c. c. 5, 8, 9 and 10. Mr. Woodhouse, and other modern writers upon prophecy may also be consulted.

as to eternal life, and in temporal matters the priest made use of the laws of the emperors."[1]

Such is the language of Nicholas, whom no one can justly accuse of neglecting the rights of his order. Fleury declares, that other popes of that age, and of a similar character, were neither sovereign princes nor temporal lords; that they did not complain of the want of temporal power, nor think that they had too much time to spare from their spiritual occupations. They were fully satisfied with the distinction between the civil and ecclesiastical powers, which one of them, Gelasius, has thus defined—"The emperors themselves in point of religion, are subject to bishops; and the bishops, in matters of state, even the bishop of the chief see, are subject to the laws of the emperors."[2]

8. But the love of power seems to be too natural to man to be declined when within his reach. During the middle ages, literature was at as low an ebb in Europe as religion, and the priests were almost exclusively possessed of the little knowledge that then dimly shone upon the world. The barbarous nations of the North that overran the Roman empire, were as illiterate as the Mahomedans of the East; and they yielded as implicitly to the dicta of the Christian priesthood, as the believers in Mahomet to the interpreters of the Koran. They embraced Christianity for no other reason than because it was the religion of the country they had subdued; and they readily transferred to the priesthood of their newly-adopted creed, the reverence which they had been accustomed to pay to the priests of their old superstition. They

Influence of priesthood increases in middle ages.

---

[1] Fleury's Hist. Lib. xiii. n. 9. Nic. Ep. 8—8. Also 3rd Diss. on Ecclesiastical History.
[2] Ibid. Diss. 4, sec. 9.

soon discovered also, that it was the best policy they could pursue to conciliate these ecclesiastics, for they were found to possess the most commanding influence over the minds of the people. The learned Florus[1] remarks, that, " generally speaking, under the Roman empire, neither emperors nor magistrates concerned themselves any more with the election of bishops than with the ordination of priests; because the bishops then had not the temporal power in their hands, as in the Grecian empire they have it not at present. But in the kingdoms that were formed upon the ruins of the Western empire, the bishops were so powerful, that it was for the interest of kings to have them on their sides."

Roman empire divided into ten kingdoms.

9. In exact conformity with the prophecy of Revelations,[2] the Roman empire was divided into ten distinct kingdoms;[3] yet all united in giving secular power to the Church of Rome, and in upholding her in all her superstitions. Though perpetually contending among themselves for minor points, yet in this they had "one mind," to "give their power and strength unto the beast."[4] They form the "scarlet coloured beast," red with the blood of martyred saints, on which the antichristian church of

---

[1] Florus was a deacon of the church of Lyons. Conc. Clar. an. 535, c. 1, &c. Fleury, Diss. 3, sec. 10.
[2] Rev. xvii. 10—13.
[3] 1. Huns; 2. Ostrogoths; 3. Wisigoths; 4. Franks; 5. Vandals; 6. Sueves and Alans; 7. Burgundians; 8. Herules and Rugians; 9. Saxons; 10. Longobards. This is Bishop Lloyd's list, from which other writers vary in some respects. Bishop Newton, Diss. on Prophecy, Diss. 14, p. 236.
[4] All antichristian governments are compared to beasts, because of the cruel and unjust means by which they acquired, maintained, and exercised their power.—Dan. vii. 11; viii. 4; Rev. xii. xiii and xvii.

Rome was seen riding in the Revelation of St.
John.

10. Circumstances thus concurring to favour their assumption of power, the prelates of the Latin church forgat the sacred character of their office, and began to exercise authority over the the nobles and monarchs of Europe. "At councils they pretended to pass sentence upon kings, as well as to determine upon matters of penance : and the kings, who knew but little of their privileges," did not think of disputing their authority in these matters. "The popes, supposing very reasonably, that they had as much, or rather more authority than other Bishops, presently undertook to regulate the differences between crowned heads ; not by way of mediation or intercession only, but by authority, which was in effect to dispose of their crowns."[1] As his own power increased, the pope was enabled to curtail that of other Bishops, and not only to divest the emperors of all ecclesiastical authority, but to interfere as he chose in their civil affairs.

11. It would detain us too long from the subject of this history, to cite the numerous instances of papal arrogance and insolence recorded by Fleury, Du Pin, and other *Romish* historians.[2] Gregory the seventh was the first pope who asserted his supremacy over all temporal rulers. He pretended *generally*, that the

---

[1] Fleury, 3rd Diss. sec. 10.

[2] Nicolas I. obliged the emperor, Louis II. to perform the functions of a groom, and to hold the bridle of his horse while he dismounted. Clement V. on one occasion, while he was at dinner, ordered Dandolo, the Venetian ambassador, to be chained under the table like a dog. These are fair specimens of the manner in which the proud pontiffs of Rome frequently exercised their usurped dominion in those days of darkness and credulity.

church might dispose of crowns and judge of sovereigns; and in *particular*, that all Christian princes were vassals of the church of Rome; also, that they were bound to pay tribute and take an oath of allegiance to her.[1] Gregory, however, notwithstanding the odious expedients to which he resorted for the purpose, did not fully accomplish the object of his ambition. Though he did not scruple to flatter the base tyrant and parricide, Phocas, in the most fulsome and blasphemous strains, yet he did not obtain his acknowledgment of him as universal head of the church of Christ. But the usurper conferred this title on Boniface IV., Gregory's successor, in terms as ample as the most grasping ambition could desire: and from that period, the year 606, till the Reformation, the means which the Bishops of Rome have used to consolidate their power, have been as nefarious as those by which it was acquired.

CENT.
IX.
Decretals of Isidore: protested against by French and other foreign prelates.
12. Of all the instruments ever invented for such a purpose, one of the most iniquitous was, "The decretals of Isidore." "In order to gain credit to this new ecclesiastical system, so different from the ancient rules of church-government, and to support the haughty pre-

---

[1] See the proofs of this assumption given by Fleury, Hist. Lib. lxiii. n. 11. This writer boldly declares, that the pope is neither impeccable nor absolute monarch even in the church, whether as to temporals or spirituals. And his remarks upon their gross abuse of the power they assumed to depose kings, and absolve their subjects from their allegiance, well deserve to be remembered. "If a monarch has committed an offence for which he deserves excommunication, this can deprive him only of the privileges of the public means of grace." "But yet for all this, his subjects should be altogether as obedient to him as they were before, in every thing that is not contrary to the law of God."—Third Diss. s. 18, "The Deposing of Kings." Fourth Diss. s. 13.

tensions of the pontiffs to supremacy and independence, it was necessary to produce the
authority of ancient deeds, to stop the mouths
of such as were disposed to set bounds to their
usurpations. The Bishops of Rome were aware
of this; and as those means were deemed the
most lawful that tended best to the accomplishment of their purposes, they employed some of
their most ingenious and zealous partisans in
forging conventions, acts of councils, epistles,
and the like records, by which it might appear,
that, in the first ages of the church, the Roman
pontiffs were clothed with the same spiritual
majesty and supreme authority which they now
assumed. Among these fictitious supports of the
papal dignity, the famous *Decretal Epistles*, as
they are called, said to have been written by
the pontiffs of the primitive time, deserve chiefly
to be stigmatised. They were the productions
of an obscure author, who fraudulently prefixed
to them the name of Isidore, Bishop of Seville,
to make the world believe that they had been
collected by this illustrious and learned prelate.
Some of them had appeared in the eighth century, but they were now entirely drawn from
their obscurity, and produced, with an air of
ostentation and triumph, to demonstrate the
supremacy of the Roman pontiffs. The decisions of a certain Roman council, which is said
to have been holden during the pontificate of
Sylvester, were likewise alleged in behalf of the
same cause; but this council had not been
heard of before the present century, and the
accounts now given of it proceeded from the
same source with the decretals, and were
equally authentic. Be that as it may, the
decrees of this pretended council contributed
much to enrich and aggrandize the Roman pon-

tiffs, and exalt them above all human authority and jurisdiction." [1]

These decretals, it is said, were forged in about the eighth or ninth century, [2] but some writers give them a still earlier date; and the doctrine that they inculcated was too acceptable to the ambitious popes not to be supported with the whole weight of their authority: but there were many Bishops of the French and Latin churches who possessed too much discernment to be imposed upon by so manifest a fraud, and whose spirits were too independent tamely to bow to the yoke thus forged for their necks. The French prelates were especially distinguished for their indignation at this insult offered to their understandings, and for their zeal in resisting this and similar impious attempts to bring them under servile subjection to the Bishop of Rome. The Abbé Fleury has shown, to the satisfaction of every ingenuous mind, that

[1] Mosheim's Ecc. Hist. Cent. 9th, c. 2. sec. 8.

[2] This is acknowledged even by Baronius, in his Annals of the year 865. Also by Cardinal Bona, who thus describes them in the third chapter of his first book of Liturgies.—" It has long been observed, by the learned, that the Decretal Epistles were all forged by some Spaniard, under the name of Isidore, whoever he was, towards the end of the seventh century; they were forged with a pious fraud, out of the sentences of the Old Canons, and of the Civil Laws, and of the Holy Fathers, who flourished in the fourth century; they are, for the most part, full of vile chronological mistakes, and are almost all written in the same style and character of writing. Riculphus, Bishop of Mentz, first brought them out of Spain into France, from whence they were disseminated over all other countries, and were commonly believed." This testimony is important, though the Cardinal was mistaken if he supposed that the Decretals were published under the name of *Isidore;* for that " would have spoiled the whole plot." It was pretended that they were the genuine writings of the former Bishops of Rome whose names are prefixed to them.—Geddes' Dissertation on the Papal Supremacy, pp. 46—51.

the pretended decretals of Isidore are utterly unworthy of credit. The same assertion is made respecting every other authority on which the popes founded their claim to universal dominion and irresponsible power, both in church and state.[1]

But in our indignation at the wrong hereby inflicted upon man, we must not lose sight of the dishonour done to God. It was the climax of those "pious frauds" which had been practised on the church, from time to time, ever since the third or fourth centuries. Having no scriptural authority for the papal supremacy, and devoid of authentic tradition or history in support of its assumption, these decretals were invented to supply the desideratum ; and to question their authenticity, was for many ages deemed a more atrocious heresy than the rejection of the Word of God. There is but one Supreme in the church and in the world ; and His dominion is righteousness and peace, truth and love. But the endeavour to maintain such a usurpation as that of Rome by frauds like the decretals, was to slander the Name, and therefore the religion, of Jesus : for it was to declare to the world, that He had delegated His authority over the universal church to one, whose rule has ever been maintained by falsehood, violence, and extortion. No wonder then that the holy and merciful Jesus has been classed with the Arabian impostor, and reproached for all the miseries brought by the papacy on mankind. Many, viewing the Christian religion only under the disguise of such *impious* frauds, have treated with scorn that hallowed name, "which is above every name," and rejected

[1] Fleury, Diss. 3, 4, on Ecc. Hist.

His religion, though blessed and blessing, as a fable " cunningly devised " by its priesthood to hold the world in bondage.[1] Why the Redeemer so long endured this indignity, we presume not to inquire : but we will praise Him for at length breaking the spell that for so many ages bound the western nations to the Roman yoke ; and we will implore Him to keep His true Church in the light of His word, lest mankind, walking in their own ways, should provoke Him again to bring them under so grievous a bondage.

Other iniquitous means to support the Papal pretensions.

13. Notwithstanding the strenuous efforts made by Nicholas, Gratian, and other popes, to establish the authenticity of these *decretals*, the opposition to them was at times so violent and so well directed, that it was found necessary to have recourse to other iniquitous expedients in defence of the papal pretensions. In the eighth century image worship was sanctioned. In the ninth century were invented the first legends, or lives of Saints, who were made to appear to

*CENT.
X.*

sanction the popes' supremacy. These were soon followed by the canonization of saints, in reward for their zeal in the cause of Rome. In the tenth century was introduced the baptism of bells ; the festival in remembrance of souls departed in unity with the Roman Church ; the institution of the rosary ; together with a long catalogue of rites and superstitions which, in days of Gospel light and freedom, are justly deemed most dishonourable to God, outrageous to the human understanding, a mockery of the feelings of the contrite and of the aspirations of

---

[1] It is too well known to require confirmation, that this was the cause of the impious treatment of the Name and the religion of Jesus Christ by the French, at the period of their revolution.

the devout, and insulting to every sentiment of
true and undefiled religion.[1]

Papal Rome now differed from Pagan Rome
in nothing but the names of her idols. When
the murderous usurper, Phocas, to conciliate
pope Boniface, gave him the celebrated pan-
theon at Rome, it was nominally converted into
a Christian Church; but it effectually retained
its original character, the Virgin Mary succeeding to Cybele, the mother of the gods; Peter,
to Jupiter;[2] and the other heathen deities
giving place to the statues of canonized saints
and martyrs. The Majesty of Jehovah was
dethroned; the mediation of Jesus superseded;
and the pope exalted as " King of kings, and
Lord of lords :" while he actually assumed
also the proudest title of the heathen emperors
of Rome, *Pontifex Maximus*.[3] At the same
time, the darkest superstitions and the foulest
practices were enlisted in support of his wicked
usurpation. In the eleventh century pope
Gregory VII. had the impiety to arrogate the
attribute of infallibility; asserting in council,

---

[1] In the Roman Church these superstitions, absurd and
wicked as they are, continue to be regarded with undiminished
reverence. For some years past it has been the policy of
her priests, in *England*, to keep such abominations as secret as
possible; and hence the hesitation of many persons in this
country to believe in their prevalence at the present day. But
of late they have been exhibited more publicly; and all who
have hitherto been incredulous on the subject, may now be convinced, without leaving England for the purpose, that Roman-
ism, in her essential character, is wrapped in the darkness of
the middle ages, notwithstanding the light of the nineteenth
century that is shining around her.

[2] It is well known that the statue of Peter in the cathedral
at Rome was originally that of Jove, the *keys* being substituted for the thunderbolts in his hand, when the image was
transferred to the Apostle.

[3] The Christian Emperors had discontinued this pagan
title for some time, when it was adopted by the Pope.

L

Pope resist-
ed by sove-
reigns of
Europe:
dawn of Re-
formation.
Inquisition
established
to extin-
guish it.

that the Church of Rome neither ever had erred, nor ever could err![1]

14. So rapidly grew into rank maturity the grossest imposition that ever darkened and enslaved the human mind. But where was the Church of Christ all the while—that Church which is composed of " a congregation of faithful men, in the which the pure word of God is preached, and the sacraments be duly administered according to Christ's ordinance in all those things that of necessity are requisite to the same?"[2] Though such a Church no where appears to have existed in the middle ages—though for many years no witness for " the truth as it is in Jesus" raised his voice against the abominations of Rome; yet it will not be doubted, by a believer in the Word of God, that " the true Shepherd" still had a little flock, in whose hearts He ruled, though "in the midst of His enemies." And as Cyrus was called by the Lord to deliver His Church from the captivity of Babylon; so, in the fulness of time, did He raise up several sovereigns of Europe to emancipate His Church from the bondage of Rome. Cyrus knew not the Lord; and he was executing his own schemes of conquest, when his triumph was rendered subservient to the purposes of Jehovah for His people's good: so also the immediate object of the European monarchs who resisted the pope, was, probably, the defence of their own power against his encroachments: but their bold protests against that haughty pontiff's claims to temporal dominion in their respective kingdoms, led, under

[1] In the sixteenth century this doctrine was confirmed by Pope Leo X. as a bulwark against the opinions of Luther. See Roscoe's Life of Leo X.

[2] Article XIX. of the Church of England.

the superintending Providence of the Almighty, to the deliverance of the true Church from the ashes in which she had for ages smouldered.

This resistance was offered so early as the eleventh century, by the emperors of Germany, Henry I., II., III., and IV.; by William I. of England, and several of his successors in the following century; and by Philip of France, together with some minor sovereigns. While they were opposing the secular domination of the pope, the churches established in their respective dominions were scarcely less active in resisting his ecclesiastical usurpation. In the twelfth century this contest was renewed by Frederic Barbarossa, Emperor of the West, against pope Adrian IV., and carried on with great spirit : and about the same period the light of the Reformation began to dawn on the Waldenses in Germany, and on several persons of eminence in England and France. To extinguish these rising beams, which are as odious to Rome, as light is to those who " love darkness " rather, " because their deeds are evil; " the Inquisition was established—a court that has been truly designated, the " depth of Satan ; for Satanical it is by the conjunction of three qualities ; indefatigable diligence, profound subtilty, and inhuman cruelty." [1] Its object was, to destroy any one, whoever he might be, that should presume to act, or even speak, against the Church of Rome ; and many of the Waldenses, and other reputed heretics, were subjected to the tortures of this, so called, " Holy tribunal." " The adoration of the host," " Transubstantiation," " Auricular Con-

CENT. XI.

CENT. XII.

CENT. XIII.

---

[1] Trapp's Popery Stated, &c. p. ii. § 12. Quoted in Johnson's Dictionary. See also " A View of the Court of Inquisition in Portugal," &c.—Geddes' Tracts, vol. i.

fession," and other abominations, were instituted about the same time, and thereby a deeper
shade was added to the gloom that shrouded the
western world—so many additional links forged
for its chains. These chains, however, were
ere long to be broken, no more, we trust, to be
riveted.

Papal autho-
rity begins
to wane.
Two popes
at the same
time.

15. Such was the policy of Rome, in order to
reclaim or put to death, on the one hand, all
that ventured to think and act as rational and
responsible beings ; and, on the other, to retain
such as were dreaming of security while sur-
rendering their consciences to the church. But
God soon turned these counsels to foolishness ;

and in the following, the 14th century, He raised
up suitable agents to vindicate the temporal and
spiritual liberties of mankind. Philip the Fair,
king of France, carried on an active opposition
against the imperious pretensions of the pope to
a temporal jurisdiction over the sovereigns of the
world. He boldly accused Boniface VIII. of
heresy, simony, and several other atrocious
crimes ; and actually demanded a general council, with a view to his deposition, a demand that
was always deemed by the pope tantamount to
a declaration of war against his assumed prerogatives.

From this time the papal authority began to
decline ; and the next step which the infatuated
pope took in order to arrest its retrogression,
tended rather to accelerate its fall. He removed
his residence to Avignon, on the Rhone, in the
South of France, merely to escape, no doubt,
from the turmoils in which he was involved in
Italy : but this step gave an advantage to his
adversaries, which they were not slow to employ
against him. They set up a rival pope at Rome,
so that the church had two popes at the same

time, each acknowledged by his partisans as the infallible and supreme ruler of the world. This schism rent asunder the vaunted unity of the Latin church.

16. In the same century arose John Wicliff, an English presbyter, who vehemently opposed the scandalous licentiousness and ignorance of the monks, and was supported in his opposition by the Duke of Lancaster and the British parliament. He translated the Bible into English, and recommended all men diligently to study the sacred volume, instead of yielding implicitly to the authority of the church in the unscriptural dogmas she put forth.

John Wicliff, the English reformer.

17. In the next century, the sovereigns of England, Germany and France, continued to oppose the insolent domination of the pope, with a determination that was rapidly gathering strength: while, on his part, he seemed to hold the sceptre with the greater tenacity, as the danger of losing it increased. At the same time, the spirit of religious liberty continued to spread, and the church of Rome was no less active in her endeavours to suppress it, torturing and destroying, wherever she had the power, all that ventured to judge in the smallest matter in opposition to her dictates. In this crusade against the religious liberty of mankind, John Huss and Jerome of Prague were committed to the flames; the laity were deprived of the sacramental cup; and it was actually declared, by a decree of the council of Constance, to be lawful to violate the most solemn engagements when made with those whom they called heretics.

CENT. XV. John Huss and Jerome of Prague burnt alive: other wicked means used without avail to stifle the Reformation.

Such were the efforts of Rome to extinguish the light of the Reformation, as soon as its dawn began to illumine the nations of the West.

But all opposition to its rising beams proved unavailing. It is somewhere written—" The Parthians shoot their arrows at the sun, and the wolves howl at the moon : but what can their impotence avail? The sun walks forth in his brightness, and the moon holds on her course, unhurt and undisturbed by the noise and the insolence below." The church of Rome, like the Sanhedrim at Jerusalem, found it hard " to kick against the pricks."[1] Jesus was persecuted in His disciples; and when He gave the word, " Hitherto shalt thou come, and no farther,"—then " her proud waves " were stayed ! The cause of His Church continued to advance in countries where it was most strenuously opposed. Some of its enemies He converted, like Saul of Tarsus, into preachers of the " faith which once they destroyed."[2] In Bohemia, the followers of the martyr, John Huss, successfully resisted all efforts to reduce them to submission to the pope : and several other nations of Europe were gradually preparing for the Reformation, which, in the following century, was introduced by Luther, Cranmer, and other devoted servants of the Lord.

Roman Church seeks to extend her dominion in the Eastern and Western worlds newly discovered.

18. [3]This review of the rise and progress of the papacy, down to the sixteenth century, will expose the fallacy of the pope's pretensions in reference to India. While the authority of the Roman church was thus rapidly declining in Europe, the discoveries in the East and West enabled her to extend her empire in both directions, and she did not omit to avail herself of

---

[1] Acts ix. 5.　　　　　[2] Gal. i. 23.

[3] This brief sketch is drawn up chiefly from Mosheim's Ecclesiastical History, Vol. ii. iii. and iv. where the facts here simply stated are given in detail.

these advantageous circumstances. Assuming the title of *Catholic*, she claimed the dominion of the universal church : and no sooner was the existence of the Syrian church in India discovered, than the papal authorities began to assail her independence, and to assert her original subjection to Rome. We are already in possession of facts enough to prove the invalidity of such an assumption. It has appeared, that the Syrian church existed and flourished in India, ages before the world had heard of the figment of papal supremacy, and that the two churches had at no time the slightest intercourse with each other, before the arrival of the Portuguese on the coast of Malabar.

19. We may now be prepared to appreciate the wisdom of Divine Providence, in closing the continent of India against the inhabitants of Europe, during the rise and progress of the papal domination. Had the church of Rome gained access to that country during the plenitude of her power, we cannot doubt, judging from her subsequent proceedings, that she would have left no means untried to destroy the identity of the church in Malabar; for the existence of that church in a state of independence, shook the foundation of her claims to universal dominion. The protection afforded to this establishment by heathen and Mahomedan rulers, presented a perfect contrast to the intolerance of Rome towards all persons and churches whose creed differed from her own. This is the admission of a Romanist, whose candour does him honour. Alluding to the violent measures adopted by his church to reduce all others to her sway, the Abbé Fleury has remarked— " What great loss Christianity suffered in Asia is very manifest. If the Saracens had held the

same principles which were received among the Latin christians of these times, they would not have suffered one Christian to live in their dominions. But this nation, though guilty of various crimes and oppressions, yet judged it to be an act of too much iniquity and cruelty; whilst the Romanists accounted it a pious deed to destroy by fire and sword all who were of a different religion from themselves, and refused to be converted." [1]

It is the custom, in an age calling itself more liberal and enlightened, to put down such statements as these, as the assertions of bigotry or the apprehensions of dotage. We maintain, that they are neither the one nor the other, but, historic facts. The whole proceedings of the Romish emissaries in India towards the Syrian Christians, will form both an illustration and a confirmation of the Abbé Fleury's remarks. Had their insidious designs and cruel efforts to reduce them from the faith of their fathers been made at an earlier period, this church might have been wholly absorbed in that of Rome: whereas, under the more righteous and liberal sway of Mahomedan and pagan rulers, as the unconscious agents of a wise and gracious Providence, she acquired a stability that long resisted all the craft and violence of her Romish enemies, to destroy her identity and independence. She now stands, if not so erect in truth and righteousness as we would fain desire, yet, as one of the most interesting monuments of ecclesiastical antiquity, and a lasting rebuke of the papal pretensions to universal dominion in the Christian world.

[1] Fleury's Ecclesiastical History, xix. Discourse, p. 20. See Jortin's Remarks on Ecclesiastical History, Vol. v. pp. 375, &c.

20. But to proceed with the history of the events that will establish the justice of this remark. The account which Vasco de Gama gave of his discoveries, encouraged several Portuguese adventurers to embark in the commerce with India. Among them was one Pedro Alvares Cabral, who was the first to bring to Europe intelligence of the Christian churches on the coast of Malabar. Having landed at Cranganore, he became acquainted with several Christians in the neighbourhood, and so far gained their confidence, that two of them, who were brothers, ventured on board his fleet, and then consented to sail with him to Europe. It was their intention to proceed from Portugal to Mosul, to visit the patriarch there, who was still the acknowledged head of their church. The names of these Christians were, Matthias and Joseph. Soon after their arrival at Lisbon, Matthias, the elder, died. Joseph then visited Rome, and proceeded thence to Venice ; but we have no account of his having accomplished his intended journey to Persia. While at Venice, he gave a description of his travels and of the Malabar Christians, which was published in Latin, under the title of " Voyages of Joseph the Indian." [1] We have no further particulars of this Joseph, than that he returned from Venice to Portugal, and thence sailed back to his native land.

A. D. 1500.

Voyage of Pedro Alvares Cabral to India : brings home two Indian Christians.

21. In the year 1502, Vasco de Gama undertook a second voyage to India, when the king of Portugal conferred on him the title of Admiral of the Indian, Persian, and Arabian Seas. In the month of February, 1502, he sailed from the Tagus with a fleet of twenty sail under his

A. D. 1502.

Second voyage of Vasco de Gama : Christians welcome him, & place themselves under his protection.

[1] This account has since appeared in several collections of travels. La Croze, p. 49.

command.　After compelling several princes on his passage to pay tribute to him, in the name of his sovereign, he arrived in safety at Cochin. The Christians, knowing that he was the subject of a Christian monarch, and concluding that he was sent to take possession of India, very reasonably expected to enjoy greater immunities under his government than they had received from their heathen and Mahomedan rulers. They, therefore, sent a deputation on board his vessel, beseeching him to take them under his own protection and that of his sovereign, and to defend them from the injustice and cruelty of the petty rajahs of the country. The deputation presented to de Gama a staff of vermilion wood, mounted at each end with silver, and ornamented with three bells : This, they said, was the sceptre of their own Christian kings, who had formerly reigned over them, the last of whom had died a short time before ; and they declared that they presented it to the Portuguese admiral in token of their submission to his master as their king.[1]　Gouvea affirms, that from this time they acknowledged themselves subjects of Portugal : long, however, before that historian wrote, which was about a century after the arrival of the Portuguese in India, they had bitter cause to lament the confidence which they so prematurely reposed in the Christianity of these visitors. Little did they suspect, that before many years had elapsed, the successors of these men would treat them with greater intolerance and cruelty than they had ever experienced from pagans or

[1] Histoire Orientale, &c.　This is a French translation of Gouvea's *Journada*, &c. or, proceedings of the Archbishop of Goa in the reduction of the Church of Malabar to the subjection of Rome.

Mahomedans. They had learned the history of their religion only from the Gospels, and a few traditions preserved among them, and were, therefore, totally ignorant of the arrogance and intolerance of the Church of Rome.

The first object, however, of the Portuguese, was to establish themselves in the country; and the admiral did not neglect the advantage to be gained from the proffered subjection of these Christian inhabitants. He received their deputation with great courtesy, and dismissed them with fair promises, assuring them of his protection when he should be better able to afford them the succour they required.

22. When the Portuguese first arrived in India, the Malabar country was divided between numerous petty princes, descendants of Ceram Peroumal's children and friends, among whom, we have seen, he divided his dominions.[1] Their power varied considerably, some commanding from one to two and three hundred, and up to a thousand men; others, from five to ten, and so on to thirty thousand: and even, it is said, to one hundred thousand;[2] but this is, probably, an exaggeration. Between these chieftains, wars were sometimes generated, which never, however, terminated in an entire separation between the parties. The three greatest powers were, the *Colastrian* Rajah to the north, the Zamorin of Calicut in the centre, and the Rajah of Cochin to the south, whose kingdom extended to Cape Comorin. At that time the Mahomedans were the chief traders on the coast, who, though not amounting to one tithe of the general population, were much courted by the several

---

[1] B. i., c. iv., s. 7.
[2] A lack. Zeireddien. Asiatic Res. vol. v. pp. 10, 11. See also Relation de L'Inquisition de Goa. ch. vii. par M. Dellon.

rajahs, and more especially by the Zamorin, who wished them to frequent his port of Calicut, on account of the duty of ten per cent. that was levied on their trade.[1] Between them and the Portuguese a commercial jealousy soon arose, which proved the cause of all the bitter hostilities that were afterward carried on, both by sea and land, between the Zamorins and Mahomedans on the one part, and the Rajah of Cochin and the Portuguese, on the other.

Rapid progress of the Portuguese, notwithstanding the opposition of Mahomedan traders.

23. Notwithstanding all opposition, the Portuguese made rapid advances to a power which, for a time, defied all native resistance, and encouraged them to assume the tone of independent sovereigns. After establishing several factories on the coast, in the year 1510, Alphonso de Albuquerque besieged and took the city of Goa, which he made the capital of the Portuguese dominions in the East. This conquest was followed by the possession of Diu, Choul, Salsette, Bombay, Bassein, and Damaun. Some of these places were obtained by conquest; others, by treaty: and the rapidity of the Portuguese advance will be seen by the date at which the last named place came into their possession—the year 1531. Their factories on the coast were at Dabul, Onore, Barcelore, Mangalore, Cannanore, Calicut, Cranganore, Cochin and Coulan (Quilon). At some of these places they were permitted to construct forts; and they obliged the Zamorin to admit of their erecting one at Calicut: but he soon expelled them from it, assisted by the Jews of Cranganore, whom he had protected against the Mahomedans. With this exception, and one or two other reverses too unimportant to notice,

*A. D.
1510.*

*A. D.
1531.*

---

[1] Eus. Renaudot. Mahomedans' first voyage to China, p. 165.

the Portuguese effectually succeeded in putting down their rivals in the Indian trade, the Mahomedan merchants sinking under their superior influence, and becoming obedient to their government and servants. All native vessels were even compelled to take *Christian* passes for their safety on the seas; nor were any indeed suffered to trade, unless in such articles as the Portuguese deemed not worth their own attention. Thus successful in Malabar, they proceeded to the opposite coast of Coromandel, where, though they did not attain to equal power, they for many years carried on a thriving commerce.

CHAPTER III.

MISSION OF FRANCIS XAVIER.

Partial success of the Portuguese missionaries in India.

1. WHILE the Portuguese were thus active in making new conquests, we do not hear that they took any notice of the Christians to whom Vasco de Gama had promised protection. Neither do they appear, until about forty years after their settlement in the country, to have given any attention to the conversion of the heathen. The government of Portugal sent out numerous Friars for the purpose; but they are charged with having taken more care to provide commodious situations and erect convents for their different orders, than to convert their neighbours to the Christian faith. And when, at a subsequent period, the Portuguese boasted of the success of their missions, the secular motives that actuated them were thus exposed by a member of their own church.—

"It is a vain conceit, if it please your Majesty," said a minister of state to Philip IV. of Spain, "that the world has entertained of the zeal of the Portuguese upon account of the conversions that have been made by them in the Indies; for it was covetousness, and not zeal, that engaged them to make all those conquests. The conversions that have been made there were effected by the Divine power, and the charity of a few particular Friars, the government and crown having no other aim therein, but the robbing of kingdoms and cities: and there were always the greatest conversions where there was most to gratify their covetousness. But where there was nothing to be had, there the people were obdurate, and not to be wrought upon. And so we see their zeal expired quickly in all places, where it was not animated by covetousness; and they who had nothing else to say but, LORD OPEN UNTO US, were not thought fit to enter into Heaven." [1]

The few friars that roamed up and down the country, were permitted to preach wherever they chose, and to erect small churches for the people whom they had collected together: but no conversions of any consequence appear to have taken place until the arrival of Francis Xavier, whose unexampled labours and success merit some detail. He was one of the first disciples of Loyola, the founder of the order of Jesuits; and as the missionaries of that society acted so prominent a part in the establishment and extension of the Romish Church in India, it may not be deemed irrelevant here to give a brief account of its origin.

2. Ignatius Loyola was born of a noble family at the castle of Loyola, in Biscay, 1491. He commenced his career as page to Ferdinand V., King of Spain. After this, he entered the army at an early age, and signalized himself by his courage and energy. At the siege of Pampeluna, in 1521, he was wounded by a cannon ball in both legs, and fell in the breach: but

History of Ignatius Loyola.

---

[1] A similar complaint is made by Manuel de Faria in the 3rd Vol. of *Asia Portuguesa.*—Geddes' History of the Church of Malabar, pp. 4—6.

the French, instead of taking him prisoner, had the humanity to convey him to the castle of Loyola, to be nursed by his family. This incident led to the institution of the order of Jesuits; and in the annals of the world, few events are to be found apparently so unimportant, leading to such consequences as have marked the course of that society.

3. While confined under the cure of his wounds, he amused himself with reading a *Life of the Saints*, and his enthusiastic mind was fired with ambition to emulate their example. Despairing, probably, of recovering the use of his limbs sufficiently to resume the active profession of arms, he resolved to change it for that of the Church. His first exercise of devotion in his new profession looked like a parting tribute to that which he had left: this was the dedication of himself to the Virgin Mary as her knight. He next devoted himself to the poor in the hospital at Marenza: and afterwards went on a pilgrimage to the Holy Land. Upon his return to Europe he prosecuted his studies with diligence, first in the Universities of Spain, and then in that of Paris, where he laid the foundation of his celebrated Order. Having presented his Institutes to the pope, Paul III., for his sanction, that pontiff referred them to a committee of cardinals, who objected to the proposed Society as unnecessary and dangerous. Upon this representation, the pope refused to confirm it: Ignatius, however, was not to be so repelled. Resolved to succeed, and considering the jeopardy into which the papal interests were then brought, through the publication and extensive acceptance of the Gospel, he saw that the most likely way to attain his object was to offer the services of his order to the pope. Ac-

cordingly, besides the three vows of poverty, of chastity, and of monastic obedience, common to most orders of monks, he now added a fourth, requiring all the members of his society to take a vow of obedience to the pope, to do whatsoever, and to go whithersoever, he should command them, in the cause of the Church, without demanding any thing from him for their services. This proposal was not to be resisted, especially in the present exigency of Rome. The pope hesitated no longer, and the order received his sanction in the year 1540.

Ignatius drew up two sets of rules for his disciples: one for their personal use, entitled, *spiritual exercises*, which contain some profitable suggestions for self-examination. The other consisted of the *Constitutions of the Order*, in which are found many things hostile to the interests of all other societies, and, in fact, incompatible with the liberty and welfare of mankind. It ought, however, in justice to the memory of Ignatius, to be remembered, that these *Constitutions*, as well as the *Secreta Monita*, which contain some rules for the members' conduct that have been justly characterized as *diabolical*, are generally attributed to Laynez and Aquaviva, the generals who succeeded Loyola. 'Innumerable writers of the Romish Church have abundantly testified,' and 'many of the most illustrious communities of that Church publicly lamented,' that the Jesuits have not only 'perverted and corrupted almost every branch and precept of morality,' but 'that they have sapped and destroyed its very foundations.'[2] The infamous *Rules* of this order

---

[2] Those who bring these heavy charges against the sons of Loyola, have taken abundant precautions to fortify them-

were not generally known until towards the close of the 18th century.

. Loyola's ostensible object in founding his society, was to stop the course of the Reformation in Europe, which, in the beginning of the 16th century, set in like a flood against the pretensions and abuses of Rome. It is probable, however, that his object was merely to signalize himself as a

selves against the reproach of calumny. The following maxims, which the whole society adopts and inculcates, will sufficiently justify their accusers.

" That persons truly wicked, and void of the love of God, may expect to obtain eternal life in heaven, provided that they be impressed with a fear of the divine anger, and avoid all heinous and enormous crimes through the dread of future punishment.

" That those persons may transgress with safety, who have a probable reason for transgressing, i. e. any plausible argument or authority in favour of the sin they are inclined to commit.

" That actions intrinsically evil, and directly contrary to the divine laws, may be innocently performed, by those who have so much power over their own minds, as to join, even ideally, a good end to this wicked action, or, who are capable of rightly directing their intention.

" That philosophical sin is of a very light and trivial nature, and does not deserve the pains of hell."—By philosophical sin the Jesuits mean an action contrary to the dictates of nature and right reason, done by a person who is ignorant of the written law of God, or doubtful of its true meaning.

" That the transgressions committed by a person blinded by the seduction of lust, agitated by the impulse of tumultuous passions, and destitute of all sense and impression of religion, however detestable and heinous they may be in themselves, are not imputable to the transgressor before the tribunal of God; and that such trangressions may often be as involuntary as the actions of a madman.

" That the person who takes an oath, or enters into a contract, may, to elude the force of the one, and the obligation of the other, add, to the form of words by which they are expressed, certain mental additions and tacit reservations."

These and other enormities of a like nature, are said to make an essential part of the system of morality inculcated by the Jesuits. Mosheim. Century 17. sec. 2. part 1. xxxv.

saint: but, whatever his real motive, when we remember the tyranny and barbarities of the Jesuits almost all over the world, it is natural for the mind to revolt at the very name of the man to whom they owe their origin. Who then can be surprized at the opprobrium which has been heaped upon his memory? Some, however, giving him credit for honesty of intention, have lent their aid to throw a veil over the injury which his society has done to the cause of pure religion. But who that considers the character and amount of that injury, can fail to regard this order as one of the severest scourges ever permitted to afflict the Church of God? Far be it from the Christian wantonly to stigmatize the character of its founder: but it is equally incumbent upon us to refrain from such conjectures as to his motives, as may tend to diminish the abhorrence with which we contemplate the miseries that he was the means of bringing upon the disciples of Christ. We know, from the instance of Saul of Tarsus, that a zealot may verily think that he is doing God service, even while persecuting His most devoted servants, and laying waste His church. But this does not render his bigotry less calamitous to its victims. There is a strong propensity in some minds to tolerate the infirmities, the excesses, and even the mischief of a man whom they look upon as meaning well, though they acknowledge his infatuation to be extreme. This will, no doubt, account for all the apologies that have been offered, by men professing a purer creed, for the extravagances of Ignatius Loyola.

They are performing, however, to say the least, a very gratuitous service, and one that is calculated to injure the cause of charity, which they, probably, mean to serve. Conceding that he was sincere, yet can sincerity in an evil cause divest it of its turpitude? Who was ever more sincere than Saul of Tarsus? But who has been louder in self-reproach, when he found, that in the days of his violence, he had persecuted " the disciples of the Lord?" Can we deem the Reformation the richest blessing mankind have received from Heaven, since the first promulgation of the Gospel, without looking upon this Ignatius as a mighty agent of Satan to resist the force, and quench the light of truth? He is gone to an infallible tribunal, to account for his motives and his deeds; and the decision of the Judge will be unaffected by the opposite interpretations, which the partialities or the malevolence of mankind may put upon them. He is, therefore, as independent of our charity, as of our reproach. But not so the living, to whom it is of vast importance to understand the character of this Society. If then charity for the *dead* requires that we 'set down nought in malice;' charity for the *living* demands that we ' extenuate nothing.' The institution itself is justly an object of suspicion and abhorrence to all who are acquainted with its history; and it is anything but charitable to mankind to give such a representation of its founder and his disciples, as may conciliate confidence, where distrust is our best security. But for this purpose, it is not necessary to suspect every jesuit to be a wicked and cruel man; far from it: and their history furnishes examples enough of an opposite character to confute so sweeping a charge. For instance, one of the first and best of Loyola's disciples was Francis Xavier, whose zeal and charity would have done honour to any cause, had they been directed solely by the word of God, instead of the interests of his exclusive order, and intolerant Church.

4. This apostle of the Papacy was, like his master, a Spaniard of noble birth. Indeed, great pains have been taken to prove his descent from the Kings of Navarre, but with what success, it is of little moment here to inquire. His father was Don Juan de Jasso, and his mother, Mary Azpilcueta Xavier, who had a numerous family, of whom Francis was the youngest. He was born April 7th, 1506, at the family Castle of Xavier, which stands at the foot of the Pyrenees, seven or eight leagues from Pampeluna. At a very early age he manifested a contemplative mind, and took much more delight in wandering alone amid the wild mountain scenery of his native land, than in the sports of the field. He was carefully educated at home under able masters, and made considerable proficiency in the classics. His predilection for study was such, that he soon determined to devote himself to literary pursuits ; and he removed to Paris in 1524, when eighteen years of age, to prosecute his studies at the celebrated university of that metropolis. Here he entered with great ardour into the study of philosophy ; and such was his success, that on taking his Master's degree, he was chosen a philosophical professor, and obtained great credit by his lectures on Aristotle.

Xavier's birth, parentage and education.

5. But he was soon to be diverted from this literary career. While the young professor was the object of general admiration, Ignatius Loyola came to Paris to complete his studies ; and hearing of Xavier's fame, he determined to become acquainted with him. Having accomplished this, he was too accurate an observer of

Loyola's efforts to gain him : he overcomes his predilection for the Society of Lutherans.

mankind not to discover in him qualities calculated to further his own designs; and with this view, he tried to persuade him to attend to divinity rather than philosophy, but for some time without avail. Ignatius, however, as we have already seen, was not to be easily repulsed. Convinced that Xavier would be an important acquisition to the society he was then projecting, he neglected no means to induce him to alter his course. Acts of kindness, flattery, affectionate entreaties, every thing that was calculated to win upon the young and ardent mind of his acquaintance, was tried, but for a long time without any apparent effect. At length, however, Xavier began to listen to him with more attention; and Ignatius, seizing a favourable opportunity, made a solemn appeal to his conscience in the words of our Lord—"What shall it profit a man if he shall gain the whole world, and lose his own soul? Or what shall a man give in exchange for his soul?"[3] He then drew so impressive a contrast between the wisdom and honour of the world, and of religion, as to cause the determination of Xavier to waver; but he could not yet consent to forego the temporal ease and advantages within his reach, for the perpetual poverty, toil, and self-denial which Ignatius exacted: nor did he at length make the sacrifice without many a severe struggle. But he had a feeling still more important to overcome than the love of literary ease. At that time several Lutherans were at Paris, in whose conversation he appeared to take much greater interest than in that of Loyola; and there can be little doubt that what he learned from them

[3] Mark viii. 36, 37.

had some influence in the formation of his character, though he was dissuaded from adopting their sentiments. It was natural for Ignatius to be alarmed at his intimacy with these persons, and to redouble his exertions to counteract their influence over his mind; and at length his success was complete.

When Xavier had once fairly entered on his new career, he followed the "spiritual exercises" of Ignatius with characteristic ardour, subjecting himself to all the privations which they enjoined. His teacher does not appear to have directed him to depend on the Holy Spirit to "mortify the flesh with its affections and lusts;" and there is no reason to suppose that he was actuated by the pure and disinterested motive of love to Christ. Ignatius had contrived to conciliate his confidence and regard, and to communicate to him no inconsiderable share of his own enthusiasm in the cause he had espoused. Nothing could be more entire than his renunciation of all that the world presents to captivate the young and ambitious, and his voluntary adoption of every thing repulsive to human nature. Ignatius, Francis, and five other converts, solemnly dedicated themselves, on the summit of Montmartre, to the service of the Pope and the Church of Rome, and faithfully did Xavier perform his vow to the last moments of his life.

6. But while he was thus contemplating a total renunciation of the world, and a life of toil and privation, his father had other thoughts for his advancement. He wrote to his daughter, the Abbess of St. Clare de Gaudia, to consult her about the removal of her brother Francis from Paris, and to obtain for him some appointment at the court of Arragon; but she dissuaded

Enters upon the work & discipline of his new calling.

him from his purpose, assuring him that her
brother 'was a chosen vessel, designed to be
an apostle to the infidel, and that one day he
would become a great pillar of the Church.'
His biographer represents this as a direct revelation from heaven to the devout Abbess, but
such pretensions can only depreciate the cause
they are intended to promote, except indeed in
the estimation of those who have an interest in
believing them. With all Xavier's zeal and
sincerity, for which we are disposed to give
him due credit, it will be seen that the interests
of pure religion were too little advanced by his
labours in the East, to believe that his mission
was of sufficient importance to the cause of
Christ to be the subject of a special revelation.
Since the Abbess appears to have been regarded
as the oracle of her family, there can be little
doubt that her brother communicated to her all
that was passing in his mind ; which will sufficiently account for her injunction to her father,
without having recourse to an intimation from
heaven for the purpose.

Is called to labour at Rome.

7. After several years spent in active labour
and patient suffering, performing long and perilous journeys on foot in the depth of winter,
and exposing himself to hardships that nearly
brought him to the grave ; he and his five companions were called by Ignatius to Rome, and
introduced to the pope, who encouraged them
to act under his direction. Xavier, having
taken orders some time before, was appointed
to the Church of St. Lawrence in Damaso,
where his faithful and energetic preaching is
said to have produced a deep impression. While
there, a dreadful famine prevailed, which called
forth all the energy of his character, and his
attention to the sufferers was, as usual, unremitted.

8. But the time drew near for his removal to the distant region of the East. While he was at Rome, Govea, a Portuguese courtier, came from the King of Portugal, John III., on an important ambassage to the Pope. This man had known both Loyola and Xavier at Paris, having been president of the college of St. Barbara while they were in residence there: and now, resuming his acquaintance with them, he was struck with admiration at their zeal, and thought them suitable persons to execute the King of Portugal's design to establish the Church in India. The king at once adopted Govea's recommendation of them; but as the presence of Ignatius at Rome was indispensable to the interests of his order, Rodriguez was appointed in his place. Xavier and his colleague complied without hesitation; and having received the pope's blessing, they departed from Rome for Lisbon in company with the Portuguese ambassador. Loyola, although seldom manifesting any emotion, however moving the occasion to ordinary minds, could not lose such a companion as Xavier without regret. He was gratified, however, at his appointment to a mission which he foresaw might raise the character and advance the interests of his order; and at parting he addressed him in these words—'Go, my brother, rejoice that you have not here a narrow Palestine, or a province of Asia, in prospect, but a vast extent of ground, and innumerable kingdoms. An entire world is reserved for your endeavours; and nothing but so large a field is worthy of your courage and your zeal. The voice of God calls you; kindle those unknown nations with the flame that burns within you.' Xavier, who had not the imperturbable spirit of his friend, was affected to tears, and

A. D.
1540.
_____
Appointed
to the Indian
Mission.

replied—'It is impossible for me to forget you, Ignatius; or not to recall to my memory that sincere and holy friendship which you have shown me. Father of my soul, when I am afar, I will think that you are still present, and that I behold you with my eyes: write to me often. The smallness of my talent is known to you; share with me those abundant treasures which heaven has heaped upon you.'

Such was his susceptibility: and when, on his way to Portugal, he refused to pay a last visit to his mother and friends, as he passed the Castle of Xavier, it must have been at no small sacrifice of his personal affections. He, probably, was afraid to trust his feelings with such an interview, or thought it his duty sternly to deny himself this tender indulgence, in fulfilment of the vows that were upon him. Happy are they who know, that they serve a Master who demands not such a sacrifice as this. It is only when the objects of our tenderest regard threaten to impede our obedience to His commands, that He requires them to be so absolutely renounced.

On his arrival at Lisbon, finding that the next fleet for India was not to sail before the following spring, he employed the intermediate time in visiting the beds of the sick and the dungeons of the Inquisition. He speaks also of the vast number of courtiers who came to him for confession, and seems to have been delighted with the appearance of religion at court. The king and queen wished to pay him every attention, and ordered apartments to be prepared for him in the palace; but he preferred a lodging in the hospital of All Saints, where he was surrounded by the sick and the dying.

9. In these labours nine months passed away; and when the time for his departure arrived, the king put into his hands four briefs, which had been received for him from Rome; two constituting him the pope's nuncio in the East, a third commending him to the King of Ethiopia, and a fourth, to all the princes of the islands in his passage. The King had ordered his cabin to be furnished with everything that could contribute to his comfort; but he could not forget his vow of poverty and self-denial, and, therefore, declined the proffered indulgence, choosing only some books, and a warm cloth to cover him during the cold and tempestuous weather that was expected off the Cape of Good Hope. Rodriguez, who had been selected for his colleague, was too unwell to accompany him; but he attended him on board the vessel, where Xavier answered a question which his friend had often put to him, in a manner that showed that he was as prepared to suffer as to do the will of God. Just as they were parting, he said, 'Rodriguez, you may remember, that when we lodged together in the hospital at Rome, you often heard me crying out in my sleep, and asked me the meaning of the words I uttered. A vision or dream was given me, in which I beheld a wide ocean lashed by the storm, and full of rocks, desert isles, and barbarous lands, hunger and thirst raging every where, with death in many a fearful form. In the midst of this ghastly representation, I cried out, 'Yet more, O my God! yet more!' I then beheld all I was to suffer for the glory of Jesus Christ; and not being able to satiate myself with those troubles which were represented to my imagination, I used these words, 'I hope the Divine goodness will grant me that in India,

A. D. 1541.

His departure for India.

which he has foreshown to me in Italy.' The spirit of this resolution is more to be admired than the judgment it bespeaks. A determination, in dependence upon Divine grace, to suffer whatever may be unavoidable in his career, ought to possess the soul of every Christian, and especially that of a missionary to heathen lands. But instead of seeking tribulation, or provoking persecution, he should rather avoid them by all means that do not involve a compromise of principle, or the neglect of duty to his Lord and the Church; and he ought to be thankful if allowed to carry on his work in peace. But if this cannot be obtained, he will deem it a privilege to suffer in the cause of his Lord.[4] It was in this mind that St. Paul was ready to encounter tribulation, even to the fellowship of his Lord's suffering, being made conformable to His death.[5] But he never courted persecution: quite the contrary. He used every lawful means to escape it.[6] How far the resolution of Xavier partook of this character, it is impossible to determine; but it will be seen, that to the end of his course, there was too much appearance of coveting affliction for its own sake, as though he thought the mere act of suffering meritorious before God. It may, probably, be said, in extenuation, that he had been educated in such notions; but this does not render the doctrine itself less objectionable, for it is not in accordance, either with the instructions or the example of the Apostles.

The vessel in which he sailed carried out the new viceroy of India, and a number of troops

---

[4] Matt. v. 11. Phil. i. 29. 2 Tim. ii. 12.
[5] Phil. iii. 10.
[6] Acts xxii. 25—29, xxiii. 6—9, xxv. 8—12. et Marg. Ref.

and passengers, amounting, together with the
ship's company, to one thousand souls. These
furnished him with ample occupation on the
passage, which took up thirteen months. His
attention to the sick and dying was unremitted,
until he was himself attacked with a malignant
fever that had nearly proved fatal: though even
in that state, it was with difficulty that his physician could prevail upon him to relax his
exertions.

A. D.
1542

10. The fleet arrived at Goa, May 6th, 1542,
when Xavier waited on the Bishop with his
credentials, and was received with all the kindness and confidence due to one so accredited.
The Bishop promised to support him in his
mission, for which he was, no doubt, thankful ;
but he sought the protection of a higher power,
without which he knew that all human aid
would be of no avail.   For this purpose he shut
himself up in one of the Churches, and spent
the whole of his first night in India in prayer ;
an example worthy the imitation of missionaries
of a purer creed.

Arrival at
Goa, and
exertions
there.

His first attention was given to the Portuguese, whom he found in a most demoralized
state.   Though Goa abounded in priests and
monks, with a Bishop at their head, yet their
admonitions had long been disregarded by men
intent on the acquisition of wealth, and the indulgence of their passions. Xavier must have
felt, that it would be in vain to endeavour to
convert the heathen to a religion, the moral
character of whose professors was so inferior to
their own.   He, therefore, set himself vigo-
rously to work to reform this state of things ;
and although there was much puerile superstition in the means he used, yet they were
such as the people were accustomed to ; and in

a short time, it is said, he had the satisfaction of observing a general improvement in their conduct.

There were several circumstances that would tend to conciliate them, and insure their attention. The novelty of his appearance and zeal; the eloquence and boldness with which he rebuked their vices; the great humility and self-denial of one whom they knew to be of such noble origin; and, above all, the countenance of the viceroy, who was known to have the King of Portugal's commands to afford him every protection: such considerations as these would, there can be little doubt, induce many to lay aside the sins against which he so ardently and steadily inveighed. But must all the honour be given to these means and motives? Notwithstanding the defect of his own knowledge, and the absence of all proof that he preached the unadulterated Gospel of reconciliation; yet may we not hope that the Holy Ghost was vouchsafed, in answer to his midnight prayer, to produce these convictions in the hearts of some whose sins he vehemently denounced, and before whom he placed the awful consequences of their lives in the future world? And may there not have been enough of the Saviour in his preaching, to encourage the humble penitent to hope for pardon and peace, through the atonement of the cross? Such a hope is too cheering amid all this darkness not to be gladly entertained.

11. While at Goa he was invited to take charge of a seminary, lately established there, for the education of native heathen youths. The students, then on the establishment, came from all the adjacent countries, and they spoke nine or ten different languages. Xavier thought

proper to decline this invitation, considering, probably, that it would interfere too much with his more appropriate duties as a missionary. But he had too good a judgment not to see the importance of the institution, and he took care to place it on such an improved footing as to render it subservient to his design for the conversion of the heathen. He called it, The college of St. Paul, and obtained its transfer to his own society; which accounts for the Jesuit missionaries in India being frequently called, *The fathers of St. Paul*.

There was another subject that demanded his immediate attention. The King of Portugal had recently sent out an ecclesiastic to ascertain the cause of the slow progress of Christianity in India: and one of the reasons assigned was, the little charity shown by the monks to their scholars and converts. It was found, that when an Indian embraced their creed, they paid no regard to his temporal wants, though left destitute by his family; and they totally neglected the orphan children of those Christians who died in poverty. It was one of Xavier's first objects to consider by what means to remedy this crying evil, which had brought a scandal upon the Church. For this purpose he prevailed upon the Christian inhabitants of Goa, to contribute towards the relief of such orphans and proselytes as might be in need of assistance; and he succeeded in establishing a seminary for the children, which was soon afterwards endowed. This useful institution was subsequently enlarged by the liberality of others, and it was found to answer the intended purpose.

12. Although thus actively employed, he was not inattenive to the primary object of his mis-

His first
visit to the
southern
coast.

sion, the conversion of the heathen, and he availed himself of every opportunity to prepare for
the work. Natives were constantly flocking to
Goa from all parts of India for purposes of trade,
and from these he obtained much information
respecting their languages, customs and religion.
When he thought himself sufficiently prepared
to enter upon the missionary field, he signified
his intention to quit Goa for the interior; but
his attention being directed to some nominal
Christians on the southern coast, he visited
them on his way. These were the Paravars,
a very low caste, who were chiefly occupied in
the pearl, chank, and other fisheries. The Portuguese had not long before rescued them from
the tyranny of the Mahomedans, and they expressed their gratitude by embracing the religion of their deliverers, though without understanding its doctrines or precepts. Xavier was
delighted to hear of this opening, and lost no
time in going among the poor people, in company with two ecclesiastics who had some knowledge of their language.

They sailed from Goa, in October 1542, with
the new commandant of Comorin, the southern
extremity of the Indian continent, where they
landed, and proceeded immediately into the interior. Here Xavier soon found the inconvenience of not knowing the native language. His
own confessions on this subject are a sufficient
rebuke for those who have thought to do honour
to his memory, by pretending that he was endowed with the gift of tongues. Having ascertained that his interpreters were not equal to
the task they had undertaken, he ceased to
address the natives through them; but with
their assistance, and that of some natives who
understood a little Portuguese, he contrived to

translate into Malabar, first, ' The words of the sign of the cross,' then, the Apostles' creed, the commandments, the Lord's prayer, the Salutation of the Angel, the *Confiteor*, the *Salve Regina*, and the whole of the Catechism. The translation of these completed, he committed to memory as much as he could, and sallied forth to propound this heterogeneous mass of truth and error, to a people whom he acknowledges to have been infidels in reality, though bearing the Christian name. How such a mind as his could expect to make them much better by merely teaching them to repeat what he was not able to explain, even though all had been true, would be unaccountable, did we not remember to what a system he had surrendered his understanding.[7]

13. He visited no less than thirty villages along the coast, the half of which only were baptized; and he thus described his mode of proceeding. "I went about, with my bell in my hand, and gathering together all I met, both men and children, I instructed them in the Christian doctrine. The children learnt it easily by heart, in the compass of a month; and when they understood it, I charged them to teach it to their fathers and mothers, then to all of their own family, and even to their neighbours.

Specimen of his mode of instruction.

" On Sundays I assembled the men and women, little boys and girls, in the chapel; all

---

[7] This expression will not be thought too strong if it is considered, that it is laid down by Ignatius as a fundamental rule of his order, that ' whatever the superior enjoins is to be simply performed with a blind obedience, not considering whether what is enjoined is good or useful, since every thought of the kind takes away the merit and weight of obedience.' This is *military* obedience indeed.

N

came to my appointment, with an incredible joy, and most ardent desire to hear the Word of God. I began with the confessing God to be one in nature, and triune in persons. I afterwards repeated, distinctly, and with an audible voice, *the Lord's Prayer*, *the Angelical Salutation*, and *the Apostle's Creed*. All of them together repeated after me; and it is hardly to be imagined what pleasure they took in it. This being done, I repeated the *Creed* distinctly, and insisting on every particular Article, asked if they really believed it? They all protested to me, with loud cries, and their hands across their breasts, that they firmly believed it. My practice is, to make them repeat the *Creed* oftener than the other prayers; and I declare to them, at the same time, that they who believe the contents of it are true Christians.

" From the *Creed*, I pass to the *Ten Commandments*, and give them to understand, that the Christian Law is comprised in these precepts; that he who keeps them all according to his duty, is a good Christian; and that eternal life is decreed to him: That, on the contrary, whoever violates one of these Commandments, is a bad Christian, and that he shall be damned eternally, in case he repent not of his sin. Both the new Christians, and the Pagans, admire our law, as holy and reasonable, and consistent with itself.

" Having done as I told you, my custom is to repeat with them, the *Lord's Prayer*, and *the Angel's Salutation*. Once again we recite the *Creed*, and at every *Article*, besides the *Pater noster* and the *Ave Maria*, we intermingle some short prayer: for having pronounced aloud the *first Article*, I begin thus, and they say after me,—Jesus, *thou Son of the living*

*God, give me grace to believe firmly this first
Article of thy Faith, and with this intention, we
offer unto thee that prayer, of which thou thyself
art the Author.* Then we add, *Holy Mary,
Mother of our Lord* Jesus Christ, *obtain for us,
from thy beloved Son, to believe this Article, without feeling any doubt concerning it.* The same
method is observed in all the other Articles,
and almost in the same manner, we run over
the *Ten Commandments.* When we have jointly
repeated the first precept, which is, *To love
God,* we pray thus: O Jesus Christ, *thou Son
of the living God, grant us thy grace to love thee
above all things !* and immediately after we say
the *Lord's Prayer :* then, immediately we sub-
join, *O holy* Mary, *Mother of Jesus, obtain for
us, from thy Son, that we may have the grace to
keep this First Commandment.* After which we
say the *Ave Maria.* We observe the same
method through the other nine Commandments,
with such little variations as the matter may
require."

This is a fair specimen of Xavier's usual mode
of proceeding with the natives, whether heathen
or nominal Christians. How he can have expected them to comprehend this confusion of
doctrine and precept, is unaccountable. Perhaps he did not expect it ; and sought only to
obtain that implicit acquiescense in all that he
told them to believe and do, which the Roman
Church inculcates as the first duty of her children. This she calls, Christian humility ; and
these poor people were, in this respect, as humble as could be desired. In fact, they were
too much obliged to the Portuguese, and too
dependent upon their power to keep them from
being again reduced under the Mahomedan
yoke, to think of withholding their assent from

whatever their preceptor told them to believe. We are not surprised then at his numerical success; nor that he himself at last became ashamed of the converts whom he had used such means to instruct.

A. D.
1543.

He spent fifteen months among these thirty villages, giving, upon an average, about a fortnight to each; and he placed over the congregations formed in this perfunctory manner, the most intelligent persons he could find among them. These he taught to repeat what he had translated, which appears to have been their principal, if not their only qualification for the important task assigned them. Though unable to instruct the people in the doctrines and precepts of Christianity, they might at least serve to keep them together, and prevent their relapsing into paganism while Xavier was away. For these catechists he was enabled to provide salaries out of the public treasury; and he built churches in most of the villages where congregations were formed.

He made some attempts to gain the attention of the brahmins also, but with so little success that he soon desisted from the effort, and devoted himself almost exclusively to the poor Paravars; and when he left them for Goa, he took with him some of their most promising youths, to be educated for the ministry in the College of St. Paul.

A. D.
1544.

Returns to
Goa with
some youths
for educa-
tion; his
second visit
to the South.

14. He arrived at Goa about the end of January, 1544, where he did not remain long: for after depositing his young converts in the college, and obtaining three companions for his journey, he was impatient to return to the South. Having assigned to each of his colleagues a district on the coast, he penetrated alone further into the country. His mode of

proceeding among a people who had never
before heard of the Christian religion, cannot
be better described than in his own words.
He thus wrote to Mansilla, one of his colleagues.—"You may judge what manner of
life I lead here, by what I shall relate to you.
I am wholly ignorant of the language of the
people, and they understand as little of mine;
and I have no interpreter. All I can perform
is to baptize children, and serve the sick, an
employment easily understood, without the help
of an interpreter, by only minding what they
want." The language spoken between Madras
and Cape Comorin is the Tamul; which was,
therefore, the language of the Paravars, as it is
at this day: consequently his addresses were
still as unintelligible to them as to the inhabitants of the interior. How extraordinary then,
that he did not wait to make himself acquainted
with their language, and carry forward the
work he had so imperfectly begun on the coast,
before he undertook to administer the Christian
sacrament of baptism, as an *opus operatum*, to
a people in total ignorance of what he was
doing. His attention to the sick they could
not but appreciate; and about this time an
opportunity was given him to perform another
service for these people, which naturally deepened the favourable impression he had already
made on their minds towards himself.

15. The *Badages*, a barbarous and powerful
tribe of freebooters of *Bisnagar*, made an incur-
sion upon the country of the Paravars, whom
they drove away, and took possession of their
villages. Xavier no sooner received this intelligence than he applied for succour to the
nearest Portuguese station; and having obtained
twenty vessels, sufficiently equipped with arms

Invasion of
the Badages
—Xavier
succours the
Paravars.

and provisions, he followed the Paravars to their place of retreat, where he found them in a deplorable condition. Many had perished with hunger and from exposure to the sun; others were dying, and all were suffering the extremity of want. But at sight of their pastor they began to revive; and when he had fed and comforted them, he conveyed them back to their homes, having heard that the Badages had retired. He also raised a subscription among his friends to repair the poor peoples' losses, and left two missionaries with them for their protection.

His preaching and success in Travancore.

16. His attention was next directed to Travancore, the rajah of that country having been induced, at the solicitation of the Portuguese, to allow him to preach in his dominions. There he found a more numerous population; and, pursuing the same course as with the fishermen on the coast, he met with even greater success. He writes that, "in one month he baptized with his own hand ten thousand idolaters. And that frequently in one day, he baptized a well peopled village. He says also, that it was to him a most pleasing object to behold, that so soon as those infidels had received baptism, they ran, vying with each other, to demolish the temples of the idols." No less than forty-five churches were immediately built for the use of these converts. Those who know the care and patience required to inculcate divine truth upon the Hindoo mind, will be able correctly to estimate such rapid and wholesale conversions. Instead of improving by experience, and taking more pains to instruct the Malabars than he had bestowed upon the Paravars, he seems to have thought that they required even less preparation for baptism, and was satis-

fied with their demolition of the Hindoo idols
and pagodas, in proof of their sincerity. But
all this intemperate zeal naturally aroused the
anger of the brahmins, who regarded the missionary as an invader of their province, and laid
snares for his destruction, from which he is said
narrowly to have escaped.

17. While thousands were crowding into the
church, and the brahmins were venting their
impotent rage against the man who was thus
thinning the ranks of their devotees, the ma-
rauding Badages invaded the country of Travancore, in greater force and better armed than
when they went against the poor fishermen of
the coast. As soon as the rajah heard of their
approach he assembled his Naires, the military
caste of Travancore, to go out against them;
but he was much more indebted to the personal
courage of the missionary than to his own
troops. Xavier, after commending his converts
to God in prayer, encouraged a party of them
to follow him against the enemy. Knowing
the effect of resolution and superstition on the
ignorant and credulous mind, he resolved to
try the experiment upon these wild robbers,
and succeeded to his fullest expectation. With
a crucifix in his hand, he ran, at the head of
his little company, towards the plain, across
which the enemy were marching in battle array.
When he came near enough to be heard, he
stopped, and called to them in a commanding
tone—" I forbid you, in the name of the living
God, to pass further, and on his part command
you to return the way you came." The effect
was instantaneous. A panic seized the fore-
most ranks, which was soon communicated to
those who followed; and in a short time the

Frightens
an army of
Badages
out of the
country.

whole army was seen flying in consternation from the field.

18. The rajah naturally attributed this deliverance to the missionary, and in token of his gratitude, immediately published an edict favourable to Christianity, and commanded his subjects to attend to the preaching of the person to whom they were so greatly indebted. Xavier, however, while availing himself of the advantages thus obtained, did not take the honour of the achievement to himself, but desired the rajah to attribute it to Jesus Christ.

The fame of this heroic deed, and his zeal in other respects, now spread far and wide, and caused many applications to be sent to him from other parts to come over and help them. Seeing the fields, in his view of the prospect, thus white unto the harvest, and that nothing was wanting but a sufficient number of labourers to enter in and reap the fruit, he wrote to Ignatius, in Italy, to Rodriguez, in Portugal, and to the doctors of the Sorbonne, in Paris, to send him an ample supply of zealous missionaries. As his moving appeal to the consciences of those whom he addressed, may be as applicable to some learned protestants of the present age, it may be useful here to insert one of his letters.

Appeals to
different
quarters in
Europe for
mission-
aries.

19. " I have often thought, to run over all the Universities of Europe, and principally that of Paris, and to cry aloud to those who abound more in learning than in charity, ' Ah, how many souls are lost to heaven, through your default!' It were to be wished, that those people would apply themselves as diligently to the salvation of souls, as they do to the study of sciences; to the end that they might render to Almighty God a good account of their learning, and of the talents which he has bestowed on

them. Many, without doubt, moved with thoughts like these, would make a spiritual retreat, and give themselves the leisure of meditating on heavenly things, that they might listen to the voice of God. They would renounce their passions, and, trampling under foot all worldly vanities, would put themselves in a condition to follow the motions of the Divine will. They would say from the bottom of their hearts, ' Behold me in readiness, O my Lord, send me wheresover thou shalt please, even to the Indies, if thou commandest me.'

" Good God, how much more happily would those learned men then live, than now they do ! with how much more assurance of their salvation ! and in the hour of death, when they are ready to stand forth before the dreadful Judgment Seat, how much greater reason would they have to hope well of God's eternal mercy ; because they might say, O Lord, thou hast given me five talents, and behold I have added other five.

" I take God to witness, that not being able to return into Europe, I have almost resolved to write to the university of Paris, and namely to our masters, *Cornet* and *Picard*, that millions of idolaters might be easily converted, if there were more preachers, who would sincerely mind the interests of Jesus Christ, and not their own concernments."

He did write these letters ; but his appeal to the university of Paris produced no other effect, than to call forth one general burst of admiration. These warm admirers of his zeal and diligence, had no ambition to follow his example. [8]

---

[8] Let us, in dependance upon the Author of wisdom and

20. Xavier paid the Paravars a third visit, and was rejoiced to find the number of converts increasing under the missionaries he had left with them : so that he had to provide for their instruction far beyond his present means. Never

grace, hope for a better result from the following stirring appeal for more labourers in India, from the pious and energetic Bishop Wilson, of Calcutta—"Oh that our cry could reach the land of our fathers! Oh that a vision, not of a single man of Macedonia, but of the hundred and thirty-four millions of Hindoos and Mahomedans who are under British sway or British influence, might present itself to the pious students at our Universities, crying, "Come over to India, and help us!"

"Englishmen! you profess to long for the opportunity of spreading the Gospel; and will you, when the opening is presented, shrink back? Shall men call themselves Christians, and see the scholar, the philosopher, the mere traveller spring forth on the distant expedition, and not imitate their example for a much higher object? Shall commerce be never weary, never disconcerted in her enterprises; and shall Christianity go to sleep? Shall the civil and military services of India be sought for with avidity by the first families in the kingdom, and shall the service of Christ be declined? Shall the privations of a voyage, the languor of an enervating climate, or the increased hazard of disease never deter men for a moment in every other profession, and shall they deter them in this?

" What can exceed the inviting prospects which India presents! The fields white for the harvest, and awaiting the hand of the reaper! Nations bursting the intellectual sleep of thirty centuries! Superstitions no longer in the giant strength of youth, but doting to their fall. Britain placed at the head of the most extensive empire ever consigned to a Western Sceptre—that is, the only Great Power of Europe professing the Protestant Faith, entrusted with the thronging nations of Asia whom she alone could teach—a paternal government, employing every year of tranquillity in elevating and blessing the people unexpectedly thrown upon its protection.

" No devastating plague, as in Egypt—no intestine wars— no despotic Heathen or Mahomedan dominion prowling for its prey: but Legislation going forth with her laws—Science lighting her lamp—Education scattering the seeds of knowledge—Commerce widening her means of intercourse—the

did missionary live more among and for the people around him: and we cannot read of his sleepless nights spent in prayer, and of his unwearied labours by day, without feeling pained at heart to think that all this exertion was in a cause which proved, in almost all other hands, more opposed to the diffusion of Divine truth, and to the civil and religious liberties of man, than any system of tyranny ever devised. After every abatement that may be made from the

British power ever ready to throw her ægis around the pious and discreet Missionary.

"Oh, where are the first propagators and professors of Christianity? Where are our martyrs and Reformers? Where are the ingenious, devoted, pious sons of our Universities? Where are our younger devoted clergy? Are they studying their ease? Are they resolved on a ministry tame, ordinary, agreeable to the flesh? Are they drivelling after minute literature, poetry, fame? Do they shrink from that toil and labour, which, as Augustine says, OUR COMMANDER ("*Noster Imperator*") accounts most blessed?

"No: the truth is, honoured brethren, our English Youth and English Clergymen are uninformed, unread in eastern story. A deathlike obscurity hangs over so distant a scene. They know little of the fortunes of the Indian Church. They think of nothing but persecutions, exile, disease, and death, as connected with the missionary life. They are held back by a false humility. They are retained by the tears of sisters and friends. Let us unite, then, in removing misconceptions —Let us join in appealing to Societies—Let us write to particular friends and public bodies—Let us afford correct, intelligible information—Let us send specific and individual invitations—And let us *pray the Lord of the Harvest, that he would send forth more Labourers into his Harvest.*

"A false notion prevails, that it is a sort of martyrdom to come out to India as a missionary; whereas the real danger is on the side of ease, not privation. A young man in the military service has vastly more to encounter. A missionary in India has more than the comforts of a good English curacy. The single real difficulty is, an increased hazard of disease. Fifty Clergymen are now wanted for India. In the southern missions of the Incorporated Society alone, Twelve are indispensable. Missionary Register, 1836, pp. 104, 105.

extravagant accounts of his superstitious and credulous biographer, who represents this missionary as an apostle in gifts and direct communications with heaven, as well as in toils and dangers; it cannot be denied that he, like Saul of Tarsus, seems to have thought that he was doing God service,[9] though most mistaken in the means he used for that end.

His converts at Manaar cruelly persecuted.

21. During his present journey to the coast, he received an invitation from the natives of Manaar to pay them a visit. The inhabitants of this island are of the same caste and occupation as the Paravars, and many were soon induced to follow their example in embracing the Christian religion. They were subject to the rajah of Jaffnapatam, on the northern coast of Ceylon, who was much incensed at their becoming Christians, and persecuted them with unrelenting rage, putting men, women and children to the sword. Notwithstanding the imperfect instruction they had received, and the short time afforded them to prove the sincerity of their profession, may we not hope that some of them were true martyrs to the name of Jesus? It is said, that six or seven hundred of these poor people were slain on that occasion, and that several died with a constancy which astounded their executioners. The usual effect of persecution was seen here. The rajah's hope thereby to suppress Christianity was more than defeated, for it produced the opposite result. He had soon the mortification of seeing his courtiers and domestics embrace the new creed, and even his eldest son, whom, in disappointed rage, he put to death. Xavier is said to have envied these sufferers their crown of martyrdom; and he

---

[9] Acts xxvi. 9—11.

naturally cherished the expectation, that the Christian religion would flourish among a people, who evinced so much fortitude in bearing the Cross. He determined, however, to defend them to the utmost of his power; and though disappointed for the present, his efforts for their protection were ultimately successful.

22. The Portuguese viceroy was then at Cambaya, whither Xavier proceeded for the purpose of engaging him to take up arms against the rajah of Jaffnapatam. He embarked at Cochin, and one of his fellow passengers was a Portuguese gentleman, but a libertine and an atheist, who gloried in his infidelity. Xavier determined to make his acquaintance, with a view to his conversion; and by his courteous manners and diverting conversation, they soon became intimate. But the man would not allow the missionary to speak to him about his soul; and whenever his sins were touched upon, he flew into a rage, inveighing against the practices of the Church, and swearing that he would never more go to confession. Xavier, nothing daunted, would then resume his milder deportment, until he had again conciliated him, but without the least relaxation from his perseverance to bring him to confession. The vessel in which they sailed touching at Cannanore, they went on shore together, and took a walk in a neighbouring wood. They had not been long there before Xavier stripped himself to the waist, and then, taking a Discipline,[1] which was pointed with wires, inflicted upon his naked body so severe a chastisement, that his back and shoulders were soon covered with blood. He then cried to his companion—" It is for

His singular expedient to convert a libertine.

---

[1] An instrument of penance.

your sake that I do this, and it is nothing to what I would cheerfully suffer for your soul. But you have inflicted a much severer penalty on Jesus Christ. Will not His passion, nor His death, nor all His blood, suffice to soften the hardness of your heart? Then, lifting up his voice, he said—" O Lord, be pleased to look on thine own adorable blood, and not on that of so vile a sinner as I am!" All this produced the desired effect. For the man immediately threw himself at the father's feet, entreated him to forbear, and promised to confess and turn from his wicked course.

This is not the only instance of Xavier's undergoing such a penance for a similar purpose ; a practice at that time very common with the monks of the Roman church, not merely to work upon a sinner's feelings, so as to cause him to be ashamed of himself, and to bring him to repentance, but to obtain his pardon : and the people were taught to believe, that the merit of such self-inflicted pain was to be purchased with money.[2] We freely acquit Xavier of so base a motive. But while in his case we would fain look upon it only as expressive of the intense interest he took in the sinner's welfare, we cannot but de-

---

[2] There have been Romanists enlightened enough to see, and candid enough to own, the absurdity of these practices. The Abbè Fleury reprobates them in becoming terms.—" The severities which a pious monk himself would suffer for the sinner, were never effectual to the healing of the latter; for sin is not like a pecuniary debt, which another may pay for the debtor, and in any kind of money : it is a disease which can only be cured in the person of the sick. Further, these penances which another performed, were condemned by a national council in England, which was held in the year 747. And they gave this remarkable reason for it : that by this means the rich would more easily save themselves than the poor, which is contrary to the express word of the Gospel."— Discourses on Ecclesiastical History, p. 164.

plore the infatuation which is thus seen to have possessed his mind. To know what toils and privations a faithful pastor undergoes for his flock, cannot fail to impress them with gratitude and love. If they have any convictions of sin, and any desire for their salvation, they will surely repent of those iniquities which cause so much painful anxiety to him who watches and prays for their souls.[3] But this is very different from these foolish, and worse than foolish penances of the monks, whose only effect could be to confirm the people in their ignorance and superstition. That Xavier could resort to the practice, how benevolent soever his intention, is another evidence of the prostration of his understanding, his absolute subjection to the carnal ordinances of his church.

A. D. 1544.

23. In the following year, 1545, he sailed again for Travancore; but the westerly winds preventing his making that coast, he concluded it to be the will of God that he should bend his course to another region. Under this conviction he bore away to the eastward, in order to visit Malacca and the Molucca isles, where the Portuguese had carried on a flourishing trade, chiefly in spices, since the year 1510. He went first to Malacca, where he arrived on the 25th September. His fame having preceded him, the natives flocked to the beach to welcome him, as soon as they heard of his arrival. There, as formerly at Goa, he found the Portuguese extremely ignorant, and abandoned to the grossest debaucheries; and again he rightly judged it to be his first duty to endeavour to reclaim them. Knowing, however, the difficulty of the task; for a sinner's pride is often more

A. D. 1545. His voyage to the Eastern isles, and successes there.

[3] Col. ii. 1, 2.

sensitive than the greenest wound; he touched their vices tenderly, not venturing at once to startle them with severe invectives, but endeavouring by kindness and courtesy to win their confidence. When he thought that he had gained the desired influence over them, he began to address himself to their wicked courses, and succeeded in bringing many to confession: but he did not wait there long enough to see whether a permanent reformation was effected in their conduct. His efforts for the conversion of the natives not meeting with the immediate success to which he had become accustomed among the Indians, he grew impatient, and soon departed for Amboyna, where he was more successful, a great number of the inhabitants embracing Christianity without delay. Here he passed some months, building churches in several villages, and preparing the most promising of the converts to officiate in them, until they should be provided with regular missionaries.

The next place he visited was the island of Ternate, where also he had to commence with the reformation of the dissolute Europeans. Here he was the means of converting a Mahomedan princess, who had lost her sons and her dominions through the wicked intrigues of the Portuguese. Her name was, Neachilé, whom, after much persuasion, he induced to embrace the Christian faith; and he baptized her by the name of Isabella. Under his instructions, she is said to have become so eminent for piety and charity, as to be more esteemed, both by natives and Portuguese, than when in the plenitude of her power.

His hazardous mission to the isles of Del Moro. 24. While at Ternate, he heard of the diabolical character of the inhabitants of the islands of Del Moro, and determined to visit them. His friends, alarmed for his safety, endeavoured to dissuade him from his purpose; but Xavier, we have seen, courted danger, and aspired to the martyr's crown. Though we would desire for every missionary of the church of Christ a more enlightened zeal than that of this apostle of his infant order, yet his answer to those who wished to detain him, deserves the consideration of every one engaged in the service of God, especially when called to an enterprise of unusual peril. Finding their entreaties of no avail, they induced the governor of Ternate to issue a decree, forbidding, under severe penalties, any vessel to transport him to those islands. He was much displeased at this attempt to constrain him, and said—" Where are those people who dare to confine the power of Almighty God, and have so mean an apprehension of our Saviour's love and grace? Are there any hearts hard enough to resist the influences of the Most High, when it pleases Him to soften and to change them? Can they stand in opposition to that gentle, and yet commanding force, which can make the dry bones live, and raise up children to Abraham from stones? What, shall He, who has subjected the whole world to the cross, by the ministry of the Apostles, shall He exempt from that subjection, this petty corner of the universe? Shall then the Isle del Moro be the only place, which shall receive no benefit of redemption? And when Jesus Christ has offered to the Eternal Father, all the nations of the earth as His inheritance, were these people excepted out of the donation? I acknowledge them to be very barbarous and brutal, and let it be granted that they were more inhuman than they are, it is because I can do nothing of my-

o

self, that I have the better hopes of them. I can do all things in Him who strengthens me, and from whom alone proceeds the strength of of those who labour in the Gospel."

He then added a pungent rebuke, saying, "That other less savage nations, would never want for preachers: that these only isles remained for him to cultivate, since no other man would undertake them. If they abounded with precious woods, and mines of gold, Christians would have the courage to go thither; and all the dangers of the world would not be able to affright them; they are base and fearful, because there are only souls to purchase. And shall it then be said, that charity is less daring than avarice? You tell me they will take away my life, either by the sword or poison; but those are favours too great for such a sinner as I am to expect from heaven. Yet I dare confidently say that whatever torment or death they prepare for me, I am ready to suffer a thousand times more, for the salvation of only one soul. If I should happen to die by their hands, who knows but all of them might receive the faith? for it is most certain, that since the primitive times of the church, the seed of the Gospel has made a larger increase in the fields of paganism, by the blood of the martyrs, than by the sweat of missionaries."

In this spirit he embarked, and many, who before would gladly have detained him, were now induced to bear him company. On landing at the first island they made, he witnessed a spectacle that would have daunted the hearts of most men, however resolute at a distance from danger. Several bodies of Portuguese, who had been recently murdered, were lying on the shore in their blood, and the savages standing over them: but on the appearance of Xavier and his company, they fled into the woods, probably concluding that they were come to avenge the murder of their countrymen. The missionary quietly followed them, and, addressing them in a conciliatory manner, induced them to return to their homes, where he afterwards laboured hard to tame their wild spirits. Knowing that " Music has charms to soothe the savage breast," he added the melody of voices to the suavity of his address, and had the satisfaction of seeing the ferocity of some yield to the influence of his gentle arts. Those whose minds were too rugged to be so mollified, he endeavoured to alarm, by leading them to the craters of their volcanos, and there making them understand, that the smoke, the flames, the showers of stones and flowing lava which they saw, were descriptive of the tortures of the damned. Indeed, he did not hesitate to tell them that " the gaping mouths of those burning mountains were the breathing places of hell." How far they understood him, it is difficult to say; but they were so far reclaimed as to permit him to move about wherever he chose, and to erect crosses and churches throughout their island: but we are not informed for *whom* these churches were erected. He does not appear to have converted any of the savages, or to have left any Christians behind; so that it is hard to imagine who could require them.

25. At Java he could make no such impression upon the barbarians. Indeed, his life was in imminent danger among them; and on one occasion, while preaching to them on the river's bank, they endeavoured to stone him to death. But, more true to the instinct of nature than to his aspirations after the glory of martyrdom, he

Royal con-
vert at
Ternate.

made his escape on a log of timber, which was lying at hand, himself thrusting it into the water, and floating upon it out of their reach.

26. From these wild regions he returned to Ternate, where he tried to convert the reigning prince, Cacil Aerio, but without effect. This man listened to the Father's instructions, out of respect, no doubt, for the Portuguese, through whose influence he had just been raised to the throne; but he showed no affection for Christianity. Indeed, he afterwards became a cruel persecutor of the converts, not sparing even his own mother-in-law, Isabella, whom he reduced to poverty. But she is said to have shone brighter in the furnace, and to have endured all her sufferings with exemplary submission as to the Divine will. How satisfactory must it have been to Xavier to witness this proof of his distinguished convert's sincerity! He prolonged his visit here several months, and spent some of his time in composing, and having translated into Malay, a catechism on the doctrines and precepts of the Gospel, which he appointed to be used in all the churches where that language was spoken. He then signified his intention to return to Malacca; and on his departure, multitudes followed him to the shore, where, as the vessel got under weigh, they raised a universal cry of lamentation that went to his heart.

A. D.
1547.
More Mis-
sionaries
arrive.

27. In her passage, the vessel touched at Amboyna, where Xavier tarried twenty days, confirming the converts. Proceeding on their voyage, they arrived at Malacca, in July, 1547, and found there three missionaries, John Beyra, Nugnez Ribera, and Nicholas Nugnez, on their way to the Moluccas. They had been sent out in compliance with Xavier's request; and he had the satisfaction of hearing from them, that seven more missionaries arrived with them in In-

dia, several of whom had remained in charge of the converts among the fishermen on the coast.

28. At this period the Portuguese obtained a decisive victory over the forces of Acheen, from the island of Sumatra; and Xavier was on the eve of embarking for Goa with the news, when the China fleet arrived, bringing a native of distinction from the island of Japan, whose acquaintance with Xavier led to important consequences. His name was Anger; he was about thirty-five years of age, rich, and of noble birth. Hitherto he had led a dissolute life, and in a quarrel had killed a man, whether intentionally or accidentally is uncertain. Disturbed in his conscience, he retreated from Coxigana, his native city, to the mountains and woods, both for the sake of the solitude they afforded, and also for the counsel and consolation of the Bonzes (heathen priests), and other recluses who had retired to the same recesses. But finding no rest there, he returned to the city, and made the acquaintance of some Portuguese, who had been at Japan two years, and were then carrying on a thriving trade. Hoping that these strangers might lead him to the rest which he sought in vain from his own country priests and their superstitions, he made known to them the uneasiness of his mind. They immediately told him of Francis Xavier, advised him to take a voyage to Malacca, for the purpose of consulting that holy Father, and assured him that he would pour the balm of consolation into his troubled soul. "A wounded spirit who can bear?"[3] And what trouble or expense will the sufferer deem too great for its recovery? The afflicted Anger did not hesitate to follow the advice of his Portuguese friends, and willingly

[3] Prov. xviii. 14.

undertook a voyage of eight hundred leagues in quest of peace of mind; but he was greatly disappointed on his first arrival to find that Xavier was away at the Moluccas. He returned home at that time; but still labouring under the same distress, was induced to make a second voyage to Malacca, which had nearly proved as unsuccessful as the former, for he arrived only just in time to catch the Father. Here he is said to have obtained, through Xavier's instructions and prayers, that composure of spirit, which he had failed to procure in solitude, or from pagan rites and priests. He soon avowed his determination to embrace the Christian faith; but Xavier recommended him to proceed with his two attendants to Goa, to be more fully instructed previous to his baptism. This advice was given with reference to the hopes which the missionary began to entertain, that this man might become the means of introducing the Gospel into the island of Japan.

29. Xavier, intending to visit the coast, sent the Japonese before him to Goa. He himself arrived at Cochin, January 21st, 1548, and proceeded without delay to make arrangements for the future supervision of the numerous congregations in the South. Appointing Antonio Criminal general superintendent, he assembled the ecclesiastics, examined their several qualifications, and gave them suitable instructions. Having himself found great inconvenience from his ignorance of the native language, he admonished them to study it without loss of time. He drew up some excellent rules for their guidance in the general affairs of the mission, that they might act in concert with each other, and in perfect obedience to their superintendent: and then he concluded his address with an earnest exhortation to them to do all things in their

power to make themselves beloved by the people, assuring them that they would thereby be able to do more good among them, than by being feared. They were to deal with the convert's faults with a due consideration for their recent deliverance from idolatry: and though he recommended them to " wink at " more than a protestant missionary would think it right to overlook, yet it is impossible not to admire the affectionate spirit that breathes through his instructions. Had his brethren, the Jesuits, in India, been always animated by a similar spirit, their instructions would have proved more permanent, and their labours would have redounded more to the Saviour's glory.

30. Xavier availed himself of this opportunity to visit the rajah of Jaffnapatam, the cruel persecutor of the Manaar Christians, and had the address to persuade him to form an alliance with the Portuguese, and take some of their soldiers into his pay. This he hoped would guarantee the safety of his poor converts. He next went to the island of Ramisseram, at the entrance of the Gulf of Manaar, for the purpose of visiting its celebrated pagoda, to which multitudes of pilgrims resort from all parts of Southern India. He was not permitted to approach it, but he lifted up his voice against its abominations, crying aloud to the assembled crowds, to turn from these vanities to the living God. None, however, gave heed to his warning, and he could only retire to fast and pray for their souls. He is said to have planted a banian shrub, in a rocky dell in the vicinity of this strong-hold of idolatry, which grew a great tree, and the shadow of whose branches afforded a shelter from the vertical sun to some proselytes, who, several years after, fixed their habitations

Conciliates the rajah of Jaffnapatam: visits Ramisseram.

around it. To this day it continues the centre of attraction to some romanists, who venerate the memory of the man by whose hand it was planted.

Returns to Goa. Baptism of three Japonese.

31. From Ramisseram he returned to Ceylon, where he embarked for Goa, being accompanied by an ambassador to the viceroy from the rajah of Jaffnapatam. They reached Goa, March 20th, 1548, and again found the viceroy absent to the northward, at the Gulf of Cambay. As Xavier was anxious to see him after so long an absence, he followed him thither, and met with a kind, and indeed, honourable reception; for he was now regarded by all classes as worthy of every attention which they could show him, or that he would consent to receive. Returning to Goa, he took up his abode in the College of St. Paul, which he was glad to find in a flourishing condition. The Japonese, Anger, was among the most diligent of the students, continuing steadfast in his Christian profession, and promising to fulfil Xavier's expectations with reference to his native country. At length, both he and his two attendants were baptized by the Bishop, D'Albuquerque, Anger receiving the name of Paul de Saint Foy. Xavier now discoursed much with him about Japan, as well as with the Portuguese who had been to that distant island; and he was not long in coming to a determination to visit it, in company with his Japonese converts. From the time that he formed this intention, his thoughts were almost exclusively given to the subject; but before his departure, he made the best arrangements in his power for the native churches in India. Five more missionaries had recently arrived, whom he distributed among the congregations; several students of the college of St. Paul were ordained, and appointed to dis-

tant churches; and not a few of the native
converts in Travancore, and even of the poor
fishermen, were deemed competent to officiate
as catechists.

32. Nor was he inattentive to the religious
wants of the Portuguese, whose reformation he
had been so instrumental in effecting. He
wrote to the King of Portugal, describing the
necessities of his subjects in India, reminding
him of his responsibilities as a Christian monarch, and entreating him, by his love for the
Lord and zeal for His glory, to send out more,
many more religious teachers. Would, that this
appeal were heard and regarded by all Christian princes and governors! Awful indeed will
be the account which they will one day have
to render of their responsibilities, unless they
are as diligent to discharge them for the glory
of God and the salvation of men, as they are to
preserve and extend their own dominions, and
exact obedience to their authority.

33. He also sent Gaspar Barzæus on a mission to Ormuz, at the entrance of the Persian
gulf, with particular injunctions to preach boldly
against the vices of that dissolute place; to be
instant in season and out of season; and to attend
with diligence and affection to persons of all ages,
and all sorts and conditions. His instructions
were, in fact, a transcript of the rules he followed
in his own proceedings, under all circumstances,
and with every description of people.[4]

Having now settled matters to his satisfaction, and appointed Paul de Camerine superior-
general, and Antonio Gomez rector of the

---

[4] These rules contain much valuable matter; and if they
were followed in the spirit in which we believe them to have
been delivered, they could not but prove a benefit to the
people.

College of St. Paul; he embarked for Japan in April, 1549. His companions were, Cozmo de Torrez and John Fernandez, besides the Japonese, Paul de Saint Foy, and his two attendants, John and Antony. They also took two missionaries to Malacca, where they were detained some time, in consequence of the dangerous illness of Alphonso Martinez, the Bishop's grand vicar, whose mind was more afflicted by reflections upon his past life, than his body was by disease. Xavier attended him with all the assiduity of true friendship, and had the satisfaction of seeing him more composed before his death; but whether his composure proceeded from faith in the Redeemer to pardon his sins and make his peace with God, we are not informed. Soon after his decease, the party for Japan again set sail, and arrived at Coxigana in the month of August, where Xavier took up his abode for some time with his disciple, Paul de Saint Foy. It would detain us too long to enter into a description of his proceedings and successes in this island. His mode of instruction, if instruction it can be called, was similar to that which he had adopted in India; and to use the words of a Jesuit missionary in South India, " his spiritual labours were crowned with far greater success" (than in India), " and laid the foundation of those once numerous and flourishing congregations of Japonese Christians, who, within a period of less than a century, amounted to more than a million of souls."[5]

[5] Letters on the State of Christianity in India. By the Abbé J. A. Dubois, Missionary in Mysore, pp. 3, 4. This mission flourished only about sixty years, when the Jesuits' intrigues and insolence brought upon the Christians a persecution which ended in their extermination. Golownin's and Krusentern's Narratives; and see Reply to the Abbé Dubois by the author, p. 86, &c.

This was the result of little more than two years' exertions, at the expiration of which period, in November, 1551, he embarked for Goa, where he remained but a short time. Still aspiring to further honours in the missionary vineyard, he soon sailed again for China; but now his course was run. When they had proceeded on the voyage as far as the island of Sancian, he was taken ill, and desired to be put on shore. His request was complied with indeed, but the officers and crew of the vessel shamefully neglected him; for they left him to die in a miserable shed, exposed to the fervid beams of a vertical sun by day, and to the cold winds by night. He expired December 2d, 1552, and was immediately put into the ground without much ceremony. But, at the request of his two friends, and ashamed, probably, of having paid so little respect to the remains of so distinguished a man, they disinterred his body, for the purpose of transporting it into India. Touching at Malacca, Pereyra, the friend of the departed missionary, had the corpse taken out of the rude case that enclosed it, and wrapping it in a gold cloth, put it into a coffin of precious wood, which he covered with a rich damask. In this state it was conveyed to India, performing on the passage, the romanists say, several miraculous cures. On its arrival at Goa, it was received with due solemnity, put into a coffin enchased with silver and *precious stones*, and enshrined in a monument of exquisite art.[6]

35. Thus terminated the career of this extraordinary man at forty-six years of age, ten and a half of which had been spent in India and the eastern isles. Had his history been trans-

Margin notes:

A. D. 1551.

Dies at the island of Sancian, within sight of China, and is conveyed to Goa for interment.

A. D. 1552.

Concluding remarks.

---

[6] Buchanan's Christian Researches, p.160.

mitted to us devoid of the absurd stories which
his biographer has crowded into it, we should
have read it with feelings resembling those with
which we peruse the lives of Fenelon, Pascal,
Charles Borromeo, and other worthies of the
Roman Church. Though these devout men
were connected with a system, many of whose
fundamental tenets are subversive of the essential doctrines of Christianity, yet their spirits
rose above their creed; and their disinterested
zeal, their fervent devotion, their simple faith
in the Lord Jesus, and their love for mankind,
command our admiration. But, in the instance
of Francis Xavier, our feelings are revolted, instead of conciliated, by the grossness of the
attempt to make his labours and triumphs subservient to the declining reputation of the Roman Church. This is sufficiently apparent
from the following paragraph with which his
Memoirs conclude.[7]

" As to what remains, if Xavier was endued
with all Apostolical virtues, does it not follow,
that the religion which he preached, was that
of the Apostles? Is there the least appearance
that a man, who was chosen by God to destroy
idolatry and impiety in the New World, should
be himself an idolater and a wicked man, in
adoring Jesus Christ upon the altars, in invok-
ing of the Holy Virgin, in engaging himself to
God by vows, in desiring indulgences from the
Pope, in using the sign of the cross and holy
water for the cure of the sick, in praying, and
saying masses for the dead? In fine, is it possible to believe, that this holy man, this new
Apostle, this second St. Paul, continued all his
life in the way of perdition, and instead of en-

---

[7] Dryden's Translation, p. 768.

joying, at this present time, the happiness of the Saints, endures the torments of the damned? Let us then pronounce, concluding this work as we began it, that the life of St. Francis Xavier, is an authentic testimony of the truth of the Gospel; and that we cannot strictly observe, what God has wrought by the ministry of his servant, without a full satisfaction in this point, that the Catholic, Apostolic, and Roman Church, is the Church of our Saviour Jesus Christ."

God forbid that so harsh an inference should be drawn against such a man: but we must also protest against this conclusion in favour of the Church of Rome, as though it were a legitimate deduction from " these testimonies, and from all the Book." The miraculous powers attributed to Xavier, which are here regarded as the testimony of God in confirmation of the doctrines which he preached, we leave to be examined when a fair attempt shall have been made to prove that he himself claimed them. When the miracles which he is said to have performed while alive, as well as the marvellous cures, pretended to have been wrought by the contact, and even in the presence of his corpse, shall have been as well authenticated as any other admitted facts in the page of history, it will be soon enough to believe them. To contend with Romish legends is to beat the air, and we have no inclination to maintain such a combat.

While, however, we suspend the consideration of these marvellous tales, merely protesting, for the present, against the unfair use that has been made of them; we need not defer our inquiry into the character of his converts, whose vast numbers have been triumphantly appealed to for the same purpose. Had their character been such as every devout and sincere Christian must have approved, it would have spoken favourably, indeed, of the moral instructions they received; but it would not have sanctioned the idolatry of the Virgin and the mass, the iniquitous traffic of papal indulgences, the holy water used for the cure of the sick, and numerous other superstitions of Rome. His converts, however, were *not* of the character here assumed. This fact we learn, not from a member of a hostile Church, nor from one of a rival order in his own Church, but from *a Jesuit missionary of thirty years' experience in the very scene of Xavier's labours*, who thus writes of him and his disciples:—" One of the first missionaries (to India) was St. Francis Xavier, a Spanish Jesuit of the greatest merit, and animated with a truly apostolical zeal, and still known under the appellation of the *Apostle of India*. He traversed several provinces of India, and is said to have made many thousand converts,[8] at a period when the prejudices of the natives against the Christian religion were far from reaching the height they have since attained."

" Xavier soon discovered in the manners and prejudices of the natives an insurmountable bar to the progress of Christianity among them, as appears from the printed letters, still extant,

[8] " It is asserted, that he baptized upwards of a million of infidels;" but the proselytes in the eastern islands are, doubtless, included in this number. Tennant's Thoughts on India, pp. 172 and 230. See the charge of Dr. Middleton (afterwards Bishop of Calcutta) to the Rev. C. A. Jacobi. Report of the Society for Promoting Christian Knowledge, 1813, p. 63.

which he wrote to St. Ignatius Loyola, his

...st Francis Xavier, entirely disheart-
...the invincible obstacles he every where
...s apostolic career, and by the apparent
...ility of making real converts, left the
country in disgust, after a stay in it of only two
or three years." [9]

This account of Xavier's reason for quitting
India speaks more favourably for his character
than all the idle and puerile stories invented to
exalt his reputation. But it does not speak so
well for his church, which was, probably, his
biographer's reason for suppressing the fact.
Considering the very superficial instruction
which, as we have seen, he gave his proselytes,
it is hard to imagine how he could have expected
them to become better Christians than are here
described? What an appalling instance does he
present of the thraldom of a noble spirit under a
system of darkness! Moving among the natives
of India with all his energy of mind, his kind
condescension and earnest entreaties, he must
have commended almost any system to a people
so unaccustomed to think for themselves as
the low caste Hindoos. But they had no foundation of scriptural instruction laid in their
minds; they wanted to be taught to build up

[9] Letters by the Abbé Dubois, pp. 2, 3. When this writer
limits the time that Xavier spent in India to two or three
years, he must be understood to omit the period of his absence
at the eastern isles. This Jesuit missionary has given a similar
description of his own converts, and those of his brethren,
stating, that they 'experienced nothing but the most distressing disappointments, and all their labours have terminated in nothing'—Letters, pp. 133—135. This important
testimony will be more appropriately considered at a subsequent period of the Jesuit missions.

themselves in the faith they had embraced, in
dependence on Divine grace to illu[...]
strengthen them, instead of being l[...]
opus operatum of the Romish ordina[...]
wonder, then, that they had little [...]
Christianity than the name. But Xa[...]
not be satisfied with this, although he knew not
how to remedy the evil. He had formed a
higher estimate of the Christian character than
these proselytes had attained, or could attain,
under such tuition, and hence the 'disgust'
with which he turned away from them. While
his church has exulted in their numbers, and
lauded them in most extravagant terms; they
fell too far below Xavier's standard, and his
honest mind was grieved to see them so unworthy of the name they bore. We honour him
for the feeling, and verily believe that the integrity of purpose which it manifested, would
have caused him to revolt at the attempt to
impose on the world with a spurious account
of his miraculous powers. We have no wish
to depreciate his memory; quite the contrary.
As a minister of Christianity, he had great
faults; but they were the faults of the system
which inthralled his mind. His personal character appears to have been unexceptionable;
and this, as well as his standard of Christian
morals for his disciples, may be fairly attributed
to the instructions and impressions he had received in early life through his protestant associates at Paris. His missionary character also,
in many respects, is worthy of admiration. For
grandeur of design and diligence in the execution; for disinterested love to man; for bold
fidelity to persons of the highest, and engaging
condescension to men of the lowest estate; for
unwearied devotion, self-denial, renunciation of

the world, intrepidity in dangers, and many
superior. stimable qualities; he has left behind
"At l example which few have surpassed
encd by e Apostles' days. Could all this pure
met in h ave been detached from the dross with
impossil it was mixed, and cast into the mould
of God's word, he would have formed one of the
brightest and best instruments ever used to
deliver mankind from the bondage of Satan,
and restore them to their rightful Lord.

Considering the essential service which this
devoted missionary performed for the see of
Rome, we are not surprised that he was canonized by the pope,[1] nor that this greatly increased his reputation with the members of the
Romish Church in the East. A Jesuit missionary to China has given the following account
of the reverence paid to the spot where his
body is supposed to have been interred in the
island where he died.

"The touch of his body consecrated the
place of his burial. That island became not
only a famous place, but also an holy land.
Even the heathen honoured it, and fled thither,
as to a city of refuge. In the mean time pirates
haunted those coasts, that no vessels dared to
go thereabouts; so that the place, where this
sacred tomb lay, was quite unknown to the
Europeans; and it is but a little while ago,
that they discovered it by a particular accident.

"In the year 1688, a Portuguese vessel

[1] Some 'Sober Questions' relating to the Canonization
of Francis Xavier, may be seen in the Portuguese MSS. presented to the British Museum by W. Marsden, Esq., vo. 9855,
entitled, Additional MSS.

The same collection contains a particular account of the
Japan Mission, which Xavier established, given in the original
correspondence of the Jesuit Missionaries from the year 1585
—1625, vo's. 9853, 9856—9860.

which, coming from Goa, had on board the
governor of Macao, was seized by a sudden
gust of wind, and forced to let the ship drive
towards these islands, do what they could. They
cast anchor between the isles of Sancian and
Lampaco, which were so near one another, as
to make a kind of haven. Contrary winds,
continuing eight days, gave father Caroccio, a
Jesuit who was on board, an opportunity of
satisfying his devout resolutions. He went on
shore, and was resolved, in spite of danger, to
go in search of the Saint's tomb. The pilot
and most part of the sailors followed him, and
they searched the whole island, but to no purpose.

" At last a Chinese, an inhabitant of the
place, imagining with himself, what it was
which they so ardently sought after, undertook
to guide them, and led them to a place which
all the inhabitants reverenced, and where he
himself began to perform actions and gestures
of piety. The father, who could not understand him, began to search about for some sign
or mark of the sepulchre, and found at last a
stone five cubits long, and three broad, upon
which were cut these words in Latin, Portuguese, Chinese, and Japonnese, *Here* XAVIER,
a man truly apostolical, was buried. Then they
all fell on their knees, and did with devotion
kiss that earth, which the tears and last groans
of that apostle had sanctified. The inhabitants
of the place came in and followed the example
of the Portuguese; even the English, for one
of their vessels came to an anchor in the same
place, came thither to honour the saint, and
prayed a great while at his tomb. Father
Caroccio some time after said mass in his pontificals, while the two vessels, the English and

Portuguese, did several times discharge their artillery, and gave marks of their common joy.

" Lastly, to preserve the memory of that holy place, they resolved to build a good square wall all round the tomb, and to dig a ditch to secure it from all inundations. In the midst between these walls, they raised the stone which they found overturned, and built an altar, as a memorial of the august sacrifice of the eucharist, which had been offered up there, which might also serve to celebrate it upon again, if either accident or devotion should carry the ministers of Jesus Christ thither any more. The people of the place did themselves assist towards the carrying on this little work, and shewed as much zeal for the honour of the saint as the Christians did." [2]

After this from a man of literature,[3] we cannot be surprised that the ignorant and superstitious inhabitants of India should be prevailed upon to invoke Xavier as a tutelary saint. There is an old idol [4] of him near Cape Comorin, to which even the heathen, as well as romanists, go on pilgrimage. Such impiety cannot be too deeply deplored. At the same time let us pray, that every future missionary of a purer creed may have grace to live as much to the Redeemer's glory, and to the extension of His kingdom in the world, as Francis Xavier lived for the reputation of his *Order*, and for the interests of the *Roman Church*.

[2] Lewis Le Comte, Memoirs and Remarks upon the Empire of China, London, 1738, pp. 355—357.

[3] L. Le Comte was one of six mathematicians sent to China by Louis XIV. of France.

[4] This idol is called, the Pagoda of Para-padri, that is, the temple, or swami house, of the great father, or minister.— La Croze, p. 302.

CHAPTER IV.

INQUISITION AT GOA.

A. D.
1560. NOT long after the death of Francis Xavier, the
Inquisition was introduced at Goa. This expedient for maintaining the cause of Rome in
India was very different from the self-denying
labours and voluntary sufferings of that devoted
missionary, whose life we have just reviewed.
This tribunal was established in Europe as
early as the twelfth century, by one Dominic,
a friar, assisted by his brethren. They were
sent throughout the papal dominions, by Pope
Innocent III., to denounce the vengeance of
the Church against all heretics, and to stir up
the sovereigns of the countries wherever they
went, to inquire minutely into the characters
and circumstances of all persons suspected of
disaffection to Rome, and to transmit a faithful
account of them to the ' Holy Office,' with a
view to their extirpation. Hence this horrid
tribunal was called the Inquisition; and in a
few years it was established in almost all the
kingdoms under the Pope's domination. The
Waldenses were among its first victims, many
thousands of them being put to death by fire
and sword. Dominic sent forth a vast number
of persons, wearing crosses, to execute this
work of destruction, and caused the friars of

his order to promise plenary indulgences to all who should assist in the diabolical crusade. His myrmidons, the cross bearers, deluged many countries with blood, and burnt alive great numbers of those whom they had apprehended.

In the year 1557, John III., King of Portugal, erected the Inquisition in his dominions, after the model of that which had long existed in Spain; and three years after, in 1560, Cardinal Henry, *Inquisitor* general of Portugal, caused it to be established at Goa. At first, both in Europe and India, the Portuguese Inquisitors proceeded chiefly against those suspected of Judaism, whom they treated with extreme severity: but they soon began to torture with equal inhumanity all who were convicted of heresy, of whatever description. And they dealt thus cruelly, not only with the heretics themselves, but also with every one supposed to have known of their heresy without divulging it. So that persons of all ranks in society stood in such awe of this tribunal, that parents informed against their children, husbands against their wives, and wives against their husbands: and none durst be seen deploring the doom of those whom they had delivered up to its officers, however close the tie that connected them, or whatever tortures they might be doomed to suffer.

The officers of this horrid institution are,— 1. *The Inquisitor General.*—2. *The Chief Inquisitors*, or counsellors of the Supreme Court. —3. *The ordinary Inquisitors*, who are commonly secular priests.—4. *The Assessors*, ecclesiastical lawyers, who are consulted by the Inquisitors. — 5. *Qualificators*, [who are commonly Dominicans, and their office is to correct heretical books.—6. *The Secretary*, who takes down the evidence given before the Inquisitor. —7. *The Advocate Fiscal*, whose office it is to prosecute the prisoner.—8. *The Treasurer*, who takes charge of the prisoners' property as soon as they are committed, and holds it subject to the Inquisitors' orders.—9. *The Familiars*, or bailiffs, whose duty it is to apprehend the accused. Noblemen have often been employed in this office.—10. *Jailers* and *Alcaides*.

The mode of receiving information against persons ; of their apprehension and trial ; their prison and tortures, with other terrific details, are so faithfully given by one who was for some time incarcerated at Goa, and narrowly escaped with his life, that his descriptions will be chiefly adopted in the following account. At the same time it should be remarked, that his statement agrees with the most authentic histories of the Inquisition in Spain, Portugal, and other Catholic countries.[1] It is also admitted, by an Inquisitor at Goa, that his descriptions of the dungeons, of the torture, of the mode of trial, and of the Auto da Fé, were, in general, just ; but he said that he judged untruly of the motives of the Inquisitors, and very uncharitably of the character of the Holy Church.[2] Of this we shall soon be able to form an opinion.

The writer in question was M. Dellon, a young French physician, who went to India to practice his profession. He commenced at

[1] See Limborch's ' History of the Inquisition,' Translated by Samuel Chandler. Also this translator's ' History of Persecution.' Gonsalvius Montanus' ' Arts of the Spanish Inquisition.' Geddes' ' View of the Inquisition in Portugal.' M. Dellon's ' Relation de L'Inquisition de Goa.' M'Crie's ' Histories of the Reformation in Spain and Italy.'

[2] Buchanan's Christian Researches, p. 166. Also The Church of England Magazine for 1837, 1838.

Damaun, a considerable station of the Portuguese about one hundred miles North of Bombay. He describes himself as a strict Romanist, who took great pains to propagate his creed, and met with considerable success. He was well versed in the Bible and the theology of his church, but too inexperienced to pay sufficient attention to his own safety in his intercourse with the Portuguese and Italian priests. Living on friendly terms with the Dominicans, and discoursing one day with a friar of their order on the subject of baptism, his remarks were more free than agreeable to his companion. He also spake disparagingly of the adoration of images, which he refused to kiss. Accordingly, he was soon suspected of heresy; and this suspicion was strengthened by his endeavours to dissuade one of his patients from placing such implicit confidence in an ivory image, which he was incessantly kissing. The sick man, a Portuguese, shocked at his impiety, as he deemed it, called him a heretic: and a short time after, another instance of the kind occurred, which tended to confirm the suspicion against him. He was equally bold in his observations upon the Inquisition, saying to a companion, who had called that office infallible, that the Inquisitors were fallible men; at the same time he exulted in the fact, that the French had never admitted that fearful tribunal into their country.

All this excited against him such a violent prejudice, that he began to fear that they would report him to the Inquisitors: for though a Frenchman, yet every one residing within the Portuguese territories was regarded as amenable to the "holy office." He determined, therefore, to anticipate them. By a law of the

Inquisition, all who accused themselves before their apprehension were absolved from any offence which they had committed against the Church : accordingly M. Dellon thought it advisable to go to the *Commissary* of the Inquisition at Damaun, with whom he had some acquaintance, and relate all that had transpired. That officer received him with apparent kindness, probably in consequence of letters of recommendation which he had brought to him from some mutual friends, and advised him to be more guarded in future. The commissary, while admitting that the ignorant people had departed from the doctrines of the Fathers in some trivial matters relating to the adoration of images, yet told him, that it did not become him to undertake to correct them. After this he took his leave, promising to be more circumspect in future ; and he naturally concluded that he should hear no more about it : in this, however, he was painfully mistaken.

A young lady residing at Damaun happened to be much admired both by the Portuguese governor and her confessor ; and the latter is said to have endeavoured to violate her chastity when at confession. The young Frenchman also paid her some attention ; and being more favourably received than the other two, their jealousy was excited, and they determined to effect his ruin. Not having any suspicion of their design, he continued to associate with them with all the confidence of friendship : until, when returning one night from the house of a lady whose daughter and granddaughter he had cured of an alarming distemper, he was stopped by an officer, and told to follow him. He knew enough by this time of the people among whom he dwelt to suspect his danger ;

but being aware also that resistance would be of no avail, he quietly obeyed. The man conducted him in silence to prison, where he was shut up without receiving any information about the charge on which he was apprehended. On requesting to see his friend, the commissary, he was informed that he was gone that day to Goa: they also told him, that he was arrested by order of the Inquisition. He now became greatly alarmed, dreading the worst; and even the visits of his friends, and their endeavours to console him, tended rather to distress his feelings: for he could not help contrasting his own situation with theirs; and nothing they said could pacify his fears in the prospect of that inexorable court, before which he knew that he must soon appear. Among his visitors were the governor of Damaun, and the priest at whose instigation, as he learned some time after, he was imprisoned. They pretended to deplore his misery, and the priest even wept over him; but he was spared, at the time, the anguish of knowing that they were tears of hypocrisy.

After a detention of three or four months, he was informed that the commissary was returned; but instead of being admitted to an audience with him, he was immediately sent to Goa, where, on his arrival, he was loaded with chains. On the following day his fetters were removed, and he was brought before the Grand Inquisitor, who inquired whether he knew the cause of his apprehension. On his answering in the negative, the Inquisitor admonished him to make a full confession; for, unlike every court of *justice*, the prisoners at *this* bar are required to accuse themselves, not being informed who are their accusers, or what is alleged against them. M. Dellon then offered freely to declare all that he could remember of what had transpired at Damaun; but his cause was postponed until one more urgent should have been disposed of. Every thing in his possession was then taken from him; and, after shaving his head, and clothing him in the dress of the prison, they shut him up in a dark dungeon.

Before entering upon this unhappy man's next audience, we will give his description of the place where he was incarcerated, and of the manner in which they treated its wretched inmates.

This jail is called, in Spain and Portugal, *Santa Casa*, that is, the holy house, everything connected with this infernal institution being esteemed Sacred. The prison at Goa was large enough to contain two hundred criminals. It consisted of several porticos, which were divided into small cells, each about ten feet square. These were built in two rows, one over the other, and all of them vaulted. The upper cells were lighted by means of iron grates, about seven feet high: the lower range were under ground, totally dark, being without any window, and narrower than those above. The walls were five feet thick. Each cell was enclosed with two doors; the inner one thick, and covered with iron, with an iron grate at the bottom. In the upper part of it there was a small aperture, through which they handed to the prisoner his food, linen, and other necessaries, and then shut it again, fastening it with two iron bolts. The outer door was entire, so that when it was closed no air could enter the dungeon; but it was opened every morning from six till eleven, for the purpose of ventilating the prison. These abodes of wretchedness were occupied by prisoners of inferior quality, and those accused of the most heinous offences.

As soon as a person is thrown into prison, he is required to give his name, and an account of his occupation. They then inquire about his circumstances; and in order to induce him to render an exact account of his property, they promise him, that if found innocent, all that he acknowledges shall be faithfully preserved, and in the end restored to him; but that if he conceals anything, it will be confiscated, though he should be proved not guilty. It appears that in Spain, prisoners were allowed some trifling indulgence in the articles of food, firing, &c. when they could afford to pay for it: but this was not the case at Goa, all, rich and poor, male and female, being treated nearly alike. The sole exception to this was that which has been intimated—those in superior circumstances being confined in the upper range of cells. Their scanty meals were brought to them three times a day, the money of the rich being expended to make provision for their poorer fellow sufferers. The prisoners in the lower range were sometimes kept in total darkness and solitude for several years, no one being suffered to visit them except their jailors, and they only at certain hours, when they took them their provisions. All this severity was intended to induce them to make a full confession of their crimes; and the hope was held out to them of deliverance, in that case, from the horrors of such an incarceration. In this, however, they were often deceived, their confessions, thus obtained, being made to form the ground of their condemnation.

When these gentler measures failed—if it be not a perversion of the term to call any part of such treatment gentle—they were put to the torture, again and again, until they had disclosed all that was expected of them. M. Dellon informs us, that in the months of November and December, he heard every day, in the morning, the cries and groans of those who were put to the *Question*, which, he says, is so very inhuman, that he has seen several of both sexes who have been ever after lame. ' In this Tribunal they regard neither age nor sex, nor a person's condition, but torture all without distinction, when it is for the interests of the Tribunal.'

The place of torture is under ground, admitting not a ray of the sun, but lighted by numerous candles. At the time of torture, the inquisitor is seated upon a kind of throne, attended by his secretary, who takes down the sufferer's confessions ; and a medical inspector, who is to determine how far the torture may be continued without actually destroying life : for it is considered a reproach to the inquisitors if any expire on the rack. The officer that applies the torture is dressed in a black linen garment reaching to his feet, which is tied close to his body. His head and face are covered with a black cowl, two small holes being left for him to see through. All this is intended to strike the unhappy victims of this diabolical system with terror : and while the executioner is preparing in their sight the instruments of torture, and stripping them to the skin, the inquisitor continues exhorting them to have compassion on their bodies and souls, and by making a true and full confession, to save themselves from the horrid *Question*.

Various modes of torture are used. One is, by stripping and binding the body. The poor sufferers, whatever their age or sex, have all their clothes removed, when they put on them a linen dress, and draw it so tight as to squeeze them almost to death. One side of the garment is then slackened; and as soon as they begin to respire again, they suffer the most excruciating agony. Sometimes the thumbs are tied so tight with small cords that they swell to a great size, and the blood gushes out under the nails. This mode of torture is applied to different limbs, and sometimes to the whole body; and the sufferers have afterwards described their pains as resembling the burning of their extremities in the fire.

What they call *Squassation*, is, perhaps, the most inhuman of all. The hands of the victim being tied behind him, and heavy weights fastened to his feet, he is drawn up by means of a pulley to a great height, and kept hanging until the hour-glass is run out, by which time all his joints are stretched to a great extent, by the weights at his feet. The rope is then suddenly slackened, and he is let down, with a jirk, nearly to the ground. This generally dislocates both his arms and his legs; but the surgeon immediately puts them in again, and the torture is repeated as soon as that officer reports that they are sufficiently recovered to bear it. Some have endured all this twice without making the required confession; but seldom has one been found courageous and strong enough to bear it a third time. We read[3] of trial by scourging, under heathen governments, but where is the barbarity in the annals of paganism to be compared to this? If it were not matter of history, it would be incredible that human beings could be

[3] Acts xxii. 24.

found capable of inflicting such excruciating torments on their fellow-creatures, or that the human body could endure them. The works mentioned at the beginning of this chapter, give several instances of persons of different ages and circumstances being put to this cruel *Question*. Even delicate females were stretched on the rack, and subjected to the horrid *squassation*, some of whom survived their sufferings, while others died soon after from their effects. But the subject is too dreadful to be further detailed. Enough has been said to show that M. Dellon had reason for the intense anxiety with which he awaited his trial.

After frequently requesting to be examined, he was at length admitted to his first regular audience, the circumstances of which he has thus described. He was led by the alcaide from his dungeon to the judgment hall, with his head, arms, and feet naked. At the door, the officer, who had conducted him, bowed with profound reverence, and then retired, leaving the prisoner to enter alone. At the farther end of the hall was placed a large crucifix, reaching almost to the ceiling. In the centre stood a table, with seats placed around it. At one end sat the secretary, and at the other the inquisitor, the prisoner sitting upon a bench on his left. He was then commanded to swear on the missal that he would speak the truth, and never divulge what transpired. After this he was called upon to declare what he had done, when he repeated what he had confessed to the commissary at Damaun, which was written down by the secretary. The inquisitor then commended him for making this voluntary confession; asked whether he had any thing more to say; and, on his replying in the negative, rang the bell for the alcaide to lead him back to his dungeon.

A few weeks after he was summoned to a second audience without soliciting it, from which unexpected circumstance he augured that they meant to set him at liberty; but he was grievously mistaken. He was again asked whether he could remember any thing besides what he had confessed; and replying, as before, in the negative, the inquisitor questioned him about his parents, his baptism, and other matters tending to show whether he had been brought up in the Roman Church. He was then made to kneel down and repeat what he had said; and after signing the secretary's paper that contained his confession, he was remanded back to jail.

This was so contrary to his expectation that he now became inconsolable; and despairing of deliverance, and, probably, dreading the *Question*, he tried to starve himself to death. His intention, however, was discovered and frustrated. He then invoked the Virgin to succour him, and endeavoured to recollect whether he had ever said anything more than he had confessed. At last, calling to mind what he had spoken at Damaun against the inquisition, he requested to be brought again before his judge, and in a few days was admitted to his third audience. After making a full declaration of all that he had uttered against the *Holy Office*, the inquisitor told him, that this was not what they expected from him: and on his again protesting that he could not call to mind anything more, he was ordered back to his cell, without his evidence this time being taken down.

He now abandoned all hope, and tried again to terminate his wretched life. Having failed in his attempt to starve himself, he pretended to be sick. Indeed, it was, probably, no pretence; for his anxiety and impatience seem to have excited him to such a degree, that when the physician was called in, he found his pulse very irregular, and his body so feverish, that he considered it necessary to take some blood from him, an operation that he repeated for sev___ days. As soon, however, as the doctor ___ him he unbound his arm again, hoping to bleed to death; but this he could not effect.

Seeing that his mind required as much care as his body, they sent him a confessor of the Franciscan Order, to reason with him, and endeavour to revive his hope. They gave him also a companion, whose society refreshed and comforted him, and in a few months he was restored to health, and recovered his spirits. His companion was then removed, when his jail became more intolerable than ever. In his melancholy and despair, he invented another method to destroy himself. Having secreted a piece of gold about his person, he contrived to make it sufficiently sharp to open a vein in each arm, by which means he lost so much blood that he fell into a swoon. A servant happening to come to his cell for some purpose, before the usual time, found him in this condition, with the blood running about the floor. Upon this discovery, the inquisitor ordered him to be secured with fetters, and closely watched; but this treatment made him the more furious, and he tried to beat his brains out against the walls and floor of the prison. Finding that severity did more harm than good, they soon removed his chains, and had recourse again to milder expedients, giving him another companion, and speaking to him in a more consolatory manner. But his mind was no sooner pacified, than they deprived him again of his associate, and left him in solitude and darkness.

In this way they continued alternately to revive and depress his feelings, for the space of about eighteen months, when he was summoned to a fourth audience.

After replying, as before, to the usual question, that he had nothing more to confess, the inquisitor read over to him the evidence of what he had said about baptism, and asked him where he had learned the doctrine of baptism by the Spirit. He answered, 'From John iii. 5,' "Except a man be born of water and of the Spirit, he cannot enter into the kingdom of God." As the inquisitor looked surprised on hearing him repeat the passage, M. Dellon begged him to interpret it: but the wary judge answered him, "The translation sufficiently explains it."

He was then asked where he had learned to speak so freely against the adoration of images, when he justified himself by appealing to the Council of Trent. The inquisitor appeared to be more astonished at this reference than the former, and referred to the passage; but again he made no attempt to correct his prisoner's interpretation.[4] Well might M. Dellon feel amazed at this ignorance in the man who presumed to sit in judgment upon him, seeing that he was so much better acquainted with the Sacred

---

[4] The following is the passage referred to in the Decrees of the Trent Council. Session 25. *De Invocatione Sanctorum et sacris Imaginibus.* Imagines Christi, Deiparæ Virginis, et aliorum Sanctorum retinendas, iisque debitum honorem et venerationem impertiendam, ita ut per Imagines coram quibus procumbimus, Christum adoremus et Sanctos, quorum illæ similitudinem gerunt, veneremur.

Q

Scriptures, and with the standard authority of their church, than his judge.

The inquisitor then told him, that what he had said against the Holy Office, showed that his designs were most pernicious; that he was a heretic; that he had rendered himself obnoxious to excommunication, and the confiscation of his goods; that he deserved to be handed over to the secular power and burned alive. We may give this unhappy man full credit for what he says of the horror that he felt when he heard this denunciation. He asserted his innocence of the charge of heresy, and expressed surprise, that what he had confessed a year and a half ago, regarding the inquisition, which was then treated lightly, should now be deemed a matter of such importance. The inquisitor denied that he had ever made such a confession, and said, that if he had, he would not have been detained so long in prison. The poor man could now hardly restrain his indignation: but happily for him, his unprincipled judge, seeing his choler rising, had him removed.

In the following month he was brought three or four times before the inquisitor, and urged to repeat what it was pretended he had confessed against the pope. He suspected that they invented this charge that they might have something plausible in the public accusation to be made against him, when brought up for judgment; but he denied it so stoutly that they desisted: and no notice was taken of the subject in his process, read at the *Act of Faith,* in which he afterwards appeared. They tried, however, to make him avow, that what he had confessed, was spoken in defence of heresy; for in that case all his property would have been confiscated: but this he resolved never to admit, feeling confident that nothing could be farther from the truth. He was most fortunate in not being put to the rack, to force from him the desired admission, for very few indeed escaped; those who confessed being tortured to discover their accomplices and teachers, and also to make them declare that their motive was heretical; and those who did not confess being put to the Question, until they made a full disclosure of all that was expected or desired.

M. Dellon now awaited with agonizing suspense the decision of his merciless judge. When a sufficient number of prisoners were collected, a day was fixed by the chief inquisitor for a jail delivery, which they call an *Auto da Fè*, or *Act a* Faith: and M. Dellon remembered to have heard, before he was cast into prison, that the *Auto da Fè* was generally celebrated on the first Sunday in Advent, because on that day is read in the churches, that part of the Gospel in which mention is made of the LAST JUDGMENT; and the inquisitors pretended by this ceremony to exhibit a lively emblem of that awful event. He was likewise convinced that there were a great number of prisoners besides himself, the profound silence which reigned within the walls of the building, having enabled him to count the number of doors which were opened at the hours of meals. He concluded, therefore, that they were ready for an Act of Faith. However, the first and second Sundays of Advent passed by without his hearing of any preparation, and he expected to undergo another year of melancholy captivity, when he was roused from his despair, on the 11th of January, by the noise of the guards removing the bars from the door of his prison. The alcaide presented him with a black habit, which he ordered him to put on, and to make himself ready to attend him when he should come again. Thus saying, he left a lighted lamp in his dungeon. The guard returned about two o'clock in the morning, and led him out into a long gallery, where he found a number of the companions of his misery, drawn up in a row against a wall: he placed himself among the rest, and several more soon joined the melancholy band. Their profound silence and stillness caused them to resemble statues, more than the animated bodies of human creatures: nothing was seen to move but their eyes. The prisoners assembled were the penitents who had confessed their faults, and declared themselves willing to return to the bosom of the Church of Rome. The women, who were clothed in a manner similar to the men, were placed in an adjoining gallery, where they could not be seen. Those unhappy beings who were condemned to be burned alive, stood by themselves at some distance, attended by their confessors, who wore long black dresses, and occasionally walked backwards and forwards.

After they were all arranged against the wall of the gallery, they received each a large wax taper, not lighted. The attendants then brought them a number of dresses, made of yellow cloth, with St. Andrew's cross painted before and behind. This is called the *San Benito*. The relapsed heretics wore another species of garment, called the *Samarra*, the ground of which was grey. The portrait of the sufferer was painted upon it, placed upon burning torches, with flames and demons all round. Those who confessed after sentence was pronounced, were dressed in the same manner, but the painted flames were pointed downward. They wore caps also, called *Carrochas*, made of pasteboard in the form of a mitre, and covered over with devils and flames of fire. All this horrid spectacle was intended to strike terror into others, to deter them from heresy.

Everything being arranged, the officers served out to each a portion of bread and figs, sufficient to strengthen them for the exertion they were about to undergo. A little before sunrise the great bell of the cathedral began to toll, which was the signal to the inhabitants of Goa to come and behold the august ceremony of the *Auto da Fè*; and the prisoners were then made to move forward from the gallery one by one. As they passed from the great hall, the inquisitor, who was seated at the door, with his secretary by him, called over the name of each prisoner, and delivered him into the hands of a particular person, who was to be his guard to the place of burning. These persons were called Parrians, or *godfathers*; and they were generally persons of respectability, who deemed it an honour to be so engaged. M. Dellon's godfather was the commander of a ship, with whom he marched forth in his turn.

The procession was commenced by the Dominican friars, who always had this honour conceded to them, in consequence of Dominic having founded the inquisition. The banner of the " Holy Office" was carried before them; in which the image of Dominic was curiously wrought in needle work, holding the sword in one hand, and an olive branch in the other, with these words, *Justice and Mercy*. Alas! where was its justice? and how[5] cruel were its tender mercies! Then followed the prisoners,

[5] Prov. xii. 10.

who walked one after another, each having his godfather by his side, and the wax taper in his hand. The women were mixed promiscuously with the men. When all those persons not condemned to die had passed, then followed the criminals who were to be burned, a large crucifix being carried between them, with its face turned to the prisoners who walked before, to denote the mercy of the Holy Office to those who were saved from the death they had deserved ; and with the back to all who followed, to signify that they had no mercy to expect. The procession was closed with the statues of those heretics who had died in prison, habited in the *Samarra*, and their bones were carried after them, shut up in black chests, with devils and flames painted all over them. The prisoners walked barefoot, and M. Dellon complains that the sharp stones of the streets of Goa wounded his tender feet, and caused the blood to stream : for they made them march through the chief streets of the city; and they were gazed upon everywhere by an innumerable crowd of people, who had assembled from all parts of India to behold the awful spectacle.

At length they arrived at the Church of St. Francis, which was this time destined for the Act of Faith, but it was usually celebrated at the Church of the Dominicans. On one side of the altar sat the Grand Inquisitor and his counsellors; and on the other, the viceroy of Goa and his court. The great altar was covered with cloth, and upon it stood six silver candlesticks with tapers burning; on a smaller altar were placed several missals. The criminals were seated, with their sureties, on a range of benches that extended from the altar to the door : they sat in the order in which they entered, those least guilty being nearest the altar. The provincial of the Augustines preached the sermon, which lasted half an hour. Treating of the inquisition, he compared it to Noah's ark, but said, that it had this advantage over it—the animals that entered the ark, came out of it after the flood, with the same brutal nature that they carried in; whereas the inquisition so far changes the persons who are detained in it, that though they enter cruel as wolves and fierce as lions, they come out meek as lambs. What a merciless mockery of the feelings of his miserable auditors, who had been subdued by torture and imprisonment!

The sermon ended, two readers mounted the same pulpit, one after the other, and read over the sentences of the prisoners, and the punishments to which they were severally condemned. After reading the sentences, they were led one by one to the altar, until as many were kneeling before it as there were missals upon it; they were then required to repeat a confession of faith after the reader. M. Dellon says, and we may well believe him, that his joy was extreme when he found that his sentence was not to be burnt, but to be a galley slave for five years. And yet, what had the poor man done to deserve such a punishment! What *Justice* or *Mercy* was there here?

When all the sentences of those not condemned to die were read over, the inquisitor, accompanied by about twenty priests, came into the middle of the church, and there repeating some form of prayer, absolved them all from the excommunication they were under, the priest in attendance giving each of them a blow. Their tapers were then lighted, to intimate, that whereas the light of Faith had been extin-

guished within their souls by the sin of heresy
and unbelief; now that they were reconciled,
they were to show forth by good works the
light which they had recovered.

This ceremony over, the inquistor resumed
his seat, when they proceeded to read the sentences of the wretched victims who were destined to be immolated by the Holy Inquisition.
Next they were handed over to the secular power,
who, with solemn, cruel mockery, was entreated
so to moderate their punishment as to prevent
the effusion of blood, and the danger of death.
The alcaide then gave each of them a slight
blow upon the breast, to intimate that they
were abandoned by the Holy Office; when a
civil officer came forward, and led them away
one by one to the stake. They were first
asked, in what religion they chose to die; and
those who answered, that they would die catholics, had the indulgence of being strangled before they were committed to the flames; but
those who resolved to die Jews or heretics, were
burnt alive. The place of burning was on the
bank of the river, where the viceroy and his
court were assembled, and where the faggots
had been prepared the preceding day. As soon
as they had replied to the question, as to the
religion in which they chose to die, the executioner seized them, and bound them to a stake
in the midst of the faggots. The day after the
execution, the portraits of the dead were carried to the church of the Dominicans. The
heads only were represented,[6] surrounded by
flames and demons; and underneath was the

---

[6] They were in general very accurately drawn; for the inquisition kept excellent limners for this purpose.

name and crime of the person who had been burned.

Such was the inquisition at Goa: and its character was the same in Spain and Portugal, and other countries, though its proceedings varied occasionally in some immaterial points.[7] For

[7] The following cases, selected from the works mentioned at the commencement of this chapter, will be sufficient to illustrate the character of this tribunal in the nations of Europe where it obtained a footing.

Maria de Cocciçao, of Estramoz, daughter of Manoel Soares Pereira, while living with her brother in Lisbon, was apprehended with two of her sisters, all three being unmarried, and came out of prison in the same Auto, acquitted of the crime laid to her charge, namely, a strong suspicion of Judaism, which she formally abjured. As the proofs against Maria were far from satisfactory, and nothing could be extorted from her to lead to her conviction, the inquisitors ordered her to be put on the rack, where, having almost got the better of the first tortures, she was at length overcome by their violence, and confessed the whole charge. The cords were immediately slackened, and the officers, taking her down from the rack, put on her clothes and carried her back to her cell. When she had recovered the use of her limbs, she was brought before the tribunal to ratify her confession. Instead of which, she stated that every thing uttered by her whilst under the executioner's hands was absolutely false; that she was and ever had been a sincere believer in Christianity; and that her confession to the contrary had been extorted by the extremity of the torments. On hearing this, the inquisitors immediately ordered her to be put again to the rack. She again sunk under its violence, and, to save her life, made the same confession as before, which was taken down in writing, while her limbs were still stretching with the cords! She was once more released and carried to her cell. As soon as she was able to appear before the tribunal, she was commanded to ratify her first and second confessions. She still, however, persisted in the same answer as before, adding, that were they to rack her a hundred times, she should always act in the same manner, so long as God afforded her strength to support the torments; that these torments and her own weakness might possibly force her again to confess that of which she was perfectly innocent; but the moment they ceased, she would revoke, and never ratify, what had been thus extorted

more than two centuries it maintained its authority, effectually preventing the diffusion of Gospel light and liberty within the territories of

from her. She farther entreated them to be assured that this was her final resolution, which no torments should induce her to alter. The inquisitors were so little affected, that they instantly commanded her to be racked a third time, the agonies of which she underwent with amazing firmness. For thus refusing to ratify her confessions, and having thrice borne the torture, which was the regular extent of punishment in the holy office, she was condemned to be whipped through the public streets by the common hangman, and then to be banished for ten years to an almost savage island. This sentence was pronounced against her when she came out at the Auto da Fe, with her two sisters, who had likewise been accused of Judaism.

Dr. Isaac Orobio was accused of Judaism by a Moor, who had been his servant, and whom he had caused to be beaten for theft. After being kept three years in prison, and interrogated several times, still persisting in denying the crimes laid to his charge, he was tortured in the following manner :— they put on him a coarse linen coat strained so very tight that his breath was almost lost, when loosing it on a sudden, this instantaneous motion put him to incredible pain. His thumbs were tied so very hard with small cords, that the blood gushed from under his nails. He was next seated on a bench, his back against a wall, wherein little iron pulleys were fixed, through which ropes were run which took hold of several parts of his body, and particularly his arms and legs; then the executioner, pulling these ropes with the utmost violence, drew his back so close to the wall, that his hands and feet, and particularly his thumbs and great toes, were so much squeezed, that he felt the most acute pains. The bench was then suddenly drawn from beneath him, so that he hung solely by the ropes, and, being unsupported, the weight of his body drew the knots still tighter, causing him inconceivable agony. An instrument in the form of a little ladder, crossed by five pieces of wood, and made sloping before, being set directly opposite to him, he received, on a certain motion of the torturers, at one and the same time, five dreadful blows on the cheek, which caused him to faint. Ropes were next fastened about his wrists, then wound round his body; after which he was laid upon his back with his feet against a wall: the executioner then drew him with all his might, so that the ropes pierced to his bones. This torture was thrice repeated, the cords being fixed round

the Portuguese, and thereby impeding the advance of Christianity in India. During this long period, who can tell how many hundred victims were sacrificed on its blood-stained altars! We pity the infatuated Hindoo females, who immolate themselves on the funeral piles of their deceased husbands; our indignation is roused when we hear that any undue influence has been used by others to induce a reluctant widow to burn; and the exertions of the Christian world have been called forth to put down the horrid practice, and pluck from the flames the helpless victims of such a superstition. Yet what is even this, compared to the system of slaughter carried on through so many generations by the inquisition, and that under the pretence of maintaining the Christian religion entire and without rebuke!

Well may we demand of them, Who hath required this at your hands? Assuredly not the God of justice and mercy; and in the sequel it will be seen, that instead of promoting the interests of the Church which these inhuman means were employed to uphold, He defeated all her priests' designs to propagate their creed

his arms, not above two fingers' breadth from the wounds which the first torture had made. The ropes now slid into the first wounds by the violence of the jerk, which occasioned so great an effusion of blood, that he seemed expiring. The physicians were then consulted, to know whether the same torture might be practised a third time without endangering his life. As these were not enemies to the doctor, they answered that he might suffer it a third time without the least danger. This declaration again saved him from undergoing again the various sorts of torture above mentioned, his sentence specifying that he should suffer successively all these different kinds the same day. Thus tortured for the last time, he was remanded to prison, where he remained above seventy days before his wounds were healed. He was at last banished for life.

in India, and thereby showed, that He gave no
countenance to their prostitution of the sacred
names which the Inquisitors inscribed on their
banner.[8]　It was not by such barbarous and un-
righteous means that Jesus Christ commanded
His religion to be propagated upon earth, when
He sent forth His disciples to preach the Gospel
to every creature.　Let us read the terms in

[8] To obviate the necessity of reverting again to this abominable institution, we may here anticipate its subsequent
history in India.　It continued to wield its iron sceptre within
the precincts of the Portuguese possessions, and sometimes
venturing to step beyond them, until the year 1775, when it
was suppressed by royal edict.　"It was the humanity and
tender mercy of a good king which abolished it," said an old
Franciscan father, who had witnessed the annual Auto da Fé,
from 1770 to 1775.　That humane king was Joseph of Portugal: "but immediately on his death, in 1777, the power
of the priests acquired the ascendant, under the Queen Dow-
ager, and the Tribunal was re-established, after a bloodless
interval of five years."　When restored, in 1779, it was
placed under certain restrictions, the chief of which were the
two following, "That a greater number of witnesses should
be required to convict a criminal than was before necessary;
and, that the Auto da Fé should not be held publicly as
before, but that the sentences of the Tribunal should be
executed privately, within the walls of the Inquisition."
　"In this particular, the constitution of the new Inquisition
is more reprehensible than that of the old one; for," as
the old father, just adverted to, expressed it, "Nunc sigillum
non revelat Inquisitio.　Formerly the friends of those unfortunate persons who were thrown into its prison, had the
melancholy satisfaction of seeing them once a year walking
in the procession of the Auto da Fé; or if they were condemned to die, they witnessed their death, and mourned for
the dead; but now they have no means of learning for years
whether they be dead or alive."　Such a suspense regarding
those whom we love is more agonizing than the most painful
certainty.　"The policy of this new mode of concealment
appears to have been this, to preserve the power of the Inquisition, and, at the same time, to lessen the public odium
of its proceedings in the presence of British dominion and
civilization."—(Buchanan's Christian Researches, pp. 167—
172.)　But the torture of feeling occasioned hereby to the

which their commission is defined, and then judge whether it gives any sanction to the horrors of this Tribunal.—" Go ye therefore, and teach all nations, baptizing them in the name of the Father, and of the Son, and of the Holy Ghost: teaching them to observe all things whatsoever I have commanded you." (Matt. xxviii. 19, 20.)

friends of the sufferers, would tend to increase the terror of its dominion; and thus its object was the more effectually accomplished by the very means which, as they pretended, were meant to moderate its operation. How extreme was this refinement of cruelty!

But such an appalling system could not long withstand the influence of the light and freedom consequent upon the growing power of the British, and in the year 1816 it was again abolished by the Prince Regent of Portugal. The Archbishop of Goa was supposed, however, to retain all the power that had been lodged in the court of the Inquisition. In Europe, this infernal tribunal was re-established soon after the restoration of the Jesuits' order: but it does not yet appear to have resumed its jurisdiction in the East; and we trust in the God of all mercy to prevent its rising again from the ruin in which its buildings there have lain these twenty years.

CHAPTER V.

FIRST ATTEMPT TO BRING THE SYRIAN CHURCH
OF MALABAR UNDER SUBJECTION TO ROME.

1. IN entering upon a relation of the attempts
made by the Romanists to reduce the Syrian
Christians of Malabar into subjection to their
Church, it is necessary to bear in mind, that
up to this period they had existed without the
remotest connexion with Rome. Ecclesiastics
employed in their subjugation, and historians
who have recorded their proceedings, have endeavoured to justify what was done, by appealing to the papal supremacy.[1]   It is asserted, as

---

[1] The following note on the papal supremacy is too important to be omitted here.

It is " worthy of remark, that on a Papist, a Jesuit of
" learning and distinction—a Professor of Rhetoric, History,
" and Philosophy in the Universities of Rome, Fermo, and
" Macerata, and, in the latter place Counsellor of the Inqui-
" sition—being employed about the middle of the last century
" to prove the Pope's supremacy, by showing from century
" to century, that since the Apostles' time to the present, it
" had ever been acknowledged by the Catholic Church, he
" soon found that he had undertaken more than it was pos-
" sible to perform ; viz. on coming to the close of the second
" century. ' Nay, says he, while, in order to support and
" maintain this cause, I examined, with particular attention,
" the writings of the Apostles, and of the many pious and
" learned men who had flourished in the first three centuries

we have seen, that all Christendom originally owed and rendered obedience to Rome; and that, therefore, she has authority to reclaim any Church or individual that may have separated from her, by such means as she may deem necessary for the purpose. It has been shown above, in the case of the primitive churches of France, Spain, and Britain,[2] that this assumption is most unwarranted; and the evidence for the independence of the Indian Church as far as the sixteenth century, is equally conclusive.

It has appeared in the foregoing pages, that hitherto the Syrian Christians of Malabar had acknowledged the Patriarch of Mosul as the head of their Church. That prelate was the

"..... ne Church, I was so far from finding any thing that "seemed the least to countenance such a doctrine, that, on "the contrary, it appeared evident, beyond all dispute, that, "during the above-mentioned period of time, it had been "utterly unknown to the Christian world. In spite, then, "of my endeavours to the contrary, reason getting the better "of the strongest prejudices, I began to look upon the Pope's "Supremacy, not only as a prerogative quite chimerical, but "as the most impudent attempt that had ever been made: "I say in spite of my endeavours to the contrary; for I was "very unwilling to give up a point, upon which I had been "taught by Bellarmin, that THE WHOLE OF CHRISTIANITY DE-"PENDED; especially in a country where a man cannot help "being afraid of his own thoughts, since upon the least sus-"picion of his only calling in question any of the received "opinions, he may depend upon his being soon convinced by "more cogent arguments than any in *mood* and *figure*. "But great is the power of truth; and at last it prevailed: "I became a proselyte to the opinion which I had proposed "to confute; and sincerely abjured, in my mind, that which "I had ignorantly undertaken to defend.'" The reader is referred to "The *Preface* to the History of the Popes," by Archibald Bower, Esq., in 7 vols. 4to. Allport's translation of Bp. Davenant on Colossians i. 18. p. 214—Translator's note.

[2] Book 2, c. 2, s. 3, 4. The same might as easily be proved of other Churches, were this the place to go further into the subject.

successor of the ancient patriarch of Persia, who took up his residence at Seleucia, on the Tigris. We have seen, from the signature of Johannes,[3] at the Council of Nice, as Bishop of Persia and the great India, that the Indian Church was dependent upon this prelate from that early period of its history : and here it is important to remark, that this statement is abundantly confirmed by writers of the Roman Church. The Abbé Renaudot, though violently prejudiced against all who differed from his creed, yet frequently mentions, in his history and liturgies, that the Nestorian Patriarchs of the Syrian Church in India derived their origin from Persia. There can be no doubt, he admits, that the Malabar Christians had professed the Nestorian heresy for above nine hundred years, and that, under the patriarch Hanan-Jesus, that sect penetrated as far as China. The Patriarchs of Persia at first took up their residence at Modena, which is the Seleucia of the Parthians. After the ruin of this city by the califs, they retired to Bagdad, whence they afterwards removed to Mosul, which many learned men suppose to have been the site of ancient Nineveh.[4]

Antony Gouvea also, a Portuguese writer, who labours hard to persuade his readers, but without an attempt to prove his assertions, that the Indian Church was at its commencement subject to Rome ; admits, nevertheless, that after the destruction of Meliapore, they were

---

[3] Book 1, c. 2, s. 9.

[4] Renaudot, Hist. Patriarch, Alexandrin, p. 188. Life of Simon, p. 42, a Jacobite patriarch of Alexandria. This work is in Latin. La Croze, pp. 51, 52. See also Renaudot's Origin of the Christian religion in China, where he gives a particular account of the Nestorians' Metropolitan cities, pp. 114—119.

so much in want of ecclesiastics that they sent
for them to the patriarch of Babylon, who consecrated and despatched three Bishops, one for
India, the second for Socotora, and the third
for Southern China. Their names were, Mar
Doua, Mar Thoma, and Mar Jonnam. On
their arrival at Cranganore, they are said to
have been so much disgusted with the place
that they immediately returned home, and sent
others in their stead.[5]

These statements are made upon such questionable authority, that they would be unworthy
of attention but for the importance of proving,
this period of our history, that the Malabar
stians had from time immemorial acknow-
d the patriarch of Babylon for their primate. This fact is further supported by the
testimony of Sozomen, who quotes the authority of Stephen of Babylon, to prove that Scleu-
cia formerly bore the name of Babylon, and
that from the fourth century it had been the
residence of the Bishops of Persia, who also
presided over the Church in India. Notwithstanding the manifest wish of Romish authors
and ecclesiastics to prove that church to be of
a different origin, it is certain, even by the evidence of their own writers, that from the first
arrival of the Portuguese in India, they never
found among the Christians there the faintest
resemblance, either in doctrine or discipline, to
the peculiarities of Rome, or any other Church
but that of Nestorius. Of the Latin language
they knew nothing, all their public services
being conducted, as at this day, in Syriac.
Neither had they ever heard of the pope of

[5] Gouvea, chap. iii. fol. v. verso colonne. *Necia et im-
piamente.* La Croze, pp. 52, 53.

R

Church of
Babylon
also inde-
pendent.

Rome, and they continued to receive their
Bishops from the patriarch of Mosul.

2. Some advocates of the papal supremacy,
seeing, probably, that this position was unten-
able without going still further back, have
carried their presumption so far as to contend,
that the Church of Babylon herself derived her
origin from Rome. This assertion they endeavour to establish on, what they call, the confession of three or four ambitious, or mendicant
friars, who, in the sixteenth century, visited
Rome, pretending to be patriarchs of Babylon,
and acknowledging that their Bishops derive
their power of ordination from the wes
fathers. Palpable as was the deception, an
some the flattery of these strangers, yet they
too acceptable to the pope not to be received
with courtesy, and they obtained from him the
recognition they desired. They came forward
at a time when the papal authority was rapidly
declining in Europe, and the Church of Rome
was too glad of any testimony in favour of her
pretensions, not to welcome " these hungry
monks " as auxiliaries to her cause.

But several Romanist writers, less personally
interested to defend the evidence of these men,
saw through the imposture, and were ashamed
of the reception that was given them at the
Vatican. The falsehood of their pretence, that
the Chaldæan Bishops owned that they received
their ordinations from the western fathers, will
appear from the whole tenor of the Synod of
Diamper, whose proceedings are hereafter to
be recorded : and all the accounts which the
Portuguese gave concerning that Church abundantly confirm this conclusion. *The men were
never owned by the Churches of which they pretended to be the patriarchs.* Father Simon,

speaking of this in his *Histoire Critique*,[6] acknowledges that "their magnifying of the
pope's power was gross flattery:" at the same
time, he thinks it was not unpardonable "in
such poor wretches," since they would not
otherwise have been suffered to approach "his
holiness," to whom they came on purpose to
make their court.   This writer observes, "that
few or none of the Oriental prelates ever applied
to the pope, unless to promote some particular
cause in which they were interested:" and
this, he says, "will account for the short continuance of those reunions with Rome which
they pretended to make."   Their end accomplished, they threw aside the mask as of no
further use.

We have seen that the prelates of Babylon
were in ancient times styled, Bishops of *Seleucia*,
a city not far from *Ctesiphon*.   Hence *Simon*,
who in the fourth century suffered martyrdom
under Sapor, King of Persia, was called
Bishop of *Seleucia* and *Ctesiphon*.   Of this city
Strabo gives the following account.—" Babylon
was the ancient metropolis of Assyria, which is
the present Seleucia of Tygris, near to which
is a great village called *Ctesiphon*, where the
kings of Parthia used to spend the winter to
spare *Seleucia*, that it might not be continually
oppressed with soldiers and Scythians: but
notwithstanding this change of the metropolis,
as the surrounding country is called Babylon,
the natives, though born in the city of Seleucia,
are called Babylonians."[7]

Seleucus, King of Syria, the officer of Alex-

---

[6] Page 93.

[7] Sozom. p. 2, 8, &c.   Eusebius Renaudot.   Translation
of two Mahomedan travellers journey to India and China in
the ninth century.

ander, who succeeded to that portion of his master's empire,[8] built Seleucia on the banks of the Tygris, and at the distance of forty miles from Babylon. It became very populous in a short time, and Pliny tells us that it was inhabited by six hundred thousand persons. The dykes of the Euphrates being broken down, spread an extensive inundation over the country; and the branch of that river which passed through Babylon, was sunk so low by this evacuation as to be rendered unnavigable. In consequence of this calamity the city became so incommodious, that as soon as Seleucia was built, all its inhabitants withdrew thither. T circumstance prepared the way for the ao plishment of that celebrated prophecy of I who, more than four hundred years before the event, and at a time when Babylon was in the zenith of her prosperity, had foretold that it should one day become entirely desert and uninhabited.[9]

In the *Bibliotheca Patrum* there is a Treatise on Paradise, composed by one *Moses Bar Cepha*, who flourished in the tenth century, and is styled, Bishop of *Bethraman* and *Bethle* and *Curator* of the Ecclesiastical affairs of *Mozul*, or *Seleucia Parthorum*.

These extracts will serve to account for the frequent use of the names here given as synonymous, when speaking of the patriarch whose authority is acknowledged by the Syrian Church of Malabar. To prove the independence of the patriarch of Babylon, in answer to the idle stories to the contrary so eagerly received at

---

[8] Book i. chap. i. sec. 17.

[9] Rollin's Ancient History, book xvi. chap. ii. sec. 2. Isaiah xlvii. Prideaux' Connection, part i. book viii. pp. 798, 799.

Rome, it is only necessary here to refer to the 33rd Canon of the Council of Nice.[1]

Canon 33.—" Let the See of Seleucia, which " is one of the Eastern cities, be honoured " likewise, and have the title of *Catholicon;* and " let the prelate thereof ordain Arch-bishops " as the other patriarchs do, that so the Eastern " Christians who live under heathens, may not " be wronged by waiting the patriarch of *Anti-* " *och's* leisure, or by going to him, but may " have a way opened to them to supply their " own necessities ; neither will any injury be done to the patriarch of Antioch thereby, seeing he has consented to its being thus, upon the Synod's having desired it of him."

From this Canon it is evident, that the Church of Seleucia, or Babylon, was originally subject to the patriarch of Antioch, the primate nearest to that city. And if, as is pretended, the Bishops of Chaldæa acknowledged that they derived their authority from the western fathers, they must have meant the patriarchs of Antioch, not the popes of Rome.[2] For after the erection of that city by Seleucus, it was for many ages honoured as " the Queen of the East ; " and when Christianity prevailed generally in Asia, it became the see of the chief patriarch of the eastern churches.[3]

To such slender authority was the pope glad to appeal in support of his arrogant pretensions. The extensive discussion it has raised may be easily accounted for and explained, if we remember that the primary object of the papacy is to maintain the supremacy of the triple crown.

[1] This is taken from the Arabic Canons, which, though not the original Canons of that Council, are yet very ancient.

[2] Geddes. Church of Malabar, pp. 12—18.

[3] Prideaux' Connection, part i. book viii. pp. 797, 798.

CHAP.
V.

For the pope to admit the independence of any other ecclesiastical superior, were to relinquish his claim to the primacy of the universal Church. Hence the cruelty, the injustice, the fraud, with which the Roman Church has endeavoured to vindicate this assumption.

First attempt against the Syrians of Malabar made by the Franciscans, with its failure.

3. The first attempts to bring the Christians of Malabar into communion with Rome, were made in 1545, by the Cordeliers, or Friars of the order of St. Francis. Of this order was Don Juan d'Albuquerque, first Bishop of Goa, who, as the pope's representative, considered himself as holding supreme ecclesiastical authority in India, and soon turned his attention the Christians of whom he had heard in countries South of Goa. He had brought with him to India a Franciscan brother, named Vincent, whom Gouvea describes as "a great servant of God." This man was sent by the Bishop to inquire into the state of the Syrian Christians, and to induce them, if possible, to acknowledge the papal supremacy.

Father Vincent, as he is called, proceeded to Cranganore, where he preached for some time without molestation; and being displeased at the sight of Christian Churches so closely resembling the heathen pagodas, he built several places of worship on a more appropriate model. The native Christians, however, were not long in detecting the real object of this friar's mission. At first they welcomed him as a Christian minister, charged with an errand of good will towards them: but they soon discovered, that instead of attending to their improvement, and affording them the protection they expected, his principal object was, to make them proselytes to a faith of which they had not yet heard, and to bring them into subjection to a church whose authority they had never acknowledged. After this discovery, Vincent perceived that they paid no more regard to his exhortations; nor could he attempt to coerce them, as he felt that he was too far removed from the Portuguese seat of government to make any use of their secular authority. But, though conscious of the difficulty of his situation, he was not slow to project a remedy. Finding that he could make no impression upon the Cattanars,[4] and that without their concurrence he could gain no attention from the people; he determined to educate some Syrian priests in his own doctrines, hoping, through them, to persuade the whole community to exchange their ancient rites and creed for those of Rome. Accordingly, he applied to the Viceroy, and to the Bishop of Goa, for permission and assistance to found a College at Cranganore; and both those authorities readily complied with his request. The establishment was soon formed, and several Syrian youths were instructed in the Latin tongue and ritual: but when they attempted to preach, it was found that all these pains had been taken to little purpose. The Syrians had allowed their sons to attend the college; but after their ordination, about which they do not appear to have been consulted, they refused to recognise their orders, would not allow them to preach anywhere to the people, and looked upon them as tools of Rome, and apostates from the faith of their fathers. Hitherto they had permitted the Portuguese to enter their churches; but now that their suspicions were awakened, they shut the doors against them, and also against their own sons who had been educated and ordained at Cranganore. It were

[4] The name of the Syrian priests.

CHAP.
V.

to forget the infirmity of human nature to imagine, that there was no human passion to stimu-
late the resistance which they offered to this
attempt to deceive them. In such a case, however, who could refuse to extenuate their anger?
But, whatever mixture there might be of human
infirmity, their proceedings did not originate in
a mere ebullition of feeling, for throughout the
whole business they were acting in obedience
to the ancient canons of their church.[5]

Second at-
tempt by the
Jesuits, also
fails.

4. Seeing the failure of this Franciscan's
attempts, and considering the mission an enterprise of too great importance to be abandoned,
the Jesuits devised another expedient. They
attributed the discomfiture of father Vincent to
his neglect of the Syrians' predilection for their
ancient language, and determined to profit by
his mistake. To diminish the force of the prejudice raised in the Syrians' minds by the
former undertaking, the Jesuits fixed upon
another spot for their establishment, the village
of Vaipicotta, about one league from Cranganore. Here they erected a college some time

A. D.
1587.

after, under the auspices of Antonio Guedes
Morales, with considerable assistance from the
King of Portugal, and the permission of the
Rajah of Cochin. The pupils of Vincent had
been perpetually reproached by the Syrians for
abandoning the language and costume of their
fathers, and assuming those of the Portuguese.
The Jesuits thought to obviate this objection,
by teaching their scholars Syriac, and allowing
them to retain the accustomed dress of the
cattanars. For a time the plan appeared to
succeed, and the establishment went on with
fair promise. This appearance, however, soon

[5] La Croze, p. 55.

proved fallacious, and the institution failed to realize the hopes of its founders. The Syrian youth, when educated and ordained by the Jesuits, could not be induced, either by commands or promises, to preach against their ancient prelates; and their teachers had frequently the mortification of hearing them, in their own college, maintain their former opinions, and even make mention of the patriarch of Babylon in their Liturgy with the respect they were accustomed to pay him.

The Jesuits were not an order of men to retire upon this disappointment, or to be content to go on with the slow progress they had hitherto made. We have seen that this society was founded for the purpose of checking the progress of the Reformation, and extending the papal authority in the world by every means that could be devised. Ignatius, it will be remembered, "bound his order by a solemn vow of implicit, blind, and unlimited submission and obedience to the Roman pontiff;" and they have not scrupled to use the most inhuman and diabolical expedients in the performance of their obligations. The infamous dogma they maintain, that the *end* justifies the *means*, has led to the perpetration of crimes, under the cowl of religion, which have outraged every principle of justice and every feeling of humanity. They have been truly characterized as "the Pope's most zealous advocates and soldiers."[7] In

---

[7] Histoire des Religieux de la compagnie de Jesus, printed at Utrecht in 1741. Mosheim, cent. 16, chap. iv. sec. 2. Jortin's Remarks, vol. v. p. 503,—" We confess and believe that the Pope of Rome is the head of the Church, and that *he cannot err.* We confess and believe that the pope of Rome is the representative of Christ, and *has full power to forgive, and retain sin arbitrarily, and to cast into hell, and to excommunicate whomsoever he pleases.* We confess that

craft, they have equalled the most unprincipled practitioner of the law; and in cruelty, the most unfeeling executioner. This character was soon exhibited in their treatment of the Syrian Christians, whose only offence was, that they had hitherto been, and showed that they meant to continue, independent of Rome.

Mar Joseph
the Syrian
Bishop, cir-
cumvented
and sent to
Europe.

5. Seeing the inutility of all attempts hitherto made to turn them from their faith, and from their allegiance to their own patriarch; and attributing their failure to the presence of the Syrian Bishop, they determined to remove him. This, however, was a hazardous enterprise, and they were convinced that they should never succeed without resorting to stratagem or force. Their intention was to send him to Portugal, with a view to his being transmitted thence to Rome, where they expected that the pope would either convert him, or, at least, detain him as long as he lived.

The prelate against whom they laid this plot, was Mar Joseph, who was consecrated for the diocese of Malabar by Mar Abdichio, patriarch of Babylon. Even Gouvea speaks highly of this Bishop, both as to his personal character, and also to his zeal in reforming abuses that had crept into the church over which he was appointed to preside. The patriarch whom this

every new thing instituted by the pope, whether it be contained in the Scripture or not, whatsoever he has commanded, is *true, divine,* and *saving, which the common man has to value more than the commandments of the living God.* We confess that the most holy pope is to *be honoured by every one with* DIVINE HONOUR, *and with the profoundest reverence, just as it is due to the Lord Christ himself,* &c."—Part of a confession of faith drawn up by the Jesuits, to which they compelled the Protestants of Germany to subscribe when they professed to return to the communion of Rome. These are the pretensions which Jesuits are sworn to defend.

Portuguese historian calls Abdichio, is the same person as Aba, or Hebed Jesus,[a] who went to Italy in the year 1562, where he assisted at the council of Trent, and gave in a confession of faith, conforming nearly to the dogmas of Rome. It is probable that Mar Joseph, whom he sent to India, professed the same creed, and that the alterations which he introduced were importations from Rome. If this conjecture be correct, it will account for the terms of commendation in which Gouvea describes, what he calls, this prelate's improvement of the ecclesiastical rites of the Syrians.

This writer, however, qualifies his favourable testimony, by adding that Mar Joseph was a Nestorian, of which he gives the following proof. He wished to be thought a Romanist, and, in order to preserve the appearance, was frequent in his visits to the Portuguese at Cochin. But they suspected his sincerity, and laid a snare for his detection. Having allowed him to take some Portuguese youths into his employment, he was very careful to instruct them in their Christian duties. On one occasion, after exhorting them to be very devout in their supplications to the Virgin Mary, as the advocate of sinners, he cautioned them against calling her the mother of God, adding, that she was only the mother of Christ. This he desired them particularly to remember, whenever they repeated the Ave Maria. The young men were startled at this doctrine, and repeated it to the Bishop of Cochin, who was expecting such an opportunity to accuse Mar Joseph of heresy.

[a] Asseman, Tom. i. pp. 536, 542. Asseman says, that Abraham Ecchellensis mentions this patriarch in his catalogue of Syrian writers, printed at Rome in 1653.

It appears that he only permitted these young persons to enter the Syrian prelate's service, that they might watch his words and actions; and he lost no time in reporting to the viceroy and the Archbishop of Goa, the information he had received. They ordered him immediately to have the Syrian Bishop arrested at Cochin, and sent to Goa, to give an account of his doctrines. On his arrival there, it was soon determined to send him to Rome, and they despatched him in a ship bound for Portugal. Gouvea does not hesitate to avow the whole of this disgraceful transaction to have been a trap set for this unwary prelate, in order that they might, with some colour of justice, remove him to a distance, hoping to make an easy prey of the flock in the absence of their shepherd.[9]

Returns to India under the auspices of the Queen, prince, and princess of Portugal.

6. When Mar Joseph arrived in Portugal, he had the address to ingratiate himself with the Queen Regent, Donna Catarina, and also with the infanta, Donna Maria, from whom he obtained permission to return to India, with marks of their royal favour. The Portuguese writers accuse him of feigning the semblance of virtue and sanctity for this purpose, and his subsequent conduct gives too much colour to the allegation. Such conduct no consideration can justify. With a righteous judge, hypocrisy never can be necessary; and with one of an opposite character, it is a Christian's duty to suffer rather than dissemble. But Mar Joseph appears to have wanted that faith in God, and that integrity of principle, which would have taught him to rest in a simple statement of his wrongs for the redress he sought. He might

[9] Gouvea, cap. iii. fol. 7.　La Croze, Histoire, &c. Liv. i. p. 58.

not have succeeded in this way; but he would
have preserved a quiet conscience, and found
this his firmest support and sweetest consolation, in all the sufferings that afterwards came
upon him for his Master's Name. But his was
not the spirit of a martyr; and there is too
much reason to suspect that he had recourse to
dissimulation, or some other means equally
culpable, to accomplish his end. He obtained
an interview with the Infant, and also with Don
Henry, a cardinal, and legate, *à Latere*[1], to the
kingdom of Portugal, to whom he pledged himself to cleanse his church from all its ancient
errors, and to do every thing in his power to
bring it into subjection to the Roman Church.
Upon this engagement, the Cardinal dispensed
with his proceeding to Rome; and he was sent
back with the Queen Regent's letters patent,
and with orders to the Viceroy of India and
the Archbishop of Goa, to restore him to his
diocese.

7. While this prelate was on the voyage back
to India, another arrived before him. The Jesuits soon found that they could not make so
easy a prey of the Malabar Christians as they
expected. Though deprived of their spiritual
head, they were too conscientiously attached to
their own communion and creed, to be forced
or deluded into a compliance with the dogmas
and discipline of Rome. When their prelate
was taken from them, and sent across the wide
ocean, they knew not whither, it was not un-

*Mar Abra-
ham, a new
prelate, ar-
rives from
Babylon.*

---

[1] A term used to designate the highest order of the pope's
legates, who are sent to represent him at foreign courts. This
dignity he conferred on his greatest favourites, who were most
in his confidence, being, when at Rome, always, *à Latere*, i. e.
at his side. When abroad, they had authority to exercise all
the papal functions.

natural for them to despair of seeing him again.
Accordingly they sent to Mar Simeon, patriarch
of Babylon, to supply his place with another
Bishop. The patriarch immediately complied
with their request, consecrated one Abraham
for the diocese, and sent him to the Serra.

The Portuguese had used great precautions
to prevent all intercourse between the Christians
of Malabar and their patriarch ; and when they
found that their vigilance had been eluded, and
that a Syrian Bishop was on his way to the
country, they endeavoured to intercept him.
Apprised of their intention, Mar Abraham travelled in disguise, and thus succeeded in gain-
ing the place of his destination. The poor
people received him with every demonstration
of joy. Since the departure of Mar Joseph,
they had been as sheep without a shepherd in
the midst of wolves, and they welcomed their
new Bishop, as their protector against the craft
and violence of the Jesuits.

Mar Joseph
arrives at
Goa ; his
dissimula-
tion de-
tected.

8. But they did not long enjoy the tranquillity of his government, which was soon disturbed by Mar Joseph's return to Malabar.
The Archbishop of Goa was greatly disappointed
at his arrival, as he had written expressly to
Portugal, that he might never be allowed to
return. Since, however, the authenticity of
his letters was not to be disputed, the Portuguese authorities were obliged to permit him to
proceed to the South ; but they did not dismiss
him without putting his sincerity to the test. As
he had been sent back with such tokens of royal
favour, in consequence of his promise to endeavour to bring over his flock to the Church of
Rome, the Archbishop and the Viceroy desired
him to take some Portuguese ecclesiastics with
him, to instruct his people in the Roman creed

and ritual. Instead of immediately complying with their demand, he required time to consider of it; and on the following day he told them, that he had received a revelation during the night which expressly forbade him to do as they wished. The Archbishop was now confirmed in the suspicion he before entertained, that Joseph had dissembled at the court of Lisbon, and immediately replied, 'And I have found a better revelation in the Holy Scriptures, which convinces me that you are not the pastor whom the Lord would have to guide this flock, but a wolf in sheep's clothing, of whom our Saviour said, " Ye shall know them by their fruits : " your fraud shall certainly be made known to the prince and princesses upon whom you have imposed ; for had they suspected your hypocrisy, they would not have honoured you with their letters of recommendation.

9. The Archbishop, however, was too skilful a politician not to discover the advantage afforded him by the arrival of another Bishop in Malabar ; and he understood too well the maxim, *Divide and conquer*, to hesitate to seize upon the opportunity to promote disunion among the people. It did not require much sagacity to foresee that the two rival prelates would soon contend for the pre-eminence, and that each would gain over a strong party to support his pretensions. By espousing the cause of either side, the Archbishop might seem to establish a claim upon their gratitude, and would hope to be more successful in his endeavours to persuade them to acknowledge the Pope's supremacy. With this view, he allowed Mar Joseph to return to his diocese, notwithstanding the recent detection of his duplicity ; and not long

Is permitted to return to Malabar, which creates a schism in the Diocese.

after his arrival, the wished for schism, like a leprosy, began to spread in the church. Many of Mar Joseph's friends rejoiced at his return, and immediately attached themselves to his interests : but the majority of the Syrians regarded him as a renegade from their ancient faith, in consequence of his compliances with the Church of Rome ; and they supported Mar Abraham, because he was quite free from popish contamination.

10. Mar Joseph now disclosed his real character. Feeling the weakness of his cause, he applied for succour to the very men of whose malicious designs against his church he had such unquestionable proof : like the unfaithful Israelites who, in danger, forsook the God of their fathers, and placed their confidence in the Egyptians, who had held them in bondage, and sought their destruction.[1] Mar Joseph complained of his rival to the Archbishop of Goa, calling him an intruder, accusing him of inculcating many pernicious doctrines, especially against the faith of Rome, and entreating that he might be removed.

This was just what the Archbishop desired and expected. He gave immediate information of the circumstance to the viceroy, who despatched orders to the commanding officer at Cochin to apprehend Mar Abraham, and send him to Goa without delay. These orders were speedily executed, as the Rajah of Cochin permitted the Portuguese troops to enter his dominions for the purpose, and assisted them with a considerable force of his own. Mar Abraham was seized and sent to Goa, where he embarked for Portugal, with a view to his being forwarded to

[1] Isaiah xxx., xxxi.

Rome, to answer to the pope for his conduct and his doctrines. As the ship in which he sailed approached the island of Madagascar, a violent gale arose, and compelled them to seek refuge in the port of Mosambique, then belonging to the Portuguese. While there, Mar Abraham contrived to effect his escape, and he proceeded to Mosul by way of Melindo and Ormus. Here he obtained from the Syrian patriarch fresh credentials, confirming his title to the bishopric of Malabar.

11. At first he intended to return direct to India, but was induced to alter his purpose when he considered the state of the country. He knew that none but his own flock would acknowledge the validity of his credentials, and that, should he succeed in rejoining them, which was most improbable, neither the Portuguese authorities, nor the heathen rajahs on the Malabar coast, would leave him unmolested. Seeing, therefore, that he must either abandon his diocese, or endeavour to regain it through the sanction of the pope, he boldly adopted the latter alternative. For this purpose he set out at once for Rome, where he arrived during the pontificate of Pius IV. When the pope had heard his story, he required him first to renounce the Syrian faith, and embrace that of Rome: then to anathematize his ancient creed, and engage to bring over the Christians of Malabar to the obedience of the pontiff. With all this he complied without hesitation, and thus betrayed as great a want of principle as his rival had shown in a similar emergency. Indeed, romanist writers charge him with an act of duplicity on this occasion, which, if true, cannot be too strongly condemned. They assert, that in the confession of faith which he

He proceeds to Rome and conforms to all that the pope requires of him.

A. D. 1566.

8

made before the pope, and carried back to India, instead of saying that the Eternal Word took upon Him human *nature*, he dexterously substituted a Syriac word which signifies *person*, or what the schoolmen call, *hypostasis*; so that, while pretending to abjure his creed, he was actually maintaining it. Whatever truth there may be in this allegation, there is too much reason to fear that he had recourse to some disingenuous means to accomplish his end; otherwise he would not have succeeded so easily in obtaining permission from the " his Holiness" to return to India. No doubt, he by this time saw enough of his adversaries to be convinced, that the justice of his cause would prove a weak ground of defence at the tribunal of Rome; and he, most probably, thought himself at liberty to use dissimulation, in order to recover what they had taken from him by violence and injustice. Such conduct, however, is indefensible, for no circumstances can justify the defence of what is right by what is wrong: but the accusation comes with an ill grace from the mouth or the pen of a romanist. The miserable man was only practising against them their own atrocious maxim—The end justifies the means.

The pope, however, was satisfied with his promise: but before he sent him away, he required him to be re-ordained by Roman Bishops. In the case of Mar Joseph a mistake had been committed, in the policy of Rome, by allowing him to return to his diocese with a recognition of his orders. It is incompatible with the pretensions of this church to acknowledge any ecclesiastical authority not emanating from herself. In the present instance, therefore, it was determined to re-ordain Mar Abraham, to which he submitted, beginning with the simple tonsure, and proceeding regularly to the order of priesthood. He was then sent to the Archbishop of Venice, with the pope's mandate. to be consecrated afresh to the bishopric of India. Whatever indignation may be felt at the arrogance of Rome throughout these transactions, it is impossible to respect the memory of a man who, to further his own present views, could submit to have such an insult offered to his own primate. The right of the patriarch of Babylon to perform all episcopal functions, was as unquestionable as that of the Bishop of Rome. But what rights, however sacred, will not ambitious men sacrifice; and what principles, civil, ecclesiastical, or moral, will they not compromise, to secure the end to which they aspire!

12. His immediate object Mar Abraham secured, the pope dismissing him with briefs addressed to the viceroy, the Archbishop of Goa, and other Indian prelates, requiring them to receive him favourably, as Archbishop of Angamale.[2]

Is re-ordained and sent back to India as Bishop of Angamale.

13. During his absence from Malabar, his rival, Mar Joseph, finding himself in undisputed possession of the see, resumed his former course, and ceased not publicly to preach the doctrines which the romanists allege he abjured at Lisbon and at Goa. This was soon reported to the Archbishop of Goa, who, with the Bishop of Cochin, transmitted an account of his conduct to the Cardinal, Don Henry, by whom at that time the kingdom of Portugal was governed,

Joseph violates his engagement to the Roman prelates —is sent to Europe, and dies at Rome.

---

[2] Gouvea says that the briefs in which all these circumstances were detailed were extant in his time, and preserved with care in the Church of Angamale, the ancient See of Malabar.—Hist. Orient. chap. iii.

during the minority of the king, his nephew, Don Sebastian. The Cardinal lost no time in writing to the pope, Pius V., from whom he obtained an order for Mar Joseph's apprehension. The order was dated 15th January, 1567, the first of this pontificate, and addressed to Don George, Archbishop of Goa, requiring him strictly to examine the doctrine and behaviour of Mar Joseph, and in the event of his proving guilty of the accusations brought against him, to send him as a prisoner to Rome. The order for his arrest was executed without difficulty, Mar Joseph having no suspicion of his enemies design. They seized him at Cochin, and shipped him off at once for Portugal, without, as far as appears, even from Gouvea, entering into the examination required. From Portugal he was forwarded to Rome, where he ended his days; but in what way, or how long after his arrival there, the historian, Gouvea, has not recorded. The abrupt manner, however, in which he closes his account of this Bishop, tends to awaken suspicion respecting the causes of his death : and from the character given of the reigning pontiff, he appears to have been capable of any atrocity. His disposition is described as so sanguinary, "that he caused every one that dissented in the least from the dogmas of Rome to be put to death, how irreproachable soever his character might be, or popular his talents and learning. We can have little doubt, therefore, that this unhappy prelate became, at Rome, the victim of the Portuguese superstition, and of the pope's inhumanity." [3]

But, whatever this miserable man suffered, we cannot vindicate his conduct : and in his

---

[3] La Croze, lib. i. pp. 62, 63.

fall we have another instructive instance of the Almighty's retribution. By his tergiversation, indeed, he did no wrong to the Romish Church, for she had no right to hold him under a restraint which tempted him to have recourse to it for his emancipation. But he had sinned against God, and, therefore, against his own soul: then can we be surprised that he who had endeavoured to establish himself by fraud, was left to be cast down by similar means? It is only while walking in the ways of the Lord, that any can feel safe in this assurance of His protection.—" He will keep the feet of his saints, and the wicked shall be silent in darkness; for by strength shall no man prevail." [*]

[*] 1 Sam. ii. 9.

CHAPTER VI.

THE NATIVE POWERS RESIST THE ENCROACHMENTS AND INTOLERANCE OF THE PORTUGUESE.

Portuguese testimony against that nation's conduct in India.

1. WHILE the Portuguese were thus harrassing the poor, defenceless Christians, they were by various means provoking the heathen and Mahomedan inhabitants to rise up against themselves. Dissatisfied with the immunities granted them, and with the lucrative commerce they were permitted to carry on, they were incessantly encroaching upon the native powers, and their insolence increased with their prosperity. In this allegation several of their own writers concur. One, especially, has described in pointed terms their avarice and tyranny, their robberies and insolence, together with the judgment of God, which their injustice, and their neglect to propagate divine truth, brought down upon them. This writer is *Manuel de Faria*, and the observations referred to occur at the close of his *Asia Portuguesa*. He says,[1] " It is remarkable, that among all the persons who have gone to the Indies, whether as governors, captains, or merchants, of which sort most of them were in truth, there has not

[1] *Ponderacion muy notable*, &c. Geddes' History of the Church of Malabar, pp. 22, 24.

been one that has raised a family of any consideration, out of the goods they have got in these parts, either there or in Portugal, though there have been several of them that have got there, one, two, three, or four millions. Now that nothing considerable of all these vast treasures should any where appear, must be for one or both of these two reasons; first, that whereas God permitted the discovery of this country, only for the propagation of His name, and the true worship (but not by such barbarous methods as the forementioned, I venture to say), these travellers have, for the most part, pursued the ends of a sacrilegious covetousness, committing many acts of injustice to fill their coffers, instead of having any regard to religion; the other is, because the most of those riches were gained by the unjust means of tyrannies, robberies, and all sorts of insolence, of which you have many instances in the foregoing history."

2. The most offensive part of their conduct, however, related to the measures they adopted for the conversion of the heathen and Mahomedans. The promoters of such a system as the Roman creed, could not venture to depend upon the simple proclamation of the Gospel. Sooner shall light blend with darkness, than the superstitions and pretensions of Rome can consist with the free publication of God's word. These are utterly incompatible. Of this the Romish priesthood have always been conscious; and, accordingly, as in the instance before us, in all their endeavours to propagate their creed, they have adopted means in accordance with its character. These allegations are confirmed by native witnesses. The writer of the following extract was a Mahomedan.

Native testimony to the same effect, and their resolution to expel them.

1st. " The believers of Malabar were established in the most desirable and happy manner, by reason of the inconsiderable degree of oppression experienced from the rulers, who were acquainted with the ancient customs, and were kind to, and protectors of, the Mussulmans; and the subjects lived satisfied and contented; but, they sinned so, that God turned from them, and did, therefore, command the Europeans of Portugal, who oppressed and distressed the Mahomedan community by the commission of unlimited enormities, such as beating and deriding them; and sinking and stranding their ships; and spitting in their faces and on their bodies; and prohibiting them from performing voyages, particularly that to *Mecca;* and plundering their property, and burning their countries and temples; and making prizes of their ships; and kicking and trampling on their (the believers') books, and throwing them into the flames. They also endeavoured to make converts to their own religion, and enjoined churches of their own faith to be consecrated; tempting people, for these objects, with offers of money: and they dressed out their own women in the finest ornaments and apparel, in order, thereby, to deceive and allure the women of the believers. They did also put *Haji's,* and other Mussulmans, to a variety of cruel deaths; and they reviled and abused with unworthy epithets the prophet of God; and confined the Mahomedans, and loaded them with heavy irons, carrying them about for sale, from shop to shop, as slaves; enhancing their ill usage on these occasions, in order to extort the larger sum for their release. They confined them also, in dark, noisome, and hideous dungeons; and used to beat them with slippers, torturing them also with fire; and selling some into bondage, and retaining others in their servitude as slaves. On some they imposed the severest tasks, without admitting of the smallest relief or exemption. Others they transported into Guzerat, and into the Concan, and towards Arabia, being places which they themselves used to frequent, in the view, either of settling or sojourning therein, or of capturing vessels. In this way they accumulated great wealth and property, making captives also of women of rank, whom they kept in their houses till European issue was procured from them. These Portuguese did, in this manner, also seize on many *Seyyuds*, learned and principal men, whom they retained in confinement till they put them to death; thus prejudicing and distressing the Mussulmans in a thousand ways; so as that I have not a tongue to tell, or describe, all the mischiefs and mortifications attendant on such a scene of evil."

2nd. " After this they exerted their utmost efforts (which they had, indeed, from first to last) to bring the Mussulmans within the pale of their religion; and they made at length peace with them, for a consideration to be paid to them of ten in the hundred."

3rd. " The Mahomedans residing principally on the sea-coasts, it was customary for the newly-arrived *Europeans* (who used to resort annually to India at the appointed seasons) deridingly to ask the persons of their own nation, settled at the seaports, whether, and why, they (these settled *Portuguese*) had not yet done away the appearance of these people, the Mussulmans? reviling thereon their own chiefs, for not abolishing the Mahomedan religion; in the prosecution of which view the heads of the Portuguese desired *Hakim* of *Cochin* to expel the *Mussul-mans* from his city, promising thereon, to prove themselves the means of his reaping double the profit which accrued to him from their traffic; but the *Hakim of Cochin* answered, ' These are my subjects from days of old; and it is they who have erected my city; so that it is not possible for me to expel them." [2]

3. From this extract it is seen, that their treatment of the other natives of India, was no better than their conduct towards the poor defenceless Christians. Their tyranny none but bondmen could endure: and the resentment it provoked was such as might be expected from men who knew their title to be free, and their power to maintain their right. Their indignation cannot be better described than in the words of Hidalcaon, a Mahomedan prince to the North,

who laid siege to Goa in the year 1570. Both in his letters to the Viceroy, Don Luis d'Ataide, and in the address that he made to his officers, when he first communicated to them his design to drive the Portuguese out of India, he assigned the violence and injustice of which they had been guilty, as the chief causes of the war.

In his first letter to the Viceroy, after having complained of some other grievances, he tells him, that " he was certainly informed, that at " Ormus, Dio, Chaul, and all the other Portu- " guese ports, his subjects' ships were all strictly " searched, and all the boys and girls that were " found on board, of whatsoever quality, Abys- " sinians or Mahomedans, were forcibly car- " ried ashore, and there detained from their " parents or masters. This, saith he, is a " matter that I cannot but be extremely of-

---

[2] Asiatic Researches, Vol. v. pp. 20, 21.

" fended with ; neither can I judge otherwise
" of your permitting such acts of violence, but
" that you have a mind to break with me, for
" if you had not, I cannot be persuaded that
" your people durst presume to commit such
" insults."

He goes on, " Let it suffice that no differ-
" ence can happen between us, but what gives
" me great displeasure, and that I am both a
" brother and an ally of the King of Portugal ;
" and do esteem you as my particular friend, to
" put a stop to this matter, that so my subjects
" may have no further cause to complain thereof.
" Besides, I am confident the King of Portugal
" will not thank any, that shall be instrumental
" in making a breach between me and him, by
" compelling my subjects thus against their
" wills to turn Christians, a practice, saith he,
" that is abominable in the sight of all the
" world ; nay, I am confident, that Jesus Christ
" himself, the God whom you adore, cannot be
" well pleased with such service as this : force
" and compulsion in all such cases, being what
" God, Kings, and all the people of the world
" do abominate. The work of turning people
" from one religion to another, if it be not done by
" the divine inspiration, and the immediate will
" of God, can never be sincere, neither can con-
" verts have any inward respect for a religion,
" which they are compelled to profess. I do,
" therefore, entreat you to see that this matter
" be speedily redressed ; but, especially that of
" taking peoples' children from them by vio-
" lence, which is a thing I stand amazed at,
" and am in duty bound to see remedied."

In his second letter, he thanks the viceroy
for an order which he had sent to Ormus, and

the other Portuguese ports, prohibiting all such violence, but at the same time tells him, that his " order was not in the least regarded; for that " the Portuguese, notwithstanding, went on " still in their former courses, to which he tells " him, if there were not a speedy and effectual " stop put, it must necessarily beget a war be- " twixt him and the Portuguese; adding, that " as he knew that neither God, nor wise Kings, " took any delight in discords, so he was cer- " tain that there was no religion in the world, " that justified the forcing of people from one " religion to another."

In his speech to his officers, he tells them, " The Portuguese at first came among us, " under the character of merchants, promis- " ing to help us to several goods that we " wanted; but that afterwards, by making of " trifling presents to some weak princes, and " other arts, they had obtained leave to build " store houses, for their wares, upon the coast; " but that instead of warehouses, they had " built fortresses, by which means they had " strengthened themselves so in India, both by " sea and land, that it was more than time " for the natives to look about them, and to " join together to extirpate such cruel tyrants, " and ravagers of so many kingdoms, and ene- " mies to the general quiet and commerce of " the world; and that for one thing espe- " cially, which was what no patience was able " to endure, their compelling the Indians in all " places, where they had power, to change their " religion."

In these transactions the Christians and the Mahomedan seem to have changed characters, the Mahomedan writing like a Christian, and the

Christians behaving themselves like Mahome-dans.[3]

4. The natives soon had reason to suspect the viceroy's sincerity in his expressions of regret at the proceedings of which they complained. For about this time the Dominican friars, under pretence of building a convent, erected a fortress on the island of Solor, which, as soon as finished, the viceroy garrisoned with a strong force. The natives very naturally felt indignant at this additional encroachment, and took every opportunity to attack the garrison. The monks, forgetful of their peaceable profession, took an active part in these skirmishes, and many of them fell sword in hand.

The Mahomedan faith has been appropriately entitled, *The religion of the sword;* and with equal propriety may we so designate the religion of these belligerent friars. The Portuguese writers give an account of one of their *missionaries,* Fernando Vinagre, who was as prompt in the field of battle as at the baptismal font. This man, though a secular priest, undertook the command of a squadron that was sent to the assistance of the rajah of Tidore,[4] on which occasion he is said to have acted in the twofold capacity of a great commander, and a great apostle, at one time appearing in armour, at another in a surplice; and even occasionally, baptizing the converts of his sword without putting off his armour, but covering it with his ecclesiastical vest. In this crusade[5] he had two

---

[3] Geddes History, &c., pp. 24—27.
        Pudet hæc opprobria nobis
        Vel dici potuisse.

[4] Called *Tadura* or *Daco,* an island in the Indian Ocean, one of the Moluccas

[5] 'These *a la Dragoon* conversions.' Geddes' History, p. 27.

assistants in the persons of his admiral, *Antonio Galvam*, and a captain, *Francisco de Castro*. These men are said to have converted five rajahs in the island of Mazacar; and the admiral is described as another St. Paul, governing all under his dominion, both with his sword and with his voice,—*a sword and a voice*, say the romanists, *worthy of a glorious eternity*.[6] Poor men! Little did they know of the spirit or the history of that holy Apostle.

5. The natives of India are accurate discerners of character, and have often correctly calculated the result of a given course of conduct. In the present instance they had the sagacity to foresee that the triumph of their oppressors would be short. A Portuguese writer has recorded, with approbation, the expression of an Indian to this effect. " Let them alone," said he, " for they will quickly come to lose that, " as covetous merchants, which they have gained " as admirable soldiers ; they now conquer " Asia, but it will not be long before Asia will " conquer them."[7]

This prediction began soon to be fulfilled; for not long after, the natives succeeded in driving the Portuguese from the island of Ito. To this they were incited by one Gemalio, a native of distinction, who thus rebuked the base intruders in a full assembly :—

" If you preach to others that there is a God " in heaven, who observes all that is done on " earth, and will certainly reward all good, and " punish all evil deeds, without believing it

---

[6] It was this Antonio who discovered the King of Portugal's special title to *the clove*, which having five points, he said, bore the King of Portugal's arms, which are the five wounds of Christ stamped upon it.

[7] Geddes History, p. 28.

" yourselves, or without practising what you
" believe, you are certainly guilty of the abomi-
" nation which such a God must detest above
" all others. You are strangers, come from the
" very skirts of the world ; and will you, who
" are the offspring of the shades, which the sun
" leaves when he goes down, presume to tyran-
" nize over us, who entertained you so kindly,
" and have been so long a sanctuary to you?
" If these be the customs of your country, you
" must know that they are what we abominate.
" Return, return therefore to your native dark-
" ness. Away to your ancient habitations,
" where the want of light will hide your ac-
" tions ; and do not come hither to commit
" them in the very apple of the eye of the sun,
" as he riseth out of his brightest cradle. You
" preach Christ crucified to us, and at the
" same time crucify those whom you have per-
" suaded to believe in him. You will make
" others to be Christians without appearing to
" be such yourselves. You must know that
" we are not ignorant of what you have done
" to the Rajah of Xael, and how you rewarded
" his great kindness and civility to you, with
" violence and outrage, and the good turns of
" his subjects with dishonouring their wives.
" We know also how you have used the Queen
" of Aram, whom, after she had lost both her
" kingdom and her husband to secure you, you
" have basely thrown off, as one who could be
" of no further use to you. Begone therefore
" immediately out of this Island, and hereafter
" never presume to set your foot, or even so
" much as to cast your eye upon it."
With this speech Gemalio stirred up the
natives to drive the invaders out of their coasts.
" Thus," says the historian, himself a Portu-

guese, " thus do we lose those places by our insolence, which we had gained by our valor." [a] In this jeopardy of their affairs, from the hostility of the Hidalcaon and other native powers whom they had irritated, the Portuguese are said to have invoked the succour of their saints, who, it is pretended, rendered them most essential service.

Portuguese
legends in-
vented in
vain for
their sup-
port.

6. The following are specimens of the achievements of these saints.—" About this time St. Francis destroyed a whole fleet of Jores who were come against the Portuguese. Though they do not pretend to have seen the saint in the battle, which was very bloody on both sides, yet a cook who belonged to a *Capuchin* convent not far off, having hid himself in the ruins of their Church, saw a friar in his own habit board the ships of the Jores' fleet one after another, whom he so terrified with his very look, as to put them all immediately to flight, and he pursued them till out of sight. This formidable friar was afterwards discovered to be St. Francis. The historian has not explained, indeed, how the saint came to be known; yet he tells us that the action was most becoming in St. Francis, who was a lively image of Christ, thus to appear and confound the enemies of Christianity, by uttering the words, *It is I*. If this story did not rebuild the *Capuchin* Church, then in ruins, the Portuguese were not so grateful as they used to be in such cases."

But this feat of St. Francis was nothing to the action which their own St. Anthony fought for them some five or six years afterwards. It was in a battle by land, wherein several saw him mowing down whole squadrons of the

---

[a] Geddes' History of the Church of Malabar, pp. 22—30.

enemy wherever the battle raged in greatest
fury, and, at the same time, extinguishing the
fire of the enemy's artillery with the sleeve of his
sacred habit. It is true, several Portuguese
fell in the action ; but they must surely have
been killed by some other weapons than fire-
arms, or at least cannon, which St. Anthony so
effectually silenced.[9]

But even these heroic deeds were surpassed
by the Apostles, James and Thomas, whose aid
was implored in the heat of battle.[1] For the
account of all this marvellous interposition in
behalf of the Portuguese, we must refer the
reader to the original record, if he has not
already read enough. Our involuntary feeling
on the perusal is, not that the Portuguese, with
such champions, triumphed in the present field,
but that they were ever defeated, and compelled
in a few years to relinquish the possessions that
were so defended. But the subject is too sad
for irony. Alas! for the prostration of the
human mind under the withering influence of
Romish superstition.[2]

What effect the friars anticipated from these
puerile legends we are left to conjecture. Probably they expected them to intimidate the
ignorant and superstitious natives, or to give

[9] Geddes', pp. 42, 43. The St. Francis here mentioned
was the founder of the Franciscan order of monks, which was
reformed in 1525 by Matthew de Bassi, under the sanction
of pope Clement VII. This was the origin of the order of
Capuchins. Mosheim, cent. 16, sec. 3. pt. i. s. xvi.

[1] J. P. Maffeii. Historia Indica, pp. 584, &c.

[2] We may here introduce the Portuguese account of an
auxiliary of a different character. In the year 1584, a famous
Amazon, who was driven out of her country by the Hidalçaon,
sought refuge at Goa. Her name was Abchi, and she is
said to have retained great wit, and the remains of exquisite
beauty, 'till the age of sixty-two, and to have fought in many
battles to admiration. Pretending to have matters of great

T

confidence to their own forces in the heat of battle: but, whatever influence they may have produced upon either party, they totally failed to increase the security of their Indian possessions, from which at no distant period they were expelled. This was a just retribution. How could they expect the righteous "Judge of all the earth" to prosper a cause, which was founded and maintained by falsehood and injustice, violence and blood? "Righteousness exalteth a nation: but sin is a reproach to any people."[3] When it is attempted to give to such impiety the sanction of religion, it is a direct challenge to the Lord to vindicate the honour of His Name; and what can such daring offenders expect but to be brought to ruin and everlasting contempt!

moment to communicate to the Viceroy, the Inquisitors put a stop to the negotiation. No one could tell why they interfered, but probably they suspected her sincerity, and a suspicion was quite enough to render her obnoxious to that tribunal. After confining her for some time in prison, they banished her to Ormus, whence she made her escape, and fled to the court of the Great Mogul, Shahbaz Khan.—Geddes, pp. 43, 44.

[3] Prov. xiv. 34.

CHAPTER VII.

CONTINUATION OF THE ROMANISTS' ATTEMPTS AGAINST THE LIBERTY OF THE SYRIAN CHURCH.

1. The jeopardy of the Portuguese affairs from the native powers, did not induce them in the least to alter their course towards the Syrian Church. Not long after the removal of Mar Joseph from India, Mar Abraham, now Bishop of Angamale,[1] arrived at Goa. He had cautiously avoided passing through Portugal, and travelled overland by way of Ormus. Rejoiced to find his rival gone, he demanded, and naturally expected, to be allowed immediately to return to Malabar, where he hoped to preside over his diocese without further interference from any quarter. In this expectation, however, he was disappointed. As he was furnished with authentic briefs from the pope, there seemed to be no just cause for detaining him; but the Portuguese had reasons for objecting to his return to the Christians of Malabar, as potent as those which had formerly induced them to send Mar Joseph among them. Their

Mar Abraham's return to Goa.

[1] It has already appeared in the foregoing pages, (chap. v. sec. 11,) as stated by Gouvea, that this prelate is described in the pope's brief as Archbishop: but he continues to be mentioned in every *history* as Bishop.—Gouvea.—La Croze. —Geddes.

design on the former occasion was to promote a schism in the church, which had succeeded, perhaps, beyond their expectation : their present object was to prevent that schism from being healed. Besides their original intention to unite the Syrians to the Church of Rome, they were now most desirous of attaching them to their civil government in India. The hostility which they had provoked from the native powers made their situation very precarious, and they would have been glad of the assistance of so numerous and respectable a body as the Malabar Christians. Nor can there be any doubt that this people would have cordially rendered them all the succour in their power, had not the Portuguese so grossly abused their confidence. Yet so infatuated were they, so blind to the turpitude of their conduct, that they did not despair of persuading the Syrians to make common cause with them against the Heathen and Mahomedans. But the arrival of Mar Abraham disconcerted them, for it threatened to subvert their design, and they determined, if possible, to prevent his return to the coast.

They soon found a plausible pretext for his detention. Without questioning the validity of the briefs which he had brought from the pope, or withholding from them the respect to which they were entitled; he was told that they suspected the sincerity of the professions he had made at Rome, and that before they could restore him to his bishopric, they must strictly examine his *briefs* and *informations*, in order to be satisfied that he had not imposed upon his holiness. The result may be anticipated. It has seldom been possible to construct a title deed of any description so correctly as to elude the subtilty of Roman Canonists. They could find enough in the most perspicuous document to neutralize its terms, especially when the pope or other ecclesiastical authorities desired it. On the present occasion they soon discovered passages sufficiently questionable for their purpose. The Archbishop took upon him to declare the pope's briefs to be null and void, as having been obtained under false pretences: and Mar Abraham, instead of being sent back to his bishopric in triumph, was confined in the Dominican Convent at Goa, where they meant to detain him until a satisfactory answer to the Archbishop's representation of the case should be received from the pope.

2. Mar Abraham was too well convinced that this would amount to imprisonment for life quietly to await the result. He, therefore, resolved to make his escape, and after several unsuccessful attempts, at length accomplished his object, upon the night of Holy Thursday, while the friars of the convent were engaged at prayers in the chapel. Having effected his passage to the continent, he hastened to Malabar, where the Christians welcomed him with unbounded joy. While both their Bishops were imprisoned by the Portuguese, they had despaired of seeing either of them again: their happiness therefore at the escape of Mar Abraham corresponded with the recent depression of their hopes, and they celebrated his return with the most joyous festivities.

Escapes from confinement there, and reaches Malabar.

Very different were the feelings with which the intelligence of his escape was received at Goa. The Archbishop and Viceroy were greatly disconcerted, and wrote immediately to the Bishop of Cochin, and all the Portuguese governors on the coast, to have him apprehended with all possible expedition, if above

ground. Expecting that this vigilant search
would be made for him, he took care to keep,
as far as possible, out of their reach, never venturing to visit any church in the neighbourhood
of Cochin, or the other Portuguese stations that
he passed.

He continued, however, to carry on a correspondence with the papal authorities, with all
the appearance of friendship: for he is said
still to have professed himself a Romanist, and
to have re-ordained all whom he had formerly
admitted to holy orders according to the rites of
the Syrian Church. If this be true, he cannot have acted with sincerity; for it is certain,
that in all other respects he preserved the
Syrian customs throughout the diocese, where
he continued to preach his former doctrines,
and in the public prayers to make mention of
the Bishop of Babylon as their patriarch.

Attends a
council at
Goa, at the
summons of
the pope,
and under
protection
of his safe
conduct.

3. He, probably, expected that his pretending to conform to the Roman Church, would
induce the papists to leave him in quiet possession of his bishopric; but he did not sufficiently
know the men with whom he had to deal, if he
thought that they could be so easily imposed
upon. Their emissaries narrowly watched him;
and the Archbishop of Goa, having reported his
conduct to the pope, Gregory XIII., that pontiff
immediately issued a brief, dated November

28th, 1578, and directed to Mar Abraham, in
which he commanded him to repair forthwith
to Goa, to assist at the provincial council that
was to be assembled there, and faithfully to
conform to all that should be decreed relating
to his diocese. Lest he should refuse to comply with this brief, under pretence of insecurity
to his person, the pope accompanied it with his
letters of safe conduct, assuring him that he

was free to go and return without molestation. On the arrival of these documents at Goa, the Archbishop, Don Vincente da Fonseca, a Dominican friar, immediately called a provincial council,[2] at which it was determined to forward to Mar Abraham the pope's brief and letter of safe conduct, together with letters of safe conduct confirmed by an oath,[3] from the Archbishop and Viceroy.

Mar Abraham did not place much confidence in these assurances of safety: yet, considering all the circumstances of his situation, and being convinced that he could not much longer escape the vigilance and growing power of the Portuguese, he determined to obey the summons, whatever were the consequences. Accordingly he repaired to the council, and assisted as desired. He was required once more to abjure the Syrian Creed, and repeat his profession of the faith of Rome: then solemnly to promise, that he would see that all the decrees of that synod, relating to his bishopric, were punctually executed, and that he would send to Goa all the heretical books to be found in the diocese, to be corrected or burned, as might be determined there: and, lastly, having confessed that there was no wine in the cup which he delivered, with the host, into the hands of the priests whom he had ordained, he was required to reordain them.[4] To this he assented without hesi-

---

[2] This was the third council held at Goa.

[3] La Croze, p. 65.

[4] What a stretch of authority was this, to invalidate the orders of a whole Church, for no other reason, and the romanists have assigned no other, than the omission to put wine into the cup used at the ordination of priests! Even in the Church of Rome, this was comparatively a modern practice. "But for *canonists* and *schoolmen*, by subtilties invented on purpose to support a late error, or to serve a present turn,

tation; and the council expressing themselves satisfied, he was permitted to go back to Malabar.

to wound Christianity in its very vitals, is a practice too common to be wondered at. " I am sure, says Geddes, the Church of Rome has much more reason to apprehend that the sacrilege of denying the cup to the laity, in the sacrament, may make her communion imperfect and ineffectual, than that this alone should make ordinations so."

" But after all this stir, this doctrine, namely, that the delivering of the bread and the cup into the hands of those that are ordained priests is essential to orders, is so far from being true, that it is owned to be a novelty by all the modern divines of any learning in the Church of Rome; and it is moreover contradicted by her daily practice: for, as all the world knows, she allows the *Greek* orders to be good, in the collation whereof she knows that the bread and cup are not given to those ordained priests."

" It is true, the council of Florence, in her instructions to the Armenians, seems to have doted into the same error with this of the Portuguese, in making that new ceremony essential to orders. But let that be as it will, it is certain, that both the present practice of the Roman Church, and all her truly learned sons, the modern schoolmen not excepted, do condemn it as an error: for which I shall only quote two of her most eminent schoolmen, and one of her ablest critics."

" Cardinal Lugo, in his 2nd Disp. *de Sacramentis,* says, " *Aliunde autem habemus, non porrectionem panis et vini determinatè requiri ex divinâ institutione, cum Græci absque illa porrectione ordinentur; ergo fatendum est Christum solum voluisse pro materiâ aliquod signum proportionatum hoc vel illud.*"

" And Becanus, in the third part of his scholastical divinity, chap. 26, of the Sacrament of Order, has as follows : " *Concilium Florentinum in instructione Armenorum solum meminit materiæ accidentalis, quæ ab ecclesiâ fuit instituta,* which was the delivering of the bread and cup, *non autem substantialis quam Christus præscripsit,* which is the imposition of hands, *Quia hæc ex Scripturis et antiquis Patribus erat satis cognita, non autem illa. Addo, si hoc argumentum valeret, posse optimè retorqueri ita, Antiqua concilia non assignant aliam materiam nisi impositionem manuum, ergo, &c.* He concludes thus, *Nota antiqua concilia assignâsse materiam à Christo institutam, Florentinum verò materiam assignâsse quam Ecclesia introduxit,* that is the latin only. By this any one

4. Not long after his return, Mar Abraham ordained his priests a third time, two Jesuits, from the college of Vaipicotta, being present at the service. They were acquainted with the Syriac language, and attended to see that no-

may see, that the Church of Rome is not so uniform a body as she pretends to be, being thus inconsistent with herself in a question of so high importance as this, viz., what is, and what is not essential to Orders; and we may see likewise, how she will break through all ancient doctrines and rules, rather than not disgrace all bodies of Christians which deny her obedience, by unchurching them by some subtilty or other; and, indeed, through the clearest evidences of matter of fact, as she does in the case of the orders of the Church of England. And, furthermore, how apt she is to look upon her own novel inventions as the main substantials of religion."

"To whom I shall only add Morinus, whose judgment in a case of this nature, is of more weight, than that of the whole tribe of schoolmen. Who in the 1st. Chap. of his first *Exercitation De Sacris Ordinationibus*, saith, *Nemo, ut mihi videtur, dubitare potest, antiquos Latinos, à quibus accepimus et ordinationes et quod sacerdotes sumus, legitimè et validè sacerdotes consecrasse, et cætera sacrarum ordinationum munia contulisse; eadem antiquorum Græcorum ratio. Certissimum enim est et evidentissimum, neminem ordinationes Græcas criminari posse, quin crimen in Latinas redundet, cum utrique mutuo alterius ordinationes probaverint: Græcusque apud Latinos, et Latinus apud Græcos sine ullâ unquam ordinationis querelâ sacra Mysteria celebraverit: pari veritatis evidentia certum est recentiores Latinos in hunc usque diem legitimas ordinationes celebrasse et celebrare, eadem ratio hodiernorum Græcorum, cum ut ex iis quæ manifestissimè* καὶ αὐτοψία *quadam demonstrata sunt, ab antiquis non differant, eosque publicè in suis ordinibus ministrantes suscipiat Ecclesia Romana, semperque susceperit.* And in his seventh Exercitation, speaking of the delivering the bread and cup into the hands of those that are ordained priests, he acknowledgeth it to be a late ceremony in the Roman Church. *Antiqui Rituales Latini, non secus ac Græci, istam instrumentorum traditionem nobis non exhibent: Quidquid spectat ad illam materiam et formam ab iis abest. Duo ritus Ordinationis editi, unus Romæ in sancti Gregorii sacramentario ex Bibliothecâ Vaticanâ, alter Parisiis ab Hugone Mainardo, ex Bibliothecâ Corbeiensi, ista omnia nobis non repræsentant duo antiquissimi Petaviani literis uncialibus scripti*

thing essential was omitted. To the other things that he had promised, Mar Abraham paid no attention, continuing to observe the ancient Syrian Creed and ritual, and to name the patriarch of Babylon in his prayers, as the head of the Church.

Apologizes for his conduct to the patriarch of Babylon, and begs him to send another Bishop to India.

5. Apprehending, or hearing, that his concessions to the Roman ecclesiastics had caused a misunderstanding in the patriarch's mind, Mar Abraham wrote to him shortly after the council, to explain the circumstances of his attendance, and his proceedings there. In his letter, which is said to have been intercepted, he told the primate that he was induced to go to Goa, purely out of fear from the Portuguese, *who were over his head as a hammer over an anvil,* and that when before the council, he delivered in a confession of faith, which none of the *Latin* Bishops were able to contradict. He then avowed himself to his patriarch, a dogmatist of the Chaldæan creed.

Thus did this poor man try to manage the two opposite authorities of Babylon and Rome; but he laboured in vain, all his tergiversation failing to secure for him the confidence of either, or the peaceable exercise of his functions.

---

qui præ cæteris eminent, duo alii secundum istos antiquissimi et egregiè splendidèque scripti, qui ampli sunt, et multa Ordinationibus illis exhibent, quæ videri possunt non necessaria, quorum unus est Rotomagensis, alter Rhemensis. Tres alii, quorum primus Senonensis est, duo alii Corbeienses, unus à Rodrado scriptus, nunc vertitur annus octogentesimus primus, alter a Rotaldo præcedente multo junior, sed copiosissimus, qui quæcunque noverat ad Ordinationes pertinere, iis ditavit Sacramentarium suum; denique unus è Bibliothecâ Thuand perantiquus, et alte. Belloracensis. In all which ancient rituals, he saith, there is a profound silence of this ceremony."
Geddes, pp. 34—37.

A. D.
1575.

At length, beginning to bend under the weight of years, worn out by the long and unremitting persecutions of his enemies, and, probably, afflicted with compunction for his frequent prevarications, Mar Abraham felt unequal to the duties of his office, and wrote to the patriarch of Babylon to send him a Bishop, to assist him while he lived, and to succeed him after his death. The patriarch complied with his request, consecrated a young man named Simeon, for the purpose, and sent him to India.

6. Mar Simeon was very kindly received by the Syrians; and, with more zeal for the integrity of their Church, than judgment under their present circumstances, they soon began to pay him more respect than Mar Abraham. The reason of this preference for Mar Simeon was, that he had held no intercourse with the *Latins:* but it was more than the young prelate could bear. Thus caressed, he was encouraged to endeavour to supersede Mar Abraham, and to assume the entire jurisdiction of the see. The consequence was, the speedy division of the diocese again into two opposite parties. Mar Simeon was patronized by a powerful Rannee of that country, called by the Portuguese Queen of Pimenta, and was permitted to establish himself in her dominions, at Carturté, one of the principal towns of the Syrians.

Mar Simeon arrives, and soon occasions a schism in the diocese.

This schism was soon followed by excommunications which the rival Bishops fulminated against each other, and the whole Christian community was thrown into violent commotion. The more numerous party adhered to Mar Simeon, acknowledging him for their lawful Bishop because free from papal contamination: but Mar Abraham appealed to the more powerful arm of the Portuguese, thus using those very means for the ruin of his competitor, which the unhappy Mar Joseph had formerly employed against himself. We cannot too deeply deplore these contentions between men holding such responsible stations in the Church, and whose duty it was, "with all lowliness and meekness, with longsuffering," to forbear "one another in love; endeavouring to keep the unity of the Spirit in the bond of peace."[5] But the ambitious Christian pays less regard to the *Church* of Christ, than the heathen soldiers paid to His *seamless robe* at the foot of the cross. It is truly afflicting to the pious mind to see these prelates so compromising the dignity, and profaning the sanctity of their office. "The servant of the Lord must not strive; but be gentle unto all men, apt to teach, patient."[6] A contrary spirit will not be permitted long to go unpunished by the Lord of righteousness and peace.

The secular character of the prelacy increases the violence of party feeling.

7. This contention was, no doubt, rendered more violent and extensive by the secular character of a great part of the Bishop's duties. Their authority extended equally over temporal and spiritual affairs within the diocese. By virtue of the immunities which the Christians had long enjoyed, the heathen princes and judges took no cognizance of their affairs, criminal cases alone excepted: so that all civil and ecclesiastical causes came within the jurisdiction of their own spiritual rulers. They paid tribute indeed to their heathen governors, and were obliged to furnish their quota of troops in the event of war breaking out: but as the wars of the country were neither frequent nor of long continuance, they felt little incon-

[5] Eph. iv. 2, 3.   [6] 2 Tim. ii. 24.

venience from this part of the conditions on which they held their privileges. The extent of the diocese was great, containing at one time upwards of 1400 churches,[7] and about the same number of country towns, or small boroughs. For many years, while in the uninterrupted enjoyment of their rights and liberties, the population rapidly increased; for the priesthood were not then, as under papal influence they afterwards became, engaged to celibacy; nor had they either monks or nuns among them; and the people very seldom took up their abode out of their native country.

8. To be the head of so respectable a community as this, was enough to fire the ambition of a young prelate, who does not appear to have taken by any means a *subordinate* view of his *secular* dignity and power. For similar reasons, we may understand Mar Abraham's application to the determined enemies of his Church to deliver him from his rival. Though Mar Simeon had been sent from Babylon at his own request, yet he wrote to the viceroy and Archbishop of Goa, describing him as an intruder into his church, and an enemy to the *Latin* faith; and desiring them to drive him out of the country. The Portuguese authorities had no such regard for Mar Abraham as to induce them for his own sake to take up his cause; yet their own interest prompted them now to do him this service. There was much more hope of their subduing the Syrians, while under the infirm and versatile Abraham, than if they had a prelate of Simeon's energy and ambition. The honour of their church also pleaded in Mar Abraham's favour; for he had received Roman

[7] About the beginning of the eighteenth century.—La Croze, p. 68.

consecration, and was appointed to his bishopric by the pope. It was, therefore, determined to give him their support, and place him in undisputed possession of his see.

Mar Simeon taken by stratagem and sent to Rome, where the validity of his consecration and orders is denied.

9. Hearing that the party of Mar Simeon was very numerous, and that he was out of their reach at Carturté, they despaired of taking him by force; accordingly it was resolved to get him into their hands by stratagem. For this purpose, they employed some Franciscan friars, who ingratiated themselves with the unsuspecting Bishop, and then, under the mask of friendship, represented to him the danger to which he exposed himself by neglecting to obtain briefs from Rome, without which, they assured him, he would always be troubled by the Portuguese, and his person would never be safe. Observing the impression made upon him by these representations, they urged him to undertake a voyage to Rome, stating it to be impossible otherwise to maintain himself in a dignity, for the sake of which he was taking so much pains.

Their stratagem succeeded. Inexperienced in the artifices of Rome, intent on the object of his ambition, Mar Simeon took no time to consider the peril he incurred by following this advice. Neither did he reflect, that the course proposed would invalidate his claim to the preference shown him by the Syrians, which, he ought to have remembered, he owed to the single circumstance of his freedom from Romish contamination. Thus heedlessly did he fall into the snare of his enemies. Having taken the precaution to appoint one Jacob, a cattanar, his vicar-general during his absence, he accompanied the friars to Cochin, whence he proceeded to Goa, and there embarked on the first ship for Portugal. Shortly after his arrival at Lisbon he was sent to Rome.

The anxiety of the Roman Church to prove the invalidity of all orders not emanating from herself, has already been shown. Accordingly, this course was adopted with Mar Simeon. He was examined by the Inquisition, and easily convicted of being a Nestorian. They then attempted to prove that he had never been consecrated, or even ordained priest. Having compelled him to anathematize his errors, they shut him up in a monastery, for the purpose, as was pretended, of instructing him in the dogmas of their Church. After a time he was brought out again, and they proceeded with his trial; at the conclusion of which the Pope, Sixtus V., pronounced sentence against him. He declared him to be no Bishop, forbade him henceforth to exercise the episcopal functions, and even prohibited him from celebrating the Liturgy, because of the alleged uncertainty of his ordination to the priesthood. With this sentence upon him, he was sent by the Cardinal Severiana to Philip II., King of Spain,[8] who placed him under the care of Don Alexio de Menezes, whom he was about to send to India as Archbishop of Goa.

10. Mar Simeon naturally expected Menezes to carry him back to India; but instead of this, he was kept in confinement at Lisbon, in a Franciscan convent, from whence he is said to have written to his vicar-general, Jacob, by every fleet that sailed to India, and in all his letters to have styled himself Metropolitan of India, and maintained his unshaken profession

He dies in confinement in Portugal: reflections on his death.

[8] This is the monarch who seized the kingdom of Portugal, which remained in possession of the Kings of Spain until the year 1640.

of the Chaldæan faith.　These letters were found some time after, in 1599, by Archbishop Menezes, when he visited Malabar, and were sent by him to the chief tribunal of the general *Inquisition* of Portugal.　It is uncertain whether Mar Simeon was alive at the time of their arrival; but if he was, it is with great probability concluded, that he was made to change his Franciscan prison for a dungeon of the Inquisition, and that they took good care that he should write no more letters to India.[9]

This is all we know of the end of this young prelate.　It was his calamity, as in the case of Nestorius, to be raised to a station of such sacred responsibility, before his religious principles were sufficiently matured for him to feel comparatively indifferent to its honours, while bearing the burden of its cares.　At any age, to fulfil the office of a Bishop well, requires a double measure of Divine grace; and when the inexperience of youth is added to all the infirmities natural to man, the difficulties are greatly augmented.　We are not surprised, then, that Mar Simeon forgot his duty to God, to the Church, and to his senior, under all the circumstances of his situation: neither can we marvel that the Lord left him in his enemies' hands, to chastise him for his pride.　But this does not exonerate the authors of his destruction.　His only offences against Rome were, that he owned another authority, and maintained a different creed,—crimes, however, that are never to be pardoned by that intolerant Church, and for which no punishment is deemed too severe.　The Portuguese historian, Gouvea, endeavours to exculpate the pope for the part

[9] Geddes, pp. 39, 40.

he acted in this tragedy, by referring to a foolish letter which Mar Simeon is said to have written to the Patriarch of Babylon, but which bears strong marks of having been forged for this purpose. In it he is represented as acknowledging himself a layman, announcing his arrival in India, describing the church there as in a very low state, and Mar Abraham as too infirm to attend to his duties. He is then made to say, that he deemed it for the service of God and for the patriarch's honour, to take upon himself to ordain priests ; and to beg that he may be confirmed in the episcopal office, and that all his ordinations may be sanctioned, by the primate's letters.[1] What must the historian have thought of his readers' credulity to suppose that they could receive all this ! What unprejudiced mind can believe it possible, that the Patriarch of Babylon would send a layman to relieve an aged Bishop in the discharge of his onerous and appropriate duties, that the Syrians would have consented to receive ordination at such hands, or that Mar Simeon himself should so little understand the nature of episcopacy as to imagine, that any letters from the patriarch could render valid the ordinations administered by an unconsecrated person ? And even if he had been guilty of the folly here imputed to him, what right had the pope to punish him for the act ? He was in no way amenable to the Church of Rome. The whole proceedings were, therefore, most iniquitous on the part of all who assisted in them ; and thus is it often seen, that the God of truth gives over His offending servants to be punished, sometimes even unto death, by those very persons who

[1] La Croze, p. 70.

U

deserve to be the sufferers, rather than the executioners of His vengeance. Thus saith the Lord, " O Assyrian, the rod of mine anger, and the staff in their hand is mine indignation. I will send him against an hypocritical nation, and against the people of my wrath will I give him a charge, to take the spoil, and to take the prey, and to tread them down like the mire of the streets. Howbeit he meaneth not so, neither doth his heart think so, but it is in his heart to destroy and cut off nations not a few." [2] As of Assyria, so of Rome, the object of all her wicked and unjust proceedings was, to maintain her proud pretensions ; and in the day of His righteous judgment will Jehovah visit upon all who are implicated in her guilt, the miseries which they have unsparingly inflicted.

Fourth Council at Goa: Mar Abraham afraid to attend: he openly avows his adherence to the Chaldæan faith.

11. Having anticipated our history for the purpose of concluding the mournful narrative of Mar Simeon's fall, we shall now retrace our steps. The removal of that unhappy prelate seemed to open to his rival the prospect of a quiet possession of his bishopric; but in this he was disappointed. The cattanar Jacob, Mar Simeon's vicar-general, refused to acknowledge Mar Abraham, and thus kept open the schism in the Church.

A. D.
1590.

The aged prelate met with further disturbance also from his old enemies, the Portuguese. In the year 1590, Don Matthias, Archbishop of Goa, called another provincial council, the fourth that had been held in India. In conformity to the brief of Pope Gregory XIII. Mar Abraham was summoned to attend, but he was too conscious how little he had fulfilled his promises at the last council to place himself again in his

[2] Isaiah x. 5—7.

enemies' power. Accordingly, he answered the summons with this proverb—*The cat that has once been bitten by a snake is frightened at a cord.*[3] By this he intimated, that he could not venture to expose himself to dangers which he believed to be inevitable, if he trusted himself again in the power of the Portuguese ecclesiastics. We may hope also, that he now felt ashamed of his former disgraceful conduct, and that he was filled with compunction at the ruin which he had brought successively upon his two brethren, Mar Joseph and Mar Simeon. Certainly his subsequent behaviour indicated a feeling of remorse, and a desire to make some reparation for the past. He dissembled no longer, boldly refused to comply with the Archbishop's injunctions, and publicly avowed his unshaken adherence to the Chaldæan faith.[4]

12. The Romanists were now furious against him; and finding that they could no longer work upon his fears, they endeavoured to blacken his character. They accused him of administering holy orders and the sacraments for money, and of admitting Christians to the communion, without previously requiring of them that confession which in the Syrian church is indispensable. These assertions are made without a shadow of proof. Criminal as Mar Abraham's conduct had been, in the means he used to secure the undivided possession of his bishopric, yet it requires much stronger evidence than these *ex parte* statements, to believe the aged Bishop guilty of such profanation.

Romanist's accusations against him.

[3] This is an Arabic proverb found in the collection of Erpenius.

[4] About this period, in the year 1591, a party of Englishmen first visited India overland. See next chapter.

CHAP.
VII.

Menezes,
Archbishop
of Goa, sails
to India,
with full
powers
from the
pope to act
in Malabar.
A. D.
1595.

13. When the account of these proceedings arrived at Rome, Don Alexio de Menezes, the newly appointed Archbishop of Goa, was on the eve of sailing for India. Accordingly the pope, Clement VIII. addressed to him the brief he issued on the occasion. It was dated 27th of January, 1595. After expressing the grief with which he learned, that Mar Abraham, Archbishop of Angamale, having sometime ago embraced the Roman faith, and rendered obedience to the holy see, as well at Rome as in the synod of Goa, was now unhappily fallen into his ancient Nestorianism, and refused to consent to have the Syriac books, that were used in his diocese, corrected and purged from the errors with which they were filled; and further, that he had committed divers acts of simony—to remedy these disorders, the pope commands Don Alexio de Menezes to make strict inquisition into the conduct and errors of that prelate; and in case he found him guilty of such crimes as were laid to his charge, to have him apprehended, and secured at Goa: afterwards, to send to Rome authentic copies of the verbal process and information, in order that the holy see might be able to form a correct judgment of the whole matter. In the mean time, that the diocese of Angamale might not suffer any temporal or spiritual inconvenience from the absence of its diocesan, the pope directed the Archbishop, in the same brief, to appoint a governor, or vicar apostolic, of the *Roman* communion, over the bishopric; and he was to procure, if possible, a man well acquainted with the Syriac language. In the event of Mar Abraham's death, he was ordered to take special care, that no Bishop coming from Babylon should be suffered to enter Malabar,

as his successor, nor any other prelate not appointed by the holy see.

Armed with these powers, Menezes embarked for India, more in the character of a crusader against an infidel nation, than in that of a Christian Bishop, to instruct the ignorant, and guide the wandering, and comfort the afflicted of Jesus' flock. He went, not as an herald of mercy, to carry glad tidings of great joy to the poor Syrians, and gather them into the fold of Christ; but as an invader, to bring them, by one unprincipled course of violence and intrigue, under the usurpation of the pope.

14. On his arrival in India, he lost no time in executing the commission with which he was charged. He began by pronouncing Mar Abraham guilty of all the crimes alleged against him, though it is not said that he examined any witnesses but those who were also his accusers. He did not issue orders for the apprehension of the aged prelate, hearing that he had retired to Angamale, which was out of the reach of the Portuguese, and that he was now too old and infirm to move out of the house; but he sent him his process, perhaps for form's sake, without, however, requiring him to appear at Goa.

His arrival, and immediate precautions to intercept all ecclesiastics from Persia.

Finding that Mar. Abraham, in conjunction with his people, had written to the patriarch of Babylon for a successor, the Archbishop issued orders to the authorities at Ormus, and all other ports to the West of the Arabian sea in possession of the Portuguese, to stop every Chaldæan, Persian, or Armenian ecclesiastic that might be on his way to India, unless he had a pass under his own hand. These orders were punctually executed. They arrived at Ormus just in time to stop a man who is said to have appeared

there with the title of Archbishop of the *Serra*.[5]
He was discovered in disguise, and immediately
sent home again.   After this, several other persons, Bishops and priests, are said to have been
stopped, when endeavouring to make their way
to Malabar, dressed in the habit of mariners.[6]
The Syrians were greatly disappointed that no
Bishop arrived, and afterwards, when they
came to know the reason, it operated to the
prejudice, rather than in favour of the papal
cause.   Their indignation was universal: and
the more they saw their Bishops and clergy
persecuted, the greater respect did they feel for
them, and the more were they exasperated
against their oppressors.   It tended to shut
their minds the closer against the dogmas which
it was attempted to force upon them, and to
increase the tenacity with which they clung to
their ancient rites and doctrines.

The fidelity
and death
of Jacob,
Mar Si-
meon's
vicar gene-
ral.

15. The Archbishop, regardless of the moral
effect of these proceedings on the Syrian community, and, perhaps, unconscious that he was
raising in their minds a barrier against his progress that no physical force could surmount,
considered his success thus far as complete, and
was encouraged to go forward with increased
ardour in the work that he had begun. His
next step was to write to Jacob, the vicar general of Mar Simeon.   To this ecclesiastic he addressed a long letter, earnestly entreating him

---

[5] A name given to the mountains of Malabar, among which
the greater part of the Syrian churches were situated.

[6] Father Trigaut, speaking of the last two Bishops sent to
India by the Nestorian patriarch, at the time that Don Alexio
de Menezes was labouring to reform the Malabar churches,
says, " *They called themselves* Metropolitans *of the* Indies
and of China."—Gouvea. Hist. of Menez.—Renaudot, Origin
of the Christian Religion in China, p. 117.

to throw away the *commission* he had received from Mar Simeon, seeing that he had been convicted at Rome of not being in orders, and to submit himself to the papal authority : at the same time he made him large promises of favour if he would comply with his injunctions. To all this Jacob turned a deaf ear, and took occasion from the attempt to seduce him from his fidelity, again to caution his people against the craft, the errors, and the presumption of Rome.

The energy of Jacob's character, and his reputation for sanctity and devotion, threatened to render him a formidable adversary to the Archbishop, had he not been soon removed by death. The Romanists have not failed to endeavour to turn this sudden interposition of Divine Providence to their own advantage. As usual, they have laboured to defame the character of a man whose integrity they could not overcome. Gouvea has invented, or repeated, a story concerning him, resembling the account that Evagrius has given of the malady with which Nestorius was suddenly seized, which is said so to have affected his tongue, that he could not speak to be heard, and that this was soon followed by his miserable end. Evagrius was a very credulous author of the sixth century, who wrote some time after the death of Nestorius. Upon such testimony do the Romanists give credit to this tale ; and they have taken it as their model for a similar invention, to account for the sudden death of the cattanar, Jacob. " He boasted," says Gouvea, " that he had received revelations, in which he had been commanded to persevere in his resistance. So great were his impudence and folly, that he dared to preach in the church of Corolongate, that the holy virgin brought forth with pain, and that she ceased to be a virgin after the birth of her Son—blasphemy that could not go unpunished: for hardly had he pronounced the words before he was smitten with the pains of Nestorius:" that is, in the tongue, which, it is said, instantly deprived Jacob also of the power of speech, and speedily occasioned his decease. [7]

Mar Abraham's death, and adherence to the Syrian creed to the last.

16. The Archbishop was not so taken up with attention to the cattanar, Jacob, as to be diverted from Mar Abraham. Though he could not obtain the presence of that aged prelate at Goa, yet he wrote to him, and also to his Archdeacon, George,[8] earnestly entreating them to renounce the errors of Nestorius, which had so long infected their church, to deliver up the manuscripts in which they were taught, and to bring their people into subjection to the pope of Rome. The Syrian Bishop returned him an evasive answer, assigning several frivolous excuses for his delay to comply with those demands. His object was to gain time; but the period now drew near for his removal to that abode, where *the wicked cease from troubling, and the weary be at rest.* [9] Feeling death approach, he laid aside all disguise, and shewed that he retained to the last his firm attachment to the ancient doctrines of his church. Two Jesuits were sent from the college at Vaipacotta to perform over him the last rites of the Roman church; but, notwithstanding their earnest exhortations, he refused to confess to them, or to receive any thing at their hands. And, to pre-

---

[7] Liv. i. c. 7 and 8.

[8] The Archdeacon was at that time the only dignitary under the Bishop of Malabar, and was employed by him as his vicar general.

[9] Job iii. 17.

vent every ground of pretence that he died in
communion with Rome, he gave express orders
that he might be buried in the Syrian church
which he had built at Angamale, and dedicated
to the Abbé Hormisdas, one of the most celebrated Nestorians of former days.

Thus ended the life of Mar Abraham.
Though we see in him little of the christian
prelate to admire, and have to deplore his dere-
liction of principle in procuring the ruin of his
two competitors; yet, with all his faults, we
cannot but sympathize with him in the cruel and
unprovoked persecutions which he endured from
the emissaries of Rome. Nor are we to judge of
his conduct by the measure of knowledge that
illumines our own brighter age. Pure and undefiled religion had long been at as low an ebb in
the Syrian, as in every other unreformed church:
and although we may hope that the record of
some of her children is on high, who in secret
mourned over the evil of their times, and the
iniquity of their own hearts; yet we have no
instances of this character in the page of history. With regard to christian principle in the
contest they maintained, all is blank. Nothing
appears in their resistance to the arbitrary
demands of Rome, but a determination to defend
the creed and the rites of their church against
all innovation, and to preserve their allegiance
to the Patriarch of Babylon: and the spirit in
which they generally persevered, forbids us to be
very sanguine in the hope, that many of them
were contending "earnestly for the faith which
was once delivered unto the saints."[1]

[1] Jude 3.

CHAPTER VIII.

PRELIMINARY MEASURES OF DON ALEXIO DE MENEZES AGAINST THE SYRIAN CHURCH.

A. D. 1597. Commencement of the English and Dutch intercourse with India.

1. THIS history has now reached the period when the attention of England began to be directed to India; a nation, whose clergy were in future times to be the first to acknowledge the independence of the Syrian church, and to endeavour to raise her from the prostrate condition in which they found her fallen.

The Portuguese had held undisputed possession of the Indian trade for almost a whole century. England and France were too fully occupied with domestic affairs, and Spain, with the prosecution of her discoveries and conquests in the western world, to think of interfering with the commerce of the East. Indeed, by the acquisition of the crown of Portugal in 1580, it became the interest of Spain to protect, rather than disturb, the Portuguese in this lucrative trade. Henry VII. of England was almost wholly employed, throughout his reign, in recovering his dominions from the disastrous effects of the intestine wars between the houses of York and Lancaster. His son and successor, Henry VIII. during the former part of his reign, was taken up with the politics and contentions of the continent of Europe, and in the latter part, with the reform of the Church of England from popery. So that he had no time, and left his subjects none, to attend to a branch of commerce of such extent and importance.

The national mind seems to have been held in suspense during the short reign of Edward VI.: a king of vast promise, but too young and tender for his subjects to enter with confidence upon commercial schemes of any magnitude, which it would require the encouragement and protection of a wise and powerful monarch to bring to maturity. The efforts of his successor, Mary, to bring the country again under the papal yoke, paralyzed the nation's energies. Under Elizabeth, they immediately began to recover from the shock they had received from Mary's cruel intolerance: but too many years of that patriotic queen's reign were employed in adjusting the nation's domestic affairs, and in repelling foreign enemies, to leave much time for extensive commercial pursuits. She ascended the throne in 1558, and reigned for the happiness, the honour, and the prosperity of her people. In 1580, the nation was encouraged to extend her commercial views, by the return of her first circumnavigator, Sir Francis Drake, from his voyage round the world. She had, however, too formidable an enemy in Spain, to venture to turn her attention to India, where the commerce was under the protection of that power, until after the destruction of the Spanish Armada in 1588. That event was followed by the overland visit of the English to India [1] in 1591, with a view to ascertain whether an opening might be effected for their commerce in that direction. In 1597, the English East India Company was incorporated, and established in

---

[1] See the last chapter, sec. 11. Note.

1600. In 1602, the year before queen Elizabeth died, the first English fleet sailed to India.

The commencement of the Dutch commerce with India was cotemporary with that of England. In 1579, they shook off the Spanish yoke, when the republic of Holland was formed; and for many years a close alliance subsisted between England and Holland, as the two leading protestant powers. The Dutch East India Company was incorporated in the year 1594, and continued long to enjoy, with the English, the most lucrative branches of the Indian trade.

But we must not further anticipate the history of the intercourse of those nations with that country, as the Portuguese were yet in possession of the commerce there: neither is it intended in these pages to refer to civil events, beyond what may appear to be necessary in order to trace and elucidate the progress of CHRISTIANITY IN INDIA.

Commission appointed for Malabar during the abeyance of the See.

2. To return to this subject. The Portuguese viceroy, Matthias D'Albuquerque, lost no time in transmitting to the Archbishop of Goa the news of Mar Abraham's death. His letter was dated February 16th, 1597, and it reached the Archbishop at the town of Damaon, where he was engaged in a visitation of his own diocese. As he was at too great a distance, [2] and occupied with business of too much importance, immediately to visit the South in person, he, in obedience to the pope's brief, nominated a Jesuit, Francisco Roz, governor and vicar apostolic of the diocese of Malabar. This ecclesiastic was subsequently appointed Bishop of the Serra,

[2] Damaon or Damaun is in the province of Guzerat, about 100 miles north of Bombay.

the first of his order raised to that dignity in India. According to Gouvea, he possessed all the necessary qualifications for the office with which he was now invested. Besides his virtues, erudition, and prudence, he was well acquainted with the Syriac and Malabar languages. In the latter, he is said to have preached with great fluency, and to have been very acceptable to the Christians where he ministered—but whether these were Syrians or Romanists, we are not informed.

But, however suitable this appointment, the council of Goa hesitated to confirm it, foreseeing that it would give great umbrage to the Syrians. Mar Abraham, before his death, had left the government of the church to his Archdeacon, George, who was held in great estimation by the people. His family, by whom he was supported, were of the first respectability in the country; and during the latter part of the deceased prelate's life, he had presided over the church in a manner that gave general satisfaction. The council, therefore, saw the inexpediency of dispossessing such a man of the office that legally devolved upon him, and bestowing it upon a stranger. Such a step could not fail still further to alienate the minds of the Syrians from the Portuguese, and to subvert all the schemes they were devising to bring them gradually to acknowledge the pope, and submit to the jurisdiction of the Latin patriarch of India. In the May following, when Menezes returned to Goa, the council met, and explained to him the reasons which had induced them to suspend his appointment. He concurred in the propriety of their proceedings; and the council resolved unanimously, that, notwithstanding the pope, in his brief, had commanded that no one should be placed in charge of the diocese who was not of the Roman communion, it was nevertheless expedient to appoint the present Syrian Archdeacon, and to associate with him Francisco Roz, and the rector of the Jesuit's college of Vaipicotta. These three were to form a commission, to manage the affairs of the diocese; and the Archbishop sent to the Archdeacon a fresh patent from himself, appointing him vicar-general. But previous to his induction into this office, he was required solemnly to subscribe to the profession of faith of Pius IV. and to place the document, with his signature, in the hands of the rector of the Jesuits, as the delegate of Menezes. With these conditions he objected to comply, alleging, amongst other reasons, that he had no occasion for any one to assist him in the discharge of his duties.

Archdeacon demurs, and is intrusted with the sole charge of the diocese.

3. The Archbishop, though aware that it was chiefly to the subscription that he objected, yet thought proper so far to dissemble as to appear to give him credit for the objection he assigned; and in order to obviate it, he transmitted to him a new patent, giving him sole charge of the diocese, without any other condition than that of requiring a profession of his faith, in conformity with the creed of the council of Trent, and with the bull of Pius IV.

The Archdeacon's object, however, was to gain time, as he and the Syrian community were in daily expectation of the arrival of a Bishop from the patriarch of Babylon : for they do not yet seem to have been aware of the precautions taken by the Portuguese, to intercept any ecclesiastic that might be discovered on his way to them. Still further to protract the adjustment of this business, the Archdeacon accepted the new patent, protesting, at the same time, that it conferred on him no authority beyond what he possessed before. And as to the confession of faith, he desired four months to consider of it, that is, until Holy Thursday, pretending that his principal reason for wishing this delay was, that he might then make the confession with the greater solemnity and publicity in the presence of the whole church. It is said, however, and probably with truth, that he only wished to put it off, in the hope that the expected Syrian prelate would arrive before the appointed day. But the Jesuits, suspecting his sincerity, urged him again to subscribe, though it seems doubtful whether this was done immediately, or whether they waited till the four months had elapsed. The Archdeacon, finding now that he could no longer evade the question, boldly told them that he would never subscribe, nor submit to their church; for that he was sure that she had nothing more to do with the apostolic church of St. Thomas, than that Apostle had to do with the church of Rome.[3]

4. After making this bold declaration of his independence, the Archdeacon assembled a synod of the cattanars and principal laymen, at Angamale, to whom he related what had transpired. Enraged at this treatment of their ecclesiastical superior, and probably apprehending the ruin of their church, they all promised, with an oath, to stand by their Archdeacon, in defence of the ancient faith in which they and their forefathers had been brought up; and they declared that they would not permit even the slightest

Archdeacon refuses to subscribe to the Roman creed, and the Syrians swear to defend him and their Church.

---

[3] It is interesting to notice the resemblance between this brave assertion of the Syrians' freedom from Roman domination, and that of Dinothus in behalf of the primitive British church, b. ii. c. 2. s. 4.

alteration to be made therein. To this resolution they afterwards added, that they would never receive any Bishop that was not appointed over them by the Patriarch of Babylon, nor suffer any Roman priest to enter their churches. These resolutions were then drawn up in form of a public document, and after swearing to maintain its contents with their lives and fortunes, they published it throughout the diocese. The whole community was immediately thrown into a state of commotion, exceeding any thing that had occurred since the first arrival of the Portuguese. The Syrians determined, not only to exclude the Latin priests from their churches, but to drive them from their villages; and two Jesuits, one at Angamale, the other at Carturté, are said hardly to have escaped with their lives. While this disturbance continued, no Roman ecclesiastic ventured to appear among them.

Menezes demands the Archdeacon's implicit submission.

5. The news of these resolute proceedings greatly disconcerted the Archbishop of Goa, whose heart was set on the reduction of this Church : but instead of being deterred by the violence of the people, his resolution to press forward seemed to gather strength with the accumulation of danger before him. He determined at once to visit the *Serra* in person, and try the effect of his presence and authority. As soon as his determination was known, the viceroy, the chapter of Goa, with the whole of the clergy, and the respectable part of the laity, waited upon him in a body, and earnestly endeavoured to dissuade him from so perilous an enterprise; but he was deaf to all the remonstrances and entreaties of his friends. At that juncture, however, war broke out between the Rajahs of Mangate and Paru; and he was thereby com-

A. D.
1598.

pelled to remain at home, as most of the Syrian
Christians lived in the territories of those two
sovereigns.   In his zeal for the pope's honour,
and for the cause of his Church, the Archbishop
was ready to brave all the perils that threatened
him, had not the Viceroy, more cautious, then
taken upon himself to command him, in the
king's name, not to depart far from Goa, while
these disturbances continued.

Thus obliged reluctantly to defer his journey
till the following spring, when he expected the
war to be over, he wrote to the Archdeacon to
that effect, entreating him in the interim, to
prepare to make the confession of faith which
he had promised; to give up all the Syriac
books in the diocese, whether orthodox or heterodox, that they might be corrected; and to
bring all his clergy and people to make their
submission to the Roman Church.   He concluded with the repetition of his request, that
all this might be executed on his arrival, for the
glory of God, and for the honour that would
redound to himself.

6. This letter alarmed the Archdeacon, as
he dreaded nothing so much as a visit from
Menezes : and with the hope of diverting him
from his purpose, he wrote immediately, apolo-
gising for withholding his subscription at the
time appointed, and assigning as his reason for
the delay, the cause that he had to be dissatisfied
with the rector of Vaipicotta, before whom it
was to be made, as well as with the whole
order of Jesuits.   At the same time, he avowed
his readiness to subscribe immediately, if the
Archbishop would appoint a friar or priest of
any other order to receive it at his hands.

Many of the Portuguese thought these reasons satisfactory, and would have persuaded the

He promises
to subscribe
before any
one but a
Jesuit.

x

Archbishop to comply with his request: but he took a very different view of the subject, regarding the excuses of the Archdeacon as a mere device to throw odium upon the Jesuits, for no other reason, as he thought, but because they were the most active and persevering in their endeavours to reduce the Syrians to the Roman faith. He hesitated, therefore, to do as was desired, for he found the Jesuits his most efficient agents in this difficult enterprise. By this indecision he created great dissatisfaction among the other orders of friars, who accused him of an overweening partiality for the Jesuits, and of sacrificing, for the gratification of that single order, the general interests of the church, and the opportunity of conciliating so many thousand souls, and thereby bringing them under subjection to the pope. The fact, however, seems to be, that the Archbishop had no alternative, if he meant to persevere in Malabar; for the Jesuits were his only counsellors in the affairs of the Syrian Church. He had himself never visited the Serra, and he found no other persons sufficiently acquainted with the Syriac language and doctrines to render him any help. Besides, the Jesuits, who had long aspired to the sole direction of the diocese, had exerted themselves in every way to gain his confidence, and up to this moment they succeeded to their entire satisfaction; for he was most reluctant to take any step without their advice and concurrence, and persisted as long as possible in his refusal to commission any one of another order to take the Archdeacon's subscription. At length, however, the perseverance of the Syrian ecclesiastic, and the importunity of the Portuguese, compelled him to yield.

7. But the Jesuits, " who sacrifice all interests and obligations to the honour of their order,"[4] never forgave him for this compliance with their opponent's demands; and they have laboured hard to prove, that, so far from its being desired by the Syrians, this people had a very great affection for them, and wished nothing so much as to be placed under their direction. In a " History of the Jesuits in India,"[5] all that the Portuguese have said of the great aversion of Mar Abraham and his Archdeacon, to the Roman Church, and particularly to the whole order of Jesuits, is flatly contradicted. It is therein asserted, that Mar Abraham had such an extraordinary regard for the Jesuits, that for some time before his death, he put himself entirely into their hands, being governed by them in all his affairs; and that the Archdeacon George had so high an opinion of their worth, that he declared to all the world, that without their assistance, he should not know how to govern the diocese after the Archbishop's death. It is moreover declared, in the said History, that when Mar Abraham was upon his death bed, he called to him the rector of the college at Vaipicotta, who was a Jesuit, and declared, in the presence of his clergy who were about him, that he committed his flock to the Bishop of Rome, as the chief pastor and prelate of the universal church; and that he commanded the Archdeacon and all his priests to obey the Jesuits, whom his *Holiness* had sent to cultivate that vineyard in all things, and to be sure to follow the doctrines that they taught, which

A. D. 1596.

Jesuits' dissatisfaction.

---

[4] Geddes, p. 48.
[5] This History was published by Pieire du Jarri, a Jesuit, and printed at *Bordeaux*, in the year 1608.

were the whole truth, and nothing but the
truth.   After this charge, he is said to have
conjured the rector, by *the love of Christ*, and the
great friendship that had always subsisted between them, to take care of the government of
his church after his death.   He then, as is asserted upon the same authority, ordered an authentic instrument to be drawn up of all that
he had said, which was to be preserved as a
testimony of his last will, and of the faith in
which he died.

The same History further declares, that this
Church was so far reconciled to the pope, in
the year 1596, that when the jubilee of Clement VIII. was published among them by the
Jesuits, they gave his holiness a thousand blessings for it, and took a singular pleasure in pronouncing his name; that during the whole time
of the jubilee, they remained in church from
morning till night, without taking any refresh-
ment; and that they were so anxious to confess
themselves to the *fathers*, that they waited in
the church in great crowds until midnight for
the purpose.

" According to this report of things," it has
been ironically remarked, " the Archbishop,
when he came into the Serra, had little more to
do than to open his arms to embrace a people,
who, being beforehand prepared by the Jesuits, were ready to throw themselves into
them."[6]   How then are we to account for their

[6] Geddes, pp. 48—50.   The same author has made the
following additional observation upon the whole of Picire du
Jarri's statement.   " But to leave romance and return to history, having only observed by the way, that it is visible from
this gross misrepresentation of those affairs, how little regard
is to be had to the Jesuits' reports of their feats in the Indies;
since to support a story purely invented for the honour of

determined resistance to his usurpation, which, as we shall see, it required all the physical power, both of the native princes and the Portuguese, that he was able to employ; all the skill and duplicity, the threats and the influence, he could bring to bear upon them, to overcome? Besides, if there is any truth in this Jesuit's narration; if his brethren were at one time so firmly seated in the Syrians' affections as he would make the world believe; it only serves to add a deeper dye to their subsequent avarice and tyranny, which, as will soon appear, provoked these Christians to rise up as one man against them. Unable longer to endure their cruel oppressions, they drove them away from the honourable and lucrative post they had usurped; and, under the impulse of this irritation, they afterwards hailed the arrival of the Dutch on the coast, as their deliverers from these ecclesiastical tyrants, and greatly contributed to their success against the Portuguese. But we must not further anticipate our History. Thus much, however, seemed to be required, in order to meet the assertions of this Jesuitical historian.

8. An affair happened about this time, which, though in itself of little moment, will serve to prove that the Syrians continued to abominate popery, and especially the Jesuits; while the conduct of Menezes in the matter, however unwarranted, will, at least, tend to show, how little he deserved the reproaches with which that unprincipled order of men have requited his services to them on so many occasions.

A Syrian youth, who had been educated by

Cattanare show their contempt of the pope and hatred of the Jesuits.

their order, they do not boggle to pretend to have an authentic instrument of the truth of it, and that drawn up by the order of a dying prelate."

the Jesuits at the college of Vaipicotta, was instructed by them to name the pope in his prayers before the patriarch of Babylon. While so engaged in the church at Carturté, he was overheard by the cattanars present, who immediately desired him to recite the prayer which the Syrians usually make for their own patriarch; and on his again naming the pope of Rome first, they beat him severely, and turned him out of the church. They also desired his father to whip him out of his obstinacy in praying for the pope, who, they said, was no prelate of theirs, nor had any thing to do with them. Menezes was soon informed of this affair, for the Jesuits left him ignorant of nothing that might turn to their own account; and he wrote immediately to the Archdeacon, expressing great resentment, and desiring him to chastise the culprits, whom he called " impudent heretics," and especially the ringleader, a cattanar, who had been more violent than the rest. This man happened to be related to the Archdeacon, who, instead of proceeding as desired, showed his approbation of what had been done. He endeavoured, however, to satisfy the Archbishop with an evasive answer to his remonstrance.

Here we have an instance, so frequent in the history of the Jesuits, of their compromise of principle to policy. It has already been remarked, that it was incompatible with the pope's pretensions ever to recognise any ecclesiastical authority not emanating from himself; and we have seen what special pains were taken at Rome to depreciate the patriarch of Babylon. But the Jesuits did not scruple to place the Syrian primate before the Archbishop of Goa, who claimed the title of Metropolitan of India, and even to name him as second in dignity and authority, provided they could thereby obtain from the Syrians an acknowledgment of the pope's precedence. This was conceding a principle, and establishing a precedent, which the poor Syrians might have turned against them, had they ever been admitted to a fair discussion of their rights: but this the Jesuits took care never to permit.

9. Notwithstanding this inattention to his own claim of ecclesiastical supremacy in India, the Archbishop was still sincerely desirous to employ the Jesuits in all his negociations with the Syrians; and it was with great reluctance that he at length yielded to the clamours of the different orders of friars, who vehemently inveighed against his hesitation to put the affairs of the Serra into other hands. Wishing, however, to preserve, as much as possible, the appearance of sincerity in his communications with Archdeacon George, and at the same time making a virtue of necessity, he at length consented to delegate a Cordelier, that is, a Franciscan friar, who had brought him letters from the Archdeacon, to receive his public subscription to the Roman faith in the Malabar language, and transmit it to Goa. He also sent him a peremptory command to chastise the cattanars, who had presumed to beat the youth for naming the pope in his prayers.

Archdeacon makes a private confession of faith to a Franciscan.

Intimidated by the repeated orders of Menezes, and by the threat of a personal visit that accompanied them, if they were not promptly obeyed, the Archdeacon at length promised to comply. With reference to the offending cattanars, he returned an answer by no means satisfactory; but he offered to confess the faith that was sent him, provided he were not required to subscribe to it in public. At the same time, he protested against his subscription being interpreted as an admission, that he had not been a true catholic until it was made. After this, he made a private profession of faith conformable chiefly to his own views, subscribed to it in the friar's presence, and sent it to Goa. But the Archbishop was greatly dissatisfied with it, both because it had not been subscribed in public, and because it was not in the prescribed form of the bull of Pius IV. Instead of abjuring the heresy of Nestorius, as he was desired, the Archdeacon contented himself with saying, that he was a *Catholic*, and that he believed what the church believed, omitting the word *Roman* in both clauses. With respect to the pope, he merely acknowledged him as a pastor of the church, without saying that he was the universal pastor of all the churches of Jesus Christ.

To satisfy the Archbishop, makes a public profession at Vaipin: proofs of his insincerity.

10. When Menezes, who easily saw through the Archdeacon's duplicity, rejected his confession, the Franciscans resolved to try once more to obtain from him a profession of faith more to the Archbishop's mind; for they seem to have thought the credit of their order involved in their success. For this purpose they proposed to him to visit Cochin, or at least, Vaipin, a village in the neighbourhood of that town, and there to do publicly, without any further delay, all that Menezes required. Anxious to divert the Archbishop from his intended journey to the Serra, and persuaded that this could only be accomplished by his compliance, the Archdeacon consented to go to the Franciscan church at Vaipin, and to do as they desired. He went accordingly; and on the day appointed, having taken his seat in an arm chair, which they had provided for him in

the church, and being surrounded by a vast concourse of the priesthood and laity, a priest read to him the prescribed confession of faith in Portuguese, and then demanded of him whether he believed in all that it contained. To which he answered, without hesitation,—*yes;* though he understood not one word of the language: and he gave the same affirmation when interrogated as to whether he acknowledged the pope to be the head of the universal church, and the Archbishop of Goa as his superior in India. The Portuguese, believing, or wishing to believe him sincere, received his confession with great rejoicing: but the Jesuits, who watched more narrowly the progress of the discussion, manifested no such pleasure at the result; for they suspected his sincerity, and their suspicion was soon confirmed.

On his return home, the Archdeacon gave to the Syrians the following explanation of his conduct. He told them that he had been to Vaipin, in order to ascertain whether his faith were sound and orthodox; that a Latin priest had read something to him in Portuguese which he did not understand; that he had avowed that the pope was the head of the Church, that is, of the Latin Church, without comprehending that of St. Thomas; and that the Archbishop of Goa was prelate of India, and Metropolitan of the Latin Bishops, but not of the Bishop of Angamale, who owed him no allegiance, and whose Church surpassed in antiquity that which the Portuguese had established. He continued afterwards to preach in accordance with these sentiments, of which the Archbishop was duly informed by the Jesuits. This prelate determined, therefore, to be trifled with no longer, and resolved, notwithstanding the continuance

CHAP.
VIII.
of the Malabar war, and all the dangers and inconveniences that were represented to him, forthwith to transport himself to the Serra: for he was convinced, that such negociations as had already passed between them would pro-duce nothing satisfactory, and that the only hope of reducing the Archdeacon and his Church to the obedience of the pope, rested on his own presence and authority upon the spot.

We cannot draw this chapter to a close, without the expression of deep regret at all the prevarication and mental reservation, too manifest in the conduct of the Archdeacon and his advisers. It is true, their provocation was great. The Archbishop's assumption of authority to command them, was past endurance by men conscious of liberty. But they seem to have understood as little as their deceased prelates, how to defend a righteous cause in the spirit of truth. We would fain believe, that their resistance to the imperious demands of Rome proceeded from a higher principle than the mere love of freedom ; but thus far we have searched their records in vain for the smallest indication of a more sacred motive. We are unwilling to think that " the lamp of God " was quite gone out in their temple ; but truth constrains us to declare, that it does not yet illumine the page of their history : and while, as freemen, we sympathize with them in their danger of bondage ; as Christians, we must protest against the means they used for the preservation of their liberty. The Almighty has oftentimes, in His inscrutable wisdom, subjected the true Church to the trial of an oppressor's rod : but in the present instance, we fear that the affliction now preparing for the Church in India, is rather to be deemed a chastisement

from the Lord for her departure from Christian
integrity. Neglecting to honour Him, by a
simple adherence to the truth, He was not
pledged for her protection. Relying upon her
own duplicity, rather than His righteous and
merciful dealing in her behalf, she lost her
glory and her defence together.

BOOK III.

—

CHAPTER I.

COMPARATIVE VIEW OF THE SYRIANS AND PORTU-
GUESE IN INDIA IN THE SIXTEENTH CENTURY.

Before entering upon the history of the expedition of Don Alexio de Menezes to the Syrian
Churches in Malabar, and of the extent of his
success in reducing them to the subjection of
Rome ; it may be useful to give a description,
both of the Syrian and the Portuguese Christians about that period. The portrait here
drawn of the Syrians' character, manners and
customs, must be free from the imputation of
partiality, as it is taken wholly from Portuguese
writers, who were not likely to invest the
Syrians with imaginary virtues, nor to attribute
to them favourable qualities which they did not
possess: and it is equally improbable that they
should describe the Portuguese as inferior to
them in morals and religion, could they have
discovered a fair pretext for giving their countrymen a superior character.[1]

[1] The first is Antonio Gouvea, already referred to in the

Of all the inhabitants of Malabar, the Syrian Christians are described as the most endowed with every natural gift, both of body and mind. With respect to person, they are generally full grown, well proportioned, and active. They are distinguishable at once from the heathen by their majestic gait. Their colour is not so dark as that of the other Indians, the brahmins alone excepted.[2] They are separated into two divisions, the origin of which has already been explained.[3] The more numerous clan inhabits the Northern districts, and is called, in the Malabar language, *Vataka Bhà-gam*, i. e. Northern Division. Those in the South are designated, *Teka Bhàgam*,[4] i. e. Southern Division. These people continue to consider themselves superior to their brethren of the North, in consequence of their descent from their common ancestor, Mar Thomas, by his first wife. In the sixteenth century, they had very few churches besides those of Diamper, Cotatte, Tourgouli, and Carturté, which are situated in the South. Their complexion is fairer than that of their brethren in the North, towards whom they long preserved a marked distinction, carefully avoiding any matrimonial connexion, refusing to inhabit the same houses

foregoing pages. He wrote, in Portuguese, the history of the Archbishop's expedition. The second, Vincent Marie de Sainte Catherine de Siéne, who was sent to Malabar, with three other friars of his order, by Pope Alexander VII., in the year 1656.

[2] The author will find it necessary occasionally, as here, to supply, from his own personal knowledge of this people, a few particulars omitted by the authorities to which he has referred.

[3] Book i. chap. 4.

[4] It appears, from La Croze, that the earlier writers on the geography, inhabitants and statistics of India, were at a loss for the meaning of these names. They are Sanskrit words, whose signification is given in the text.

with them, and even to employ their cattanars.
But, notwithstanding this unsocial feeling, they
have always cordially united and acted with
them in defending and promoting their religion.
In these respects the Syrian community seemed
for a long period to be of one heart and one
mind.

In general, they are very industrious, and,
though an uneducated people, have a good
measure of common sense, as they have frequently proved by the counsel they gave to others
under trying and difficult circumstances. They
are described as very courteous to strangers, and
rather formal: prolix in their discourse, accompanied with very graceful action; and abounding
in proverbs, also in historical and fabulous tales.
These manners, however, and this circumlocu-
tion, are not peculiar to them, being common
to most eastern nations.

They pay strict attention to the fifth commandment, to honour their father and mother,
applying it, as the Church of England does, in
her catechism for children, to all their governors
and teachers, spiritual pastors and masters.
They never sit in presence of their parents, seniors, elder brothers, ministers, or superiors of
any description, until desired; and when once
seated, they do not think of rising again before
they are dismissed. In their assemblies, none
speak but the oldest and most eminent persons
present, the younger never presuming to open
their lips unless questioned by their elders.
And when children are addressed by their
father, or scholars by their master, they put
the left hand upon the mouth, as though to
hold their breath in mute attention, or to prevent its passing on the speaker.[5] When two

[5] Job is probably alluding to a similar custom when, des-

Syrians meet on the road, the younger puts out his arm and presents his hand to the elder, at the same time respectfully bowing his head. This token of reverence is paid also to their cattanars, and to secular persons holding honourable situations in the state.

These courteous manners contributed, in great measure, to preserve that peace and unity, for which the Syrians were distinguished above all other inhabitants of India, before the arrival of Romish ecclesiastics to sow among them the seeds of division. They are also regarded as one cause of that suavity observed in their general deportment, which is so agreeable to strangers.[6] In these respects, they may read an important lesson to Christians boasting greater light, and a higher degree of civilization. Much is implied in the Apostolic injunction, " be courteous ; "[7] and a neglect to observe it in the various relations of life, has deprived many a Christian community of the peace that Jesus Christ bequeathed to His disciples.[8]

The Syrian Christians are described as remarkable for their curiosity, and are said to listen with great avidity to anything new or

cribing the respect paid to him in his prosperity, he says, " The princes refrained talking, and laid their hands on their mouth," (Job xxix. 9,) that is, when he spake to them. This mark of respect is universally observed by Hindoos also, when addressed by their brahmins or superiors.

[6] This courtesy is not peculiar to the Christians, being generally observed in most other respectable natives of India. Portuguese writers give a similar description of the Chinese, saying, that although the ceremonies established by law and long usage in China, appear tedious to foreigners who are unaccustomed to them, yet that they are found to prevent irritation and endless disputes among a people who are naturally choleric.

[7] 1 Peter iii. 8.   [8] John xiv. 27

strange. Like the other natives of the country, they are very superstitious, and much addicted to omens and prognostics. Tuesdays and Fridays they consider unpropitious, and avoid as much as possible entering upon any undertaking on those days.

The females are very graceful in their deportment, and in their general conduct, modest and retiring. Notwithstanding the heat of the climate and their freedom of intercourse with their neighbours, they are seldom or ever known to violate the law of chastity. It has been presumed, that the very early age at which they marry, contributes not a little to preserve them in this integrity of character; but why may we not also ascribe it to their regard for the seventh commandment? The other natives of the country marry at the same tender age, and their women are much more restricted in their intercourse with the world; but they are by no means equally exempt from reproach in this respect.

The dress of the women corresponds with their character. It consists of a cloth which covers the body, and almost the whole of their legs. They wear also a small waistcoat, with short sleeves, called a shouldery, which covers the breast. When they go to church, or pay a visit to their Bishop, they envelop themselves in a long white cloth, which is drawn over the head, and reaches to the ground, leaving nothing but the face to be seen. Their ornaments are not unlike those of the Hindoo women. Upon the right arm they wear large armlets of gold, or silver, which are well wrought. Sometimes these ornaments are solid and very heavy; but in general they are hollow, and contain a few small stones, which make a tinkling sound to the swing of the arm. Like all other women of the country, they go barefoot, and wear large anklets of silver, or brass, according to their husbands' and fathers' circumstances. Their occupations are wholly domestic.

The dress of the men is much more simple, consisting of a small piece of white cloth passed round the waist, and extending to the knees : the superior quality of this cloth, and the cleanliness of their persons, are all that ordinarily distinguish the rich from the poor. But when at church, or in the presence of native princes or their superiors, the rich wear a light dress, not unlike a surplice, embroidered, sometimes with great taste, on the sides and behind. At the visitations of their Bishops they are particularly neat in their apparel, and are fond of anointing their bodies with perfumes. Like the women, they let their hair grow long, none cutting it but the aged, those who have been on pilgrimage to the sepulchre of St. Thomas at Meliapore,[9] and persons who have taken upon them the vow of celibacy. But the hair is not suffered to hang loose, being neatly gathered together in a tuft upon the top of the head, and fastened with a pin, surmounted by a gold or silver cross, or some other ornament. When persons of distinction among them marry, they decorate the hair with gold or silver roses. Instead of the turban worn by the Hindoo and Mahomedan, the Syrians sometimes cover the head with a silk handkerchief, two ends of which are suffered to fall on the left shoulder. They wear also a coloured girdle round the waist, which is generally red, and serves the

[9] These pilgrimages have long been discontinued, and vows of celibacy are now seldom made.

purpose of a purse, or pocket,[1] as they put in
the ends of it their money, betel, and anything
else that they have occasion frequently to use.
But the rich prefer to carry their betel in a
small pouch under the right arm.

In front of their girdle they were accustomed
formerly to carry a large knife, like a poniard,
highly tempered, and having a long metal handle; sometimes the handle is made of gold, and
beautifully wrought. From the end of this
handle are suspended chains of the same metal,
to one of which is fastened a steel wherewith to
sharpen the poniard; to another, a small metal
box, which contains quick lime. This lime is
prepared in a peculiar manner, to improve the
flavour of the betel leaf, which they, in common
with all the other natives of India, both men
and women, are continually chewing. To the
other chains are appended instruments for

[1] There can be little doubt that this was the form of the
purse mentioned by our Lord, (Matt. x. 9.) The original
word is ζώνη, a girdle, from the Heb. זנר to encircle, or gird
round. The disciples were commanded by their Lord to provide no money, εις τας ζωνας, literally, in their girdles,
which were, probably, made into a kind of purse, as is still
usual in other Eastern countries, besides Judæa and India.
Thus Dr. Shaw, (Travels, p. 227,) speaking of the dress of
the Arabs in Barbary, says, "One end of their girdles, being
doubled back and sewn along the edges, serves them for a
purse, agreeable to the acceptation of the word ζωη in the
Scriptures, which in Matt. x. 9, and Mark vi. 8, we render
a purse." The Roman soldiers used in like manner to carry
their money in their girdles; whence in Horace, Qui zonam
perdidit, means one who has lost his purse, Ep. ii. lib. ii.
lin. 40: and in Aulus Gellius, lib. xv. cap. xii., C. Gracchus
is introduced saying, "Cum Romá profectus sum, Quirites,
zonas quas argenti plenas extuli, eas ex provincia inanes
retuli."—Those girdles which I carried out full of money
when I went from Rome, I have at my return from the province brought home empty. See more in Wetstein, on Matt.
x. 9. Parkhurst, Gr. Lex. Harmer's Observations, vol. i.
pp. 28, 29.

cleaning the teeth and ears, and a pair of pin-
cers, with which they remove the thorns that
often run into their naked feet. All these imple-
ments are generally used by the other natives
of India also, who are seldom unprovided with
them.

The Syrians are very active, and their bodies
flexible, owing to the copious use of cocoa-nut
oil, with which their joints are rubbed from infancy. In former times they seldom appeared
abroad without being well armed. Besides the
poniard just described, a few carried matchlocks, or rude muskets : others would bear a
lance, at the end of which were suspended steel
rings, which made an agreeable sound when
the lance was in motion. But the greater part
of them carried only a naked sword in the right
hand, and a buckler on the left arm. They
were trained to the use of these weapons at the
early age of eight years, and continued the
exercise till twenty-five ; which accounts for
their using them with such dexterity. They are
very expert huntsmen, and excellent soldiers : [2]
we are not surprised, therefore, that they were
formerly held in such estimation by the sovereigns of the country. A native prince was
respected or feared by his neighbours, according to the number of Syrians that he had in his
dominions.

They have always been esteemed and patronised by their rulers, as much for their
general fidelity and regard to truth, as for their
skill and military prowess. But, notwithstanding their warlike appearance, their disposition
was always very peaceable : and such is their

[2] This activity and independent character of the Syrians
gradually declined, after the subjugation of a great portion of
them to the Church of Rome.

character at present, as quarrels, much less murders, are rarely heard of among them. When they entered church, they deposited all their arms in the porch, which then presented the appearance of a guard house: and after divine service, every man would take up his own weapon again without the least confusion, and walk quietly home.

In remarking upon this pacific character of the Syrians, in the year 1656, the Roman missionary, Vincent Marie de S. Catherine de Siéne, acknowledges that he was unable fully to express his admiration of what he observed. For he says, that he could not help contrasting it with the frequent assassinations that he was accustomed to see or hear of, both in Italy, and in all the colonies of the Portuguese in India. How much more consistent then would it have been with this conviction, and more becoming the office of a Christian minister, to have exhorted his countrymen to follow the example of these Syrians, rather than strive so violently as he did to make them proselytes to a creed, which failed to restrain the sanguinary spirits of its professors.

The Syrians formerly carried on a lucrative trade in pepper, which is one of the chief productions of their country; and also in the produce of the palm tree, which they cultivated within the enclosures before their houses. They have always been esteemed for their scrupulous fidelity in commercial transactions. To the poor they are very charitable, and treat even their slaves with kind attention. Indeed, instances have not unfrequently occurred of their adopting them, when they have had no children; and even where they had families of their own, they still took a parental interest in their slaves, bequeathing to them their liberty by will, and leaving them legacies, sometimes to a considerable amount.

In the use of food they are very temperate, their principal meal consisting of boiled rice, with salt, milk, ginger, and a few other simple ingredients made into a wholesome condiment.[3] On particular occasions, and when entertaining their friends, they indulge in the use of sugar, butter, and salt fish ; and these are considered great delicacies. In consequence of their living so much upon vegetables, they seldom venture to take animal food without suffering severely from indigestion. They are equally remarkable for their sobriety, none but the lowest of them ever taking wine, ardent spirits, or fermented liquors. Those who have any regard for their character seldom think of tasting any thing stronger than water or milk : nor do they suffer any inconvenience from this abstinence. Indeed, it contributes so effectually to the preservation of their health, that they make hardly any use of medicine, are strong and active, and attain to a great age. It is worthy of remark, that they have a very limited knowledge of the medicinal properties of the herbs that abound in their country—one sufficient proof that they have but little occasion for them.

As to the administration of law in criminal causes, they depended upon the heathen princes to whom they were tributary : but in civil and ecclesiastical matters they were under the jurisdiction of their own Bishop, who, conjointly with his Archdeacon, adjusted all their disputes, in the two-fold capacity of pastor and judge.

---

[3] This is the composition of the currie generally used in India.

If any one had the temerity to dispute his sentence, he was severely punished. But these powers have since been curtailed.

[4] Notice has already been taken of the privileges granted them by Ceram Peroumal, the distinguished prince of Malabar, who lived in the 10th century. In virtue of these grants, the Syrians took precedence of the Naires, the nobility of the country, and were second only to the brahmins, who are regarded as decendants from brahma, the Hindoo creator. To this caste even the rajahs of Malabar, in common with all other Indian princes, pay extraordinary deference. The Syrians at one time ranked next to them, and were regarded by the laws of the country as the protectors of all artizans—goldsmiths, founders, carpenters, blacksmiths, &c.[5] If a heathen of any of these castes received an injury, he applied to the Christians for redress; and they did not fail either to grant, if in their own power, or to obtain for him, if a case under other jurisdiction, the satisfaction he desired.

They were never subjected to the authority of provincial governors, but depended immediately on the rajah, or prime minister, of their country. Whenever their immunities were invaded, they all united in their defence, unawed by any rank or power which the offender might possess. If a heathen struck a Christian, he was sentenced to die, but was allowed to atone for his offence by going to the church, and carrying in his hand an offering of gold or silver, according to the quality of the person assaulted. In their care to maintain their precedence, they

[4] Book i. c. 4. s. 7.
[5] These and all other professions are divided in India into families or castes.

avoided coming in contact with persons of inferior caste, and would not touch even a Naire. When walking out, they frequently raised their voices to give notice of their approach, that persons of inferior caste might move out of their way.[6] If any one refused to pay them this mark of respect, though he were a Naire, they are said to have claimed the right of killing him on the spot. The Naires, though themselves regarded as the nobility, and at present forming the chief military force of Malabar, yet paid the Christians great deference, and esteemed it a high honour to be regarded as their brethren.

It would be tedious to enumerate all the privileges which the Syrians of former days enjoyed; neither is it necessary in this place, as there will be frequent occasions to refer to them in the sequel. But we may mention one or two, which are of sufficient consideration to show that these Christians were formerly almost on a par with their sovereigns. They were allowed to have a military force of their own, which was composed chiefly of Shanars, the caste that cultivates the palm tree. Besides the brahmins, they were the only inhabitants of the country permitted to have enclosures in front of their houses. They possessed the right of mounting, and travelling on elephants, a distinction peculiar to them and to the heir appa-

---

[6] This practice is not peculiar to the Christians of Malabar, brahmins and all persons of distinction being treated with similar respect. *Slaves* are required to shout as they go along, that they may be informed if any one of respectability is approaching, when they hide themselves till he has passed. Does not this furnish another illustration of the tokens of reverence which Job received in the days of his prosperity? " The young men saw me, and hid themselves : and the aged arose and stood up." Job xxix. 8.

rent of the sovereign. They were allowed to
sit, even on a carpet, in presence of the rajah
and his ministers of state; an honour conceded
also to foreign ambassadors. During the sixteenth century, the rajah of Paru proposed to
extend this last named privilege to the Naires
in his dominions, but the Christians immediately
declared war against him if he persevered; when,
conscious of his inability to enforce it in opposition to their will, he was obliged to leave
matters on their ancient footing.

All these immunities and honours rendered
the dignity of their Bishop so considerable,
that, as the Italian missionary, Vincent Marie,
has testified, he was as highly esteemed as a
king. We cannot be surprised, therefore, at
the Jesuit's anxiety to possess themselves of an
office invested with such authority, and so calculated to exalt their order in the estimation of
the native princes. But, as in Japan and Abyssinia, so here, their consummate ambition and
intolerance marred their design, and provoked
the natives to expel them, before they had become firmly seated in the episcopal chair which
they usurped.

After this description of the Syrian Christians,
extracted from the works of their restless and
implacable enemies, and published at the very
time when they were making every effort to dis-
solve the unity of this church, and identify it
with that of Rome; we shall give, from the
same authorities, the character of the Roman
church, as it then existed in India. It consisted chiefly of Portuguese, who are thus
described by a Carmelite missionary of their
own.

" The Christians who live in the Portuguese
colonies in India are composed of three classes.

The first are the soldiers, who came from Portugal, and are called *Regnicoles*.[7] The second are called, *Métifs*,[8] the descendants of the former. The third are the slaves that have been converted to the faith. The first class, the nobility among them excepted, are the dregs of Portugal; for the most part a seditious people, covered with crimes, and banished from their country. The second class are ill educated, extremely effeminate, and abandoned to all kinds of sensual indulgence. The third are a wild race, totally incapable of instruction, and ferocious in the extreme. In a climate so warm as that which these people inhabit, their natural propensity to evil is always on the increase: indeed, many of them actually believe vice to be necessary. It is incredible with what enmity and thorough malevolence they persecute one another, and that for the most trivial offence. Such is their immodesty, that we cannot venture to describe it. The men and women live in continual idleness, passing all their days together perfectly naked, without the least respect for each other, or any regard to the difference of sexes. They are incessantly chewing betel, cardamoms, and areca, which are heating and intoxicating drugs. They are also perpetually smoking tobacco. This mode of living is enough to set their bowels in a flame, which are already almost burned up by the heat of the climate they inhabit. From these general causes, one can easily comprehend what must be the conduct of this people: but I will gladly omit a

[7] The natives of the kingdom of Portugal.

[8] That is, mongrel or mixed breed; their fathers being Portuguese, and their mothers natives of India, generally of the lowest castes.

more particular detail, in order to spare the reader's feelings.[9]

This description, appalling as it must appear, is, however, somewhat flattering : for the *Métifs* and *Slaves* are introduced for the purpose of diverting the reader's attention from the infamy of the *Regnicoles ;* whereas, those two debased classes are just what these, their fathers and instructors, made them. The general character of the people is qualified by the exception made in favour of the nobility, in order to avoid giving offence to the whole nation of Portugal : but every author, whether ancient or modern, who has undertaken to describe them, has concurred in giving them the same character. We have seen the state of debauchery in which Francis Xavier found them. Linschot, who has entered much into the offensive details, plainly shows, that there was no corruption of manners more infamous or more general than that of the Portuguese in India.

And yet, these composed the church to which the Syrian Christians were invited, yea, commanded, upon pain of excommunication and death, to join themselves ! Who can wonder that they shrunk with abhorrence from such a community ? The very proposal was an insult to their feelings and understanding. With all their ignorance and imperfections, they were to the Portuguese, as light to darkness, as salt to clay. How revolting then to every pious senti-

---

[9] Vincenzo Maria, Lib. ii. c. 18. p. 202, 203. *La Christianità che vive*, &c. See La Croze, pp. 87—89, where the other Italian and Portuguese authorities are all given. To the testimony of the missionary here quoted might be added that of Linschot, Tavernier, and other travellers, all Portuguese or Italians, and therefore interested in giving the best account they could of this people.

ment or feeling, and even to the dictates of common sense, was the attempt, under the pretext of imparting to them superior religious blessings, to unite such a people with these base invaders of their country. What other effect could have resulted from such an amalgamation, than the extinguishing of the little light which their own church had preserved, and the loss of the Christian savour they might yet retain? Heathen conquerors have frequently adopted the Gods of the nations they subdued. Happy had it been for the Portuguese if they had so far followed the example, as to trim their own waning lamp by the brighter torch which they found burning in Malabar, instead of labouring to extinguish it.

CHAPTER II.

THE FIRST VISITATION OF DON ALEXIO DE ME-NEZES, ARCHBISHOP OF GOA.

1. THE Archbishop of Goa, seeing that his negociations with the Syrians were not likely to produce the desired result, determined to visit them in person, and fixed a day for his departure. When the viceroy and the clergy at Goa heard of his intention, they entreated him not to expose himself to such imminent danger; but he returned them only this answer, *That his life was but too secure in this case, seeing he had never merited enough to entitle him to the honour of being a martyr.* Lest, however, his humility should deceive him in passing this judgment upon himself, he did not think proper to rest his security upon his want of merit to suffer, and therefore provided himself with a strong escort for his protection. What a contrast to the confidence of Ezra in his God, when about to pass through much greater perils on his way from Babylon to Jerusalem. He and his companions united, in fasting and supplication, to seek the protection of heaven; for he said, "I was ashamed to require of the king a band of soldiers and horsemen to help us against the enemy in the way: because we had spoken unto the king, saying, The hand of our

A. D. 1599.

Menezes' passage to the Southern coast.

His prepa-
rations for
the siege of
Cunahle.

God is upon all them for good that seek him ; but his power and his wrath is against all them that forsake him." [1]

2. Before a man can exercise such trust in the Lord, he must have the testimony of an upright conscience that he is doing His work. But Menezes was engaged in a very different service, and placed his reliance on corresponding means of defence. He was commissioned by the council at Goa to act as their envoy to the native princes of Malabar, and to treat with them concerning peace and war. For some time past the Portuguese commerce had been annoyed by a nest of Mahomedan pirates, who infested the Malabar coast. It was known that in the first instance they had been encouraged by the Zamorin of Calicut, for the express purpose of distressing the Portuguese,[2] with whom, as we have seen, he had just cause to be offended. Their first leader was one *Pate Marca*, a Mahomedan of a daring spirit, to whom the Zamorin had granted permission to build a fortress in his dominions, which he called *Cunahle*. Here the pirates gathered the spoils they took from the Portuguese both by sea and land, which soon accumulated to a vast amount. On the death of *Pate Marca*, he left the command of this fortress to his nephew, Mahomet Cunahle Marca, who was captain of the pirates at the time of Menezes' visit to the coast. He was not inferior to his uncle in courage or dexterity ; and he had so increased the strength of the place, that it was become one of the strongest fortifications in India. Marca and his crew no longer confined their depredations

---

[1] Ezra viii. 21, 22.
[2] Asiatic Res. vol. v. pp. 24, 25. See book ii. chap. ii. sec. 22.

to the Portuguese, but had the hardihood now to attack the subjects of the Zamorin himself.

The destruction of Cunahle and this daring banditti was the first object of the Archbishop, who embarked at Goa, December [3] 27th, 1598, on board a galley, strongly armed, and commanded by Don Alvaro de Menezes, supposed to have been a near relative of the prelate. When they reached the bar of Cunahle, they were joined by the whole of the Portuguese Armada, commanded by the viceroy's brother, and were saluted by all the guns and music of the fleet. Menezes immediately called a council of war; and having listened to the several opinions of the officers respecting the best mode of attacking the fortress, he despatched their resolution to the Council of State at Goa. He also took advantage of the Zamorin's rage against the pirates, to invite him to combine with the Portuguese for their destruction. Indeed, without the assistance of that prince, they could not hope to reduce the place.

3. After completing these arrangements for the siege, the Archbishop proceeded with a strong convoy to Cannanore; and having remained there sixteen days, he sailed direct to Cochin, where he arrived, January 26th, 1599. The place of landing being inconvenient, a temporary flight of stairs was prepared for him; and he was received with great splendour and acclamation, the Bishop, the Governor, Don Antonio de Noronha, and the whole city, being assembled to do him honour.

On the following day, when the magistrates

His arrival and proceedings at Cochin.

[3] La Croze says September, but this would be allowing three months for the passage to Cochin, which, in fair weather, is easily made in a few days. Both Gouvea (p. 73) and Geddes (p. 53) mention December.

of Cochin came to pay their respects to him, he told them of his determination to reduce the Syrian Christians to the obedience of Rome before his return to Goa, and demanded their assistance in the undertaking, which they readily promised.

The day after, he called the council of the city together, and strongly recommended them to co-operate in the siege of Cunahle. Convinced, by his representations, that they were specially interested in wresting that fortress out of the hands of the pirates, they immediately raised and armed one hundred and fifty men at their own expense, and sent them on five strong vessels, with a quantity of all kinds of ammunition, to join the armament before Cunahle. The Archbishop also, to animate them in the enterprise, sent with them one of his best yatchs, manned with his menial servants.

Rajah of Cochin's policy to detach him from the Zamorin defeated.

4. The rajah of Cochin does not appear to have been at all consulted in the business, but he could not remain a quiet spectator of the Archbishop's zeal in these military operations. For some years past it had been the policy of the Cochin rajahs to prevent a reconciliation between the Zamorin and the Portuguese, in order that they might keep the latter dependent upon themselves, and engross their trade. The reigning prince, therefore, watched with anxiety their present proceedings; for he foresaw that the success of those two powers against the pirates would lead to their permanent coalition, and he determined, if possible, to separate them, by destroying the confidence of Menezes in his rival's friendly professions. With this intention he sent his chief justice, one Joan de Miranda, of Cochin, to wait upon the Archbishop, and inform him, that he had received

intelligence that might be relied on from his spies in the Zamorin's cabinet, that instead of joining the Portuguese in the siege of Cunahle, he had determined to cut them all off as soon as they landed on his coast, in revenge for the numerous injuries they had done to his ancestors. He therefore pretended, that he considered himself bound, by a sense of duty to the King of Portugal, who was his friend and *Brother in arms*, to make the Archbishop acquainted with the impending danger.

But Menezes was too crafty a politician to be taken with such a stratagem. Few men living understood better than he the intrigues of princes, and the way of turning them to his own purpose. He returned his grateful acknowledgments to the rajah for the intelligence, but at the same time declared his intention to trust the Zamorin on the present occasion. The reason he assigned for placing this confidence in one who was thought to have deserved so little to be trusted, was, that the Portuguese had no cause to fear the treachery of any one, seeing that they had sufficient power to avenge themselves on all who should deceive the King of Portugal, either in peace or in war. This, no doubt, was intended to deter the rajah himself from attempting to interfere with the expedition; but the Archbishop's real inducement for relying on the Zamorin's fidelity was, that the destruction of the pirates was now become as much the interest of that prince as of the Portuguese themselves.

The rajah, however, would not be turned from his purpose without making a more formidable attempt to accomplish it. Finding that his plot had not succeeded, he resolved to divert the Zamorin from sending an army against Cu-

z

nahle, by immediately declaring war, and commencing hostilities against the Caimal, or prince of Corugeira, the Zamorin's friend and ally. Having, with incredible expedition, raised an army of six thousand men for the purpose, he sent to inform the Archbishop that he intended to wait upon him before he marched. Though Menezes did not pay him the compliment of going out to meet him, yet he received him with great courtesy; and having exchanged civilities, the Archbishop first informed the rajah of his intention to visit all the Christian churches in Malabar, in order to reclaim them to the true Christian faith, from which, he affirmed, they had greatly swerved; and that since many of those churches were within his dominions, he expected his co-operation in so good a work. The rajah having promised his assistance, Menezes then said, that there was another favour which he must not deny him, and that was, to defer his war with the Caimal till Cunahle was taken. The rajah gave many reasons for refusing to comply with this request, all of which the Archbishop over-ruled; and he pressed him so hard upon the point, that before they parted, he made him promise to disband his army.[4]

The siege of Cunahle has too little connexion with this History to be narrated here: but it is of importance to know the part which the Archbishop acted in promoting the expedition, in order to understand the belligerent character of the man, who was come to convert an entire church to the faith of Rome. From such a beginning, the Syrians would know what they had to expect from his visit. He soon showed, that he could direct with equal energy the cannon

[4] Gouvea. chap. vi. Geddes, pp. 53—56.

of Portugal and the bulls of Rome, and that he was more ready to fight than to preach his way to peace.

A.D.
1599.

5. Having made satisfactory arrangements for the siege, Menezes proceeded to the work of hostility against the Syrians. His first step was, to send a civil request to the Archdeacon to come and speak with him at Cochin; but having waited several days without seeing him, or even receiving an answer to his message, the Archbishop concluded, and with good reason, that he was afraid to venture into the city. In order to remove his fears, he sent him a letter of " safe conduct," promising, with an oath, that he would not question him about any thing that had passed.

Opens his proceedings against the Syrians: gains the rajah of Cochin.

The Archdeacon now felt himself in a great dilemma. He was quite awake to the danger of putting himself in the power of Menezes, notwithstanding his " safe conduct;" for past experience had taught him how little confidence was to be placed in the word of a Roman ecclesiastic, when it threatened to obstruct the interests of his Church. But he saw also, that resistance could not long avail him; for he had ascertained that the Archbishop was now supported by the rajah of Cochin. That prince had, no doubt, demurred, when called upon to fulfil his promise to assist in the reduction of the Syrians, being, probably, unwilling to give up so many good subjects. He could not but suspect also, that the meditated subjugation of that people, was undertaken for no other purpose but to add strength to the arms of Portugal, which were already sufficiently powerful to overawe the native princes. He therefore thought proper to throw some impediments in the way of the Archbishop's arrangements;

z 2

these, however, the prelate's superior policy enabled him to surmount. The principal lever that moved the rajah was a golden bribe of twenty thousand ducats,[5] for which paltry sum, he sold the best and bravest of his people into the hands of a relentless enemy. Verily, " It is better to trust in the Lord than to put confidence in princes."[6]

Syrian
Archdeacon
meets him
with a
strong es-
cort at
Cochin.

6. The Archdeacon assembled a great number of cattanars, and the most respectable inhabitants of the different parishes, to consult together what measures it were best to adopt in this emergency. It was unanimously agreed, that he should wait on the Archbishop, seeing how dangerous it would be to provoke him any further : for they feared lest he should exert his influence to ruin them all at once, by putting a stop to their pepper trade, on which they chiefly subsisted. They believed also, that he had the native princes so completely at his command, that he could induce them, if he chose, to sacrifice all their lives and property at his pleasure. Besides, they concluded that he would soon be obliged to return to Goa, and flattered themselves that when he was gone, they might resume their former course. But all this shows that they did not yet know the character with which they had to deal.

Upon these considerations, it was determined to yield to the pressure of necessity just so far, as to avoid being overwhelmed by the gathering storm. They agreed to allow the Archbishop to say mass and preach in their churches— a concession that seemed to have the sanction of their own records, which enjoined the offering of

---

[5] La Croze, p. 100. The golden ducat was valued at nine and sixpence : consequently the bribe amounted to £9,500.
[6] Psl. cxviii, 9.

such civilities to any foreign Bishops that might visit them. But as to any acts of jurisdiction, which they thought it probable that he would attempt to exercise; such as a visitation of the diocese, conferring orders, excommunicating, and other episcopal functions; it was resolved to put him off as well as they could with excuses, and to throw impediments in his way until the time for his return to Goa. By these means they hoped, without incurring the displeasure of so powerful an enemy, to preserve their affairs in their present position until the arrival of the Syrian Bishop, for whom they had written to the patriarch of Babylon.

Having published this decision throughout the diocese, a strong guard was provided to escort the Archdeacon to Cochin. He set out with 3000 men well armed, and under the command of a captain, called a Paniquais.[7] These captains were not unlike feudal lords, having sometimes from 4,000 to 6,000 men at their command, who were trained by themselves to the use of arms; and they were much feared in the country, being always very courageous and desperate enemies. Accordingly Menezes made an attempt to conciliate some of them, inviting them to visit him at Cochin as their friend : but, aware of his design, instead of attending to his invitation, they took an oath,[8] according to the custom of the country, to act with all their force against him, if he should attempt to offer any violence to their Archdeacon, or any one of their cattanars. When these men had taken such a vow upon them they were desperate in fulfilling it, fighting against any force,

---

[7] The name of an independent chieftain of Malabar.
[8] Literally, made themselves *Amouços*.

however unequal, even " two against a thousand,"[9] till they or their enemies fell.

While one of these Paniquais escorted the
Archdeacon to Cochin, a second was engaged
to meet and protect him there. Hearing how
strongly he was defended, the Governor of Cochin, Don Antonio de Noronha, thought it expedient to go out peaceably to meet him, and
conduct him to the Archbishop's palace. Menezes received him courteously, as though nothing had happened ; and the Archdeacon knelt
down and kissed his hand, in which act of
reverence he was followed by all the cattanars
and Christians in his train. The Archdeacon
then introduced the two Paniquais, who, when
all were seated, took their stations at the right
and left of the Archbishop's chair, with their
broad swords drawn, and surrounded by their
attendants in the same attitude of defence.
Before the business commenced, a serious affray
had nearly taken place ; for on closing the hall
door to keep out the crowds that were pressing
in, those without concluded that this was done in
order to secure the Archdeacon, and they were
on the eve of bursting open the doors to rescue
him. They cried aloud, that now was the time
to show their regard for their religion and Archdeacon, and to die in their defence. But they
were soon pacified by the cattanar stationed at
the door to keep order, who assured them that
the Archdeacon was in no danger, and entreated
them to remain quiet and do nothing, until they
should hear the Paniquais within call for assistance.

The tumult being appeased, the Archbishop
proceeded to business ; and after much discus-

9 La Croze, p. 101.

sion, it was finally agreed that he should go on the following day to Vaipicotta, where the Archdeacon and his cattanars engaged to meet him. This he selected as the first church to be visited, because of the Jesuits' college there. It is with great probability concluded, that Menezes was dissatisfied with this concession, but that he was afraid to attempt any thing further at this first interview, in consequence of the force that he saw prepared to resist his demands.[1]

7. Having made the necessary arrangements for his voyage,[2] the Archbishop and his retinue embarked on seven boats, being accompanied by Roque de Mello Pereyro, a former governor of Malacca, with two more boats, and by John Pereyra de Miranda, afterwards governor of Cranganore, with another. Thus honourably attended and well guarded, he set forth; and on his arrival at Vaipicotta, he was conducted by the Jesuits and their scholars to the college. There he put on his pontificals, and marched in procession to the parish church, attended by all the inhabitants of the village. He then mounted the pulpit, with his mitre on his head and crozier in his hand, and delivered a long discourse on John x. 1,—"He that entereth nót by the door into the sheepfold, but climbeth up some other way, the same is a thief and a robber." From these words he laboured to prove, that none were true pastors but those who entered by the door of the Roman Church, and were sent forth by the Pope, who was

---

[1] La Croze, p. 102.

[2] The travelling in the interior of Travancore is principally on the backwater, and on the rivers that flow into it; which will account for the frequent use of the term, *voyage*, instead of journey.

Christ's Vicar on earth ; and that since none of their former Bishops had been sent by that high authority, but by the schismatical Bishops of Babylon, they were all thieves and murderers of the flock. The historian, Gouvea, describes this sermon as so full of pious and devotional sentiments, that it drew tears, not only from the Portuguese, but also from the natives present. These, however, must have been tears of sympathy, from seeing the others weep, as they could not understand one word of the language in which Menezes preached.

After the sermon, he desired the congregation to assemble again next day, to be confirmed, a ceremony of which the few Syrians present had never before heard. At the time appointed, he explained to them the nature of the rite and its effects ; and then, with no other preparation of the candidates but that of a solemn procession for their sins, he proceeded to confirm them. With the exception of the sacraments of Baptism and the Lord's Supper, there are few services of the Church of more importance, or attended with greater benefit than this, when the candidates are carefully examined and instructed in its nature and use, and the ordinance is administered with due solemnity. But when this, or any other religious service, is so grossly profaned, as it was on the present occasion, it can tend only to grieve the devout, and to bring religion into greater contempt with the ungodly.

At the time of confirmation he explained the doctrine of purgatory, of which also they had never heard until then : and the service concluded with the celebration of mass, in which the whole of the inhabitants of Vaipicotta are said to have joined.

The Archdeacon had not yet made his appearance, for he suspected what Menezes would do, and determined not to give to his proceedings the sanction of his own presence. He and the cattanars, therefore, deferred their journey to Vaipicotta until two days after the Archbishop's arrival. Menezes could not but conjecture the cause of this delay, yet thought it expedient to refrain from noticing it, and to receive the Archdeacon as though nothing had occurred to displease him. He then explained the course he proposed to adopt for the reformation of the Church; and the Archdeacon, in his turn, so far dissembled as to seem to approve of his plan.

8. This appearance of condescension, however, Menezes found it difficult to sustain much longer. Indeed, it ended here. For some time he quietly attended the Syriac matins and vespers, though he did not understand the language, until informed that they persevered in praying for the Patriarch of Babylon, as Universal Pastor of the Church.[3] He was then greatly enraged to think that he should have been present when such an indignity was offered to the pope, and resolved to suffer it no longer. He said, that he regarded the Patriarch of Babylon as a Nestorian schismatic and a heretic, and refused to listen for a moment to the proposal of the Jesuits, to compromise the matter with the Syrians for the present, and to refrain from interfering with the obnoxious practice until possessed of sufficient power to

Menezes'
violence
against the
patriarch
of Babylon
enrages the
populace,
whom the
Archdeacon
appeases.

[3] 'A title that all Patriarchs, as well as the pope, have assumed to themselves for some hundred years: nay, by what Gregory I. has said of that title, I do not know but the pope might be one of the last that assumed it.'—Geddes, page 61.

enforce obedience to his mandates. They assured him that if he thus prematurely exposed his designs, the Syrians would not again admit him into their churches, and that all hope of conciliating them would then be lost. But Menezes was too impetuous to enter into this Jesuitical policy, and remained inflexible. He declared his persuasion, that it was impossible to hold communion in prayer with Christians so far removed from the truth ; for that, according to his sentiments, they could not offer him a greater insult than by recognising in the Church, especially while he was present, any other universal pastor than the pope of Rome. He could not but feel piqued also at being so taken in by the Syrians ; but he soon had his revenge.

Accordingly, without communicating his design to any one, he assembled, in his private apartment, the Jesuits who presided over the college, the Archdeacon and Cattanars, and there addressed the latter with great energy, endeavouring to convince them that the pope was the only head of the Church on earth, and that the Bishop of Babylon was a heretic and schismatic. He then pulled out of his pocket a sentence of excommunication, written in Latin, and commanded his secretary to read it with an audible voice. When finished, he desired his interpreter to explain it in Malabar to all present who did not understand Latin. In this document he forbade all persons in the diocese of Angamale, whether seculars or ecclesiastics, to give in future the title of *universal pastor* to the Patriarch of Babylon. He asserted, that this title belonged only to the Roman pontiff, the successor of St. Peter and Vicar of Jesus Christ ; he therefore commanded them henceforth to make no mention of the Syrian

patriarch in their Liturgy, or in any public
prayers, but to regard him as a Nestorian
heretic, excommunicated from the Roman
Church.

When this document had been read and interpreted, Menezes called upon the Archdeacon
and two senior cattanars to sign it. But the
Archdeacon, grieved at what he had heard,
naturally felt embarrassed, and hesitated to
comply. The Archbishop, without relaxing in
his demand, or giving him time to recover from
his consternation, called to him abruptly—' Sign
it, Father,' for it is full time to lay the axe at
the root of the tree.' Thus taken by surprise,
the Archdeacon seems to have lost his self-
possession ; for he signed the document without uttering a word. The two senior cattanars
then followed his example ; and immediately
the excommunication was affixed to the gates
of the church, and the assembly broke up.

When the cattanars and elders heard what
had been done, they were greatly enraged, and
ran together to the lodgings of the Archdeacon,
where they made loud lamentation, crying out,
" That the Archbishop of Goa was come with
his Portuguese to destroy their religion ; that
he had insulted their Patriarch by whom they
had been governed for above twelve hundred
years." This uproar brought the inhabitants
of the village together, who readily joined in
the cry. After exclaiming against the Arch-

In India ministers of religion are generally addressed by
this title, Padre, i. e. father.

N.B.—Not to attach undue importance to this exclama-
tion, it may at least be regarded as tending to confirm our
conclusion, that this Church was under the jurisdiction of the
Primate of Persia in the fourth century. (Book i. ch. ii.) It
was evidently the current opinion in Malabar at that time,
and remains so at the present day.

bishop with bitter vehemence, venting a thousand curses on his head, and bewailing their misery, in having strangers thus intruding among them to overturn the religion in which they had been born and bred; the people told their cattanars, that if they would suffer them to take vengeance on these intruders, they would either expel them out of their country, or die in defence of their religion.

The Archdeacon went out to the people, and signifying to them by signs that he desired to be heard, they held their peace; when he addressed them to the following effect, saying— " That there was a time for all things, and that this was a time for dissimulation, not for revenge; that he had indeed signed the excommunication of their Patriarch, but that he acted purely out of fear; for they were to consider, that, besides the force which the Archbishop had brought with him, he had engaged the Rajah of Cochin, within whose territories they were then assembled, to protect him in all that he did; and that that prince would assuredly avenge any insult offered to Menezes, on their lives and estates. As to himself," he said, " he was resolved to die in defence of the religion of his country, rather than consent to the introduction of popery;" adding, " the Portuguese, if they liked their own religion, might live in it, in God's name, and he knew nobody that would trouble them for it: but that he saw no reason why they should thus disturb and persecute people in their own country, because they would not turn papists, or change their own religion for theirs: and that, as to the Archbishop, the reason of his being so furious to destroy the authority of the Patriarch of Babylon was, that he might make himself Pri-

A. D.
1599.

mate of the Indies; to which he hoped that none of the Christians of Malabar would ever consent, or be persuaded to forsake their ancient religion for that of popery."

To this the whole multitude assented with loud acclamations, crying, "That they would lose all they had in the world, and even their lives, rather than consent to such a sacrifice." Here the matter ended, probably because none of the Paniquais were present, who would, doubtless, have proceeded forthwith to violence. The Archdeacon did right in preventing this, and in suppressing the fury of the people. It is not for Christians to avenge themselves, but rather to "give place unto wrath:" for it is written, "Vengeance is mine; I will repay, saith the Lord."[4] Had the Archdeacon acted upon this principle, and resisted the proud pretensions of Rome with the meekness of piety and the firmness of integrity, he would have taken up a position from which Menezes would have found it impossible to dislodge him. But when intimidated to sanction the excommunication of his Patriarch, he made a compromise of principle which gave to his adversary an advantage that he never could recover. Besides, the remembrance of this concession could not fail to disturb his peace, and, consequently, to impair his energies for the growing contest. So true is the proverb, "The fear of man bringeth a snare: but whoso putteth his trust in the Lord shall be safe."[5]

9. The Portuguese, however, were not satisfied with these proceedings. They had other interests to preserve besides those of the church;

Portuguese remonstrance against his violence disregarded.

---

[4] Rom. xii. 19. Deut. xxxii. 35.
[5] "Shall be set on high." M. R. Prov. xxix. 25.

and feeling the jeopardy in which the Arch-bishop's temerity had placed them, they could not forbear to complain of his having acted in a manner so contrary to the advice of all about him. They also urged upon him the necessity of embarking without delay on one of his gallies, and fleeing beyond the reach of danger. But Menezes paid no regard either to their remon-strances or their advice. He told them plainly, that he was engaged in the cause of God, and that he would defend it to the last. And when they ventured to blame his precipitate excom-munication of the Patriarch, and to declare that it was nothing but an act of ungovernable zeal, with little or no light; he replied, that he was so far from repenting of what he had done, that he would do it again if necessary; and that, instead of retreating to Cochin, he was deter-mined to go the following morning to Paru.[6]

Two Syrian
ecclesiastics
join him.

10. Hitherto all parties but his own imme-diate attendants seem to have been opposed to his proceedings. But he was aware that the Portuguese durst not abandon him, and that the Rajah of Cochin was bribed to defend him while within his dominions. He knew, therefore, that he incurred very little danger by proceeding with his visitation. But that night a circum-stance occurred which led immediately to his procuring two important accessions to his party, one of whom proved a more effective agent than he had hitherto found for his purpose. Two Indian priests, from the college of the Jesuits, who lodged in an apartment next to that of Menezes, discoursed together upon what had just happened, and purposely spoke loud enough for him to hear what they said. "This Arch-

[6] Geddes, pp. 62, 63.

bishop," said they, " proceeds against the Holy
Patriarch only through envy, and we need
not obey a mandate which is so manifestly unjust." These men were, probably, instigated to
this conduct by the Jesuits, whose wily policy
the violence of Menezes tended to defeat. The
Archbishop, overhearing them, conjectured what
was their reason for speaking so loud; and
having called them in, sharply rebuked them for
their assurance in discoursing together upon
subjects which they did not understand. " And
for you," added he, " to debate upon such
heresy in my hearing, greatly aggravates your
impertinence." Perceiving, however, that his
rebuke produced little effect upon them, he very
adroitly lowered his tone. Desiring them to sit
down before him, and turning the subject of
discourse, he assumed a kind and condescend-
ing manner, and proceeded to instruct them in,
what he called, the doctrine of salvation. This,
according to his views, consisted in implicit
obedience to the Roman church, an obedience,
without which all Christians, he said, were in a
state of condemnation. He then, says Gouvea,
returned to the subject of their Patriarch, telling them, that he was an heretic, for whom it
was therefore unlawful to pray in the church.
Having spent a great part of the night in discoursing with these men to the same effect, in
the morning, before dismissing them, he gave to
each a beautiful picture enchased in silver, together with some ecclesiastical ornaments, with
which he had provided himself at Goa for such
occasions. By this means he completely won
over these two ecclesiastics; and before they
parted, he embraced them with tears in his
eyes, calling them his sons, and exhorting them
to continue submissive to the true church.

This exhortation had the desired effect upon them, for from that time they both attached themselves to his person ; and one of them, who had been the Archdeacon's intimate friend, ultimately became a most efficient instrument in obtaining that ecclesiastic's submission.

His violence at Paru ineffectual.

11. Paru,[7] whither Menezes proceeded on the following day, is the metropolis of a kingdom in which the noblest body of Syrian Christians reside. These people were strongly attached to their own Patriarch, and the most violently opposed to every thing that savoured of popery, as they had on several occasions sufficiently manifested. Some time before, two native youths of this town, named Don Jorge du Cruz and Don Joan du Cruz, had been sent by the Portuguese to Rome, in the pontificate of Gregory the Thirteenth, who paid them great honour, and granted them many indulgences for their church. Amongst others, he permitted them to erect *an elevated altar*,[8] the use of which, the Syrians could not then understand : for they, according to the practice of the primitive Christians, and of all the eastern congregations, had only one table, standing in the place of the altar, in each church. When these priests attempted to introduce the privileges granted them by the pope, their countrymen not only treated the indulgences with contempt, but refused to allow the men, although of the noblest families in the country, to officiate in any of their churches. Their own brethren and kindred took the lead in persecuting them, and finally compelled them to leave the kingdom, when

[7] Or Parour, near Cranganore.
[8] Un Autel priviligié.

they sought refuge among the Portuguese at Cranganore.

The Christians of Paru, though thus disaffected toward the Roman church, had, according to agreement, prepared great festivities for the reception of the Archbishop; for they hoped, by entertaining him with such hospitality, to divert his mind from entering upon any business. But having heard the night before he came, of the insult he had offered at Vaipicotta to their Patriarch, they changed all their festive preparations into arms, and were so much incensed against him, that they sent only eight or ten persons to meet him at his landing, and conduct him to the Archdeacon.

Though Menezes could see nothing but grief and dejection in every countenance, yet he seemed to take no notice of their sorrowful appearance; and, giving them his cross to carry before him, he followed them direct to the church. When he arrived there, he found it full of men, armed with swords and lances, bows and muskets. Not a single woman or child was to be seen amongst them. Observing this hostile preparation, and apprehensive lest his Portuguese guards and attendants should come to blows with the people, he commanded them all to return to their boats, except two priests, whom he retained to assist him in the ceremonies he was about to perform.

Having put on his pontificals, and pronounced a benediction on the people, he preached to them for an hour and a half; and the purport of his discourse was to prove, that there was but one true religion, which was the Roman; and that all Christians were under an indispensable obligation to submit themselves to the Pope. When he had finished his sermon, he explained to the people the rite of confirmation, which he called a sacrament. Thus far they listened to him in silence: but when he called upon them to come to be confirmed, they could endure it no longer, and began to cry out with great vehemence, that they would never be confirmed by him, it being a service which none of their prelates had ever used; that it was no sacrament of Christ's institution, but an invention of the Portuguese to make them their slaves, by setting a mark on their foreheads, and giving them a box on the ear; that though the inhabitants of Vaipicotta had basely submitted to be buffeted and enslaved by him, yet that they would never endure it, nor suffer him to touch their own beards, or their wives' and daughters' faces; that he might go home in a good hour to his Portuguese, and let them alone with their religion; but that if he persisted in disturbing them thus, he should pay dearly for his presumption.

Menezes listened to all this with apparent composure, and when they had done, resuming his seat, he endeavoured to persuade them that confirmation was a sacrament, asserting, but without attempting to prove from Scripture, that it was instituted by Jesus Christ himself. Perceiving, however, that his words were of no avail, and that the tumult rather increased than subsided, he rose up, and, advancing towards them, with his crozier in his hand and his mitre on his head, thus addressed them—" This is the true and catholic faith which I preach to you; Jesus Christ taught it to His disciples, and St. Thomas preached it in these parts; all true Christians admit this doctrine, and I am ready to die for it. I shall not leave this country until I have established it by my preaching or my blood. If you wish to shed it, in order to prove this truth, approach me, you are armed; and I am not in a state to defend myself. The pastor does not fight; he has no other function than to feed his sheep. I have removed all the Portuguese, and here stand alone in the midst of you."

With this he moved forwards, apparently much discomposed. What effect he expected all this gasconade and show of determination to produce on the assembly, is uncertain. As he spoke in Portuguese, very few could understand one word of what he said: and if they had, they were not a people to be moved by sound, and vehemence, and gesticulation, where they looked for argument; nor were they of a spirit to quail before the anger of his mitred brow. They were as ready to die for their religion as he was for his; but they were too noble-minded to raise a weapon against an unarmed man, how great soever the provocation he had given them. It would have yielded them no satisfaction to shed the prelate's blood: all that they desired of him was, to leave them in the quiet enjoyment of their religion. Probably they felt some respect also for his office, though they owed none to his person. When, therefore, he drew near to them, they made way for him to pass, and allowed him to move on in any direction he chose without offering the slightest molestation.

But this was not what he wanted. Their forbearance, instead of appeasing, appeared only to irritate him the more. Seeing that he had made no impression upon the assembly, he began again to speak aloud in praise of his doctrine, and challenged all who dared to enter the lists, to argue with him in public. He had

CHAP.
II.

been informed, that the Archdeacon had on the preceding night assembled the principal inhabitants of Paru, and induced them to promise never to renounce the Patriarch of Babylon. To this Menezes next alluded, saying, " They hold the light in abhorrence, and seek places of darkness for their nocturnal assemblies, that they may teach falsehood." This roused the Archdeacon, and threw him off his guard. Understanding the insinuation, he cried with great vehemence, " Who are they that teach heresies in the dark, and preach no where but in corners." Without waiting for an answer, he rushed out of the church; but soon returned, with eight or ten children, whom he had picked up in the streets; and presenting them to the Archbishop, he said, that these were all that he could persuade to be confirmed; that the women could not come, being otherwise engaged; and that no adults would consent to receive confirmation at his hands. Menezes had, no doubt, felt some relief to his spirit even in the displeasure which he had awakened in the Archdeacon's breast: for few trials are harder for an angry man to bear, than to see those whom he addresses apparently indifferent to his wrath. While, therefore, the Archdeacon was absent, he resumed his composure, and continued to converse with the people; but when he saw him return with these few children, and heard his apology for not presenting more, he could not but feel the affront offered to a rite, to which he attached so much importance. Nevertheless, being more practised in the art of dissimulation than his antagonist, he concealed his indignation : and receiving the children with tokens of affection, he embraced them, saying, that the church, like a good mother, loved all her children alike; and that when some forsook her, she did not cease to welcome others, and admit them to the kingdom of heaven.

Finding, however, that this apparent condescension was unheeded by the people, and that no more came forward to be confirmed, he determined to leave them, and proceed on the following day to Mangate. He then retired to his boat, followed by the Archdeacon and all the men in arms, who had been with him at church. Dissembling the chagrin that he must have felt at his reception here, he invited the Archdeacon to embark with him : and although the people suspected that his object was to secure the Archdeacon's person, they encouraged him to go, assuring him, that if he went with a good courage he need fear no one, for that they would take care to put to death any man who should dare to hurt him.

The Portuguese historian[9] gives an account of two conspiracies said to have been formed about this time against the life of Menezes; but there is so little appearance of truth in either of them, that, concurring in La Croze's opinion that they are not worth repeating, and that if related, it were easy to expose their absurdity,[1] I shall pass them over. There is nothing in the character or history of these people that can render them liable to the suspicion of acting so base a part. Had they desired the life of this their enemy, he had recently put himself in their power, and dared them to the deed. Whereas, they had shown, that nothing was further from their wish than to harm him, and they had suffered him to depart in peace. Probably the historian was

[9] Gouvea, chap. 11, pp. 154—162.
[1] La Croze, p. 113.

anxious to give his hero the glory of at least braving the *perils* of martyrdom, though he could not adorn him with its *crown*.

12. The Archbishop proceeded from Paru to Mangate, the capital of a small kingdom on that coast. On his arrival there he was received without any ceremony, and conducted by a very small company of persons to the church. This he found filled with goods and women, who had sought refuge there from the effects of the war which then raged between the rajahs of Mangate and Paru. Having endeavoured to comfort these poor people in their trouble, expressing sympathy with them in the losses they had already sustained, and in the dangers to which they were still exposed, he gave them his blessing, and preached to them as usual against the errors in which, he asserted, they had been brought up. Finally, he exhorted them to be obedient to the Pope, and then returned to his boat.

Gouvea[2] gives an account of an interview between Menezes and an old man at this place, which was calculated to console him under the discouraging circumstances of his visit. That writer relates, that on the evening of the same day, the Archbishop received a visit from a venerable cattanar, with a white beard, eighty years of age, who bore a good character, and sincerely desired to obtain salvation. This man, respectfully accosting the prelate, conjured him by the love of Jesus Christ, to tell him the truth on every subject about which he was come to question him. He reminded him, that if he did not deal with him faithfully, he would have to answer unto God for his soul. He then

---

[2] Gouvea, chap. 12. La Croze, livre 2nd.

said, that he desired to know for certainty whether the Pope was the head of the universal church, and vicar of Jesus Christ upon earth: whether our Saviour had annexed to the see of Rome the sovereignty over all believers, and had limited salvation to those who paid their obedience to the pontiff. On the other hand, he put it to his conscience to declare, whether the doctrine which he had that day taught, did not proceed from some emulous or jealous feeling on the part of Rome towards the church of Babylon, as he had often heard it affirmed by his Bishops. He added, that although he was eighty years of age, and one of the oldest cattanars of the diocese, he had never till that day heard of this primacy of the Pope, nor had it ever entered into his head; he therefore intreated Menezes to undeceive him in the matter, and teach him faithfully what he ought to believe. In conclusion, he again charged him to remember, that if he led him into error, God would call him to account for deceiving his soul.

The Archbishop, says Gouvea, could not listen to this discourse without shedding tears. He was moved with compassion towards these poor people, and filled with indignation against their pastors who had deceived them, and held them for so many years in a state of such blindness. " After some pious remarks," Menezes took in his hand a cross that he wore on his breast, which, says his credulous historian, " was made of the wood of the actual cross of our Saviour," and then, addressing the old man with great solemnity, declared, that what he preached proceeded neither from emulation nor jealousy; that it was the true and pure catholic religion, without which there could be no salvation ; and that all the objections of schismatics were lies and artifices, whereby the evil Spirit sought to seduce them, and lead them to hell.

It is said that the good old man possessed more simplicity than understanding, and so it would appear from his answer to this speech. For he replied, that since a person of so much consideration as Menezes had assured him of all this, he would henceforth believe it to be true. And he is reported to have kept his word ; for that in all the opposition which the Archbishop afterwards encountered, he adhered to him with an inviolable attachment. The whole account, however, looks very suspicious, and is unsupported by any authority. It is so very unlikely, considering the fidelity of the Syrians, and especially of the cattanars, to their own Patriarch, that this man should instantly have renounced him, at the word of a stranger, for another Patriarch of whom he had never heard before ; and all the circumstances of the interview are so precisely what Menezes may naturally enough be supposed to have wished to happen, at such a crisis of his campaign ; that we cannot but suspect the story to have been got up to support the appearances of a cause in jeopardy.

His fruitless visit to Cheguree.

13. As Menezes, while at Mangate, was informed that some Paniquais were in pursuit of him from Paru ; and the inhabitants also were in hourly expectation of their enemies ; he shortened his visit, starting in the evening for Cheguree, where he arrived at daybreak on the following morning. Cheguree being within the dominions of his friend and ally, the rajah of Cochin, he there felt himself secure. The Archdeacon also had a residence at this place,

and *is said* to have invited Menezes to come and spend a few days with him, promising to wait for him there.[3] The Archbishop, as soon as he arrived, sent to inform the cattanars and inhabitants of the place, and to desire them to meet him at the church. The only answer he received to his message was, that the doors of the church were shut, and that there were none but women in the town, who did not care to say what had become of the men. He was, therefore, induced to remain quietly in his boat until the cool of the evening, when, no one appearing to welcome him, he proceeded with his own attendants to the church, and desired them to open the doors, that he might offer up his evening devotions at the altar.

During the night he was informed that the Archdeacon was in the town, and had shut himself up in his house, resolved not to appear again in the Archbishop's presence. According to this assertion, he seems to have been forgetful of his promise to entertain Menezes, and of the duties of hospitality. Whether it is more probable that he should have invited such an enemy to his habitation, and afterwards broken his word; or that the story of his invitation was invented to throw discredit upon his character, the reader will judge. The Portuguese, however, who accompanied the Archbishop, were by this time heartily tired of their fruitless and hopeless campaign. Hearing of the Archdeacon's determination, they went in a body to Menezes, accompanied by the Jesuits and his own confessor, and represented to him the utter inutility of proceeding further with his visita-

---

[3] Gouvea, chap. 12.

tion. They entreated him to retire at once to
Cochin, and not to expose the second per-
sonage[4] of the Portuguese authority in India
to such repeated insults, and to the manifest
peril of losing his life. Menezes thanked them
with much tenderness for their attention, but
at the same time protested, that nothing should
turn him from his purpose ; that he would persevere unto death, even though he were compelled to travel alone through the country,
with nothing but his staff in his hand ; that
he felt himself bound to preach to the people
the true Catholic doctrines, because, in the
quality of Metropolitan of India, he occupied
the place of the Apostle St. Thomas ; and,
lastly, that he had put his confidence in that
holy Apostle, who would assuredly favour his
enterprise, and procure for him from God the
succour and constancy that he so greatly
needed.[5]

What an example of perseverance is here
presented to the Christian missionary! Can we
see all this fortitude, this self-denial, this energy, exerted to maintain the figment of the
papal supremacy, and to promulgate the *exclusive* dogmas of Rome, without being roused
to at least equal exertion to proclaim the true
Catholic doctrines of the Cross, and the Re-

---

[4] The Archbishop of Goa ranked next to the Viceroy.

[5] We may now conjecture the Romanists' motive in receiving
the tradition of St. Thomas's labours in India. By adopting him for their tutelary saint, they were the more likely to
gain credit for their pretensions among an illiterate people.
It is worthy of remark also, that, by Gouvea's own showing, in the passage cited in the text, (chap. 12.), Menezes
avows his confidence in the *direct intercession* of that Apostle,
without the slightest allusion to Jesus Christ, the only Me-
diator between God and Man, 1 Tim. ii. 5.

deemer's sole right to universal dominion? While
we shrink from the arrogance of Menezes; while we abhor his intolerance, and deplore his infatuation; let us not fail to learn a lesson of diligence in a better cause, from his fidelity to the Church of Rome.

CHAPTER III.

DISHONOURABLE CONDUCT OF THE ARCHBISHOP.

Menezes'
attempt at
conciliation.

A. D.
1599.

1. The Archbishop, though determined not to relinquish his undertaking, yet now saw the expediency of altering his course: and having silenced for the present the importunities of those about him, he retired to his cabin, where he wrote to the Archdeacon in more conciliatory terms. After some warm expressions of friendship, he assured him, with an oath, that he remembered nothing of what was past; that he had no intention to do him any harm, but only desired to benefit the souls of men, and to deliver them from their errors; that if he would only do him the favour to come and discourse with him once more, he had no doubt that he should be able to convince him, out of the Holy Scriptures and from the doctrines of the Church, of the truth of all that he had taught. Judging of the Archdeacon by most other men, he reserved to the last what he, probably, considered his strongest argument. He knew well, that ambition is natural to the human heart, and therefore closed his epistle with a promise to do great things for him, if he would but

A. D.
1809.

submit himself unreservedly to the Roman Church.

This letter was delivered to the Archdeacon that night, and it met with no unfavourable reception. When he had read it, he called the cattanars together, and told them that it was disreputable to hide themselves any longer, and to decline treating openly on religious matters with the Archbishop, who accused them of dogmatizing in secret, and of presuming to withhold his sentiments from the world. He then delivered it as his judgment, that they ought to wait on Menezes, and hear what he had to say; but that they should take a sufficient guard to prevent his detaining them as prisoners. To this proposition all agreed, and they went, attended by a vast body of Christians, armed with swords, spears, and muskets. When they sent to inform the Archbishop of their arrival, and to say, that if he would come ashore they were ready to enter upon the conference to which he had invited them; he replied, that the sun was then too hot to stand exposed to it all the time that it would take to hold their discussion, and that it would be more convenient for all parties to assemble on board his boat. Seeing that the boat's stern was aground, and that it was surrounded by their own people, both on shore and in the water, which was very shallow, the Archdeacon and his two cattanars ventured to go on board. In the cabin, besides the Archbishop's confessor and a number of priests, they found assembled the Jesuits, who had accompanied him from place to place, and several Portuguese laymen.

2. The Archdeacon began with an apology for not coming sooner, as he had promised : and he attributed the delay to the people, who were

Public conference with the Archdeacon and cattanars.

greatly displeased with the Archbishop's proceedings. He told him without reserve, that all his attempts to separate them from the Patriarch of Babylon, to whom they had been subject more than a thousand years, only caused them to adhere the more tenaciously to his authority. He owned that they had not received him with that courtesy which he might have expected; which indeed they intended to have shown him, had he not fallen so foul on their Patriarch, and chosen to call him an excommunicated heretic; whereas, they knew him to be both a true catholic, and a most holy man. He further complained of his attempts to introduce into the diocese several novelties, which neither they nor their forefathers had ever heard of before.

To all this Menezes replied, that he was sure they were not ignorant that the Patriarch of Babylon was an avowed Nestorian; and not to trouble them with any arguments to prove that all Nestorians must be heretics, he would only ask them one question, which was, Whether they believed the Gospel of St. John? To this they answered in the affirmative, and added, that they would die rather than deny any thing that was revealed therein. " Well then," rejoined the Archbishop, " pray tell me, how you can reconcile what St. John saith,— *The Word was made flesh, and dwelt among us,*[1] with what your Patriarchs and Bishops

---

[1] John i. 14. The discrepancy on which the Archbishop here animadverts arose from his use of the Vulgate, the only version with which he appears to have been acquainted. His words are—*Verbum caro factum est*—according to the Vulgate rendering of ἐγένετο. This appeared to the Syrians to lead to the confusion of the two natures, and to give occasion to suppose, that the Divine Nature had been turned into flesh. In truth, the Latin translation does so express it, as though,

have taught you, to wit, *that the word did not make itself flesh, and that Christ was not God, and that God did not make himself man*—for do you not sing in your churches, in the service for the Nativity, that the Word did not make itself flesh, as the unbelieving Romans teach, but did only dwell in Christ as in a Temple.[2] Now, after this, how can you say that you admit the Gospel of St. John, and that you are Christians, seeing that you err in the fundamental doctrine of the Incarnation of the Word? Why do you wish me to refrain from preaching these truths unto you? Why do you shun me, and even desire to put me to death?"

It is said that the Archdeacon returned no answer to this challenge, but the cause of his silence is not explained. The Syrians were orthodox on the doctrine of the Incarnation, but probably the unintelligible assertions of Menezes, and the positive tone in which he delivered them, confused the minds of the Archdeacon and his Cattanars, unaccustomed as they were to such imperious dictation. Otherwise, it were easy for them to have replied, that the Word

in the Original, ἐποιήθη (was made) had been used, instead of ἐγένετο, (literally *became*). Accordingly, the Vulgate rendering, and consequently the Roman dogma founded upon it, is heretical. The Syriac version is more faithful to the original, and answers to this Latin sentence—*et verbum caro fuit.* The Armenian, which is thought more ancient than even the Syriac, gives the same sense. Not to mention the Egyptian, which in this place appears ambiguous; the Sclavonic, which is of the ninth century, gives a correct rendering of the Greek text, and also of the Syriac and Armenian versions. In the Portuguese translation of the New Testament by Jean Ferreira d'Almeida, this passage seems to be accurately given--*E aquella Palarra encarnaü.*—La Croze, p. 118. Appendix, pp. 21, 22.

[2] In his objection to this expression, Menezes exposed his ignorance of the original, where the word, ἐσκήνωσεν, is literally, he tabernacled, or, dwelt as in a tabernacle.

was not converted into flesh, but merely inhabited a human body, thereby assuming the nature of man into a personal union with the Godhead. He was made " in the likeness of sinful flesh ; "[3] took upon Him the form of man ; became subject to all the infirmities and sufferings, exposed Himself to all the privations and temptations, and, at last, submitted to the death, which man inherits. Thus in every respect, short of sinful passion and actual transgression, He became flesh, and " was in all points tempted like as we are, yet without sin."[4] He tabernacled among men, in order, by His life, to magnify the Law and make it honourable ; and by His death, to pay its utmost penalty. Hence His obedience was performed, and His sufferings were endured, in substitution for all that believe in Him. And hence the necessity for Him to assume the nature of man, for whose transgressions he undertook to make atonement unto God.[5]

The Pope's supremacy and Roman infallibility asserted and disproved.

3. It is not certain whether the Syrians entered sufficiently into these objects of the Incarnation of the Word ; but the interpretation of the doctrine which Menezes attributed to them was perfectly orthodox, and no reason can be assigned for their declining to maintain it, except their temporary embarrassment. According to Gouvea,[6] the Archdeacon, without taking any notice of what had been said, turned

---

[3] Rom. viii. 3.　　　　[4] Heb. iv. 15.

[5] Phil. ii. 5— 8.—" Let this mind be in you, which was also in Christ Jesus : who, being in the form of God, thought it not robbery to be equal with God ; but made himself of no reputation, and took upon him the form of a servant, and was made in the likeness of men : and being found in fashion as a man, he humbled himself, and became obedient unto death, even the death of the cross."

[6] Ch. xii. p. 171.

abruptly to the subject of the Pope's pretensions. "Your Lordship would fain persuade us," said he to the Archbishop, "that none can be saved who are not obedient to the Church of Rome. This, as far as I could ever see, St. John has no where declared. Besides, we have in our archives a letter of St. Caius, Bishop of Rome, wherein he confesseth that he had nothing more to do with the Church of Babylon, than the Church of Babylon had to do with his Church. We possess also another letter, which is called, in our records, the Letter on the Lord's Day, and is said to have been dictated by our Lord, to have been written by an Angel, and to have fallen from Heaven on a Sabbath day, while the people were assembled in Church. In that letter the same truth is affirmed respecting the independence of the Church of Babylon." He and the Cattanars then went on to refer to other legendary tales and writings of the same description, until the Archbishop, interrupting them, said, "Why do you stop at these obsolete fables, when you have the light of the Gospel to guide you, which is more brilliant than the sun, and the words of Jesus Christ, who expressly commended His sheep to the care of St. Peter and his successors. After the Saviour's ascension, St. Peter was chief in the Church, and prelate over the other Apostles: and the successors of St. Peter have the same authority over all who exercise the Apostolic functions, that is to say, over the Bishops, Archbishops, and Patriarchs of the whole world. Why did our Lord, after His resurrection, commend His sheep only to St. Peter? Why, in the time of His passion, did He command only St. Peter to confirm his brethren? Why did He not say to any other

2 B

CHAP.
III.
Apostle, that he had prayed for him that his faith might not fail? He evidently showed thereby, that He had appointed that Apostle the prelate of the whole world, and universal pastor of the Church: that He had constituted the chair of St. Peter the sovereign see, to rule and judge all the rest: that while the Catholic faith would be fallible in them, its infallibility should be secured in St. Peter's see by the special assistance of the Holy Ghost, which the Lord Jesus had obtained for him from His Father, so that he might be able to confirm and teach the rest."

Gouvea, instead of giving the answer of the Syrian ecclesiastics to this harangue, proceeds with the narrative as though they returned none, probably intending us to infer, that they thought the Archbishop's argument unanswerable. Indeed, he everywhere speaks of that prelate more in the language of panegyric, than of history: none, however, but a romanist, himself blinded by the fable of the infallibility of his Church, would have considered such a speech as this creditable, either to the understanding or the theology of an Archbishop. The ingenuity indeed of Menezes and his Church, in thus converting to the honour of St. Peter his thrice repeated denial of his Lord with oaths and execrations, an event that filled the Apostle himself with grief and shame, we cannot fail to admire; but a more manifest perversion of Holy Writ is hardly to be found. The three questions of this prelate might have been answered in almost as few sentences. We need only consider—

First. When our Lord thrice commended His sheep to Peter, He asked him each time,

" Lovest thou me ?" [6] The Apostle, instead of
being conscious of the honour that it is here
pretended was then conferred upon him, " was
grieved," because of the repetition of his Lord's
question.   He could not but feel that it implied
a doubt of his love, and he would remember,
with remorse, that he had recently given too
just cause for such doubt.   Consequently, before " the chief Shepherd " restores him to the
office of feeding His flock, He requires the open,
the unequivocal avowal of his love to be repeated, just so often as he had denied Him.
The other disciples had given no such reason to
question their fidelity to their Master: He,
therefore, leaves them, without repeating the
instructions which they had already received, to
gather, to feed, and attend His sheep.   The dis-
crimination then in this case was any thing
but honourable to Peter.

Second.   The Lord commanded him to
strengthen his brethren, because he had experienced more of Satan's devices than they, when
that enemy sifted him as wheat ; and more of his
Lord's power, in keeping him from utterly falling away.[7] By the forwardness of his zeal, in
protesting his readiness to defend his Master
even to the death, he had shown himself less
conscious than the other disciples of his infirmities : [8] for this reason, probably, he was given,
for a short time, into the hands of Satan.   His
fall wrung from his heart the bitterest tears he
had ever shed ; and it taught him to warn his
brethren of the malice and craft of the enemy.
Attributing his recovery to his Lord's power and
compassion, he learned, by an act of grace
second only to that which had regenerated his

[6] John xxi. 17.   [7] Luke xxii. 31, 32.
[8] John xiii. 36—38.
2 B 2

heart, to encourage his brethren to hold fast their confidence in the same Lord, at all times and under all circumstances.

Third. Jesus prayed equally for all His Apostles, in their capacity as pastors of His flock.[9] His special prayer for Peter was only in consequence of his special fall.

This Apostle then, so far from being invested with any authority over his brethren, was the least entitled to such a distinction. He knew better than to assume the preeminence which the Roman church ascribes to him. On no occasion did he presume to dictate to the other Apostles. If any one might claim this precedence, it was John, the disciple whom the Lord loved the most.[1] If any one appears to have been acknowledged by the rest as their leader, it was James, who presided at the apostolic council at Jerusalem.[2] If any one seems to have spoken with authority to his brethren, it was Paul, who, at Antioch, withstood EVEN PETER " to the face, because he was to be blamed." [3]

Both parties agree to hold a Synod, and in the interim to abstain from interfering with each other.

4. On such a foundation do the romanists build their Pope's supremacy, and the infallibi- lity of their church. Truly is it a foundation of sand. Why should the silence of these Syrians to the questions of Menezes be attributed to their incapacity to answer him? It is quite as probable that, in common with many divines of the English, Scotch, and other orthodox churches, they thought it a fruitless task to un- dertake to controvert such manifest absurdities, in a conversation with one so deeply interested

---

[9] John xvii.
[1] John xiii. 23 ; xix. 26 ; xx. 2 ; xxi. 7, 20.
[2] Acts xv.   [3] Gal. ii. 11—14.

to maintain them.   But, whatever was the
cause of their apparent inattention to his arguments, it is evident from what followed that
they made no impression upon their minds.   It
was at length, however, agreed, that a Synod
should be called, as early as convenient, to determine questions of faith ; and that in the
mean time the Archbishop should be at liberty
to visit any of their churches, to preach in them,
and give the blessing.   But the Archdeacon in-
sisted on his neither confirming persons, nor
performing any other Episcopal function within
the diocese ; and that he should not be received
as their primate, but as a Bishop merely on a
visit to them, and acting so far by sufferance.

Seeing that these were the best terms that
he was likely at present to obtain, Menezes
signed the agreement, and the Archdeacon and
cattanars followed his example.   It was further
arranged, that the Synod should be held before
Whitsuntide ; and the Archdeacon, who, it was
agreed, should accompany the Archbishop, promised to desist from stirring up the people
against him, and from going about with troops
of armed men.   This agreement produced but a
temporary tranquillity, being soon infringed by
Menezes.

5. Immediately after this arrangement, the
Archbishop proceeded by water to Canhur,
whither the Archdeacon followed by land, not
venturing to trust himself in the boats, where
he would have been in the power of the Portuguese.

*At Canhur
they sepa-
rate.*

At Canhur the prelate was very courteously
received, the Archdeacon having prepared his
way, by informing the people that he did not
come among them as their Bishop, but merely
as a stranger, to pay them a friendly visit.   On

this understanding, they permitted him to preach in their church. Though he so far kept to his agreement as to do nothing but preach and give the blessing, yet in his sermon, which was very long, he availed himself of the opportunity to expatiate on the errors of Nestorius; also on the truth and supremacy of the Roman church, and on the obligation of all other churches to render unto her implicit obedience. This gave great offence to the people; and the Archdeacon, justly regarding it as taking an unfair advantage of the indulgence that had been shown him, and a violation of the agreement so recently concluded between them, felt himself much aggrieved, and resolved to go no further in his company. He therefore went to him, and, pleading indisposition, begged to be excused from proceeding, as he desired to retire to Chegurée for medical assistance. Menezes, having no longer any wish for his detention, allowed him to depart; and they met no more until the Archdeacon gave in his adhesion to the Roman communion, an event that was preceded by a series of outrages unparalleled in the history of any church but that of Rome.

Archbishop proceeds to the South.

6. The ill success of the Archbishop in the five churches which he had already visited, convinced him that the further he went to the North, the opposition would increase; for the Archdeacon had taken up his abode there, where he was generally beloved. He determined, therefore, to proceed to the southward, both because, as the Archdeacon had less authority there, he hoped to meet with better success among the people; and also, because the political affairs of the Portuguese demanded his immediate presence in that direction. In pursuance of the instructions he had brought with

him from Goa, it was necessary for him to hasten to Coulan,[3] a fortress in Travancore, about one hundred miles from Cape Comorin, belonging to the Portuguese. It was a place of great importance to them, being a considerable mart for cotton, pepper, ginger, cardamoms and other articles of merchandize. At that time the Portuguese trade, and even their safety there, was threatened by a fort which the Rajah of Travancore was erecting in the neighbourhood. The demolition of this fort was the principal object of the Archbishop's visit.

7. He commenced his journey thither on the first of March, halting in his way at a castle within two leagues of Cochin, where the governor and the Bishop of that city paid their respects to him. Having communicated to them his design, he proceeded direct to Porca, where the rajah of that country, who had been expecting him for some days, welcomed him with great demonstrations of joy. In this place he found a small church belonging to the Syrians, to which he went in the evening, and was kindly received by the Christians. For this reception he was indebted to the attention of the rajah, who professed a great friendship for the Portuguese, and had commanded the people, on pain of his displeasure, to comply with all that the Archbishop might desire.

After preaching and giving the blessing, Menezes repaired to the house of the principal cattanar, to lodge for the night. Here the rajah

At Porca he receives a friendly visit from the Rajah.

[3] Or Quilon. In remote times this was a sea port of considerable note, and the town is said to have been built, A. D. 825. The Christians, as well as the Hindoo natives of this part of Malabar, commence their era at the period of its foundation; and it is mentioned by Marco Paolo, in the year 1295. The brahmins here possess a very ancient temple dedicated to Siva.—Hamilton.

paid him a visit before he retired to rest, accompanied by a vast number of his people well armed, and a retinue of pages carrying flambeaux. He was gorgeously apparelled, and covered with gold and jewels. All this display was intended to impress the Archbishop with a high notion of his magnificence and power, as he had a request to make which he considered of great importance. After courteously saluting him, and taking to himself the credit of protecting the commerce of the Portuguese from pirates, and performing other services for that people, he said, that he hoped these good offices would be deemed sufficient to entitle him to the honour of being called *Brother in arms* to the king of Portugal, as the rajah of Cochin had been. The Archbishop's answer showed that he knew how to render the rajah's ambition available for his own purpose. After returning his civilities, he said, that what he had asked was an honour that the king of Portugal never conferred on any sovereign until he had merited it by some signal service. However, he promised to do what he could to obtain for him the distinction to which he aspired. This interview lasted two hours, and it was near midnight when the rajah took his leave.

This prince is described as a young man of short stature, but well proportioned, and distinguished among the rajahs of Malabar for his valour and courtesy. He called himself Nambraché, that is, High Priest. He is said to have been very zealous in his devotions, having nine hundred idols in one temple, to each of which he presented daily an offering and a short prayer. While thus engaged, he was loaded with ornaments, and these superstitions employed him from six in the morning till noon.

During this time he gave audience to no one, and attended to no secular business whatever. Not that he was peculiar in these exercises, as it was customary for all the rajahs of Malabar to devote their mornings in a similar way to the worship of their idols : and, assuming that they attributed their prosperity and safety to those images, we cannot but admire their zeal, and think it worthy of the Christian's imitation in his daily supplications to the only true God. Shall the torch of superstition eclipse the lamp of Christian devotion? This be far from the children of light! Not indeed that the Sacred Scriptures require them to spend so much time at their devotions: yet they are to be in the spirit of prayer all the day long.

8. Early on the following morning the Arch-bishop went to church, where, in open violation of the solemn compact into which he had so recently entered, he said mass, and afterwards confirmed the whole congregation. It is to be feared, from this and other numerous instances of the kind, that there is too much truth in the historian's assertion,[5] that " none but fools will ever expect that papists will observe any such promises longer than the first opportunity they have to break them." The present case certainly tends to confirm it. Menezes had, as we have seen, expressly engaged, by the agreement of Cheguree, not to administer confirmation until the promised Synod had been held: but he acted here, says another historian, according to the infamous maxim of his Church, that no one is bound to keep an engagement contracted with heretics.[6] The service, how-

Marginal note: Violates his agreement with the Archdeacon.

---

[5] M. Geddes, p. 72.

[6] La Croze, p. 126. This maxim was justified by the councils of Lateran, and the decrees of popes Gregory IX. and Innocent III.

ever, went off without commotion; which is to be attributed both to the rajah's commands, and also to the influence of the Jesuits, who had an establishment at Porca, and had laboured hard to reconcile the people there to the Church of Rome.

9. The Archbishop's call to the South being urgent, he set out that evening for Coulan. The journey was long and perilous, as it lay through a country whose inhabitants were hostile to the Portuguese. But the rajah of Porca provided him with a strong escort, commanded by a confidential officer of his own, who preserved him once from imminent danger by the way, and brought him in safety to his journey's end. On his arrival at Coulan, he learned that the Portuguese had just sustained a considerable loss on the coast: this intelligence, however, did not deter him from prosecuting the object of his mission. Under pretence of visiting a church near the fort, which the rajah of Travancore was building, he took a view of the works; and finding them nearly finished, and concluding that they would soon receive a garrison, he lost no time in despatching a messenger to the commander-in-chief of the Portuguese forces before Cunahle, desiring him to bring the whole of his armada without delay to demolish this erection. He assured him, that if he came immediately he would have no difficulty in executing the task, for that he would find none but workmen to resist him.

10. The Portuguese commandant was not unprepared for this order; for, at the commencement of the siege of Cunahle, though at that time, as at present, the rajah of Travancore was at peace with the Portuguese, the Archbishop left secret instructions with that

officer, to proceed immediately after the fall of Cunahle, with the whole of his force, and destroy the fort in question. The pirates, however, held out longer than was expected; so that Menezes had the mortification of seeing the work nearly completed: and while looking for the armada to come and destroy it, he received despatches, informing him that the Portuguese had failed in an assault upon Cunahle, and been beaten off with great slaughter; that the commander had retired to Cochin to have the wounded cured, and would soon wait upon the Archbishop, at Coulan, for further orders.

At this news Menezes was exceedingly distressed, both on account of the number of persons of quality that were killed in the action, and also because he had reason to fear that it would greatly encourage the native princes in their opposition to the Portuguese, whom they had hitherto been accustomed to regard as invincible. To obviate such a consequence, he did not hesitate to despatch letters to all the rajahs of Malabar, in which he asserted, that the Portuguese had obtained a great victory before Cunahle; and though obliged to acknowledge that it was purchased with the blood of several brave men, among whom were some of his own kindred, who were very dear to him, yet he had no doubt that at the next attack they would carry the place.

Thus, in less than a fortnight, this Archbishop, this Apostle of the Papacy, this primate of all India, perpetrates three crimes, either of which were sufficient to brand with infamy the name of any christian, whatever his station in society. He first violates a most solemn engagement within a week after it was made: he next treacherously orders the destruction of a fort that belonged to a prince with whom his nation was at peace : and he, lastly, circulates notorious falsehoods, in order to anticipate a result which he deemed of sufficient political importance to justify the deception. Were such the services for which it is thought he would have been canonized, had he not lived to return to Europe, and exposed his real character to the world ? [1]

Having sent off the letters containing this false intelligence respecting the state of things before Cunahle, the Archbishop, too anxious to repair the defeat they had sustained to await the commandant's arrival, set out himself for Cochin, to devise measures without delay for the improvement of their affairs. The peace they had made with the Zamorin of Calicut, seems to have been considered only as a temporary suspension of hostilities, or rather, a union of their forces for their mutual accommodation, both being equally interested in the destruction of the pirates. That prince, however, had acted with so much fidelity, and his co-operation was so essential to the success of the enterprise, that Menezes proposed to render the peace between them permanent. The expediency of

[1] Manuel de Faria. Asia Portuguesa, tom. iii. " This illustrious prelate, had he never returned to Spain, had, in " all probability, been made a saint before this time, where, " through the difficulty there is in the managing of high " posts, whether offered to him or procured by solicitations, " he lost all the glory he had acquired in the Indies, in the " opinion of the world."

" His high posts in Spain, which the author saith he doth " not know whether he procured by solicitation or not, were " the *primacy of Braga*, and viceroyship of Portugal, under " Philip III., for two years, and the presidentship of the " council of state of Portugal at Madrid, in which office and " court he died."—Geddes, pp. 74, 75.

this measure was too obvious not to meet with
the unanimous concurrence of the council at
Cochin; but, before it could be concluded, it
required the Viceroy's confirmation.

11. Accordingly, the Archbishop transmitted
the despatches for this purpose to Goa, and
then proceeded with his visitation. From Cochin he went direct to Molandurtè, a Syrian
town of some importance. Here the Christians received him with such tokens of friendship, that he ventured again to violate his agreement with the Archdeacon, by administering
the rite of confirmation, and performing other
episcopal functions. The only opposition he
seems to have met with here, was from a cattanar, who was suffering from the leprosy.
Though not in a state to take a very active part
against the prelate, yet he succeeded in persuading several persons to join him in refusing
to hold any communication with this foreign
Bishop.[8]

*Visit to Mo-
landurtè,
where he
again vio-
lates his
agreement
with the
Archdea-
con.*

12. While at Molandurtè, Menezes received
the Viceroy's despatches, confirming the peace
with the Zamorin, and requiring him, together
with the Governor and the Bishop of Cochin,
to repair immediately to Vaipin to sign the treaty.
This result was not effected without jesuitical artifice. The Zamorin had a nephew, Uniare
Cherare, who was his prime minister. This
man had been privately baptized by Francisco
Roz, who allowed him to retain the profession
of paganism, lest he should lose his uncle's confidence, and, with it, the opportunity of serving
the Portuguese. From the time of his baptism,
Uniare, being president of the Zamorin's cabinet, had communicated to the Portuguese all

*Concludes a
permanent
peace with
the Zamo-
rin. In-
stance of
jesuitical
artifice.*

[8] La Croze, p. 126.

the secrets of state, and gradually disposed
the members of council, and even the Zamorin
himself, to entertain a more favourable opinion
of them. The Archbishop, instead of condemning either the prince or the jesuits for this
scandalous dissimulation, actually confirmed it:
for, on a subsequent occasion, he administered
to the prince the rite of confirmation, with the
same secrecy, and giving him the same infamous
dispensation which he had received from the
jesuit at his baptism. Here we have another
practical illustration of the abominable maxim
of the Roman Church, already noticed—*the end
sanctifies the means*. To secure the fruits of
this traitor's perfidy to his sovereign and his
kinsman, they sanctioned, yea, encouraged his
hypocrisy.[9] If the Apostle pronounces their
damnation just, who resolved to do evil that
good might come;[1] what judgment would he
have given against such men, whose *end* was
as perfidious as their *means*?

9 Geddes' History, p. 77.   1 Romans iii. 8.

CHAPTER IV.

PROGRESS OF THE ARCHBISHOP'S ENCROACH-
MENTS.

1. HITHERTO the Archdeacon had conscientiously observed the terms of his agreement,
and abstained from all interference with Menezes; but now his forbearance was no longer
compatible with his duty to the Church of
which he was the temporary guardian. He,
no doubt, considered the compact cancelled by
the Archbishop's repeated violation of its conditions; and very fairly attributing that prelate's growing assurance to his own quiescence,
he at length began to publish excommunications against him and the Syrians who should
join him. He wrote to all the Churches, cau-
tioning them not to have any thing more to
do with a prelate who had behaved so unfaith-
fully towards them; and also to the native princes
of Malabar, to put them on their guard against
the Archbishop and his designs. He saw sufficient reason to assure them, that Menezes arro-
gated to himself the ecclesiastical jurisdiction
of the country, for the purpose of making the
Syrians vassals to the Portuguese.[1] This design

A. D.
1599.

The Arch-
deacon and
native
princes
oppose
Menezes.

[1] It will be seen, by the 24th Decree of the 9th Session of
the Synod of Diamper, that this suspicion was too well founded.

they already suspected, and it had given them no little uneasiness. The rajah of Cochin, especially, was fully aware of the prelate's intention, and awake to the danger that threatened his own dominions; and he ventured, as far as he could, to endeavour to impede the Archbishop's progress. He began by making the Christians of Molandurté, who were his subjects, pay dearly for their kindness and submission to Menezes, imposing upon them a heavy tribute, from which they were not relieved for many years. He also commanded them, on pain of death, to repair to their Archdeacon at Angamale.

He resolves to hold an ordination at Diamper —attempts ineffectually made to prevent it.

2. While these proceedings intimidated the Syrians, they were calculated to have the opposite effect upon the determined spirit of the Archbishop. Having despatched his business with the Zamorin, and being encouraged by his favourable reception at Molandurté, he set out for Diamper, the ancient seat of several Bishops of Malabar. His great object in his present migrations was, to form a strong party among the Syrians, that through them he might gain access to the whole community: and having remarked that the Cattanars retained a close attachment to the prelate who ordained them, he resolved to commence his proceedings with the ordination of as many as he could persuade to receive orders at his hands. At this time the circumstances of the diocese favoured his design, for he had succeeded in keeping the see in abeyance for two years. Consequently, there had been no ordination during that period: and concluding that many would be desirous and ready to present themselves for the purpose, he gave notice of his intention to hold a public ordination at Diamper on the

Saturday before the approaching Palm Sunday.

This plan succeeded, though not at first to his wishes, nor without opposition. Affecting ignorance of the Archdeacon's dissatisfaction at what he had hitherto done, he wrote to inform him of his intention, and to invite him to be present and assist at the solemnity. The Archdeacon was much grieved at this determination to anticipate the approaching council, and replied, "That it was contrary to the late agreement they had made together, and that it would put an end to the affair of the Synod, which the Archbishop seemed so much to desire, since the principal question to be debated therein was, *Whether he was their Prelate or no.*"

But Menezes suspected that the Archdeacon talked so much about the Synod only to amuse him and gain time, in the hope that he would soon be compelled to return before he had done anything of importance. Indeed, Gouvea goes so far as to charge the Archdeacon with the first infraction of the treaty at Chegurèe; because, as that historian asserts, without attempting to explain how he ascertained the fact, he never meant the Synod to be held.[2] Enough, however, has here been adduced to show, that the Archbishop alone was guilty of breach of faith; for he did not suffer a week to elapse without breaking the agreement that he had signed. It cannot be pretended that he was under any constraint when he put his signature to the deed; for at the time he actually held, in a manner, possession of the Archdeacon's person, who, therefore, if any one, had cause to complain of coercion.

[2] Chap. xiii. p. 190.

2 C

The suspicion, however, of the Archdeacon's duplicity, furnished the artful prelate with an excuse for setting him at defiance. He wrote him word, "that nothing should hinder him from conferring orders at the appointed time: and not only so, but that he would exercise all other acts of episcopal jurisdiction, in obedience to the Pope's briefs, to whom all the churches of the world were subject." These "Briefs," it will be remembered, were in his possession, when he signed the agreement to abstain from the acts which he now shamelessly avows his determination to perform.

The Archdeacon, finding him so bent upon holding an ordination, and, probably, wishing to appear ready to make some concession, re-joined, "that since he was resolved to do it, right or wrong, he begged of him to ordain none but *Latin* [3] candidates." To this the Archbishop replied, "that he should ordain both *Latins* and *Chaldæans;* for that it was his business to put an end to that distinction, by bringing all Christians into one fold under one universal Shepherd, who was the Pope."

Seeing that he thus gloried in the shame of violating the act of Chegurèe, the Archdeacon was convinced that nothing he could do would stop so unprincipled a man in his career. But he determined, notwithstanding, to use all his influence with the native authorities to prevent the intended ordination, or, at least, to reduce the number of candidates as low as possible. He suspected that Menezes would ordain all that came to him, without exacting the usual fee; for he knew enough of that prelate to see, that he had sufficient sagacity to discover the

---

[3] This name is given to all the *native* youths educated at the Jesuits' college, as well as to Portuguese students.

advantage that would accrue to him from this affectation of disinterestedness. While it gained him more credit with the people, it would tend to attach those whom he ordained the closer to his person. By this means he would also alienate their minds from their own Church, and seriously affect the Syrian Bishops' revenues, which were derived chiefly from these and other dues received annually from the clergy. The precedent of gratuitous ordinations being once established, the Archdeacon foresaw the difficulty, should the Providence of God ever favour them with happier times, that would lie in the way of future prelates to recover their established rights. It was therefore his duty, as the legal guardian of this orphan Church, to protest against, and, if possible, prevent an innovation, alike unnecessary and mischievous.

For this purpose he wrote in pressing terms to the rajahs of Cochin, Angamale, and Mangate, who had for some time been the friends and protectors of Menezes, entreating them to use their interest with him to dissuade him from his purpose. The rajah of Cochin he especially urged not to permit the ordination to take place within his dominions. On receipt of this remonstrance, those princes wrote to the Archbishop, earnestly requesting him not to confer orders before the proposed general Synod of all the Christians in Malabar : but their letters proved as unavailing as that of the Archdeacon. Menezes replied to them all in the same strain,—" That in matters relating to the Christian Law he could have nothing to say to them ; that he gave no account of his conduct to infidels, to whom the secrets of Christianity were unknown ; that in every thing else he should obey them, in justice and equity; and, finally, that the administration of orders which he was about to confer, was included in those things in which they had promised him their favour and assistance."

Besides soliciting the intervention of these princes, the Archdeacon published an edict throughout the diocese, forbidding all Christians, upon pain of excommunication, to receive orders from the hands of Menezes. He circulated another document, commanding all Cattanars and Christians not to suffer the Archbishop to enter any of their Churches, nor to be present at any of his masses and sermons. Besides the ecclesiastical censures which they would incur by their disobedience, he warned them of the disgrace and chastisement that would fall on them from their sovereigns.

To the cattanars and inhabitants of Diamper he addressed a special olla,[*] commanding them to prevent the Archbishop from holding an ordination in their Church, or exercising any other jurisdiction. This order arrived too late, as he had already preached twice on two successive days, and confirmed several persons, without the slightest interruption. But the Archdeacon's commands were no sooner made known, than the people raised a disturbance against Menezes; and the senior cattanar immediately went to him, and, in his own name and that of every other cattanar in the place, desired him to quit the town, and not to set his

---

[*] Olla, i. e. leaf. This is the Palmyra leaf, which is cut in strips, and written upon with a stylus, or pointed iron pen. This seems to have been the only mode of writing used in India before the introduction, by Europeans, of pen, ink and paper. To this day their Vedas and Shasters are composed of these strips of Olla strung together.

foot in their church again, nor to confirm any
more: telling him, at the same time, that with
them this ceremony was most unnecessary, as
they anointed their children's heads with oil at
their baptism, which was all the confirmation
they required.

The Archbishop appeared to take no notice
either of the man, or of what he said ; but,
calling the other cattanars around him, began
to instruct them in the nature of this rite.   It
has been shrewdly remarked, that he ought to
have done this before, had not his understanding
been filled with more heat than light: that he
acted without any rule to guide him, and abandoned himself to an intemperate zeal which led
him into many faults that would have ruined
him, but for the fear in which the native princes
stood of the Portuguese power.[5]

The Archdeacon now redoubled his entreaties
with the rajah of Cochin, to exert all his authority to prevent the approaching ordination.
Accordingly, that prince sent a positive command to the governor of Diamper to stop the
service if begun, and to threaten with his displeasure and severest chastisement, all who
should present themselves to the Archbishop
for holy orders.   The Naires of the place came
several times in a body to the door of the
church, where they struck their bucklers in
token of hostility, and cried aloud, that the
Archbishop had nothing to do with the Christians of that country, who were subject to their
own king : and rather than suffer him to pass,
they threatened to assassinate him and all his
followers.

These menaces induced the attendants of

⁵ La Croze, p. 131.

Menezes to station sentinels at his chamber
door every night; but he himself walked about,
affecting to be unmoved by all the noise and
opposition raised against him. It is difficult to
say whether his confidence and perseverance
were occasioned by " his prejudices," which
are said always to have served him in lieu of
articles of faith; [6] or by his knowledge of the
natural timidity of the heathen, who either
feared or respected the Portuguese too much
to provoke their resentment. At all events, he
was persuaded, as will soon appear, that they
durst not offer any injury to his person.

On the eve of the day fixed for the ordination, an officer of rank in the service of the
rajah of Cochin, who was governor of a neighbouring town, happening to pass Diamper, in
company with several Naires, met the Archbishop on the road. Accosting him with
haughty mien and eyes flashing with anger, he
reproached him with having come amongst
them only to insult the gods of the country,
to overturn their laws, to abolish the ancient
customs of the Christians, and to seduce them
from their allegiance to their rightful sovereign.
" You shall pay for it, said he; for we will kill
you, and all the Christians of the country who
join you : that others may learn by your example
not to presume to attempt to establish new laws
in our state." The Archbishop not understanding him, a native priest in his company interpreted what the man had said ; when he turned
from him with a contemptuous smile. In a
short time, however, he sent him an answer
more becoming his sacred office, but little in
accordance with his proceedings. He desired

[6] Ses préjugez, qui lui tenoient lieu d'articles de Foi.—La
Croze, p. 131.

them to tell him, "that he had done nothing
but what was according to the commands of
the Great and only God, who made heaven and
earth, and without whose will no one could do
him any harm." Had this expression of confidence in the Almighty been supported by a
corresponding behaviour, it would have deserved
admiration, and might have won the attention
even of the heathen. But how could they
honour that God, or think Him better than
their own, whom this prelate professed to be
serving, while using so much violence, arrogance, and injustice? The officer, instead of
being appeased by his more conciliatory message, went away in a rage.

3. On the following morning, the governor
of Diamper, in obedience to the rajah's commands, circulated a notice to all the inhabitants, to remain at home as prisoners for the
day. He forbade them, under pain of confiscation of their goods, to move out of their
houses, or to go to church, or to hold any communication with the Archbishop. But these
precautions were of little avail. Menezes and
his party seem to have expected an order to
this effect from the Governor, and took care to
anticipate him, by collecting all the candidates
in the church on the preceding evening, and
remaining shut up with them there through the
night. Next morning the service was performed,
without the knowledge, or even suspicion, of
those who were so anxious and vigilant to prevent it. There were thirty-eight candidates.[7]
The Archbishop began with requiring them to
abjure the Nestorian creed ; then, to profess
that of Pius IV. ; afterwards, to swear alle-

Thirty-eight candidates ordained.

7 Geddes says thirty-seven, (p. 79.) Gouvea, (ch. xiv.)
J. F. Raulin, (p. 29,) and La Croze, (p. 133,) say, thirty-eight.

giance to the Pope; to renounce for ever the Patriarch of Babylon; and solemnly to engage never to admit any other prelate to their church except those sent from Rome. The service was then concluded in the usual form. In this manner did he succeed in executing, what was then thought, a masterpiece of policy. "It was thus," says Gouvea, "that Menezes began to secure in this country a number of persons who remained faithful to him, and never abandoned his interests."

Hostile disposition of the Naires towards him at Mangalan.

4. After the conclusion of this service, the Archbishop quietly retired from Diamper. Easter approached, and he determined to spend the passion week at Carturté, in the dominions of the Rannee of Pimenta. In the way thither, he visited several churches, and met at some of them with a friendly reception; at others he was less kindly received, the people refusing even to see him. At one place, called Mangalan, he is said to have been in great danger from a troop of Naires, who were seeking to murder him. Being informed of their intention, and that they had already surrounded his boat, with their guns [8] shouldered and matches lighted, Menezes took the precaution of moving to the opposite bank of the river. The Portuguese historian greatly exaggerates his danger on this occasion. To those at all acquainted with the country and its inhabitants, the whole description will wear the aspect of romance. Had the Naires, the military caste of Malabar, been so intent on killing him as is pretended, it is very unlikely that they would have suffered his boat

---

[8] *Matchlocks* were used in India till within the present century, when the natives began gradually to adopt the European musket. But the *matchlock* is still used in the interior, chiefly by native huntsmen.

to be removed : neither, if it had been shifted to the opposite bank of the river, which is narrow, would it have been out of their reach. Besides, whatever degree of danger may have *appeared* at the moment to surround the Archbishop, it is evident, from all that we have hitherto seen, and from what occurred afterwards, that their sole object was to alarm him, for the purpose of inducing him to retire to Cochin or Goa. No doubt he himself perceived this ; for he continued to move about quietly in the midst of them, thereby giving them frequent opportunities to put him to death, had such really been their intention.

5. From Mangalan, he proceeded to Carturté, where he arrived April 1, 1599, on the Friday before Palm Sunday. Early on the following morning he went to church, said mass, and preached. At the conclusion of the service, he desired the people not to fail to come to church again next day, as he had something of importance to communicate to them. It was here that he first practised a trick upon the natives, which was afterwards frequently repeated, both by himself, and other missionaries of his church who followed him. The inhabitants of India are generally very proud of being admitted to the confidence of their superiors, and persons in authority. The Malabar Christians especially, are said to be greatly pleased to have a secret intrusted to them, and to keep it with fidelity. Gouvea himself avows, that it was by this artifice Menezes ingratiated himself with the Syrians, and promoted his cause among them.

6. After he had dismissed the congregation, he retired to his boat, inviting several of the most considerable persons among them to follow

him. When they came, he spared neither money nor promises to win them over to his party; and two of their number he selected for special notice, pretending that he thought them the most deserving of this attention. Their names were, Iti Mato Mapula, and Iti Mané Mapula.[s] We are not told the nature of the secret which he intrusted to them; but they were sufficiently flattered by his confidence to attach themselves to him, and, subsequently, they became of essential service to his cause. By such means was he gradually insinuating himself among this people, for the purpose of undermining their fidelity to their Patriarch, which he found was not to be taken by assault.

Tries the
effect of
pomp and
music,
which at
first give
general dis-
satisfaction,
as also his
interference
with their
offerings
and ser-
vices.

7. He was not equally successful with the cattanars and people in general, who would not listen with patience to his discourse. Without appearing to notice this, he resolved to try what effect the Portuguese music would produce upon them, hoping that it would charm the common people, and reconcile them to the Latin service, to which they seemed to have a great aversion. With this view, he sent for a full choir from Cochin; and on Palm Sunday, high mass was performed with all the pomp and ceremony that he would have observed at Goa. But it failed to make the desired impression. Both cattanars and people were so far from being enchanted by the music and pompous

---

[s] *Iti*, is a very common appellation in Malabar. It has been supposed to be a title of respect, corresponding with the English, *Sir, (Dominus)*; but this is not likely, as it is frequently borne by persons of inferior station. *Mapula*, is, probably, a contraction of *Maha Pulla*, literally, great child. This is, undoubtedly, an honourable title, and given both to Syrians and Mahomedans. Joseph de Sancta Maria. Itin. in Indiam, p. 107. See J. F. Raulin. Hist. Syn. Diamp. p. 30. Note.

ceremony, that, " if they liked it ill before, they were now perfectly disgusted : as, in truth, none but they that place all religion in external performances can do otherwise,—there being no passion which that service will not excite in its spectators sooner than devotion."[9] This remark is most correct. The people could take no more part in this service than in the performances of a theatre in an unknown tongue.

These proceedings of Menezes prevented the regular services of the Syrian Church ; and for that reason they gave general dissatisfaction, notwithstanding all his attempts to make them acceptable. He also put a stop to the offerings of the people, which form the chief part of the cattanars' revenue. It was customary at the principal festivals of the church, for each communicant to pay a single Fanam, a small coin of the country, worth about fourpence.[1] This voluntary contribution the Archbishop affected to pronounce an act of simony, and his panegyrist, Gouvea, applauds his decision. How then, it is justly demanded, will they defend the exactions of the Roman Church, at their masses, especially for the dead, and other services?[2]

8. Besides this interference with the offerings of the Church, he attempted to introduce a practice of which they had never before heard, that of *Auricular confession*, to which he called every one, preparatory to taking the sacrament. This was regarded as a fresh griev-

Introduces auricular confession:

[9] Geddes, pp. 80, 81. Gouvea asserts, that the people were delighted with what they heard, and with the Archbishop's discourse, of which, by the way, they did not understand one word, for he preached in Portuguese. He acknowledges the dissatisfaction of the cattanars, but attributes it to their avarice. Ch. 14. p. 210.

[1] The gold fanam of Malabar is worth sevenpence.

[2] La Croze, p. 136.

ance. In conformity with the doctrines of the Chaldean Church, from which they had hitherto been supplied with Bishops and teachers, they were as much attached to the Sacrament of the Eucharist, as they abhorred the Roman confession. These two points, however, Menezes resolved, if possible, to carry on the present occasion—the abolition of the offerings, and the introduction of auricular confession : and for this purpose, he took upon himself to forbid the celebration of the communion in the Syriac service on Palm Sunday. At this also the cattanars took fresh alarm. Holy Thursday was always kept by this people with great solemnity ; but they began to fear, that if the Archbishop went on at this rate, without interruption, he would exclude them from their own church on that day. There was another church at Carturté belonging to the Syrians of inferior caste,[3] in which they requested him to celebrate the approaching festival : but he refused to listen to their proposal, saying, that so long as he remained in their country, he would set his face against all simony, whether in these churches, or any other.

Opposed by
a cattanar
at the head
of a band of
men.

9. Though his arbitrary conduct was calculated to provoke the resentment of the people, yet he had secured a sufficient party from among them to protect him from violence. But he and his friends could not prevent the general feeling of indignation. On the same evening that he had treated the cattanars with so much arrogance, one of them, the son of a principal inhabitant, assembled a company of about thirty persons, who began publicly to complain of his proceedings. Moved by their representations,

---

[3] The descendants of Mar Thomas by his concubine.

A. D.
1599.

the people rose immediately, and sought every opportunity to insult those in the Archbishop's train. Gouvea asserts, but neglects to state where he gained his information, that their intention was to come to close quarters as soon as possible, and to take that opportunity to assassinate the Archbishop; but that he, seeing what was likely to happen, shut himself up in a secure place, and desired his Portuguese attendants to put every thing out of sight that they saw was offensive to the Christians. With this order they complied, from respect for their prelate, says this historian, but not without a great sacrifice of their own feelings; for that it was most painful to them to refrain from acting with the usual valour of the Portuguese; and, he adds, they found it hard to endure the least affront from a people, towards whom they uniformly carried themselves, as though born to domineer over them, instead of tamely submitting to their insults.[4] When our author delivered these sentiments, he little thought how soon the righteous God would raise up a power, both wiser and more valiant, to avenge the cause of this injured people, and drive their oppressors from their most valuable possessions on the coast.

10. The cattanar who had raised this disturbance, left Carturté, at the head of his band, to go to the Archdeacon, who had retired to Angamale, and inform him of all that had happened. At the same time, two persons went from another quarter to the palace of the Rannee of the country, which was two leagues from Carturté, to represent to her, that the Portuguese prelate was using his utmost exertions to deprive her

The Rannee orders him to depart.

---

[4] Gouvea, p. 212. La Croze, p. 137.

of her authority over her Christian subjects, and to bring them under subjection to the Portuguese. Gouvea calls these men rebels, a name that he gives to all that refused to submit to Menezes: but it was never more undeserved; for, instead of opposing one invested with lawful authority over them, they were merely resisting his arbitrary usurpation. The rajah of Turubelé,[5] the Rannee's adopted son, and presumptive heir to her throne, had already given her the same intelligence; and this, added to the remonstrances of the two Christians, induced her to send one of her chief ministers, to notify to the Archbishop, that he and his train were to leave her dominions in three days, under pain of death.

This order Menezes received on the Tuesday of the Holy Week, and returned a short answer that was calculated for the present to stop further proceedings against him. He replied, that the Portuguese were friendly towards her Highness; that for himself, he had no other intention but to serve her as far as he could in all matters, not contrary to the laws by which he was bound; and that, as concerning his departure, he would send an explicit answer the next day. This reply produced the expected result, causing the Rannee to suspend the execution of her orders: but the Archbishop saw the necessity of exerting himself still further to avert the displeasure of so powerful a princess, who, without reckoning the troops of the rajah of Turubelé, could in any emergency assemble thirty thousand footmen in arms. She was, moreover, less dependent on the Portuguese than the other sovereigns of Malabar, and was,

---

[5] Thurubale. Gouvea.

therefore, to be treated with more deference. So entirely was this imperious Bishop influenced in all things by expediency, rather than principle.

These considerations induced him at once to send away part of his train, and to take such other precautions against the Rannee's displeasure as his prudence might suggest. But he concealed from his own people the motive of his proceedings; and, having called them together, told them, that as it was his intention to winter [6] in these parts, he wished those who were married to retire with their wives to Cochin or Goa. He then dismissed them all, without giving any one time to reply, apprehending, no doubt, the reluctance of some to leave him behind.

11. He next applied himself to the answer which he had promised to send to the Rannee's envoy on the subject of his own departure. He began by declaring positively that he would not leave the country: and then, artfully classing himself with the Syrian prelates, who had, from time immemorial, been allowed to visit the churches of Malabar without molestation, he said, that in the present affair he did not question the royal authority to command; that he bore no prejudice against it, but, on the contrary, ordered the Christians everywhere to obey their lawful kings in all secular matters; that, whatever he did, he was only acting according to the law of the Christians, whose abuses he came to reform; that the same Christians had received many privileges from their ancient

He dissembles with her, and bribes her officers to protect and assist him.

---

[6] India being north of the line, the winter, properly speaking, is as late there as in Europe. But Menezes alluded to the rainy season, or S. W. Monsoon, which sets in on the Malabar coast in the month of April, and continues about four months.

kings; and that her Majesty ought to remember, that for fifteen hundred years strange Bishops had visited Malabar, without a single instance of any former sovereign having banished one of them from the country; so far from it, they had always treated them with marks of distinction, though not in alliance with the sovereigns from whose country those prelates came; that it was, therefore, most unaccountable, that the Rannee should behave towards him in so different a manner, especially when it was considered, that he was the second person in India of the Portuguese nation, with whom her Highness was at peace; finally, that if she put him to death, he would be rewarded, and his assassins chastised by his God, not to mention the Portuguese, who certainly would not leave his death unavenged.

It cannot but be observed with what consummate art Menezes, in this letter, conceals the broad distinction that subsisted between the churches of Syria and Rome, and assumes equal authority with prelates of the former communion, of whom he is speaking, to visit and reform the Indian church. He knew, however, that this deception was not likely to be detected by a heathen princess and her officers, with whom, therefore, he expected his reasons to have all the force of legitimate arguments. Whether or no this was the case, it is hard to say; as he was too well aware of the avaricious disposition of the natives, not to accompany his epistle with much weightier reasons than it contained. Iti Mato and Iti Mané, the two Syrians who had attached themselves to his cause, were the bearers of this letter; and with it, they presented to the Rannee's prime minister some presents of considerable value, in the Archbishop's

name. These had the effect of so far dispersing
the threatened storm, that no more opposition
was made at present to his sojourn in the country: but both the Rannee, and the rajah of
Turubelé, continued to be ill affected towards
him, and secretly to annoy him in every possible manner.

12. Convinced that little dependence was to
be placed on his negociations with the Rannee,
Menezes took more effectual precautions for his
personal security. For this purpose he bribed
the commanding officer of the place with a large
sum of money, to have the environs of Carturté
traversed every morning and evening, and twice
during the night, in order to disperse any persons that might be suspected of having a design
against him. Hence it is obvious, that, notwithstanding his apparent defiance of danger on
former occasions, he was as susceptible of fear
as other men when he really believed that there
was cause for alarm. This continued as long as
he remained in the town; and, thus secured
from harm, he was enabled to conduct the daily
services of the holy week with as much pomp
as he could have displayed at Goa, in the midst
of his own clergy. When he had gone through
the Latin ritual, he permitted the cattanars to
perform their Syriac services, and even conde-
scended to assist them, says Gouvea, to the great
satisfaction and edification of the people.

Having secured the principal officers in authority, and a strong party among the cattanars
and people at Carturté, he now ventured to advance more rapidly with his encroachments.
On Holy Wednesday, after divine service, he
assembled the cattanars, and delivered to them
a discourse upon the consecration and benediction of *holy oils*, the use of which was wholly

Celebrates passion-week with great pomp, and the various popish ceremonies.

2 D

unknown to them, but they listened to him in silence. This apparent acquiescence encouraged him on the following day to go through the service in question, with the usual solemnities, at which all present are said, by his panegyrist, to have been much edified. He next proceeded to enclose the host[7] in a pix, or small shrine, another practice hitherto unheard of by these people. But they were now prepared to behold with admiration whatever he did; and the novelty and pomp of these superstitions so delighted them, that they became more and more attached to him every ceremony that he performed. These services, they said, were deserving of all praise, and they openly acknowledged that the ceremonies of the Roman church far surpassed those of their own. After this, Menezes proceeded to the concluding service, which is said to have deepened this favourable impression in their minds, and completed their conversion. Robed in his pontificals, with the mitre on his head, he first washed, and wiped with a towel, the feet of all the cattanars of the place, and then kissed them—an act of humility which, it is affirmed, drew a flood of tears from the eyes of all present, and excited in them the most lively feelings of devotion. The services of the day were then concluded with a sermon, preached by the Jesuit, Anthony Toscan, who explained, apparently with much zeal and piety, all the mysteries which, as he pretended, were comprised in the ceremonies they had just witnessed.

Such a pompous display was well calculated to work upon the susceptibilities of an ignorant people, and so to answer the Archbishop's pur-

---

[7] The wafer consecrated at the mass of the Roman church.

A. D.
1599.

pose. But when it is affirmed that they were edified thereby, and excited to devotion, it is necessary to know what meaning we are to attach to these expressions. If we are to understand by them, that the simple people were rapidly *built up* as members of the church of Rome, and became more and more *devoted* to the Archbishop's cause, then the propriety of the terms may be conceded. But it is impossible for the reasonable mind to imagine, how such an exhibition could " build them up in the most holy faith" [s] of the Gospel, or produce in them the feeling of devotion towards that God, Who " is a Spirit," and Who is to be worshipped, not with such carnal ordinances as these, but " in spirit and in truth." [*] If it were ever in the contemplation of Menezes and his assistants to produce any thing like these sentiments, then his own historian has done him great injustice. For Gouvea has not recorded that he uttered one word calculated to turn men " from darkness to light, and from the power of Satan unto God." [l] It is impossible to discover, even from that writer's elaborate account of the Archbishop's proceedings, that they could have any other tendency, than to transfer his proselytes from the comparative simplicity of their own church, to the superstitions and idolatries of Rome.

13. This effect was strikingly exhibited in the service of the following day, which was Good Friday. The Syrians attached great importance to the adoration of the cross at that festival: here, therefore, the ceremony of the Roman church seemed to them a confirmation of their own ; and this circumstance, together

Adoration
of the cross.

---

[s] Jude 20.   [*] John iv. 23, 24.   [l] Acts xxvi. 18.

with the splendour and parade with which, according to the Roman ritual, Menezes performed it, filled them with ecstasy. Loudly did they express their astonishment that any could be induced to speak ill of the Archbishop, seeing that he celebrated and exhibited with so much zeal the mysteries of the faith. "Thus did the prelate show how well he understood the art of attracting to his party an illiterate people, by dazzling them with a pompous display of ceremonies to which they were unaccustomed. [2]

14. Under the influence of these impressions, which the partizans of Menezes did not fail to cherish, the principal cattanars and laity proceeded to the church, where the prelate and his attendants were chanting matins according to the Latin liturgy. They had together talked over all that had transpired during the past few days, and had come to the conclusion, that what the Archbishop had preached to them must surely be the truth, and that, therefore, to resist him would be to fight against God. This led them immediately to determine to throw themselves at his feet, to implore his forgiveness for the past, and without reserve to swear allegiance to the Pope.

Violent in-
terruption
to the ser-
vice—Me-
nezes' party
prevails.

15. But the harmony with which matters were thus proceeding was soon interrupted by the arrival of the cattanar, who at the commencement of the business had raised a disturbance, and then went to inform the Archdeacon of what had occurred. He now returned in haste, bringing an excommunication against all who should receive the Archbishop for their pastor, or in any way assist him in his designs. Entering the church during divine service, he

---

[2] La Croze, pp. 141, 142.

stood aloof. But Menezes, whose eye nothing could escape, observed him, and sent him a message by a cattanar instantly to leave the church, which, he said, was no place for an excommunicated rebel like him. The man laughed at this order, and returned for answer, That he would not quit the church for one who was not his Bishop, and that he regarded his excommunication no more than the dirt under his feet, the Romish prelates having nothing to do with the Serra. The Archbishop, whose feelings were all alive to maintain the jurisdiction he had assumed, could not endure this insult. Knowing the importance of promptitude in such circumstances, and feeling secure of support from the Syrians whom he had already gained, he immediately commanded the service and music to cease, and, turning to the spot where the man stood, ordered him to draw near. On his treating the summons with contempt, several cattanars went to him, and dragging him into the Archbishop's presence, held him there, while Menezes sharply rebuked him, demanding how he had dared to rebel against him and the Roman church, in placing himself at the head of a band of renegades, and that at a time when his duty required him to be celebrating divine service in church. The cattanars who stood over him, seeing that he gave no answer, and probably putting a favourable construction upon his silence, conjured him to submit, promising that the Archbishop would absolve him from his excommunication. Expressing no reluctance to yield, Menezes spoke to him again, desiring him, in milder terms, only to declare his belief that the Roman pontiff was chief of the church of Jesus Christ, and his vicar on earth, and that whosoever does not obey him will lose eternal salvation. The man still remaining unmoved, Menezes held out to him his breviary,[3] and desired him to swear upon the holy Apostles that he *believed all that he was going to hear.* This was an unconscionable demand indeed! and one to which no man could yield until bound by the mental bonds of popery. Upon this cattanar it produced no such effect; and his brethren, seeing that all endeavours to make him open his lips were of no avail, at last forced him on his knees, and holding him down, desired him to beg the Archbishop's pardon: to which he resolutely replied, "That he would die rather than do that, or any thing else whereby he should acknowledge him for his prelate." Finding that he was neither to be terrified nor persuaded into compliance, and fearing lest the example of his resistance should embolden others who had not yet joined his party, Menezes ordered him immediately to be turned out of the church. At this the cattanar cried aloud, "That he would not be turned out of a place where he had more right to be present than the Archbishop: that the church belonged not to him, and had no dependence on the See of Rome." This declaration threw the whole assembly into confusion. As several relations and friends of the man were present, the congregation was instantly divided into two parties, the one endeavouring to keep him in, and the other to turn him out. Menezes, knowing the strength of his party, and judg-

---

[3] The book containing the daily service of the church of Rome, as contradistinguished from the Missal. In Spain, Portugal and Italy, it was generally identified with the Bible, and called, as here, the holy Apostles. Very few even of their ecclesiastics knew more of the Sacred Scriptures than what they learned from the extracts contained in their Breviary and Missal.

ing it better to leave them to carry on the contest, quietly withdrew to the choir, and commanded the service and music to be resumed, as though nothing else was going on in the church. It happened as he expected. His proselytes paid no attention to the music, but maintained the struggle, until they had overpowered the opposite faction, and succeeded in turning out the refractory cattanar, together with all his associates.

16. After service, the Archbishop retired to his lodging, which was over the church, the cattanars having appropriated for his accommodation one of their own apartments.[4] The same night, those who had intended to make their submissions to him in the morning, came to his room, and desired an interview with him. This he readily granted, and received them courteously. As soon as they entered, they threw themselves at his feet, and reproached themselves for their past resistance to his authority, for which they pleaded ignorance of the matters in question. They then abjured the errors and supremacy of the Patriarch of Babylon, and engaged in future to pay unreserved obedience to the church of Rome. Menezes, overjoyed at their submission, raised them one by one from the ground; called them his spiritual children; and told them, that after having enjoyed the consolation of delivering them from their ancient errors, he no longer regarded their former opposition, and that he was resolved in future to give them proofs of his tender regard. They then entreated him to instruct them further, and repeated, with ardent protestations, their

---

[4] In most of the Syrian churches there is a suite of rooms for the use of the unmarried cattanars.

determination to do whatever he should command them.

As the majority of the cattanars and inhabitants of Carturté joined in this submission to
Rome, that city is to be regarded as the first
conquest of Menezes: and it gave him the
greater satisfaction, when he remembered the
determined opposition which they had shown
when the Jesuits first visited them, and also
considered the effect that the example of so
important a place was likely to produce on the
other churches of the country. It will be seen
in the sequel, that in this respect his anticipa-
tions were realized.

Attempts to
depose the
Archdeacon
—a confer-
ence first
proposed.

17. In the true spirit of his church, he lost
no time in putting these men's sincerity to the
test.   The first use he resolved to make of them
was, either to subdue or ruin the Archdeacon,
George: and for this purpose, having addressed
his new converts in a confidential manner, and
assured them that it was his intention to do
nothing further without their advice; he in the
the same breath declared, that he could no
longer endure the Archdeacon's rebellion, and
was therefore determined at once to depose
him, and put another in his place. The person
whom he named for the office was a cattanar,
named Thomas Curia, a near relative of the
Archdeacon's, and a person of good character.
In this step, however, they were not prepared
to go along with him, for they did not like the
proposal.   George was born at Corolongate,
about two leagues from Carturté, where many
of his relatives and friends resided; and he was,
moreover, generally beloved. Although, therefore, these men were sufficiently captivated
by the pomp and ceremonies they had witnessed, to apostatize from the faith of their

fathers, yet they had not learned to show such implicit subjection to the church which they had adopted, as to sacrifice a friend in obedience to her commands. Accordingly, they took Menezes at his word, and, instead of yielding the prompt obedience he desired, ventured to advise a different course. They acknowledged that he had too much cause to be displeased with the Archdeacon, yet endeavoured to extenuate his contumacy by pleading the inexperience of his years. They also attributed his opposition more to the evil counsellors by whom they said he was surrounded, than to himself. For these reasons they entreated Menezes, before he declared his place void, to try the effect of a conference with him; and they recommended that a deputation should be appointed to wait upon him, in order to admonish him, and endeavour to prevail upon him to conform. They next begged to be allowed twenty days for the purpose, and promised, that if he did not submit within that time, they would renounce him, and acknowledge any other Archdeacon whom Menezes might appoint. To this proposal the Archbishop assented, knowing that it was much more important to his cause to gain, than to excommunicate the Archdeacon; for he foresaw that a strong party would remain attached to him, if he maintained his allegiance to the Patriarch of Babylon; and that the diocese would be thereby kept in a state of perpetual schism. Accordingly, six of the oldest inhabitants were next day appointed to wait upon him; and they exerted themselves with their utmost ability to persuade him to submit to the Archbishop; but their efforts were of no avail.

18. The concluding ceremonies of Passion-week were performed during the absence of

Holds a second ordination— receives a visit from Francisco Roz.

these commissioners. On Easter-eve the Archbishop held a second ordination, at which the candidates were very numerous; and among them were several whom the public officers had hindered from presenting themselves on the former occasion. Thus did Menezes gain a considerable accession of strength; for those whom he ordained looked upon him alone as their diocesan, and assisted him effectually at the approaching Synod, and in all his subsequent measures. In fact, they considered themselves identified with his cause.

On the same day, while affairs were advancing with so bright a prospect, Francisco Roz, the Jesuit, arrived at Carturté. At that time he was the teacher of Syriac in the college at Vaipicotta. Hearing of the success of Menezes, he came to congratulate him upon it; and, when mass was over, he told him, "That he could hardly believe himself in the same Carturté, where, not many months ago, desiring to say mass, he was obliged to have the doors opened for him by the Rannee's officer; and when he elevated the host, all the people shut their eyes that they might not see it. It was there also that they beat one of his pupils for naming the Pope in his prayers; and when he showed them an image of our Lady, they cried out, AWAY WITH THAT FILTHINESS, WE ARE CHRISTIANS, AND FOR THAT REASON DO NOT ADORE IDOLS OR PAGODS."

Thus, by the testimony of Romanists themselves, we learn in what abhorrence the Syrians held the worship of images before they were corrupted by the abominations of Rome. It was natural for this Jesuit to exult in the transformation which had been effected at Carturté; for he considered not the day, when those who, in this manner, and in such a cause, compass

sea and land to make proselytes,[5] will find their
laughter turned to mourning, and their joy to
heaviness.[6]

19. There were two churches at Carturté,
and early on the morning of Easter day, the
Archbishop was conducted in grand procession
from one of them to the other, both congregations, who had never before united in their religious services, now combining to do honour
to Menezes; and, together swearing allegiance to
the Roman Church, they tendered their pledges
to him as her representative. The brahmins
and other heathen of the place, as well as the
Syrians who continued faithful to their own
Patriarch, saw the imminent peril into which
their respective religions were brought by these
proceedings, and united for their mutual defence.
Hearing of the intended procession, they resolved, if possible, to prevent it: but finding
themselves not strong enough for this, in consequence of the military guard with which the
governor of Carturté defended the Archbishop,
they determined to interrupt him as much as
they could. The Portuguese historian asserts,
that the devil had great power in these parts
before the introduction of the true, that is to
say, the Roman faith; and that the brahmins
and their associates hired one of his agents to
accomplish their present diabolical purpose.
They are accused of having engaged the most
infamous sorcerer in the whole country to kill the
Archbishop during the procession;[7] and it is said
that he undertook to perpetrate the infernal deed

[5] Matt. xxiii. 15.   [6] James iv. 9.
[7] To this day sorcery is practised to a fearful extent by
some castes of heathen in India: but there is no reason to
suppose that the Syrians ever followed their infamous
example.

by a charm that had never yet failed him : but that the Christians in the procession, seeing him beginning his magical tricks, instantly seized him, dragged him before the governor, and loudly demanded justice against him. That officer was too much interested in the protection of Menezes not to attend to their application. He despatched a messenger to the Rannee without delay, to acquaint her with the circumstance; and an order was as promptly returned by her to have the sorcerer empaled. A sharp stake fastened to the ground was to be run through his body, and the man left to die upon it a lingering and agonizing death.[8] The Archbishop, however, would not hear of his being put to such torment, and procured a commutation of his sentence. He was banished to Cochin, and there condemned for life to row in the Portuguese gallies.

To return to the procession, which ended without further disturbance. The remaining services of the day were then performed, and conducted with great magnificence, the Archbishop, in his robes, presiding in both churches. The Jesuit, F. Roz, preached on the occasion, in the Malabar language, on the two usual topics,[9] Nestorianism, and the implicit obedience due to the Church of Rome. Not a

---

[8] Till within these few years the heathen governments were most inhuman in the infliction of punishment on criminals, and in torturing their prisoners of war. The improvement that has latterly taken place in this respect is to be attributed to the influence of European example.

[9] These are the words in which Gouvea describes the sermon. They are taken from the French translation of his history published in 1609.—" Le peuple entrant dans l'eglise, " l'Archeuesque luy donnoit la benediction : puis le Reuerend " Pere François Roz monta en chaire, fit la predication en " langue Malabare, discourant tout le long du sermon de

word was said, according to the showing of their own historian, on the all-important and appropriate theme, of Jesus' resurrection from the dead; "Who, as at that season, was delivered for our offences, and was raised again for our justification."[1] These Romish ecclesiastics uniformly preached and acted, as though they thought that they had nothing to do with the example of an Apostle of the New Testament, who "determined not to know any thing among" the Churches that he established or visited, " save Jesus Christ, and him crucified."[2]

In the course of the day, Menezes confirmed all that presented themselves for the purpose: but some still had courage enough publicly to object to it; and they left the church in great anger, exclaiming, that they had no need of such a ceremony to be performed among them.

20. After service, the cattanars and people celebrated their Nercha,[3] or feast of Charity, to which they invited the Archbishop. In many of the churches certain revenues were dedicated to the maintenance of these feasts, which were held at Easter and at some other festivals. The provisions at these entertainments were of the simplest kinds, consisting of the fruits of the country, rice and vegetables. No beverage was allowed except pure water.

Syrians' feast of charity— dissertation on the practice.

" l'obeissance, qui doiuent tous les Chrestiens à l'eglise Ro-
" maine: et combien sont fouruoyez du chemin de salut ceux
" qui contredisent à l'Archeuesque, et a ce qu 'il preshe et
" pretend." The other topic of his discourse, Nestorianism, is mentioned by La Croze (p. 148): but enough, we presume, has already been said on the subject in these pages.
    [1] Rom. iv. 24, 25.   [2] 1 Cor. ii. 2.
   [3] Geddes, p. 86. Gouvea writes, *Narché* ; La Croze, *Nerka.*

The feast was held in the porch of the church, where the tables were spread. The Bishop always presided when present, and implored a blessing on the food: if absent, this duty devolved on the senior cattanar. In the division of the food, the Bishop received a treble, the cattanars, a double, and the laity, a single portion.[4] In this preference shown to the Bishop and priests, they were, probably, guided by the Apostle Paul's injunction, who seems to be referring to a similar distribution when he gives this charge to Timothy,—" Let the elders that rule well be counted worthy of double honour, especially they who labour in the word and doctrine. For the Scripture saith, Thou shalt not muzzle the ox that treadeth out the corn: and, The labourer is worthy of his reward." [5]

Fatigued with the services of the day, Menezes desired to be excused from assisting at the Nercha: and having stayed to pronounce the blessing before the repast, he retired to his apartment. He was soon followed, however, by two cattanars, bearing his portion of the feast, which consisted of a large bunch of figs, some cakes made of rice, and several dishes of vegetables dressed in the usual manner of the country. This he received with many tokens of affection; and he was, doubtless, highly gratified with this unequivocal acknowledgment of him for their prelate.

The existence of this practice in the Syrian

---

[4] Geddes says, that "The bishop received one half of the provision, the priests a quarter, and the people a quarter among them," p. 85. Gouvea and La Croze are followed in the text. If the whole were divided into six equal parts, the Bishop's treble portion would be one half, that is, three sixths: and the cattanars would have two sixths. *Only one sixth,* therefore, would remain for the laity, instead of *a quarter.* See Raulin, Syn. Diamp. p. 226, Note *b.*   [5] 1 Tim. v. 17, 18.

Church is an additional proof of its antiquity. It has been identified with the " feast of charity," mentioned by St. Jude;[6] and is supposed to be alluded to by St. Peter,[7] and St. Paul. The latter Apostle is thought to have abolished the custom, in consequence of the intemperance and disorders with which the feasts were attended.[8] Whether the *agapai* of St. Jude coincided with the Nercha of the Syrians, it is hard to determine : but if we may not assign to the practice an apostolic origin, it certainly existed in the primitive Church. Clement of Rome, of whom St. Paul speaks with so much honour,[9] evidently refers, in his epistle to the Corinthians, written towards the close of the first century, to a similar profanation of the sacred feast, which that Apostle's epistle had only for a season corrected.[1] The nature of those feasts may be learned from the famous letter of Pliny, the ninety-seventh, written to the Emperor Trajan at the beginning of the second century. He was the Roman governor of Bithynia, and thus described the Christians of that province. " That they were accustomed on a stated day to meet before daylight, and to repeat among themselves a hymn to Christ as to a God (quasi Deo), and to bind themselves by an oath, with an obligation of not committing any wickedness, but, on the contrary, of abstaining from thefts, robberies, and adulteries; also, of not violating their promise, or denying a pledge; after which it *was their custom to separate, and to meet again at a promiscuous harmless meal.*"[2]

---

[6] Verse 12.   [7] 2 Peter ii. 12.
[8] 1 Cor. xi. 22—33.   [9] Phil. iv. 3.
[1] Lardner's Credibility of the Gospel History, Vol. i. part 2. Milner's Ch. History, Vol. i. pp. 122—129.
[2] " Morem sibi discedendi fuisse, rursusque coëundi ad ca-

There can be little doubt that this is a description of the Christian *Sacrament*, and subsequent *feast* of *Charity*.

Towards the close of the second century this custom was thus described by Tertullian, the earliest Latin[3] father whose writings are extant. " In refuting the calumnious accusations of the Pagans, he speaks of the Agape, or feast of charity. ' Its object,' he says, ' is evident from its name, which signifies love. In these feasts, therefore, we testify our love towards our poorer brethren, by relieving their wants. We commence the entertainment by offering up a prayer to God ; and after eating and drinking in moderation, we wash our hands, and lights being introduced, each individual is invited to address God in a Psalm, either taken from the Scriptures or the produce of his own meditations. The feast concludes, as it began, with prayer. Tertullian does not expressly say, but it may be fairly inferred, that the materials of the feast were furnished out of the oblations made at the eucharist ; a portion of which appears also to have been allotted to the support of the martyrs in prison. When we read the above description of the Agape, we cannot but participate in the regret " that has been expressed[4] " that scandal should have occasioned the discontinuance of an entertainment, so entirely consonant

---

piendum cibum, promiscuum tamen et innoxium." Pliny's Letters, Book x. let. 97, 98. Milner's Ch. Hist. Vol. i. pp. 144 —148.

[3] He was a native of the province of Africa and city of Carthage.

[4] This reference is to Rev. Dr. John Hey, late Norrisian Professor of Divinity in the University of Cambridge. Bishop of Lincoln's Ecclesiastical History of the Second and Third Centuries. Illustrated from the writings of Tertullian, pp. 162, &c., and 428, 429.

to the benevolent spirit of the Gospel. If, however, we may believe Tertullian, the grossest abuses were introduced into it even in his time : for we find him, in the tract de Jejuniis, charging the orthodox with the very same licentious practices in their feasts of charity, which the pagans were in the habit of imputing—and, according to the statement in the Apology, falsely imputing to the whole Christian body.[5]

In the third century, Cyprian also, Bishop of Carthage, in his 34th epistle to that Church, alludes to "the feasts of charity" which they were accustomed to keep at stated seasons ; and, at the same time, speaking of Aurelius and Cellerinus, two confessors, he reminds the people, that the clergy were said to be honoured according to the proportion they received of the public offerings.[6]

In the following century, Chrysostom, Bishop of Constantinople, thus describes the feast of charity and its origin. " The first Christians " had all things in common, as we read in " the Acts of the Apostles ; but when that " equality of possessions ceased, as it did even " in the Apostles' time, the *agape*, or love-" feast, was substituted in the room of it. Upon " certain days, after partaking of the Lord's " Supper, they met at a common feast ; the " rich bringing provisions, and the poor who " had nothing being invited."[7]

[5] On these contradictory assertions of Tertullian, the learned prelate has remarked, " that the truth probably lies between them. Abuses did exist, but neither so numerous, nor so flagrant, as the enemies of the Gospel, and Tertullian himself, after he became a Montanist, alleged." Ib. p. 430.

[6] Presbyterii honorem designasse nos illis jam sciatis, et sportulis iisdem cum presbyteris honorentur, et divisiones mensurnas æquatis quantitatibus partiuntur. Geddes, p. 86.

[7] Encyclopædia Britannica on *Agape*.

2 E

The antiquity, then, of this practice is undoubted ; and it was always attended with the
receiving of the Holy Sacrament, the only question being, whether it was celebrated before or
after that ordinance.   Cave inclines to the
former opinion :[8] but the more general belief is,
that it followed.

In the history of this feast we have another
humiliating instance of human infirmity.   Entertainments that were given originally for the
sole purpose of promoting unity and brotherly
love, too soon degenerated into riotous banquet-
ings ; and the house of prayer, in which they
were kept, was converted into a scene of drunk-
enness, and all manner of excess.   After many
fruitless attempts to correct these abuses, they
were generally abolished.   The Council of Laodicea, about the middle of the fourth century,
peremptorily forbade them, under the name of
charity feasts ; prohibited the clergy who were
invited from carrying any meat away with them
to their own houses ; and commanded " that
no one should eat, or prepare beds or tables
for that purpose, in the house of God."[9]   The
third general council of Carthage, held in 397,
" forbids all feasting in the Church in general
to the clergy, except in case of necessity, when
they were upon a journey, and could not otherwise be entertained ; and orders that the custom should be discontinued as much as possible
also in the laity."[1]   Austin, in writing against

---

[8] Cave's Prim. Christ., part i. ch. 11.   Monfaucon,

[9] Du Pin, 4th century.   Council of Laodicea.   Chapters 27
and 28.   Ὅτι ὁ δεῖ ἐν τοῖς κυριακοῖς ἢ ἐν ταῖς ἐκκλησίαις, τὰς
λεγομένας ἀγάπας ποιεῖν, καὶ ἐν τῷ οἴκῳ τῦ Θεῦ ἐσθίειν καὶ ἀκούβιτα-
ςρωννύειν.

[1] Con. Carth. iii. c. 30.   Ut nulli episcopi vel clerici in
ecclesia conviventur, nisi fortè transeuntes hospitiorum ne-

Faustus, the Manichee, fully admits the abuses attending these entertainments; declares that, nothing but necessity induced the Church to tolerate them in any form; and that they would be discontinued as soon as practicable, without doing too great violence to the minds of a weak people, who had a predilection for this long-established custom.[2]

In this manner was the feast of charity gradually discontinued almost throughout Christendom. In the western world it seems to have lingered longest in *England*, Pope Gregory having, for certain considerations, conceded this indulgence to the English, long after its abolition by the councils of Laodicea and Carthage.[3]

This dissertation on the feast of charity will not be thought irrelevant in this place, if the importance of establishing the antiquity of the Syrian Church in Malabar be duly considered. They had preserved the custom from the first ages of the Church in all its primitive simplicity; a satisfactory proof of their independence of Rome, where it had long been discontinued, and of the comparative superiority of her character.

21. To proceed. On the evening of Easter day the Archbishop walked through the town,

Menezes visits and relieves the sick.

cessitate illic reficiantur. Populi etiam, quantum fieri potest, ab hujusmodi conviviis prohibeantur. Vid. Con. Afric. Can. 42.

[2] Aug. cont. Faust. lib. 20. c. 21. Qui se in memoriis martyrum inebriant, quomodo à nobis approbari possunt, cum eos, etiam si in domibus suis id faciant, sana doctrina condemnet? Sed aliud est quod docemus, aliud quod sustinemus, aliud quod praecipere jubemur, aliud quod emendare praecipimur, et donec emendemus, tolerare compellimur. Bingham's Christian Antiquities, B. viii. ch. 10. sec. 1.

[3] Pour certaines considerations, lesquelz furent rendus et concedez aux Anglois par le Pape Sainct Gregoire. Cardinal Cesar Baronius. 1 Tom. Annal. anno 57. Gouvea, ch. 16.

visiting the sick, whom he relieved with money, and comforted with spiritual advice. Nor did he forget at the same time to declare, that such was the duty of every prelate, and the common practice of all Roman Bishops; but that their own prelates had shamefully neglected it. This, as may be supposed, did not fail to produce a very high opinion of the piety and humanity of Menezes, among a people so remarkable for their simplicity of manners. Not suspecting the integrity of his motive, they began immediately to extol him to the skies, as much more humble and charitable than the Chaldean Bishops. In this insidious manner was the foundation effectually laid for their complete subjugation.[4]

Favourable reception at Nagpili.

22. On the following day the Archbishop visited Nagpili, about half a league from Carturté, where the Syrians had a church. At this place resided the late senior cattanar, Jacob, who had been the vicar-general of Mar Simeon. Here Menezes preached, baptized several infants, and confirmed a great number of young persons. He also reconciled several cattanars to the Roman Church. The facility with which he succeeded here, is accounted for by the proximity of the place to Carturté, where most of the inhabitants had been in attendance during the whole of passion week, and joined in the service.[5] They were prepared, therefore, to welcome the prelate in their own village, and tender him their oath of allegiance.

Reflections on his successes.

23. And here notice may be taken of the surprise which has been naturally expressed, at the Archbishop's successes among a people with whom

[4] Geddes, p. 86. Lee's Brief History.
[5] Gouvea, Ch. 16. p. 241.

he could hold so little intelligible communication.[6] He found no difficulty in conversing with the native princes and officers, who generally understood Portuguese: but that he should have been so forcible a preacher, as is pretended, among the Malabar Christians, who comprehended not one word of his language, nor he of theirs, is thought most astonishing; and his successes appear inexplicable. And so they would be, had he simply depended on his preaching to effect the desired result. But when we consider to what expedients he resorted, to seduce them from the religion of their fathers, we cannot be astonished at the rapidity of his progress. Few people so poor as they were, could have resisted the temptation of money, which he set before them; and few, so ignorant, would have been proof against the attractions of pomp and splendour. He gave them such as he had; and the effect produced corresponded with the means used. He had not faith to say unto the soul, bowed down with spiritual infirmity—" In the name of Jesus Christ of Nazareth rise up and walk."[7] He knew not the charm of His Name, nor the light of His Gospel, nor the unction of His Grace. How then could he bless them with the tidings of salvation? Had he gone to them in a right spirit, on the errand of mercy, we should have been at no loss to account, upon religious principles, for such a sensation as he produced. For then we might have ascribed it to the Spirit of God, which clothes His word with power, making it the instrument of converting men from sin to holiness, and from error to truth. But seeing that he addressed himself only to the vanity of the human mind,

---

[6] Geddes, pp. 86, 87.   [7] Acts iii. 6, 7.

and to the depravity of the heart, his achievements are to be regarded as little more than the ordinary effects of covetousness and superstition on the infirmities of mankind. These speak to the needy and the ignorant, in language sufficiently intelligible for the purpose of such a man as this Archbishop of Goa.

CHAPTER V.

MENEZES' CONTINUED PROGRESS: OVERCOMES THE ARCHDEACON.

1. AFFAIRS being arranged at Carturté so much Menezes revisits Molandurté. to his satisfaction, on the evening of Easter Monday the Archbishop set out for Molandurté, where he had before been well received. But he now met with a different reception, not one person going out to welcome him at the place of landing, though only a quarter of a league from the town, and the doors of the church being shut against him. They held back, however, more from fear, than from any alteration in their feelings towards Menezes. In consequence of the attention they had before paid him, the Archdeacon had redoubled his complaints against them to the rajah of Cochin; and that prince, besides imposing a heavy fine upon their Church, had sent some of the chief inhabitants of the place to the Archdeacon, bound as prisoners. It was this severity that intimidated the people, and caused them to shun the Archbishop's presence.

2. Finding how matters stood, and fearing His complaints there against the rajah of Cochin. lest a tumult should be raised if he appeared among them, he did not leave his boat: but, resolving to have recourse to arguments more

effective than any that might be drawn from
Holy Scriptures or reason, he wrote immediately to the Governor of Cochin, Don Antonio de Noronha, desiring him to send the
rajah's prime minister to him at Molandurté,
where he would wait for him. He was well aware,
says Gouvea, that the reduction of the Malabar
Christians would distress the rajah, who, by
that means, in case of a rupture with the Portuguese, would be deprived of the service of at
least fifty thousand of his best musketeers. Under
this apprehension, it could not fail greatly to annoy
him to see the measures now taking to bring this
brave and numerous body of men under the jurisdiction of the Portuguese prelates, who would always combine with the viceroys of Goa, to promote their temporal interests, expecting thereby
to secure their services, even against their native
prince. As, however, it was important to maintain even a nominal sovereignty over them, and
this could only be done by keeping on good
terms with the Portuguese, the rajah resolved
to preserve the appearance of friendship, and
gave a verbal assent to all that the Archbishop
desired; but, at the same time, he determined secretly to exert himself to prevent the subjugation of his Christian subjects to the Church of
Rome.

Accordingly, the governor of Cochin had no
difficulty in prevailing upon him to allow his
minister to wait upon the Archbishop. When
that officer arrived at Molandurté, Menezes
made bitter complaints against the rajah for his
oppression of the inhabitants, and for his violence in sending some of the chief men in
custody to the Archdeacon: and all this was
done for no other reason, he said, but because
of the kind reception they had given him on his

former visit to the place. The minister did what he could to pacify him, promising to acquaint his master with what he had said, and assuring him, "That if any thing were amiss the rajah would certainly redress it, and give him all the satisfaction he could desire." To this the Archbishop abruptly answered, "That he expected no kindness from his master, since he had already denied him so small a favour, as to order the muskets that were kept in the choir of the church to be removed to a more suitable place: that he had indeed promised that it should be done, but that he understood that the muskets were there still." The minister, either not thinking, or fearing, to ask him what *he* had to do with the church, quietly answered, "That the officer of the place was to blame for that, and not his master, who, to his knowledge, had given the order required."

3. Thus the Archbishop showed that he knew, both whom to brow-beat, and whom to bribe. He required the minister to prove his friendly disposition by going with him to the church, and there pacifying the peoples' fears. This he did immediately, desiring those present, in the rajah's name, to do whatever the Archbishop commanded them. But though he spake thus in the hearing of Menezes, he privately caused it to be known, that the rajah would be much better pleased with their adherence to their own Archdeacon and their ancient customs, than with their submission to the Archbishop. The people, however, chose to follow his open exhortation, rather than his secret suggestion. As soon as he had taken his departure, Menezes entered the church, where he officiated, it is said, greatly to the satisfac-

tion of the assembly. Many present were in their hearts favourable to the Portuguese; and although the day before they durst not meet the Archbishop, yet now, without any other apparent cause than the prime minister's public injunction to obey him, they gave in their adhesion to the Church of Rome.

But the heathen inhabitants were not tranquil observers of these proceedings. The evening had hardly closed, when thirty Naires, armed with matchlocks, came to the persons in attendance upon the Archbishop, and told them, that their prelate had better retire without advancing any further into the rajah's dominions; that if he persisted in his enterprise, they would pay him as he deserved for all the trouble that he had occasioned their prince; and that as for the Christians of the country who had welcomed him, they should do so no longer without having cause to repent of their treacherous conduct. When these threats were reported to Menezes, he affected to treat them as unworthy of his notice.

Archdeacon still holds out.

4. Just as he had made up his mind to leave Molandurté, a native priest, of the Portuguese diocese of Cochin, returned from the Archdeacon, to report the result of a commission with which Menezes had charged him to that ecclesiastic. This man was related to him, and, though now of a different communion, it was expected that one with whom he was nearly connected would be more likely to make a favourable impression upon his mind, than a stranger. But the answer received from the Archdeacon disappointed this expectation. He admonished Menezes to desist from his rash crusade; told him that it was in vain to expect the Christians to comply with his wishes; and

warned him, that in all his proceedings he put his life in imminent danger, for that the principal rajahs of Malabar, and especially the rajah of Cochin, were resolved to favour the Christians who maintained their ancient rites and government; and that, in case of necessity, they would raise an army of one hundred and fifty thousand Naires for their defence.

5. This letter was publicly read, and it had the effect of dividing the Archbishop's party. Some were of opinion that he ought immediately to withdraw, and have nothing more to do among them. Others, more determined to cleave to him, thought that they treated the Archdeacon with too much consideration; that he ought rather to be excommunicated, and his person seized. Menezes, who understood human nature well, knew that an appearance of lenity would tend to confirm this favourable disposition towards him, and to reconcile the party that had manifested some opposition. He therefore answered, that meekness and patience were virtues which the Son of God had taught them when upon earth; and that those who thought he had not acted right while among the Christians, should pray to God to inspire him with more wisdom and a better spirit, that he might be able henceforth to conduct himself in a manner more certainly for the peoples' benefit. "This was truly the most sure way of succeeding," says Gouvea, "and therefore this good prelate had these words of the Psalmist perpetually on his lips,—*Bene patientes erunt ut annuntient*,[1] which he interpreted thus,—That they who preach the word

Menezes' affected forbearance—Specimen of his knowledge of Scripture.

[1] Gouvea's reference is to Psalm xci., where, in the Vulgate, these words occur. In the original Hebrew, the LXX and English versions, the passage will be found, in Psalm

of God to hard hearts, ought to have great patience. And truly the patience and forbearance of the Archbishop, both in his labours, and also in his tolerance of the rebellion of this Archdeacon and his adherents, was the best remedy for propagating Christianity in these regions, and that which obtained all that he aimed at. For had he adopted any other mode of conduct, he would have failed in every thing, as he himself confesses to this day." Enough has been seen already, and more remains to be related, of the arrogance and intolerance, the subtilty and violence of this man, to enable us rightly to interpret this encomium. Father Du Halde also speaks in terms equally flattering of the learning and great knowledge of the Scriptures, which Menezes, and other Roman Theologians in India possessed.[2] The present instance is, certainly, no very satisfactory proof of this assertion, if the Archbishop could really think that the passage quoted was descriptive

---

xcii. 14, 15: דְּשֵׁנִים וְרַעֲנַנִּים יִהְיוּ Literally, they shall be fat and flourishing, or green, (viz. Those that be planted in the house of the Lord, &c. See Job xv. 32. Psalm xxxvii. 35. Cant. i. 16.) To shew that the Lord is upright, &c. In the Septuagint ἐν παθοῦντες ἔσονται κ.τ.λ.: They shall be at their ease: which may correspond with the Latin—bene patientes. But the words, Ut annuntient, which Menezes joined to the foregoing verse, for the purpose of making it speak the sentiment which he desired to express, manifestly belongs to the verse at the head of which it stands, even in the *Vulgate*, from which Menezes must have quoted the text. This the celebrated Bishop of Meaux has remarked, in his notes on the Psalms, p. 301. Whether this perversion of the passage were made in ignorance or with design, it will suffice at least to show, how little this Archbishop of Goa was entitled to the commendations that are bestowed upon him for his knowledge of Holy Scriptures. Gouvea, ch. xvi. pp. 248, 249. La Croze, p. 152. See note.

[2] Du Halde. See the epistle before the twelfth selection of his 'Edifying Letters,' p. 17. La Croze, p. 153.

A. D.
1599.

of the conduct he was pursuing. Knowing, as we do, his design against the Syrian Church; his previous attempts, and present determination, to subdue the Archdeacon by any and by every means; when we read of his *meekness* and *forbearance*, we cannot but think his spirit more accurately described in a passage of another Psalm,—" The words of his mouth were smoother than butter, but war was in his heart: his words were softer than oil, yet were they drawn swords." [3]

6. From Molandurté, Menezes went a second time to Diamper, where he had held his first ordination. Here the prime minister of Cochin met him, according to appointment; and they held an animated discussion under the porch of the church. The Archbishop began, by complaining of the opposition that he had met with from the governor of the place, who, he said, not only prevented all the Christians from resorting to him, but encouraged the heathen, and especially the Naires, who were the Rajah of Cochin's subjects, to deride and menace, both himself, and the Christians of his train. When the minister attempted to offer an apology for the governor, the Archbishop interrupted him; and, throwing himself into a violent passion, he struck the cane he held in his hand three times on the ground, exclaiming, with great vehemence—" Don't offer to speak to me. I know " your heart too well, and the ill-will that you " bear towards all that concerns me and the " Christian law. But there is one that I blame " more than you, and that is your master, who, " 'though *Brother in Arms* to the King of " Portugal, suffers me to be thus ill-treated in

His second visit to Diamper— his violence of temper.

[3] Psalm lv. 21.

" his own country. But you may tell him
" from me, that the King of Portugal shall
" know how I have been used by him, and
" that it will not be long ere he shall smart
" for it."

The minister endeavoured to pacify him, and
assured him, that his master knew nothing of
what had happened at Diamper when he was
there before, and that as soon as he should be
made acquainted with it, he was sure that he
would make examples of all those who had in any
manner given offence to the Archbishop.   This
apology, instead of appeasing Menezes, threw
him into a greater rage.   He vociferated again,
saying, that it was all a trick to impose upon
him; that in matters of such importance the
people would not have dared to act as they did
unless they had received orders to do so; that
every fault found with his proceedings was mere
pretence, invented for the sole purpose of deceiving the viceroy, and the Portuguese governor of Cochin, in order to gain time; and that
he had treated too often with kings, and knew
their tempers too well, to be made to believe
that they would not enforce obedience whenever
they chose.

From the temper exhibited by the prelate at
this interview, we may know what credit to
attach to the repeated assertions of Gouvea,
that the heathen were constantly forming plots
against the Archbishop's life.   All this hector-
ing on the part of Menezes does not bespeak a
consciousness of danger; nor can it be imagined
that the prime minister would have submitted
so tamely to his insolence, had there been any
intention to hurt him.

The same historian, probably anxious to extenuate this unbecoming violence in a Christian

Bishop, makes an observation tending to prove
its necessity. He says, that among these infidels,
in affairs of importance, modesty and humility
are of no use ; because these virtues are unknown to them ; and that there exists among
them nothing but pride and arrogance. [4]

Seldom has a more unfounded assertion been
made than this. Another historian [5] has justly
remarked, " I do not know what to think
of this reflection. All the accounts of ancient
and modern travellers give a very different testimony respecting the dispositions of these people." It is true, that the natives of India
generally are themselves most violent in their
passions, and seldom exercise the least patience
or forbearance towards one another. But in a
religious teacher, whether their own Gooroo, or
the minister of another religion, they look for an
entire subjugation of the temper : and instead of
being unable to appreciate meekness and patience in one holding that sacred office, they
would pay no attention whatever to his instructions if he did not exhibit these virtues.

As to Menezes, who, according to Gouvea,
was softness itself towards the Christians, he
should have added, *only when they in all
things submitted to his dictates*—yet he abused,
and treated with an air of superiority, not only
the native officers, but the rajahs themselves.
Whenever he held a disputation with any one
whom, by reason of his dependence upon the
Portuguese commerce, or his dread of their
power, he knew that he could insult with impu-

[4] Gouvea, c. 17. p. 251.
[5] La Croze, p. 154.

nity, he did not fail to address him in the impetuous tone of a lord and master.

On the present occasion, his vehemence and threats seem to have alarmed the minister, who assured him again, that his master always had favoured, and always would favour, his designs in the Serra. The Archbishop, taking him at his word, said, " I shall soon know that. If " you are sincere, you will directly call all the " Christians together, and command them, in " the king's name, to acknowledge me as their " prelate, and to unite themselves to the church " of Rome, to which the king of Portugal him- " self is subject, and all true Christians spread " over the whole earth. They must also for " ever renounce the Archdeacon and his party, " and, in one word, do whatever I command " them." To this the minister instantly ac- ceded ; and having assembled the Christians in the porch of the church, he commanded them, in the presence of Menezes, to obey him as their Archbishop in all things, on pain of the rajah's high displeasure. Then, assuring them that this was the will of his majesty, he told them, that they were to give no heed to any persons who should speak to them to the contrary.

He had scarcely finished, when the prelate sar- castically whispered in his ear—" Take care, Sir, " to say in private the reverse of what you have " now said in public, as you did at Molandurté. " Then I shall be convinced that you do but " dissemble in every thing for the purpose of " deceiving me." The officer, instead of being disconcerted by the detection of his duplicity, laughed at the Archbishop's sarcasm, and turned the subject of discourse. He said, that he had affairs of more importance to negociate with him, and that he had come to declare the Rajah's mind upon them.

A. D. 1599.

7. Upon this the assembly was dismissed, when the minister entered into discussion with Menezes about some debts which the Portuguese state had contracted with the government of Cochin; and also about a pension that his master had formerly been accustomed to receive, but which he had lately said nothing about, though it had been withheld for several years. This was just what the Archbishop wanted. He instantly seized the opportunity which this complaint gave him, to press his own demands with increasing urgency. " How can the rajah," said he, " expect me to settle his affairs, while " he opposes mine? When he shall have ac- " complished all I desire with respect to his " Christian subjects, then will I treat on his " behalf with the king of Portugal and the " Viceroy, and his interests shall always be " dear to me."

Private interview with the prime minister of Cochin.

8. With this answer the minister retired; and the Archbishop lost no time in assembling the congregation in the church, to whom he preached a sermon; and, in conclusion, he commanded them to go home, and come again next day, to be confirmed by him, and to have their children baptized. With this injunction they complied; and as all passed off quietly on the occasion, he ventured to open his mind to them respecting the measures which he intended to pursue towards their Archdeacon. He told them, that they were not ignorant how that man had rebelled against him, his venerable prelate, delegated by the Roman pontiff himself, who was Jesus Christ's vicar upon earth, and whom the Saviour had invested with full power and jurisdiction over all the churches of the world. He

Determines to excommunicate the Archdeacon.

2 F

further said, that he had been compelled to depose the rebel, and to pronounce him excommunicated, as an abettor of heretics, and associated with infidel kings against the Christian religion: that he had thought it fitting to explain to them his conduct, that they might all unite with him, and abandon an ecclesiastic, who, after repeated remonstrances, had yet shown no inclination to yield him due obedience.

The falsehood of this accusation must be obvious to every one, unless we concede the papal assumption of universal authority in Christendom, and consent to identify Christianity herself with the church of Rome. While Menezes accused the Archdeacon of associating with infidel kings, to whom, as sovereigns of the country, the Syrians were entitled to look for protection; he ought to have remembered, that he was himself using every means to secure the assistance of those very powers for the subjugation of the Syrian church.

The people, however, were either too simple to detect the fallacy and inconsistency of what he said, or too obsequious to raise a question against it. They are reported to have been satisfied with all they heard, and even to have gone so far as to censure their Archdeacon's pertinacity. With so little difficulty did this intemperate and artful prelate gain over the congregation of Diamper.

Contrasts his own charity with the parsimony of the Syrian Bishops.

9. In the evening he visited the sick inhabitants, and gave alms with a liberal hand to the widows and orphans of the place. We may conjecture with what motive he dispensed his bounty, from the address with which he accompanied it. He told the people here, as he had done elsewhere, that what he did was their prelate's duty, instead of taking money

from them, as their former Bishops had done. This was disingenuous in the extreme, and showed how little his gifts deserved the name of charity. It has been justly remarked, " That he forgot to tell them, that whereas their former prelates had lived altogether upon alms, having no settled revenues to maintain them, by reason of their residing under princes who were infidels ; he had above twenty thousand crowns a year in rents that were certain. Besides, by having represented to the government, that what he was doing in the Serra was a great service to the state of Portugal, he had the command of the public treasury at Goa, which was never so full as at the present time, the Viceroy, Don Matthias de Albuquerque, having in the year 1597 left in it eighty thousand ducats, besides an immense quantity of jewels.[6]

" This *trick*, for," says the historian just cited, " it deserves no better name," together with the haughty tone which he assumed in his conferences with the native princes and their officers, caused many Christians to wish themselves under the jurisdiction of Portuguese prelates : for they saw that they would not allow their rulers to tyrannize over them ; but would espouse all their quarrels, and protect them in their rights, which their own Chaldean prelates were never able to do. Poor people! little did they know that they were escaping from the *whip*, to be chastised with scorpions.[7]

10. By such methods had the Archbishop now reduced three of the most considerable places in the diocese, Carturté, Molandurté, and Diamper, with several adjacent villages.

Archdeacon alarmed at his progress, and doubtful how to act.

---

[6] Geddes, p. 91. [7] 1 Kings xii. 11.

Besides these, he felt himself sure of all the churches in the kingdoms of Porca, Gundara, Marca, and Batimena, whose rajahs had already commanded their Christian subjects to obey him in all things. The Archdeacon began now to feel considerable alarm at the rapidity of his progress, fearing lest he should soon lose Angamale itself, the metropolitan church, and the place of his own residence. Considering the crisis to which affairs seemed to be reduced, and the impossibility of his contending much longer with so powerful and subtle an adversary, he felt himself driven to the alternative, of either submitting to the Church of Rome, or preparing to be sent as a prisoner to Portugal. Escape from the country was impracticable, Menezes having, as already stated, completely blocked up all the ports, to prevent the arrival of any ecclesiastics from Babylon. In this juncture, the Archdeacon does not appear to have remembered the believer's refuge in times of peril. Had he determined to pursue what he knew to be his duty to the Church, in a Christian spirit, and with confidence in the Lord, then he might have exulted, with Zion of old, " Behold, God is my salvation; I will trust and not be afraid." [8] But losing sight of this impregnable bulwark,[9] his mind began to vacillate; and hence ensued more trouble to himself, and more mischief to his Church, than, we may venture to say, would or could have arisen had he faithfully stood his ground.

Menezes
endeavours
to frighten
him into
submission.

11. A cattanar who was with him on a visit, observed his embarrassment; and, instead of encouraging him to persevere, went, and treacherously informed Menezes of his perplexity

---

[8] Isa. xii. 2.   [9] Isa. xxvi. 1.

how to act. The Archbishop, delighted with
this intelligence, immediately wrote him a long
and spirited letter, at the conclusion of which
he endeavoured to work upon his fears, saying,
" That although he could not compel him to
appear before the human tribunal of the
Church,[10] where he would be condemned and
chastised as he deserved; yet he cited him
to appear before the judgment seat of God,
where he would have to answer for the souls
bought with the blood of Jesus Christ, that
were now burning in hell, through his revolt
and disobedience, which had kept them from
being reconciled to the Roman Church, out
of which there is no salvation. In conclusion,
he said, that this citation would take effect in
a short time, and that he had much rather
have averted it, according to the laws of brotherly love; that he did not address him in
that respect as a prophet, but as a man who
felt assured that God would never abandon His
Church, and that the glorious Apostle, St.
Thomas, would intercede with God for the
Christians of the country, against those who
were opposed to their welfare." This letter
appears to have made a strong impression on
the Archdeacon's mind. " The Malabars," says
Gouvea, " are much given to auguries, and this
poor ecclesiastic, as weak as the rest, took the
Archbishop's words as presages of his approaching death." This, according to the same
historian, joined to an internal inspiration of
the Holy Spirit, caused him to adopt a more
temperate resolution, and to answer the letter
in a manner that indicated a tendency to reconciliation.

[10] The Inquisition.

CHAP.
V.
___
Finds the
people of
Naramè
in arms to
resist him;
applies to
the heathen
governor for
assistance;
the place
abandoned.

12. Before his answer arrived, the Archbishop, having finished his business at Diamper, proceeded to Naramè,[1] a considerable village of the Christians, which he found in arms, the inhabitants having bound themselves by an oath never to forsake their religion, which they called the law of St. Thomas, nor to abandon their Archdeacon, but to defend them to the last drop of their blood. Accordingly, when the Archbishop was about to land, and proceed to the church, they called out to him to stay where he was, for that the church doors were shut, and that not an individual in the place would hold any communication with him. Though this resistance was most unexpected, yet Menezes met it in his usual manner. As the village was within the dominions of the Rajah of Cochin, he sent immediately for the governor, desiring him to come on board his boat, for that he had something very important to say to him. Here is another proof, how little he scrupled himself to make use of heathen governors to subdue this inoffensive people, and to maintain his usurpation over them; whereas, he had just urged it against the Archdeacon as a heinous offence, and one for which he deserved to be deposed, that he had recourse to the same powers, to aid him in defending the liberties, the constitution, the very existence of the church, of which he was the lawful guardian.

When the governor came on board, Menezes desired him to go directly to the village, and do for him there, as had been done at Molandurté and Diamper. The man promised to comply with his request; but when he came on shore, intending to cause the church to be opened, he found no one in the village; for the

[1] Naraine, Gouvea.

people, hearing of his arrival, and concluding for what purpose he was come, had hid themselves, in order to avoid being compelled to violate the oath they had so recently taken. Upon reporting his ill success, the Archbishop flew into a violent rage, and nothing could persuade him, that the governor had not himself secretly instigated the people to this resistance. But for this suspicion he had no shadow of ground. Whatever the immediate cause of this opposition, the governor does not seem to have taken any part in it. The villagers now carried their determination so far, as to refuse to sell any fresh provisions to the Archbishop and his train; so that they were reduced to the necessity of living for several days upon the rice and biscuit which they had brought with them.

13. The vexation of Menezes, on account of this resistance, was soon relieved by the Archdeacon's reply to his letter, which arrived about the same time. The substance of this communication was, that he acknowledged himself at length overcome by the irresistible force of truth, and that he would now submit himself to the Roman Church: he also implored " the prelate of the Portuguese " to forgive all his past faults. Menezes was too much rejoiced to receive such a letter from him not to yield to his supplication; at the same time, he took care not to disclose his feelings immediately. He did not fail, says Gouvea, to be on his guard against the usual deceptions of heretics, of which he was well aware. Accordingly, assuming the appearance and tone of gravity, he said to the cattanar who brought the letter, that he had been so often deceived by the Archdeacon, that he knew not how to trust him again. But he wrote to that ecclesiastic himself in a more conciliatory strain,

Receives a submissive letter from the Archdeacon.

congratulating him on this beginning of his conversion : nevertheless, in order to render it more
sure, he said that he must exact of him an oath,
and his subscription to ten preliminary articles,
without which he could enter into no treaty with
him.   God was powerful enough, he added, to
defend His Church, without the Archdeacon's
concurrence.

14. The following were the articles he drew
up for the purpose.

" 1st. That the Archdeacon should abjure
" the errors of Nestorius, and of all his sectaries,
" especially Diodorus and Theodorus, whom
" the Malabar Christians esteemed as saints.
" That he should confess them to be accursed
" heretics, and condemned for their errors, which
" they held until death.

" 2dly. That the Archdeacon should confess
" and declare, in every place where he should
" go in company with the Archbishop, that
" there is no law of St. Peter, nor a law of St.
" Thomas; but that there is only one law of Jesus
" Christ our Lord, preached throughout the
" world by all the Apostles.

" 3rd. That he should subscribe the confes-
" sion of faith which the Archbishop had sent
" to him from Goa, when he made him gover-
" nor of the bishopric, after the death of the
" Archbishop Mar Abraham.

" 4th. That he should deliver up all the
" Syriac books of the diocese, as well his
" own, as those which had belonged to the
" former Archbishops, in order that those which
" needed it might be corrected, and that the
" rest might be burned.

" 5th. That he should promise and swear
" obedience to the Pope as St. Peter's succes-
" sor, and Christ's vicar upon earth, chief of his

" Church, father, master, doctor, and supreme
" head of all Christians, and of all Bishops,
" Archbishops, Primates and Patriarchs in the
" world; that he should confess that all men
" owe him obedience, and that none can be
" saved without.

" 6th. That he should anathematize the
" Patriarch of Babylon as a Nestorian heretic,
" schismatic, and separated from the obedience
" of the holy Roman Church. That he should
" swear not to obey him in anything, to have
" no intercourse nor any communication with
" him whatever : that he was not to receive his
" letters, nor give him any answer to them.

" 7th. That he should likewise swear not to
" admit any Bishop or prelate into the diocese,
" unless he were sent by the Roman Pontiff,
" and recognized by the Archbishop of Goa;
" and that whomsoever he might send he should
" obey him as his true pastor.

" 8th. That he should recognise the Arch-
" bishop Menezes for his prelate delegated by
" the Apostolic see; that he should in all
" things be subject to his commands so long
" as the diocese should be without a proper
" pastor.

" 9th. That he should circulate letters to
" assemble a Synod of the Diocese, in that place
" which should seem most convenient to the
" Archbishop, in order to treat upon matters of
" the faith : that all the priests and all the
" persons selected by the churches to attend
" should assist there, and that the Archdeacon
" should swear to assent to whatever shall be
" there decreed.

" 10th. That he should go with the Archbishop
" peaceably, whithersoever he went, without
" any armed persons except his attendants,

" and that he should accompany him in all his
" visits to the churches."

One or two observations may be made upon
these articles before we proceed. The first
shows, that Menezes and the other Roman
divines in India, were as undeserving of the
Father Du Halde's commendations for their
knowledge of ecclesiastical history, as for their
acquaintance with the Holy Scriptures. Diodorus of Tarsus is here classed with the Nestorians; whereas, he died in the fourth century,
and Nestorius arose in the fifth century. The
Archbishop ordered this father to be condemned
as an accursed heretic, for errors which he is
said to have " held until death." This accords
with no history extant of the life of Diodorus,
of whom it may be said, that few of the fathers
of that age have left behind them so unsullied
a reputation. We have no means of knowing
what were his views upon the incarnation of
the Lord Jesus, his works being destroyed;
but Du Pin, himself a romanist, has judiciously
and candidly remarked—" There is no great
probability, that one who was praised, esteemed,
and cherished by Meletius, St. Basil, St. Gregory Nazianzen, St. Epiphanius, and even by
St. Athanasius and his successors, Peter and
Timothy of Alexandria; who was also considered in a General Council as one of the
most learned and most orthodox Bishops of all
the East; and, in short, who was the master of
St. Chrysostom, should be guilty of so gross an
error as that of Nestorius."[2]

[2] Du Pin. Fourth Century. Art. Diodorus of Tarsus.
Raulin, by way of apology for Menezes, says, that he seems
to have called these two fathers Nestorians, because he knew
them to have been imbued with a similar doctrine. Hist.
Syn. Diamp. p. 36, note b. It is to be regretted that he did
not give his authority for this conclusion.

The only show of reason adduced in support of this allegation is, the circumstance, that Theodore of Mopsuestia was the pupil of Diodorus. We shall soon see how little Theodore himself deserved this Archbishop's malediction : but were it otherwise, the candid reader will agree, with Du Pin, that "it would not follow as a matter of course, that he learned his error from his master, since we daily see heretical disciples, who have had orthodox masters. Should not the faith of St. Chrysostom rather serve to justify Diodorus, than the error of Theodorus to condemn him?"

With respect to Theodore, he is reproached with having held the errors of Nestorius, in consequence of his intimacy with that heresiarch in the early part of his life : but this accusation was not brought against him until some time after his death, when, at the fifth General Council, his conviction was obtained by the intrigues of ecclesiastics.[3] He is described as one of the most learned men of his time. "We must observe," says the historian, "in favour of this excellent ecclesiastic, so renowned for the sanctity and simplicity of his manners, that he abandoned the doctrines of Nestorius, and thus effaced the stain he had contracted by his personal attachment to that heretic, and to John of Antioch."[4]

Such were these two men, of whose condemnation Menezes speaks in such unqualified terms. How deeply is it to be deplored, that such passionate ignorance should pass for enlightened zeal ; and that decisions so ill founded,

---

[3] Du Pin.   La Croze.
[4] Mosheim, cent. 5, ch. ii. sec. 10. Note h. See also ch. iii. sect. 3, 5.

CHAP.
V.

Assumption
of Roman
Supremacy
—Baronius'
perversion
of Cyprian's
sentiments.

should be so dogmatically laid down as established truths !

15. The Archbishop's ten articles are framed upon these two fundamental tenets of the Roman Church :—" Implicit obedience to the Pope ; " and, " Denial of the Papal supremacy is the sole cause of heresy."

Every Roman Bishop swears at his consecration, that he will contend with, and persecute to the utmost of his power, heretics, schismatics, and rebels against his Lord, the Pope, and his successors.[5] Here we see with what fidelity Menezes redeemed his pledge, and with what perseverance he laboured to enforce his doctrine of implicit obedience, upon those who had never owned the papal authority.

Cardinal Baronius, a cotemporary of Menezes, has laid down this tenet, " that there is but one single cause of heresy, which is, denying the pope's supremacy." This he endeavours to impose upon the world as the judgment of Cyprian ;[6] whereas, nothing is more certain than that the African prelate said not one word

---

[5] The express words in the oath are—" hereticos, scismaticos, et rebelles Domino nostro papæ vel successoribus ejus, pro posse persequar, et impugnabo."

[6] The words of Baronius are—" Cyprianus sæpe et firmiter contestatur, non aliunde abortus esse hæreses et nata schismata, quam inde quod sacerdoti Dei non obtemperatur, nec unus in Ecclesiâ ad tempus sacerdos, et ad tempus Judex vice Christi cogitatur ; quem esse Petri successorem, Romanum Pontificem, pro constanti, et absque aliqua controversia sæpius asseverat." See the Bishop of Worcester's Charges, 1722 and 1728. This was the celebrated President of Magdalen College, the champion of the liberties of Oxford, and not of Oxford only, but of England ; for he took one of the first steps in that resistance to the papal encroachments, that were sanctioned and commanded by James II., which ended in the removal of that king from the throne.—*Thoughts on the Separation of Church and State, by Dr. Burton.*

to this effect. The Cardinal quotes three of his epistles, which, if it could be proved that he is therein speaking only of the Bishop of Rome, would furnish grounds for the opinion attributed to him. But, instead of this being the fact, that venerable father is alluding to himself, and every other Bishop in the universal Church, when he says, " that heresies and schisms " would in great measure be prevented, if in " that place where they first sprang up, due " deference were paid to the testimony and " authority of the Bishop with his Presbyters." There is nothing whatever in these epistles that favours the jurisdiction of the Bishop of Rome, more than that of any other of his order. It is true, on one occasion he wrote to Cornelius, the Roman prelate, describing the episcopal power and responsibility in very unqualified terms. But his object was, not to exalt him above his brethren, but to animate his drooping spirits: for he was so much depressed, in consequence of the divisions which the Novatian heresy had occasioned in his Church, as to forget the duties that such an exigency demanded of him. The language of Cyprian's letter is that of a senior counselling a junior, not the qualified tone of a suffragan to his metropolitan.[7]

When we remember the expedients to which the papal advocates resorted at the time of the Reformation to support their sinking cause, and their unblushing perversions of the Word of

---

[7] It should be remembered, as fully proved in a former part of this work, (book ii. ch. ii.) that the Bishop of Rome did not assume the pre-eminence which he has since maintained, until many ages after Cyprian. How unfounded then must be the assertion, that that prelate designed to support those arrogant pretensions, of which he had never heard.

God for the purpose, we cannot be surprised at the use which this learned Cardinal so unfairly made of the writings of this celebrated Bishop of Carthage. Baronius was the confessor of Pope Clement VIII., who created him a cardinal in 1596, and afterwards made him librarian to the Vatican. No doubt, gratitude to his patron, combined with his zeal for the honour of his Church, induced him to fabricate so respectable an authority in defence of the papal pretensions. But it cannot be expected of those who have no such personal motive to obscure their perception of truth, that they should look with his partial eye, upon circumstances which have been perverted to so base a purpose.

Menezes allows the Archdeacon twenty days to consider the Articles.

16. To proceed. When Menezes had put his signature to the above recited articles, he wrote to the Archdeacon, allowing him twenty days to consider their terms ; and if then not fully resolved to subscribe to them, he forbade him to appear in his presence. In order to secure the fidelity of the bearer, who was a cattanar, he required him, before his departure, to swear allegiance to the Church of Rome, and to promise, upon oath, to return, and have nothing more to do with the Archdeacon, in the event of his refusal to sign the articles.

Rajah of Cochin promises to assist him in reducing the Christians.

17. Having dismissed the messenger, the Archbishop returned to Cochin, where his principal business was, to engage the Portuguese governor of that city to join him in an urgent request to the Rajah of Cochin, that he would assist him more cordially in his design, to unite the Syrians with the Church of Rome. In order to induce the governor to enter into his views, he represented to him the vast importance of such a union to the Portuguese interests in India ; an object,

he said, which he had all the while as much in view, as the governor himself could have it at heart. While engaged in this conference, the Rajah, hearing of the Archbishop's arrival, came to visit him, when Menezes availed himself of this favourable opportunity, to press home his request. The governor also seconded his application with so much zeal, that before they parted, the Rajah renewed his promise, to command his Christian subjects to obey the Archbishop in all that he should desire. With this he was satisfied for the present, and returned to Cranganore,[8] there to compose, with the assistance of the Jesuits, the decrees for the approaching synod. Recent events having caused him to feel confident of a favourable result to their deliberations, he was now more sincere than heretofore in the expression of his readiness to hold the assembly; for he hoped thereby, either to confirm the Archdeacon's adhesion to Rome, or to neutralize any further opposition that he might raise.

18. He had very little rest however at Cranganore, and his confidence in the Rajah's sincerity was soon shaken; for the day after his arrival, he received letters from the Zamorin of Calicut, informing him, that the Rajah of Cochin had actually begun war upon his ally, the Caimal, or reigning Prince of Corugeira; and that if the forces of the enemy were not stopped immediately, he would be compelled to withdraw his

His confidence in the Rajah soon shaken.

[8] Cranganore was formerly one of the principal towns of the Malabar Christians. Gouvea speaks of a tradition preserved there, which relates, that St. Thomas, after having established the faith, set up a cross in the town, that was to be seen in his time. This historian, with his usual credulity, states, that many miracles were wrought by this wonderful cross, for the confirmation of the faithful, and to the admiration of the heathen. Chap. 18.

army from before Cunahle, which, he said, there could be no doubt, was all that the Rajah wanted. As soon as the Archbishop had read these letters, he despatched a messenger after the Rajah, who had already set out, entreating him not to attack the Caimal till after the reduction of Cunahle, since it would inevitably divert the Zamorin from the siege of that fortress, before which his army still lay, in expecation of the return of the Portuguese Armada in the spring. He wrote also to the governor of Cochin and the commissioners of the treasury, desiring them to come to him immediately. They obeyed his summons without delay; and after discoursing with them on the critical state of affairs, he requested them to go after the Rajah, and stop him on his march.

Suspects the Mangate rajah of preventing the Archdeacon's submission— threatens him.

19. Before he left Cranganore, a letter arrived from the Archdeacon, assuring him of his readiness to subscribe all the articles which he had sent him, but declaring that he could not possibly wait upon him in so short a time as he had fixed. Menezes immediately suspected the cause of this delay, and was prompt with his remedy for its removal. Hearing that the Rajah of Mangate, in whose territories the Archdeacon then resided, was very much averse to his submission, he sent to that prince a servant of his own, with a splendid retinue, to let him know, that if he dared to hinder the Archdeacon from coming to him, the King of Portugal should know of it: and he assured him, that that great monarch was resolved to avenge all the wrongs that were done to him in the Serra, to the utmost of his power. This threat produced the desired effect. The Rajah was too dependent upon the Portuguese, to provoke the resentment of a man of the Archbishop's temper and station. He,

therefore, sent him word, that the Archdeacon might wait upon him whenever he pleased; that he should not interfere, and had never thought of interfering to hinder him. Notwithstanding this, the Archdeacon did not make his appearance; "having, in truth, no stomach to the morsel the Archbishop had prepared for him." Menezes, therefore, sent two Jesuits to him, to let him know, that this was his last admonition, and that, if he did not come to him in eight days, he would certainly depose him, and put another in his place.

20. The governor and commissioners who went after the Rajah of Cochin, overtook him, and prevailed upon him to suspend hostilities, and retrace his steps. He resolved to take Cranganore in his way back, where he arrived, with twenty of his chief Naires, besides his usual train. The Archbishop, as soon as he heard that he was ready to come on shore, went to the landing place of the castle to meet him, and he there behaved towards him with greater appearance of civility than before. After an exchange of compliments, they proceeded together to a hermitage, at a short distance, where they held a private conference for a considerable time. At length the Rajah called in his prime minister, and some of the chief men, together with the commandant of the castle, and several of the Archbishop's attendants. In presence of this company, Menezes thanked the Rajah for desisting from the war of Corugeira, and also promised him the thanks of the King of Portugal. At the same time, he said, that this must not hinder him from acquainting his Highness, that he had cause to be much dissatisfied with the usage which he had received from him. The Rajah then desired to know what

Overcomes the Cochin rajah by his violence and insolence.

2 G

had displeased him; assuring him, that there was nothing he so much desired as to satisfy him in all things. The Archbishop replied, "with a frowning countenance:"—"The confidence with which the " King of Portugal, my master, and your High- " ness'brother in arms, ordered me to come alone, " without any apprehension of danger, into these " parts,[9] with a view to restore the Christian " law, which is corrupted and fallen into decay, " was founded upon his knowledge, that in your " dominions there are many of these churches " placed under your immediate protection.   As " heir and successor to the Kings of Diamper, " the former sovereigns of these Christians, you " are bound to defend and succour them as those " princes did, into whose rights and possessions " you have entered.   Besides, your Highness is " brother in arms to the King of Portugal, and " the most powerful sovereign on the coast of " Malabar; which caused the King, my master, " to think that you would protect me in all " perils, and that you would assist me to ob- " tain what I expect from all the Christians of " these countries.   In this persuasion I am my- " self come from Goa, having left my own " diocese to strengthen myself in these parts, " which are so far from my home, and at . " such a distance from the sea, and from the " arms and protection of my own nation.   But " I see that I was mistaken in my confidence.   I " have been in the countries of all the sove- " reigns of Malabar, and in none of them have

9 This is the first time that we hear of this order from the King of Portugal. It is no where said when he received it; nor is any attempt made to reconcile it with the entreaties of the viceroy, and other public authorities, that he would not expose himself to the dangers of which they forewarned him, if he should venture to visit the southern coast.

" I received worse treatment than in those of
" your Highness. Indeed, they have all ho-
" noured me more than you have. Within your
" dominions I have been exposed to many in-
" sults, and a thousand incivilities from your
" governors and Naires. The Christians, your
" subjects, have been persecuted and loaded
" with taxes, for no other reason, but because
" they received me with civility : and I myself
" have been threatened every day with a vio-
" lent death."

Here the prime minister abruptly interposed,
desiring Menezes to let his majesty know what
affronts or injuries he had received in any part
of his dominions. This threw the prelate into
a violent rage, and he vociferated—" Sir, no
" one knows them better than you do, for they
" were done before your own eyes. You chose,
" however, to wink at them. Nay, I do not
" know but that you had a hand in procuring
" them : so do not, I pray you, pretend to be
" ignorant of them, nor offer to conceal them
" from your master."

The Rajah then protested that he had never
heard of any wrong or insult offered to the
Archbishop in any part of his territories. This
Menezes flatly contradicted, telling him, that it
was no such thing ; for that he had himself frequently informed him by letter, what he had
endured from his subjects, but could gain no
redress ; that the insults offered him, and the
impediments thrown in his way, had never been
remedied, as he expected, and as they ought to
have been, considering how much the Rajah
was indebted to the Portuguese. " Your High-
" ness imagines," said he, " that I want to stir
" up your Christian subjects against you :
" whereas you should rather reflect that the

" Portuguese, so far from wishing to deprive
" you of your subjects, are obtaining fresh sub-
" jects for you every day.　To them are you
" indebted for all that submit at this time
" to your authority.　When the Portuguese
" first entered into alliance with the Rajah of
" Cochin, he was the poorest sovereign in Ma-
" labar, and had the fewest subjects.　But now,
" you have been exalted by the Portuguese to
" a state of wealth and power far exceeding all
" the rest.　Yet, instead of rendering them
" a due acknowledgment for such obligations,
" your Highness prefers the Archdeacon, your
" subject, to me, and to the whole state of the
" Portuguese, who have so often shed their
" blood in your defence, and in that of your
" predecessors.　Wherefore, for the future, I
" will complain of no one but the King, my
" master, for sending me from a palace at Goa,
" where I lived at my ease and in splendour,
" to wander up and down the Serra to be
" abused as I have been.[1]

To this insolent harangue the rajah replied,
by asking Menezes what he meant; telling him,
that the treatment he had received in his dominions did not merit such complaints; and
desiring him to instance in what particulars he
had been aggrieved. Menezes rejoined, that the
worst that could be done to a man was to kill
him, and that this was what the subjects of his
Highness had repeatedly attempted to do to him;
not to mention other insults to which he had been
exposed. He then entered into the particulars of

---

[1] Geddes has justly remarked, that " this does not agree
" very well with what is said before of his going into the
" Serra purely out of zeal and devotion, and contrary to all
" that the viceroy and others could say or do to hinder him."
p. 101.

of what had happened at Molandurté and Diamper, and openly charged the Rajah with encouraging the Archdeacon in his rebellion against him. The only proof he gave in support of this allegation was, that he had granted several ollas to that ecclesiastic to obtain supplies of provision; whereas he had never given one to himself, though he had often desired it, and especially a decree, ordering all his Christian subjects to submit to him. The Rajah quietly promised to speak to the governor of Cochin, to send to the Archbishop an olla, with the edict that he desired. This irritated him still more; for he thought the Rajah used him contemptuously, when he talked of treating with the governor about that which was his own immediate concern. He, therefore, told him, that it had always been his practice to put him off with delays; that for his own part he desired none of his ollas; and that the Christians of St. Thomas, had they been true Christians, would never have suffered their kings to intermeddle with religious matters; especially infidel kings and idolaters, as he was, who, knowing nothing of the true God, worshipped stocks and stones, and even devils, instead of God; that for his part, he could not but marvel at his Highness, who, though he took no heed to the laws of the Jews and Mahomedans in his kingdom, yet presumed to blend the laws of the Christians with his own; that he was indeed surprised at his countenancing the Archdeacon, while in a state of rebellion against his own prelate; and at his favouring those who adhered to the Patriarch of Babylon, in opposition to the Pope, though he knew nothing of the difference between those prelates; that he would do well, therefore, to leave his Christian subjects to him, who was their true Bishop, and not meddle with matters that he did not understand. In conclusion, he said, that as for the Archdeacon, he had determined, that if he did not come and submit to him by the next Saturday, he would turn him out of his place, and put another into it; and that he could not but look upon him as a very bad Christian, if it were only for his having communicated the affairs of Christianity to his Highness, whom all the world knew to be an infidel.

The Rajah is said to have been " desperately angry" at what Menezes had said about his religion and his idols. He was too prudent, however, to touch on that tender subject, and coolly answered, " You may expect the Archdeacon, one Saturday, two Saturdays, three Saturdays." At this the Archbishop flew out again, and, striking his cane upon the ground with great violence, exclaimed, " I will not expect him one, two, and " three Saturdays; but if I live, I will depose " him if he does not come and submit before " the next. He deserves to be deposed, if for " no other reason, for having dared to com- " promise the interests of Christianity, by en- " gaging your Highness in its affairs, though he " knows you to be an infidel."

The Rajah could not but stand amazed at the overbearing spirit and the injustice of this man, in exclaiming so vehemently against the Archdeacon for endeavouring to interest him in matters, which he himself laboured so hard, in so unchristian a temper, and with so little scruple, to compel him to patronise. Seeing, however, that the more they talked, the more furious he grew, and raised his voice the higher; and thinking, no doubt, that the question at issue between the Archdeacon and Menezes was not

worth all this contention; he put on a cheerful
countenance, and said to him, with great good
humour. " Well, they shall do as you desire.
" There is nothing I have studied so much as to
" please your Lordship."   This at once pacified
the Archbishop, who replied, that it was what
he had always expected from his Highness.
He then apologized for throwing himself into
such a passion ; expressing a hope, that the
Rajah would not be surprised at it when he
knew, that he was pledged to maintain the
cause of Christianity to the utmost, and that for
the least of its interests he was bound in duty to
sacrifice his head, should any one choose to cut
it off.   To this the Rajah made answer, " Your
" head is as dear to me as my own.   If I knew
" of any that sought after it, they should not
" keep their own upon their shoulders much
" longer.   I will be answerable for whatever
" may happen to you."

In order to turn the conversation, the Rajah
began to complain of the misconduct of the
Portuguese in his dominions; and the Archbishop was not backward, in his turn, to promise
him satisfaction, engaging to do him justice in
all that was reasonable.   They then discoursed
for some time on matters of less importance: and
when the Rajah rose to depart, the Archbishop
accompanied him to the landing place, where
they exchanged protestations of friendship, and
parted on good terms.

21. When we consider the forbearance of
this heathen prince towards a stranger, who
had so rudely insulted himself, his officers, and,
above all, his gods, we must confess that he
exhibited a temper much more becoming a
Christian, than that displayed by the Archbishop.   Little does this prelate seem to have

A. D.
1599.

*Inconsist-
ency of his
behaviour
with the
character of
a Christian,
and the
office of a
Bishop.*

studied the character which our Lord required His disciples to learn—to be, like Him, "meek and lowly in heart."[1] Nor did he show that he was much better acquainted with St. Paul's description of a Christian Bishop,[2] who, besides other essential graces mentioned by the Apostle, must be " of GOOD BEHAVIOUR, NOT READY TO QUARREL, and OFFER WRONG, as one in wine;[3] but PATIENT, NOT A BRAWLER." Had St. Paul commanded, instead of prohibiting, such behaviour; or, could it be shown that the Bible anywhere, directly or indirectly, sanctions the defence of religion by such means as the Archbishop used; then there would have been some reason in the excuse he offered for his passion. Whereas now, it is utterly indefensible; for it was an outrageous violation of every precept and example of the New Testament, and committed by the very person who claimed to be regarded as the first Christian prelate and teacher in India.

At the Rajah's command, the Archdeacon submits, and subscribes articles in private.

22. He knew, however, that this mode of proceeding was the most likely to attain his object; and, therefore, he did not scruple to give all considerations of Christian propriety and consistency to the winds. If it failed, as it necessarily must, to commend to the heathen the religion of the meek and lowly Jesus; it at least served the cause of the Archbishop's master at Rome, and that satisfied his conscience. For it led immediately to the Archdeacon's submission; and, shortly after, to that of a great portion of the Syrians. The Rajah was too wise a politician to endanger his interests with the Portuguese by again provoking a man of the Archbishop's rank and disposition.

---

[1] Matt. xi. 29.   [2] 1 Tim. iii. 2—4.
[3] Μὴ πάροινον, Marginal Reading, Authorized Version.

Although the prelate had actually interfered to prevent the Christians from submitting to the temporal jurisdiction of the Rajahs of Cochin, Mangate, and other princes to whom they were subject; yet the Rajah felt that he had no alternative, but either to humour him, or to incur the displeasure of his government. Incapable of appreciating the consequences of sacrificing the liberty of his Christian subjects to his own political expediency, as soon as he returned home, he wrote to the Archdeacon, desiring him to come without delay, and submit to the Archbishop. He wrote also to the Rajah of Mangate, in whose dominions that ecclesiastic then resided, that in case he found him reluctant to do as required, he was to compel him to obey.

This letter was too much for the Archdeacon's Christian principle. There is reason to fear that he placed more confidence in man than in God: for when he saw himself abandoned by the powerful monarch who had hitherto protected him, instead of exercising faith in the arm of Omnipotence, to bring to nought his enemy's designs, he wrote immediately to the Archbishop, as the Rajah required, declaring that he was now ready to throw himself at his feet, and obey all his commands, within the time that he had prescribed. He begged, however, to be permitted to wait upon him any where but at Cranganore; for as that fortress belonged to the Portuguese, he was afraid of trusting himself there, lest he should be seized and sent to Goa. The Archbishop complied so far with his request, as to appoint the meeting at the Jesuits' College at Vaipicotta. The Archdeacon arrived there first, with a numerous company of cattanars and respectable Syrians, and waited in the church the arrival of Menezes. As soon as the prelate entered, the Archdeacon came forward, and throwing himself at his feet, made his humble confession in the words of the prodigal. " 'Father, I have sinned against heaven, and " in thy sight, and am no more worthy to be " called thy son ' : [4] I do humbly beg pardon " for all my resistance and faults, which have " been great indeed." This humiliation is to be attributed to his fears, rather than to any change that had taken place in his sentiments. Menezes, who was intimately acquainted with human nature, could not but suspect this ; yet it answered his present purpose to give him credit for sincerity. Raising him from the ground, he embraced him with apparent tenderness, and assured him that he forgat all that was past. He said also, that God's mercy in reducing him at last to the Catholic Church, was greater than the malice of the Devil, which had been the cause of his not returning sooner ; that he would certainly receive that great reward which is reserved in heaven for those who bring so many souls to the purity of the faith, as he was convinced that he would do by his example ; that he would therefore have him subscribe the profession of Faith and the ten articles without delay.

Before complying with this requisition, the Archdeacon begged to speak a word in private to Menezes, promising afterwards to do whatever he commanded. His request being granted, when they were alone, he declared himself ready to give his subscription publicly if the Archbishop desired it ; though he ventured to suggest, that it would be more advisable for the present to subscribe in private, on

[4] Luke xv. 21.

account of those Christians who were not yet so well instructed as they ought to be : but that before the meeting of the Synod, at which he promised to sign the documents before all the assembly, he hoped to be able to prepare them to receive whatsoever should be therein determined ; and this he thought that he should accomplish more effectually if they knew nothing of his having already submitted to the Roman Church. The Archbishop saw the expediency of conceding thus much, and answered, "That although a profession of faith was so much the better by how much the more publicly it was made, yet that he so far approved of the reason that he had given for the opposite course, as to dispense with his making it openly on that occasion. They then repaired, in company with the Jesuit, Francisco Roz, to the Archbishop's lodgings, where, having shut the doors, the Archdeacon knelt down before a crucifix which stood on the table, and, laying his hands on the Missal, swore to the ten articles, and also to the profession of faith. Menezes, suspicious of his recanting, then required him to put his signature to them, that he might not be able afterwards, however inclined, to deny what he had done.

23. On the following morning, when the cattanars were assembled, the Archbishop acquainted them with his intention to call a Synod very speedily; to which they all assented. It was next debated where it should be held, and Angamale was named as the most suitable place, being the metropolis of the diocese; but to this Menezes had three objections — First. Because the Christians there, were, of all the Syrians, the most devoted to their ancient religion.—Secondly. Because it

It is determined to hold the Synod at Diamper.

was not in the dominions of the Rajah of Cochin, who was more dependent on the Portuguese than the other princes of Malabar, and, therefore, most to be relied on for protection.— Thirdly. Because it was too far from the Portuguese garrison of Cochin. These objections showed that he still had a suspicion of their sincerity. No one, however, ventured to offer any remark upon them ; and it was unanimously resolved, that the Synod should be held in the town of Diamper, which was at no great distance from Cochin ; and also, that it should be opened on the 20th of June, 1599, being the third Sunday after Whitsuntide.

Both parties issue summonses to their respective flocks to attend.

24. In pursuance of this decision, the Archbishop and Archdeacon issued their letters (ollas), summoning a sufficient number of priests, and all the procurators [5] of their respective jurisdictions, to assemble at the town of Diamper on the day appointed, and to come with full powers to treat on all matters relating to the Church at the Diocesan Synod to be holden there. These letters bore date the 11th of May, allowing six weeks to prepare for the business, which interim the Archbishop did not fail to improve to his own purpose.

Visit from the Caimal of Angamale.

25. Before he left Vaipicotta, the Caimal of Angamale, who went by the name of *The black rajah* of Malabar, came to pay him a visit. The Archbishop received him very courteously ; and at parting, according to the eastern custom with persons of state or property, gave him a handsome present. It consisted of several pieces of very rich cloth, with which he had provided himself at Goa to a large amount, for the purpose, as already stated, of making pre-

[5] The duties of these Officers were similar to those of the English Church-Wardens.

sents in the Serra. The Caimal, who is described as a violent and inhuman prince, was so
delighted with his present, that he promised
Menezes to see him obeyed in all things.

26. When the Caimal left him, the Archbishop returned to Cranganore, where he immediately set to work, assisted by Francisco
Roz, to compose the decrees for the Synod.
They were all written with his own hand ver-
batim, as afterwards published by himself: and
when finished, he had them translated out of
Portuguese into Malabar. Then, having observed that the Syrian churches were without
altars, he consecrated a stone altar for every
church in the Serra.

*Menezes
finishes the
decrees for
the Synod.*

27. His next step was, to engage all the
neighbouring princes and their chief officers,
though they were heathen, to assist him, which was
accomplished without difficulty. So much again
for his consistency, in thus doing the very thing
that he had alleged as the poor Archdeacon's
chief offence, and as proving him unworthy of
the Christian name.

*Engages
heathen
princes and
officers to
support him.*

28. The only thing now remaining to be
done was, to secure a majority of votes at the
approaching Synod, which, he flattered himself,
was to be the consummation of his labours.
This he effected by ordaining no less than
fifty cattanars on Trinity Sunday, in the church
of Paru, having previously required them to
abjure their ancient communion, and subscribe
the creed of Pope Pius the Fourth. These,
together with the youths whom he had before
ordained, were devoted to his cause, and they
made together about two thirds of the cattanars
at the Synod. He also took measures to secure
the votes of several of the most considerable of
the procurators, by making them valuable pre-

*Holds an
ordination,
and uses
other means
to secure a
majority at
the Synod.*

sents. To the leading man among them he gave a cross, set with diamonds of great value; and another equally valuable he presented to an aged cattanar, who had been the friend and companion of their late prelate, Mar Abraham.

Thus did he prepare successfully to act the farce of a general Synod: for it deserves to be regarded as no better than a farce, both because he had already laid claim to the jurisdiction, and performed the episcopal functions; that is to say, he had done all the business, which it was the chief, and the avowed object of the Synod to determine whether he was, or should be, authorized to do: and also because, instead of leaving every one to deliberate and vote according to the dictates of his conscience and judgment, he used every expedient he could devise to destroy the freedom of the assembly. By holding out to the Portuguese the prospect of commercial advantages from his success, he obtained their unanimous support. By threats, promises or bribes, he induced the most influential of the heathen rajahs and their officers, either to promote his object, or, at least, to withdraw their opposition. By intimidating the Archdeacon, ordaining a majority of clergy, caressing some already in orders, and with presents conciliating the chief of the laity, he prepared them all obsequiously to listen to the decrees which he had already composed for their acceptance. An assembly convened under such circumstances cannot rightly be called a Synod, the object of which was always understood to be, freely and fully to discuss the ecclesiastical affairs of a given province. Whereas, nothing was further from the intention of Menezes than to allow of any discussion whatever, having already determined all the matters to be brought before the assembly, and secured their concurrence.

29. These nefarious proceedings have not met with universal approbation even in the Roman Church. Father Simon was heartily ashamed of them, and attributed to them the failure of all attempts to secure the permanent attachment of this people to the Pope. He has judiciously and candidly remarked—" All that these methods have hitherto produced, serves only to let the world see by what means the Roman religion has been established in the East, which he that knows will not wonder, that all the re-unions which have been made with the people we call Schismatics in those parts, have been so short lived."[6] Had Menezes and his colleagues trodden in the steps of the Apostles; had they placed before the Syrians the single object of serving the Lord Jesus Christ; had they faithfully proclaimed His Gospel to them, and relied on His power and promise to make it effectual to the conversion of souls; the result would have been very different indeed. It is true, the pretensions of the Pope could no more have withstood such a declaration of the truth, than the darkness of night can withstand the rising day. And since the primary object of this Archbishop was to uphold the papacy, the means he used, though most antichristian, corresponded, at least, with the end he had in view. But they were infamous to the last degree, and ere long they brought down the righteous judgment of heaven, to the overthrow of the cause which they were employed to establish.

Father Simon's candid remarks on his conduct.

[6] Simon's *Histoire Critique*, or, Critical History of the Old Testament, p. 109. Geddes, p. 108.

CHAPTER VI.

ACCOUNT OF THE JEWS IN MALABAR.

In the last chapter, the Archbishop of Goa, when addressing the Rajah of Cochin, was said to have alluded to THE JEWS in his kingdom.[1] A colony of this scattered and afflicted people had been settled on the coast of Malabar, particularly at the town of Cochin, from time immemorial; and a brief account of them cannot but interest every Christian, who sympathizes with them for their fathers' sake, and, for Jesus' sake, devoutly seeks their restoration to God.[2]

There are two distinct classes of this interesting nation, the one called the Jerusalem or *White* Jews; the other, the ancient or *Black* Jews. The white Jews reside at Cochin, or rather in the suburbs, at Mattachery, called also Jews' Town, which is about a mile from the city. The black Jews also have a synagogue there, and several families live near it; but the great body of that tribe inhabit towns in the interior of the province.

The white Jews have preserved the following

---

[1] Sec. 14.

[2] This account is drawn up principally from Dr. Buchanan's *Christian Researches,* pp. 215, &c.

narrative of the events relating to their first arrival in the country. The original document is written in the Hebrew language, and has been handed down to them by their fathers.

" ' After the second temple was destroyed, (which may God speedily rebuild !) our fathers dreading the conqueror's wrath, departed from Jerusalem, a numerous body of men, women, priests, and Levites, and came into this land. There were among them men of repute for learning and wisdom ; and God gave the people favour in the sight of the king, who at that time reigned here, and he granted them a place to dwell in, called Cranganore. He allowed them a patriarchal jurisdiction within the district, with certain privileges of nobility ; and the royal grant was engraved, according to the custom of those days, on a plate of brass. This was done in the year from the creation of the world, 4250, (A. D. 490) ; and this plate of brass we still have in possession. Our forefathers continued at Cranganore for about a thousand years, and the number of heads who governed were seventy-two. Soon after our settlement, other Jews followed us from Judea ; and among these came that man of great wisdom, Rabbi Samuel, a Levite of Jerusalem, with his son, Rabbi Jehuda Levita. They brought with them the SILVER TRUMPETS, made use of at the time of the JUBILEE, which were saved when the second temple was destroyed ; and we have heard from our fathers that there were engraven upon those trumpets the letters of the ineffable Name.[3] There joined us also from Spain, and

[3] " This circumstance of the *Jubilee Trumpets* is to be found in a similar account of the Jews of Malabar, published in the " History of the Works of the Learned," for March, 1699.

other places, from time to time, certain tribes of Jews, who had heard of our prosperity. But at last, discord arising among ourselves, one of our chiefs called to his assistance an Indian king, who came upon us with a great army, destroyed our houses, palaces, and strong-holds, dispossessed us of Cranganore, killed part of us, and carried part into captivity. By these massacres we were reduced to a small number. Some of the exiles came and dwelt at Cochin, where we have remained ever since, suffering great changes from time to time. There are amongst us some of the children of Israel, (Beni Israel,) who came from the country of Ashkenaz, from Egypt, from Tsoba, and other places, besides those who formerly inhabited this country.'

"The native annals of Malabar confirmed the foregoing account, in the principal circumstances, as do the Mahomedan histories of the latter ages; for the Mahomedans have been settled here in great numbers since the eighth century.

"The desolation of Cranganore, the Jews describe as being like the desolation of Jerusalem in miniature. They were first received into the country with some favour and confidence, (agreeably to the tenor of the general prophecy concerning the Jews, for no country was to reject them) and after they had obtained some wealth, and attracted the notice of men, they were precipitated to the lowest abyss of human suffering and reproach. The recital of the sufferings of the Jews at Cranganore, resembles much that of the Jews at Jerusalem, as given by Josephus.

It is not necessary to suppose that these trumpets belonged to the Temple; for it is well known, that in every considerable town in Judea there were Jubilee trumpets."

The brass-plate mentioned in the foregoing narrative was "given them by a native king. It is written, of course, in the *Malabar* language and character; and is now so old that it cannot be well understood. The Jews preserve a Hebrew translation of it, which they presented to me: but the Hebrew itself is very difficult, and they do not agree among themselves, as to the meaning of some words. I have employed, by their permission, an engraver at Cochin, to execute a fac-simile of the original plate, on copper.[4] This ancient document begins in the following manner, according to the Hebrew translation:[5]

" 'In the peace of God, the King, which hath made the earth, according to his pleasure. To this God, I, Airvi Brahmin, have lifted up my hand, and have granted, by this deed, which many hundred thousand years shall run——I, dwelling in Cranganore, have granted, in the thirty-sixth year of my reign, in the strength of power I have granted, in the strength of power I have given inheritance, to Joseph Rabban.'

" Then follow the privileges of nobility; such as permission to ride on the elephant; to have a herald to go before to announce the name and dignity; to have the lamp of the day; to walk on carpets spread upon the earth; and to have trumpets and cymbals sounded before him. King Airvi then appoints Joseph Rabban to be ' Chief and Governor of the houses of congregation, (the Synagogues), and of certain districts, and of the sojourners in them.' What

---

[4] " The original is engraved on both sides of the plate, the fac-simile forms two plates. These are now deposited in the Public Library at the University of Cambridge."

[5] A copy of this Hebrew translation also was sent to the University by Dr. Buchanan, with other MSS.

CHAP.
VI.

proves the consequence of the Jews at the period when this grant was made, is, that it is signed by seven Kings as witnesses. 'And to this are witnesses, King Bivada Cubertin Mitadin, and he is King of *Travancore*. King Airla Nada Mana Vikriin, and he is the *Samorin* King. Veloda Nada Archarin Shatin, and he is King of *Argot*. The remaining four Kings are those of *Palgatchery, Calastri, Carbinah,* and *Vara-changur*. There is no date in this document, further than what may be collected from the reign of the prince, and the names of the royal witnesses. Dates are not usual in old Malabar writings. One fact is evident, that the Jews must have existed a considerable time in the country, before they could have obtained such a grant. The tradition before mentioned assigns for the date of the transaction, the year of the Creation, 4250, which is, in Jewish computation, A. D. 490." We have already seen, that the celebrated rajah of Malabar, CERAM PEROU-MAL, granted extensive privileges to the Christians and Mahomedans in his dominions; [6] and the Jews also partook of his generosity.

[7] The synagogue of the white Jews is a light, airy building, and decorated with some taste: while the assembled Israelites, being partly composed of merchants from Bagdad, Bussorah, and other parts of Asia, each clad in the costume of the country from which he came, increase the interest of the scene. The chanting of the Hebrew service is very melodious. They possess a copy of the Pentateuch, beauti-

---

[6] B. i. c. 4, ss. 7 & 8.

[7] In 1820, the author visited Cochin, and he is now writing from memoranda which he made at the time of what he heard and saw. This is the case also with the other parts of this chapter not marked with inverted commas.

fully written upon a long roll of parchment, and rolled up upon two rods : and when they unroll it to read, it is so contrived that it always opens upon the portion appointed for the day.[8] The sacred roll has a silken covering, is decorated with silver ornaments, some of which are intended to represent Aaron's bells, and it is preserved in an enclosed recess at the end of the synagogue, opposite the gallery where it is read. It was carried with great solemnity to the desk; and during the reading of the Law, the chief persons of the synagogue went, one at a time, and stood for a few minutes in silence by the reader : and when each moved onward to the gallery, the rest gave him this Hebrew salutation as he passed—"The honour is yours." As he returned, they said—" Peace be unto you." It must be confessed, that there is much puerile ceremony, and unbecoming levity, at different parts of the service.[9] But for this, the

---

[8] This will illustrate the act of our Lord in the synagogue at Nazareth (Luke iv. 17). " And when he had opened (unrolled, ἀναπτύξας) the book, he found the place where it was written," &c. The simple arrangement is, to unroll the (I believe) *right* rod, and when the given portion is read, to roll it up upon the *left* rod—and so on to the end of the roll.

[9] For instance ; though the assembly appeared to be deeply interested in the chanting of the service, yet the singer had no sooner finished, than, descending from the gallery, he came into the centre of the synagogue, and proceeded immediately to put up to auction the honour of performing the following parts in the ceremony about to take place. 1st. That of drawing aside the curtain before the recess in which the Law was deposited. 2nd. That of carrying the sacred roll into the gallery where it was to be read. 3rd. That of reading the portion for the day :—and 4th. That of carrying the book back again to its place. The first honour was knocked down to a little boy, who ran immediately to the curtain, but was stopped before he reached it, as it was not to be drawn before all were ready for the removal of the roll. The incident, however, seemed greatly to amuse the whole assembly, except

reverence manifested for the word of God would interest the Christian mind. In the transit of the Pentateuch across the synagogue, the men ran themselves, and carried their children, to kiss the silver ornaments and silken covering of the sacred roll. During the service, the men wore a fine muslin shawl thrown loosely over their heads, in obedience, they said, to the command contained in Numbers xv. 37, &c. : but these plain white muslins do not answer to the description of the " fringes in the borders of their garments," and the " ribband of blue " upon them, which are there commanded to be worn.

The BLACK JEWS are a distinct race. " It is only necessary to look at " their countenance " to be satisfied that their ancestors must have arrived in India many ages before the White Jews. Their Hindoo complexion, and their very imperfect resemblance to the European Jews, indicate that they have been detached from the parent stock in Judea many ages before the Jews in the West ; and that there have been intermarriages with families not Israelitish." The woolly hair of some, and their resemblance to the negro in other respects, favour the conclusion that they were originally a mixed race from Africa : but others appear so much like the natives of India, that it is sometimes difficult, at first sight, to distinguish them from the Hindoo. By a little closer obser-

---

the Christian visitors, who were pained to witness such a profanation of sacred things. The money raised on the occasion is appropriated to the officers and repairs of the synagogue; and a Jew of some intelligence defended the practice, on the plea, that those who intended to bid for the honour of reading the Law, were induced to improve themselves in private, that they might read it well.

vation, however, the Jewish contour of their countenances cannot be mistaken. " The White Jews look upon the Black Jews as an inferior race, and as not of a *pure* caste : which plainly demonstrates that they do not spring from a common stock in India."

" The Black Jews communicated," to Dr. Buchanan, " much interesting intelligence concerning their brethren the ancient Israelites in the East : traditional indeed in its nature, but in general illustrative of true history. They recounted the names of many other small colonies resident in northern India, Tartary, and China, and gave him a written list of SIXTY-FIVE places.[1] He conversed with those who had lately visited many of these stations, and were about to return again. The Jews have a never ceasing communication with each other in the East. Their families indeed are generally stationary, being subject to despotic princes ; but the men move much about in a commercial capacity ; and the same individual will travel through many extensive countries. So that when any thing interesting to the nation of Jews takes place, the rumour will pass rapidly throughout all Asia.

He " inquired concerning their brethren, the Ten Tribes. They said that it was commonly believed among them, that the great body of the Israelites are to be found in Chaldea, and in the countries contiguous to it, being the very places whither they were first carried into captivity ; that some few families had migrated into regions more remote, as to Cochin and

---

[1] In 1820—Of White Jews at Cochin there were about forty families, and of Black Jews, about one hundred families. In the Asiatic Researches, Vol. x. may be seen an account of the Jews in Ceylon in the tenth century.

Rajapoor, in India, and to other places yet farther to the East; but that the bulk of the nation, though now much reduced in number, had not to this day removed two thousand miles from *Samaria*. Among the Black Jews he could not find many copies of the Bible. They informed him, that in certain places of the remote dispersion, their brethren have but some small portions of the Scriptures, and that the prophetical books were rare; but that they themselves, from their vicinity to the White Jews, have been supplied, from time to time, with the whole of the Old Testament."

In the Jews' burial ground at Cochin, " some of the tombs are handsomely constructed, and have Hebrew inscriptions in prose and verse. This mansion of the dead is called, by the Jews, *Beth Hairin*, or, ' The House of the Living.' "

The Children of Israel are dispersed over other parts of India,[2] and another opportunity

[2] At the beginning of the year 1808, Dr. Buchanan " visited Cochin a second time, and proceeded afterwards to Bombay, where he had an opportunity of meeting with some very intelligent men of the Jewish nation. They had heard of his conferences with the Cochin Jews, and were desirous to discuss certain topics, particularly the prophecies of Isaiah; and they engaged in them with far more spirit and frankness, he thought, than their brethren at Cochin had done. They told him, that if he would take a walk to the bazar in the suburb, without the walls of Bombay town, he would find a Synagogue without a *Sepher Tora*, or book of the Law. He did so, and found it to be the case. The minister and a few of the Jews assembled, and showed him their Synagogue, in which there were some loose leaves of prayers in manuscript, but no book of the Law. The author did not understand that they disapproved of the Law; but they had no copy of it. They seemed to have little knowledge of the Jewish Scriptures or history. This only proved what he had been often told, that small portions of the Jewish nation melt away from time to time, and are absorbed in the mass of the heathen world. Nor is this any argument against the truth of the prophecy,

will occur, in the sequel, more appropriate for
the consideration of their present state and
future prospects. Although they do not actually form a part of this History, yet the final
prosperity of the Christian Church is too intimately associated with the restoration of the
Jews, not to render every vestige of them, in
foreign countries, a matter of interest to the
believer in the promises of God. They are at
present cast out indeed from the favour of Jehovah, but they are not cut off from hope of a
return. They are still rooted in the Almighty's
purposes of mercy : though some of the branches
are broken off, yet have they the assurance
that they shall be grafted in again : and when
brought back to the God of their fathers,
through the Messiah of their prophets, who can
tell to what extent they may be the heralds
of mercy to the yet unredeemed nations of the
earth? " For if the casting away of them be
the reconciling of the world, what shall the
receiving of them be, but life from the dead ? " [3]
While then we sympathize with them in their
desolation, may we not hope that it is one of the
Divine purposes in dispersing them over the face
of the earth, that they may be prepared, when
" His set time for their deliverance shall come,"
to convey the glad tidings of salvation around
their several homes? Their dispersion through
all countries may be regarded as favouring this
expectation. Every where are they ready,
waiting only the quickening of God's Spirit,

---

which declares that they should remain a separate and distinct
people ; for these are mere *exceptions.* Conversions to
Christianity in the early ages would equally militate against
the prediction, taken in an absolute sense."

[3] See this argument conducted to its conclusion in St.
Paul's Epistle to the Romans, ch. xi.

CHAP.
VI.

and the enlightening of His word, to go out into the waste places of the earth, and proclaim the universal invitation of the Gospel. Devoutly is this consummation to be wished, both for Jews and Gentiles: and fervently do we pray for the time when they shall be united in one fold, under one Shepherd, JESUS CHRIST, the LORD.

APPENDIX

TO

BOOK THIRD, CHAPTER SIXTH.

———

MANUSCRIPTS OBTAINED BY DR. CLAUDIUS BU-
CHANAN FROM THE JEWS AT COCHIN.—CHRIS-
TIAN RESEARCHES, pp. 232 — 236. TENTH
EDITION.

" Almost in every house I find Hebrew books,
printed or manuscript; particularly among the
white Jews. Most of the printed Hebrew of
Europe has found its way to Cochin, through
the medium of the Portuguese and Dutch commerce of former times. When I questioned the
Jews concerning the old copies of the Scriptures, which had been read in the synagogues
from age to age; some told me that it was
usual to *bury* them when decayed by time and
use. Others said that this was not always the
case. I despaired at first of being able to procure any of the old biblical writings; but after
I had been in the country about six weeks, and
they found that I did not expect to obtain them
merely as presents, some copies were *recovered*.
The white Jews had only the Bible written on
parchment, and of modern appearance, in their
synagogue; but I was informed that the black

Jews possessed formerly copies written on *Goat-skins;* and that in the synagogue of the black Jews there was an old record chest, into which the decayed copies of their Scriptures had been thrown. I accordingly went to the synagogue with a few of the chief men, and examined the contents, which some of them said they had never looked at before, and did not seem greatly to value. The manuscripts were of various kinds, on parchment, goat-skins, and cotton paper. I negotiated for them hastily, and wrapped them up in two cloths, and gave them to the Jews to carry home to my house. I had observed some murmuring amongst the bye-standers in the synagogue, while I was examining the chest: and before we appeared in the streets, the alarm had gone forth, that the Christians were robbing the synagogue of the Law. There were evident symptoms of tumult, and the women and children collected and were following us. I requested some of the more respectable Jews to accompany me out of the town; but I had scarcely arrived at my own house at Cochin, when the persons who had permitted me to take the manuscripts, came in evident agitation, and told me I must restore them immediately to calm the popular rage. Others had gone to complain to the chief magistrate, Thomas Flower, Esq. And now I had lost my spoil, but for the friendly counsel and judicious conduct of Mr. Flower. He directed that all the manuscripts should be delivered up to him, and, that there should be no further proceedings on the subject without his authority. To this the Jews agreed. There was some plea of justice on my side, as it was understood that I had given a valuable consideration. In the mean time he allowed a few days to pass, that the minds of the people might become tranquil, and he then summoned some of the more liberal men, and gave them a hearing on the subject. In the mean time I thought it prudent to retire from Cochin, for a day or two, and went to Cranganore, about sixteen miles off, to Colonel Macaulay, the British Resident at Travancore, who was then at the house of Mr. Drummond, the collector of Malabar. On my return to Cochin, Mr. Flower informed me that all the manuscripts were to be returned to my house; that I was to select what was *old*, and of little use to the Jews, and to give back to them what was *new*. The affair ended, however, in the Jews permitting me generously to retain some part of the *new*.

‘ I have since made a tour through the towns of the Black Jews in the interior of the country, *Tritoor, Paroor, Chenotta*, and *Maleh*. I have procured a good many manuscripts, chiefly in the Rabbinical character, some of which the Jews themselves cannot read; and I do not know what to say to their traditions. A copy of the Scriptures belonging to Jews of the East, who might be supposed to have had no communication with Jews in the West, has been long considered a desideratum in Europe; for the Western Jews have been accused by some learned men, of altering or omitting certain words in the Hebrew text, to invalidate the argument of Christians. But Jews in the East, remote from the controversy, would have no motive for such corruptions. One or two of the MSS., which I have just procured, will probably be of some service in this respect. One of them is an old copy of the Books of Moses, written on a roll of leather. The skins are sewed together, and the roll is about forty-eight feet in length. It is, in some places, worn out, and the holes have been sewed up with pieces of parchment. Some of the Jews suppose that this roll came originally from Senna in Arabia; others have heard that it was brought from Cashmire. The Cabul Jews, who travel into the interior of China, say that, in some Synagogues the Law is still written on a roll of leather, made of Goats' skins dyed red; not on vellum, but on a soft flexible leather; which agrees with the description of the roll abovementioned.[1]

'Ever since I came among these people, and heard their sentiments on the prophecies, and their confident hopes of returning to *Jerusalem*, I have thought much on the means of obtaining a version of the NEW TESTAMENT in the Hebrew language, and circulating it among them and their brethren in the East. I had heard that there were one or two translations of the Testament in their own possession, but they were studiously kept out of my sight, for a considerable time. At last, however, they were produced by individuals in a private manner. One of them is written in the small Rabbinical, or Jerusalem cha-

[1] "Mr. Yeates, formerly of All Soul's College, Oxford, and editor of the Hebrew Grammar, has been employed by the author for the last two years, at Cambridge, in arranging and collating the Hebrew and Syriac MSS., brought from India. His collation of the Roll of the Pentateuch above mentioned, is now finished, and is printed in a thin quarto volume. The University, with great liberality, resolved that this book shall be printed at their expense, for the benefit of Mr. Yeates; and Dr. Marsh, (the present Bishop of Peterborough,) the learned editor of Michaelis, has written a Note on the character and comparative importance of the manuscript, which will form a preface to the work."

racter; the other in a large square letter. The history of the former is very interesting. The translator, a learned Rabbi, conceived the design of making an accurate version of the New Testament, for the express purpose of *confuting* it. His style is copious and elegant, like that of a master in the language, and the translation is in general faithful. It does not, indeed, appear that he wished to pervert the meaning of a single sentence; but depending on his own abilities and renown as a scholar, he hoped to be able to controvert its doctrines, and to triumph over it by fair contest in the presence of the world. There is yet a mystery about the circumstances of this man's death, which time will perhaps unfold: the Jews are not inclined to say much to me about him. His version is complete, and written with greater freedom and ease towards the end than at the beginning. How astonishing it is that an enemy should have done this! that he should have persevered resolutely and calmly to the end of his work! not indeed always *calmly*, for there is sometimes a note of execration on the Sacred Person who is the subject of it, as if to unburden his mind, and ease the conflict of his labouring soul. At the close of the Gospels, as if afraid of the converting power of his own translation, he calls heaven to witness that he had undertaken the work with the professed design of opposing the ' *Epicureans*,' by which term he contemptuously means the Christians.'

THE END OF VOL. I.

PRINTED BY
L. AND G. SEELEY, THAMES DITTON, SURREY.

Date Loaned

MAR - 8 1973		
USE FOR ONE MONTH		
FEB - 5 1990		

CPSIA information can be obtained at www.ICGtesting.com
Printed in the USA
LVOW121611110712

289684LV00006B/192/P

9 781173 583064